NINJA Foodi
XL PRO AIR FRYER
OVEN COOKBOOK

The Complete Guide with 600 Easy and Affordable Air Fryer Oven Recipes, to Bake, Fry, Toast the Best Meals with Your Ninja Foodi Air Fryer Oven

600
EASY
RECIPES

Summer Huoen

Table of Content

Chapter 4 Fish and Seafood 34

Chapter 5 Poultry 57

Chapter 6 Meats 79

Chapter 7 Vegan and Vegetarian 100

Chapter 8 Vegetable Sides 117

Chapter 9 Wraps and Sandwiches 123

Chapter 10 Appetizers and Snacks 127

Chapter 11 Desserts 139

Chapter 12 Holiday Specials 152

Introduction

Have you ever wondered how it would feel to have a kitchen device that can bake, whole roast, dehydrate, air fry, pizza, broil, toast, bagel, and reheat all in one place? Well, you need not wonder much because your Ninja Foodi XL pro air fryer oven does exactly that! Now, nothing can stop you from preparing all your favorite meals and that of your loved ones because you have everything you need right in one unit and at no extra cost.

The Ninja Foodi XL doesn't just serve the multi-purpose function; it comes with a wide range of features and functions that make it a must-have in your kitchen for absolutely all your cooking needs. What's more? Your Ninja Foodi XL pro air fryer oven is your best pick to save time, space and conserve energy.

In this book, you will learn all you need to know about the Ninja Foodi XL pro air fryer, including its features, functions, and tips to help you optimize your Ninja Foodi XL pro air fryer oven to bring the best results.

More than you having the knowledge of the functions and features of the oven, I have painstakingly presented you with 500 Ninja Foodi XL pro air fryer oven and a 1000-day meal plan to get you prepared for the days ahead and make it easy for you to make the choice of using your air fryer oven. I can see you becoming an expert at the use of the Ninja Foodi XL pro air fryer oven. All you need is to follow the procedures and steps in this guide.

Let's get started!

Chapter 1 The Ninja Foodi XL Pro Air Fryer Oven 101

My encounter and use of the Ninja Foodi XL Pro Air Fryer Oven Makes come to the conclusion that it is a multi-purpose kitchen device that offers high functionality and convenience. With my conviction, I will let you know what the Ninja Foodi XL pro oven is, what it looks like, its features, and the benefits you stand to enjoy from it.

What is the Ninja Foodi XL Pro Air Fryer Oven?

As much as I have used a lot of oven before now, I can boldly tell you that the Ninja Foodi XL Pro Air Fryer Oven is a special type of oven. The specialty I found in it lies in the fact that it cooks large meals two times faster than the average full-sized oven. This oven allows you to bake all your favorite meals faster and to your taste. Unlike average ovens, the Ninja foodi XL pro air oven combines the functions of a toaster oven and an air fryer in one convenient package. This differentiates it from other types of air oven and enables it to offer functionality at its best, you can trust me on this.

The oven is built with brushed stainless steel that is aesthetically furnished with rounded corners and is equipped with a control pad. In terms of size and length, the Ninja Foodi XL is wider and shorter than an average toaster oven.

Features of the Ninja Foodi XL Pro Air Fryer Oven

Unlike every other oven I have seen, the Ninja Foodi XL Pro Air Fryer Oven is equipped with many unique features. I was amazed at how well the oven performs at its maximum best. **You can see the leading features it possesses for yourself:**

True Surround Convection

With its 10x convection power, the Ninja Foodi XL pro air oven works faster in baking and produces crispier and juicier outcome than a traditional full-sized oven.

Extra Large Countertop Oven Capacity

Another feature that I love about the oven is its two-level even cooking that requires no rotation. The extra-large countertop oven capacity enables it to fit into a 5-Lb chicken, two 12-in pizzas, a sheet pan of vegetables, and a 12-lb turkey.

Digital Display Handle

Another good feature of the oven that makes me take a step further to learn more about it is that it ensures that there is an optimized oven rack position that illuminates based on the function chosen. This digital display handle ensures that whenever the door is opened, the display settings freeze to stop any accidental changes that may happen during the cooking process.

Air Fry Function

Are you just like me, who loves to have his foods well fried and in a healthy manner? Then, the Ninja Foodi XL pro air oven is your sure bet. It has an air fry feature that fries your meals the healthier way when compared to the traditional full-size convection oven by ensuring up to 75% less fat in your meals.

Benefits of Ninja Foodi XL Pro Air Fryer Oven

I have enjoyed several benefits since I purchased my Ninja Foodi XL pro air fryer oven. In this chapter, I will show you some of the benefits you will enjoy while using the Ninja Foodi XL Pro Air Fryer Oven.

Taste

I am always delighted whenever I see my meals giving a nice taste and with the Ninja Foodi XL pro air fryer oven, I get the best taste for my meals. The oven cooks your meal faster than the conventional oven, which ensures that your meals are healthier and tastier. All your veggies and meat will boil faster when you use the Ninja Foodi XL Pro Air Fryer Oven . This ensures that all your meats and veggies retain their moisture as they are cooked at a shorter time frame. Your veggies will not only be healthier because their moisture is retained, but they will also be crunchier and crispier, thereby making mealtime fun!

Time-Saving and Convenience

If you are like me, who sometimes have moments that I need to get my meal done in time, then you need this oven. The Ninja Foodi XL pro air fryer Oven cooks faster. Just as it does for me, it offers a convenient way to cook your meals. The Ninja Foodi is just over a cubic foot and it can accommodate two trays of food. This allows you to cook a larger amount of meals in a shorter time frame. So, instead of cooking in bits as you would with a conventional oven, you can save time and cook large portions of food in a low time frame while you get to do other things.

User Friendly Led Controls

I am sure you don't want to be stressed while cooking Well, nobody wants to be stressed, not even me. And the good news is that, the Ninja Foodi XL Pro Air Fryer Oven comes with bright, intuitive, LED, Touch controls which point out the four different levels to help you make the best use of the ten functions the Ninja Foodi led control offers.

With the Ninja Foodi XL Pro Air Fryer Oven, you can perform different tasks easily. You can pause the cooking process, so you check to see how your meal is doing, and the temperature settings will continue immediately after the cooking process continues.

In the convection fan settings, there are four separate categories (maximum, high, medium, and low) which automatically corresponds with the function you choose while cooking.

The oven also comes with an Oven Light Button, which comes on by default when your kitchen device starts. Its LED timer counts down based on the type of cooking function you use. It also comes with many heating elements and air flow velocity that has been specifically tailored to correspond to whatever cooking function you choose.

Build and Design

I was able to get a beautiful oven that comes with a nice design when I got my Ninja Foodi XL pro air fryer oven. The oven comes with great design and structure. It is built with durable stainless steel, and the front doors are made with shatter-proof tempered glass to ensure safety whenever the doors are flung open.

Its touch controls and LED are located at the pull-down handle to enable easy and convenient access. Its heat dissipation vents are located at the top of its two sides and also at its back. The Ninja Foodi XL pro oven also comes with a three-foot heavy electrical cord for protection which makes it safer to use.

Energy Saving

Let me burst your bubble. Do you that a large conventional oven consumes about 4 000 watts of electricity? Yes. However, the Ninja Foodi XL pro air fryer oven consumes 1,800 watts which shows that it saves power than the average oven. Not only will you be able to save time, but you will be able to save money too!

Ten Cooking Functions

I enjoy the ability of the oven to play ten roles in my kitchen. Yes, the Ninja Foodi XL pro oven offers ten different functions, which make it a multi-purpose oven. You can bake, air fry, whole roast, dehydrate, Pizza, Broil, Toast, Bagel, and reheat. This means you don't have to buy different kitchen devices as your Nina Foodi XL pro oven offers different functions for you to optimize.

The Ninja Foodi XL Pro Air Fryer Oven's Functions

As I have mentioned in the last part of the chapter above, the oven performs ten different functions making it an awesome choice for me. And I am sure you will enjoy it too. Check out the functions you will enjoy with the Ninja Foodi XL pro air fryer oven.

AIR FRYING

I love air frying so much and this oven gives me the opportunity to do what I love. The air frying function is just one of the many tasks you can use in the air fry oven. It has a large rack size that enables you to fit over three pounds of foods successfully in it and fry. This will allow you to fry large meals all at once, saving you time and energy. Air frying is so thorough it helps me to control my calorie intake and produces food with seventy-five percent less fat when compared to traditional frying methods.

AIR ROASTING

This conventional oven presents the best chance of air roasting. The technique and dexterity the range provides in air roasting will knock your socks off with little time. The oven also comes with a well-detailed recipe booklet that will guide you on how to use it to roast several items easily with excellent results. It can be used for air roasting of different proteins, vegetables, and spices. You can air roast proteins as large as three pounds and produce excellent results for all the ingredients involved.

TOASTING

The oven's large rack size also ensures efficient toasting of many slices of bread without squishing them. The results you will obtain from toasting are second to none as it toasts bread evenly and gives you a toast with a beautiful golden-brown shade if that is what you want. The different degrees of toasting mean that it will produce the right shade of toast necessary as there are various options tailored to your taste. Lovers of bagel can also benefit from this oven as it has an impressive- bagel setting that gives you a uniformly brown bagel shade.

BAKING

If you are in love with baking, the oven is your sure bet. You can use this oven for baking different items using the shallow pan or the sheet pan. The shallow pan is suitable for frying large things like cakes, muffins, and even bread, while the sheet pan will give you the best quality of evenly baked cookies and biscuits like that of a full-size oven. The large rack size ensures you can bake a family-sized meal at once in the oven. The oven has a timer that can be set based on your desired outcome for the material you are baking. The oven comes with a thermometer that will give you the exact temperature as cooking goes on.

AIR BROILING

The oven gives you an evenly and uniformly result on both sides. For example, if your chicken breast, the result you will get is juicy and sufficiently browned-looking meat on both sides. This excellent result is also produced within 20 minutes irrespective of the predetermined degree of air broiling.

DEHYDRATION

This oven is equipped with the ability to perform dehydration at low fan speed and low temperature to create balanced and chip-like dehydrated foods for different occasions. This oven presents you with an excellent alternative to a traditional air fryer; the rack size also ensures that you are able to dry more food than a conventional toaster oven.

KEEPING FOOD WARM

The oven was designed with a rear heat source, high-velocity fan, and a surrounding airflow that makes it able to keep food at serving temperature over a long period of time. After cooking, you can leave cooked items in the oven and eat after a few hours at a serving temperature. It also has stainless steel as a handle which can prevent excess heat loss from the cooked item.

REHEAT

The oven can also act as a microwave and heat food items back to your desired temperature.

Ninja Foodi XL Pro Air Fryer Oven Accessories

I am a fan of the accessories that come with the ninja foodi XL pro air fryer oven. They make it easy for me to use the oven for my culinary purposes. The oven comes with five accessories. **They are:**

- **Sheet pan**
- **Wire rack**
- **Air fry basket**
- **Roast tray**
- **Crumb tray**

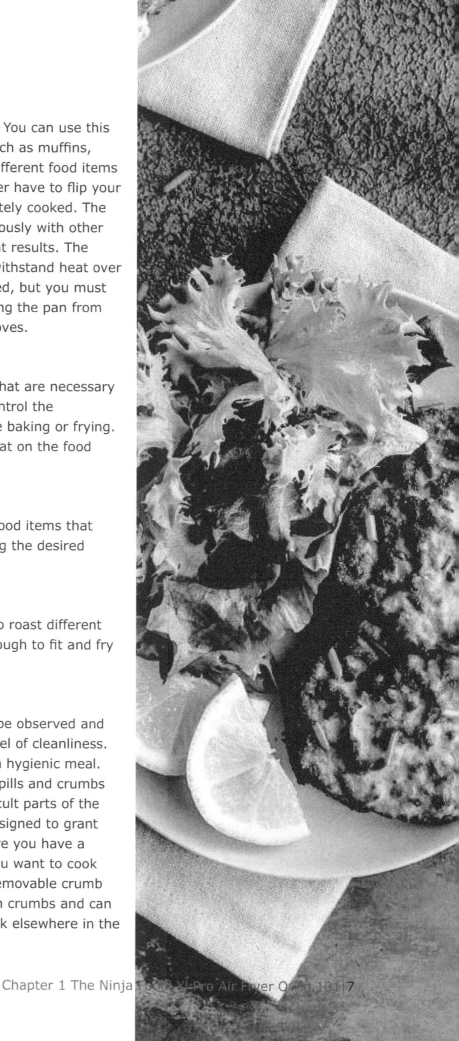

➤ Non-stick sheet pan

The oven comes with two sheet pans. You can use this pan for baking different food items such as muffins, cake, biscuits, etc. It can also roast different food items 360 degrees; this means you no longer have to flip your food items to ensure they are adequately cooked. The sheet pan can also be used simultaneously with other accessories and still generate excellent results. The non-stick option means the pan can withstand heat over a long period without getting destroyed, but you must take proper precautions when removing the pan from the oven, such as wearing cooking gloves.

➤ Wire Rack

The oven comes with two wire racks that are necessary to allow good air circulation and to control the temperature of the food items you are baking or frying. The wire rack reduces the effect of heat on the food items present in the oven.

➤ Air Fry Basket

It is a large basket capable of fitting food items that weigh up to 4 pounds without affecting the desired result.

➤ Roast Tray

The roast tray offers you the ability to roast different food thoroughly. The oven is large enough to fit and fry a whole chicken on the roast tray.

➤ Crumb Tray

One of the most important factors to be observed and maintained while cooking is a high level of cleanliness. A clean oven is beneficial to produce a hygienic meal. While cooking, there would be small spills and crumbs stuck to different and sometimes difficult parts of the oven. However, this oven has been designed to grant you access to all components to ensure you have a clean oven ready for you whenever you want to cook again. This access is because of the removable crumb tray that has been designed to contain crumbs and can also be removed to remove other stuck elsewhere in the oven.

Tips on Cleaning and Maintenance

I have been enjoying my Ninja Foodi XL pro air fryer oven because I understood that needed to care for it. I will share tips on how you can maintain and clean your oven so that it will serve you as much as you want. Follow the tips I share below:

- To ensure you roast meat and vegetables to the best degree, press the level 2 button and only use oils that were produced to withstand high heat and a high smoke point for general cooking.

- Ensure you clean thoroughly after every use

- Before you start cleaning, make sure you turn off this machine and allow it to cool down.

- You should not only the racks and look for crumbs make sure you leave the interior walls and glass door clean after each use. You can use a damp sponge to clean off oil stains.

- Do not apply harsh abrasives on the oven interiors and exteriors as they would damage them.

- Leaving your oven clean can be enhanced by placing an aluminum foil in the bottom sheet pan to minimize oil spillage and littering crumbs.

- Do not cover holes on roast trays with aluminum foil.

- You should also clean the exterior of the oven with a damp cloth after applying a spray solution to the sponge used. Do not spray the solution on the door.

- You can also clean the air-fry basket by spraying it with cooking oil and then followed by light brushing.

- Although the oven doors are made with tempered glass to ensure safety, they can still be damaged by scratching.

- To ensure your food is well cooked, the oven works at high temperature, which means oven doors and surfaces will be hot so ensure you protect your body-hands before opening the oven. You can wear protective gloves.

- The accessories were not only designed for your comfort and efficiency; they were designed to be durable if properly maintained. You can maintain the accessories such as air baskets, roast trays, sheet pans, etc., by hand washing them.

- Ensure you never leave it unattended and provide necessary ventilation all around.

- Do not put accessories like sheet pan, roast tray, and crumb tray in dishwater; only soak the sheet pan and roast tray if there are tough grease stains on them. You should only soak them in warm soapy water, and after which, you will make use of a non-abrasive brush to clean them off thoroughly.

- You should only return the materials to the oven if after thoroughly drying them with clean materials.

Troubleshooting Guide

From my experience, I discovered that even though the Ninja Foodi XL pro air fryer oven is very straight-forward and easy to use, certain minor technicalities can be possibly encountered. So I will share answers to some questions you may have when using the Ninja Foodi XL pro air fryer oven.

1. Why Is the Oven Not Turning On?

If your oven isn't turning on, ensure your power cord is well plugged into the socket. Then, reset the circuit breaker and press the power button.

2. Can the Sheet pan be used in place of the air fry basket when using the air fry function?

Yes, you can. However, the crispiness of your meals may differ.

3. Can I set the unit to its Automatic Settings?

In order to restore the default settings of your oven, press the Light and 2 LEVEL buttons together for about 5 seconds.

4. Why do the heating elements turn on and off?

It is not unusual for the heating elements to turn on and off. This is because the oven has been structured to control the temperatures specific to every function by adjusting the power levels of each heating element.

5. Why is steam emitting from the door of my oven?

This occurrence is not unusual as meals that have high moisture content tend to emit more steam that exceeds the inside of the door to the counter.

6. Why is my Ninja Foodi XL emitting smoke?

To avoid this, make sure you use the roast tray on the heated pan whenever you cook greasy meals or whenever you use the air roast, whole roast, and air fry functions. However, if you have done all of this and the smoke persists, remove the accessories and run a toast cycle on shade 7. This will clear up the grease responsible for the smoke.

7. How do I clean the Sheet Pan?

If food remains are stuck on your sheet pan, then soak your sheet pan in water before you begin to clean. You can line the sheet pan with aluminum foil or parchment paper when you are cooking to make cleaning easier.

8. Why did my circuit breaker fall off while using my oven?

The Ninja Foodi XL pro air fryer oven consumes 1800 watts of electric power. This means it must be inserted into an outlet on a 15-amp circuit breaker. You must also ensure that your Ninja Foodi XL pro air fryer oven is the only device that is plugged into your circuit breaker whenever you are using a 15-amp circuit breaker.

9. Why does my Ninja Foodi XL oven seem like it's still in use after I turn it off?

It is normal for your Ninja Foodi XL pro air fryer oven to appear to still be on after it is turned off. This is because the cooling fan will keep running after your Ninja Foodi XL oven is off. The cooling fan will stop running immediately when your Ninja Foodi unit reaches below 95°F.

Chapter 2 Breakfasts

Italian Bacon Hot Dogs

Prep time: 5 minutes | Cook time: 15 minutes | Serves 4

3 brazilian sausages, cut into 3 equal pieces
9 slices bacon
1 tablespoon Italian herbs
Salt and ground black pepper, to taste

1. Take each slice of bacon and wrap around each piece of sausage. Sprinkle with Italian herbs, salt and pepper.
2. Select the AIR FRY function and cook the sausages in the air fryer oven at 355ºF (179ºC) for 15 minutes.
3. Serve warm.

Potato and Kale Nuggets

Prep time: 10 minutes | Cook time: 18 minutes | Serves 4

1 teaspoon extra virgin olive oil
1 clove garlic, minced
4 cups kale, rinsed and chopped
2 cups potatoes, boiled and mashed
⅛ cup milk
Salt and ground black pepper, to taste
Cooking spray

1. In a skillet over medium heat, sauté the garlic in the olive oil, until it turns golden brown. Sauté with the kale for an additional 3 minutes and remove from the heat.
2. Mix the mashed potatoes, kale and garlic in a bowl. Pour in the milk and sprinkle with salt and pepper.
3. Shape the mixture into nuggets and spritz with cooking spray.
4. Put in the air fryer basket. Select the AIR FRY function and cook at 390ºF (199ºC) for 15 minutes, flip the nuggets halfway through cooking to make sure the nuggets fry evenly.
5. Serve immediately.

Bacon and Egg Cup

Prep time: 5 minutes | Cook time: 15 minutes | Serves 1

2 eggs
4 ounces (113 g) bacon, cooked
Salt and ground black pepper, to taste

1. Select the BAKE function and preheat MAXX to 400ºF (204ºC). Put liners in a regular cupcake tin.
2. Crack an egg into each of the cups and add the bacon. Season with some pepper and salt.
3. Bake in the preheated air fryer oven for 15 minutes, or until the eggs are set.
4. Serve warm.

British Breakfast

Prep time: 5 minutes | Cook time: 25 minutes | Serves 2

1 cup potatoes, sliced and diced
2 cups beans in tomato sauce
2 eggs
1 tablespoon olive oil
1 sausage
Salt, to taste

1. Select the BAKE function and preheat MAXX to 390ºF (199ºC) and allow to warm.
2. Break the eggs onto a baking dish and sprinkle with salt.
3. Lay the beans on the dish, next to the eggs.
4. In a bowl, coat the potatoes with the olive oil. Sprinkle with salt.
5. Transfer the bowl of potato slices to the air fryer oven and bake for 10 minutes.
6. Swap out the bowl of potatoes for the dish containing the eggs and beans. Bake for another 10 minutes. Cover the potatoes with parchment paper.
7. Slice up the sausage and throw the slices on top of the beans and eggs. Bake for another 5 minutes.
8. Serve with the potatoes.

Bagels Bake
Prep time: 10 minutes | Cook time: 15 minutes | Serves 4

1 cup unbleached all-purpose or whole wheat flour, plus more for dusting
2 teaspoons baking powder

¾ teaspoon kosher salt
1 cup 0% Greek yogurt, drained of any liquid
1 egg white, beaten

1. In a medium bowl, combine the flour, baking powder, and salt and whisk well. Add the yogurt and mix with a fork or spatula until well combined.
2. Lightly dust a work surface with flour. Transfer the dough to the work surface and knead for 2 to 3 minutes by hand until it is smooth and slightly tacky. Divide the dough into 4 equal balls. Roll each ball into a ¾-inch-thick rope and join the ends to form bagels. Brush the tops with the egg white and sprinkle both sides with a topping of your choice, if desired.
3. Select the BAKE function and preheat MAXX to 280ºF (138ºC).
4. Working in batches, place the bagels in the air fryer basket in a single layer. Bake for 15 to 16 minutes (no need to flip), until golden. Let cool for at least 15 minutes before cutting and serving.

Cinnamon Walnut Muffins
Prep time: 15 minutes | Cook time: 10 minutes | Makes 8 muffins

1 cup flour
1/3 cup sugar
1 teaspoon baking powder
¼ teaspoon baking soda
¼ teaspoon salt
1 teaspoon cinnamon
¼ teaspoon ginger
¼ teaspoon nutmeg
1 egg
2 tablespoons

pancake syrup, plus 2 teaspoons
2 tablespoons melted butter, plus 2 teaspoons
¾ cup unsweetened applesauce
½ teaspoon vanilla extract
¼ cup chopped walnuts
¼ cup diced apple

1. Select the BAKE function and preheat MAXX to 330ºF (166ºC).
2. In a large bowl, stir together the flour, sugar, baking powder, baking soda, salt, cinnamon, ginger, and nutmeg.
3. In a small bowl, beat egg until frothy. Add syrup, butter, applesauce, and vanilla and mix well.
4. Pour egg mixture into dry ingredients and stir just until moistened.
5. Gently stir in nuts and diced apple.
6. Divide batter among 8 parchment paper-lined muffin cups.
7. Put 4 muffin cups in air fryer basket and bake for 10 minutes.
8. Repeat with remaining 4 muffins or until toothpick inserted in center comes out clean.
9. Serve warm.

Cheddar Avocado Quesadillas
Prep time: 10 minutes | Cook time: 11 minutes | Serves 4

4 eggs
2 tablespoons skim milk
Salt and ground black pepper, to taste
Cooking spray
4 flour tortillas

4 tablespoons salsa
2 ounces (57 g) Cheddar cheese, grated
½ small avocado, peeled and thinly sliced

1. Select the BAKE function and preheat MAXX to 270ºF (132ºC).
2. Beat together the eggs, milk, salt, and pepper.
3. Spray a baking pan lightly with cooking spray and add egg mixture.
4. Bake for 8 minutes, stirring every 1 to 2 minutes, until eggs are scrambled to the liking. Remove and set aside.
5. Spray one side of each tortilla with cooking spray. Flip over.
6. Divide eggs, salsa, cheese, and avocado among the tortillas, covering only half of each tortilla.
7. Fold each tortilla in half and press down lightly. Increase the temperature of the air fryer oven to 390ºF (199ºC) and switch from BAKE to AIR FRY.
8. Put 2 tortillas in air fryer basket and air fry for 3 minutes or until cheese melts and outside feels slightly crispy. Repeat with remaining two tortillas.
9. Cut each cooked tortilla into halves. Serve warm.

PB&J Oatmeal with Banana

Prep time: 10 minutes | Cook time: 25 minutes | Serves 4

Cooking spray
2 large very ripe bananas (the riper the better)
2/3 cup quick-cooking oats (uncooked)
½ teaspoon baking powder
Pinch of kosher salt
½ cup unsweetened almond milk (or any milk you desire)
5 tablespoons peanut butter powder (such as PB2)
1 tablespoon honey
1 large egg
1 teaspoon vanilla extract
½ cup blueberries
4 tablespoons grape preserves

1. Generously spray a 7-inch round cake pan with cooking spray.
2. In a medium bowl, mash the bananas well with a fork. In another medium bowl, stir together the oats, baking powder, and salt.
3. In a large bowl, whisk together the milk, peanut butter powder, honey, egg, and vanilla. Mix in the bananas until well incorporated, then add the oat mixture and combine. Fold in the blueberries. Pour into the prepared baking dish and spoon the jelly over the top by the teaspoon.
4. Select the BAKE function and preheat MAXX to 300ºF (150ºC).
5. Place the baking dish in the air fryer basket. Bake for 25 minutes, or until the top is golden brown and the oatmeal is set in the center. Remove and set aside to cool for 10 to 15 minutes. Slice into 4 wedges and serve warm.

Banana Butter Bread

Prep time: 10 minutes | Cook time: 22 minutes | Makes 3 loaves

3 ripe bananas, mashed
1 cup sugar
1 large egg
4 tablespoons (½ stick) unsalted butter, melted
1½ cups all-purpose flour
1 teaspoon baking soda
1 teaspoon salt

1. Coat the insides of 3 mini loaf pans with cooking spray.
2. In a large mixing bowl, mix the bananas and sugar.
3. In a separate large mixing bowl, combine the egg, butter, flour, baking soda, and salt and mix well.
4. Add the banana mixture to the egg and flour mixture. Mix well.
5. Divide the batter evenly among the prepared pans.
6. Select the BAKE function and preheat MAXX to 310ºF (154ºC). Set the mini loaf pans into the air fryer basket.
7. Bake in the preheated air fryer oven for 22 minutes. Insert a toothpick into the center of each loaf; if it comes out clean, they are done.
8. When the loaves are cooked through, remove the pans from the air fryer basket. Turn out the loaves onto a wire rack to cool.
9. Serve warm.

French Toast Sticks

Prep time: 10 minutes | Cook time: 6 minutes | Serves 4

2 eggs
½ cup milk
⅛ teaspoon salt
½ teaspoon pure vanilla extract
¾ cup crushed cornflakes
6 slices sandwich bread, each slice cut into 4 strips
Maple syrup, for dipping
Cooking spray

1. In a small bowl, beat together the eggs, milk, salt, and vanilla.
2. Put crushed cornflakes on a plate or in a shallow dish.
3. Dip bread strips in egg mixture, shake off excess, and roll in cornflake crumbs.
4. Spray both sides of bread strips with oil.
5. Put bread strips in air fryer basket in a single layer.
6. Select the AIR FRY function and cook at 390ºF (199ºC) for 6 minutes, or until golden brown.
7. Repeat with the remaining French toast sticks.
8. Serve with maple syrup.

Creamy Sausage and Cauliflower
Prep time: 5 minutes | Cook time: 45 minutes | Serves 4

1 pound (454 g) sausage, cooked and crumbled
2 cups heavy whipping cream
1 head cauliflower, chopped

1 cup grated Cheddar cheese, plus more for topping
8 eggs, beaten
Salt and ground black pepper, to taste

1. Select the BAKE function and preheat MAXX to 350ºF (177ºC).
2. In a large bowl, mix the sausage, heavy whipping cream, chopped cauliflower, cheese and eggs. Sprinkle with salt and ground black pepper.
3. Pour the mixture into a greased casserole dish. Bake in the preheated air fryer oven for 45 minutes or until firm.
4. Top with more Cheddar cheese and serve.

Baked Buttermilk Biscuits
Prep time: 5 minutes | Cook time: 5 minutes | Makes 12 biscuits

2 cups all-purpose flour, plus more for dusting the work surface
1 tablespoon baking powder
¼ teaspoon baking soda

2 teaspoons sugar
1 teaspoon salt
6 tablespoons cold unsalted butter, cut into 1-tablespoon slices
¾ cup buttermilk

1. Select the BAKE function and preheat MAXX to 360ºF (182ºC). Spray the air fryer basket with olive oil.
2. In a large mixing bowl, combine the flour, baking powder, baking soda, sugar, and salt and mix well.
3. Using a fork, cut in the butter until the mixture resembles coarse meal.
4. Add the buttermilk and mix until smooth.
5. Dust more flour on a clean work surface. Turn the dough out onto the work surface and roll it out until it is about ½ inch thick.
6. Using a 2-inch biscuit cutter, cut out the biscuits. Put the uncooked biscuits in the greased air fryer basket in a single layer.
7. Bake for 5 minutes. Transfer the cooked biscuits from the air fryer oven to a platter.
8. Cut the remaining biscuits. Bake the remaining biscuits.
9. Serve warm.

Cherry Tarts with Creamy Vanilla Frosting
Prep time: 15 minutes | Cook time: 20 minutes | Serves 6

Tarts:
2 refrigerated piecrusts
⅓ cup cherry preserves

1 teaspoon cornstarch
Cooking oil

Frosting:
½ cup vanilla yogurt
1 ounce (28 g) cream cheese

1 teaspoon stevia
Rainbow sprinkles

Make the Tarts
1. Select the BAKE function and preheat MAXX to 375ºF (190ºC).
2. Place the piecrusts on a flat surface. Using a knife or pizza cutter, cut each piecrust into 3 rectangles, for 6 total. (I discard the unused dough left from slicing the edges.)
3. In a small bowl, combine the preserves and cornstarch. Mix well.
4. Scoop 1 tablespoon of the preserves mixture onto the top half of each piece of piecrust.
5. Fold the bottom of each piece up to close the tart. Using the back of a fork, press along the edges of each tart to seal.
6. Spray the breakfast tarts with cooking oil and place them in the air fryer oven. I do not recommend stacking the breakfast tarts. They will stick together if stacked. You may need to prepare them in two batches. Bake for 10 minutes.
7. Allow the breakfast tarts to cool fully before removing from the air fryer oven.
8. If necessary, repeat with the remaining breakfast tarts.

Make the Frosting
9. In a small bowl, combine the yogurt, cream cheese, and stevia. Mix well.
10. Spread the breakfast tarts with frosting and top with sprinkles, and serve.

Chicken Breakfast Sausage Biscuits

Prep time: 5 minutes | Cook time: 15 minutes | Serves 5

12 ounces (340 g) chicken breakfast sausage

1 (6-ounce / 170-g) can biscuits
⅛ cup cream cheese

1. Form the sausage into 5 small patties.
2. Place the sausage patties in the air fryer oven. Select the AIR FRY function and cook at 370ºF (188ºC) for 5 minutes.
3. Open the air fryer oven. Flip the patties. Air fry for an additional 5 minutes.
4. Remove the cooked sausages from the air fryer oven.
5. Separate the biscuit dough into 5 biscuits.
6. Place the biscuits in the air fryer oven. Air fry for 3 minutes.
7. Open the air fryer oven. Flip the biscuits. Air fry for an additional 2 minutes.
8. Remove the cooked biscuits from the air fryer oven.
9. Split each biscuit in half. Spread 1 teaspoon of cream cheese onto the bottom of each biscuit. Top with a sausage patty and the other half of the biscuit, and serve.

Cheddar Egg and Bacon Muffins

Prep time: 5 minutes | Cook time: 15 minutes | Serves 1

2 eggs
Salt and ground black pepper, to taste
1 tablespoon green pesto
3 ounces (85 g)

shredded Cheddar cheese
5 ounces (142 g) cooked bacon
1 scallion, chopped

1. Select the BAKE function and preheat MAXX to 350ºF (177ºC). Line a cupcake tin with parchment paper.
2. Beat the eggs with pepper, salt, and pesto in a bowl. Mix in the cheese.
3. Pour the eggs into the cupcake tin and top with the bacon and scallion.
4. Bake in the preheated air fryer oven for 15 minutes, or until the egg is set.
5. Serve immediately.

Simple Blueberry Muffins

Prep time: 10 minutes | Cook time: 12 minutes | Makes 8 muffins

1⅓ cups flour
½ cup sugar
2 teaspoons baking powder
¼ teaspoon salt
⅓ cup canola oil

1 egg
½ cup milk
⅔ cup blueberries, fresh or frozen and thawed

1. Select the BAKE function and preheat MAXX to 330ºF (166ºC).
2. In a medium bowl, stir together flour, sugar, baking powder, and salt.
3. In a separate bowl, combine oil, egg, and milk and mix well.
4. Add egg mixture to dry ingredients and stir just until moistened.
5. Gently stir in the blueberries.
6. Spoon batter evenly into parchment paper-lined muffin cups.
7. Put 4 muffin cups in air fryer basket and bake for 12 minutes or until tops spring back when touched lightly.
8. Repeat with the remaining muffins.
9. Serve immediately.

British Pumpkin Egg Bake

Prep time: 10 minutes | Cook time: 10 minutes | Serves 2

2 eggs
½ cup milk
2 cups flour
2 tablespoons cider vinegar
2 teaspoons baking powder

1 tablespoon sugar
1 cup pumpkin purée
1 teaspoon cinnamon powder
1 teaspoon baking soda
1 tablespoon olive oil

1. Select the BAKE function and preheat MAXX to 300ºF (149ºC).
2. Crack the eggs into a bowl and beat with a whisk. Combine with the milk, flour, cider vinegar, baking powder, sugar, pumpkin purée, cinnamon powder, and baking soda, mixing well.
3. Grease a baking tray with oil. Add the mixture and transfer into the air fryer oven. Bake for 10 minutes.
4. Serve warm.

Mozzarella Sausage Pizza

Prep time: 10 minutes | Cook time: 6 minutes | Serves 4

2 tablespoons ketchup
1 pita bread
⅓ cup sausage
½ pound (227 g)

Mozzarella cheese
1 teaspoon garlic powder
1 tablespoon olive oil

1. Select the BAKE function and preheat MAXX to 340ºF (171ºC).
2. Spread the ketchup over the pita bread.
3. Top with the sausage and cheese. Sprinkle with the garlic powder and olive oil.
4. Put the pizza in the air fryer basket and bake for 6 minutes.
5. Serve warm.

Cornmeal and Ham Muffins

Prep time: 10 minutes | Cook time: 6 minutes | Makes 8 muffins

¾ cup yellow cornmeal
¼ cup flour
1½ teaspoons baking powder
¼ teaspoon salt
1 egg, beaten

2 tablespoons canola oil
½ cup milk
½ cup shredded sharp Cheddar cheese
½ cup diced ham

1. Select the BAKE function and preheat MAXX to 390ºF (199ºC).
2. In a medium bowl, stir together the cornmeal, flour, baking powder, and salt.
3. Add the egg, oil, and milk to dry ingredients and mix well.
4. Stir in shredded cheese and diced ham.
5. Divide batter among 8 parchment paper-lined muffin cups.
6. Put 4 filled muffin cups in air fryer basket and bake for 5 minutes.
7. Reduce temperature to 330ºF (166ºC) and bake for 1 minute or until a toothpick inserted in center of the muffin comes out clean.
8. Repeat with the remaining muffins.
9. Serve warm.

Lush Veggie Omelet

Prep time: 10 minutes | Cook time: 13 minutes | Serves 2

2 teaspoons canola oil
4 eggs, whisked
3 tablespoons plain milk
1 teaspoon melted butter
1 red bell pepper, seeded and chopped
1 green bell pepper, seeded and chopped

1 white onion, finely chopped
½ cup baby spinach leaves, roughly chopped
½ cup Halloumi cheese, shaved
Kosher salt and freshly ground black pepper, to taste

1. Select the BAKE function and preheat MAXX to 350ºF (177ºC).
2. Grease a baking pan with canola oil.
3. Put the remaining ingredients in the baking pan and stir well.
4. Transfer to the air fryer oven and bake for 13 minutes.
5. Serve warm.

Speedy Coffee Donuts

Prep time: 5 minutes | Cook time: 6 minutes | Serves 6

¼ cup sugar
½ teaspoon salt
1 cup flour
1 teaspoon baking powder

¼ cup coffee
1 tablespoon aquafaba
1 tablespoon sunflower oil

1. In a large bowl, combine the sugar, salt, flour, and baking powder.
2. Add the coffee, aquafaba, and sunflower oil and mix until a dough is formed. Leave the dough to rest in and the refrigerator.
3. Remove the dough from the fridge and divide up, kneading each section into a doughnut.
4. Put the doughnuts inside the air fryer oven. Select the AIR FRY function and cook at 400ºF (204ºC) for 6 minutes.
5. Serve immediately.

Air-Fried Avocado Tempura

Prep time: 5 minutes | Cook time: 10 minutes | Serves 4

½ cup bread crumbs
½ teaspoons salt
1 Haas avocado, pitted, peeled and

sliced
Liquid from 1 can white beans

1. Mix the bread crumbs and salt in a shallow bowl until well-incorporated.
2. Dip the avocado slices in the bean liquid, then into the bread crumbs.
3. Put the avocados in the air fryer oven, taking care not to overlap any slices. Select the AIR FRY function and cook at 350ºF (177ºC) for 10 minutes, giving the basket a good shake at the halfway point.
4. Serve immediately.

Mushroom and Yellow Squash Toast

Prep time: 10 minutes | Cook time: 10 minutes | Serves 4

1 tablespoon olive oil
1 red bell pepper, cut into strips
2 green onions, sliced
1 cup sliced button or cremini mushrooms
1 small yellow

squash, sliced
2 tablespoons softened butter
4 slices bread
½ cup soft goat cheese

1. Brush the air fryer basket with the olive oil.
2. Put the red pepper, green onions, mushrooms, and squash inside the air fryer oven and give them a stir. Select the AIR FRY function and cook at 350ºF (177ºC) for 7 minutes, or until the vegetables are tender, shaking the basket once throughout the cooking time.
3. Remove the vegetables and set them aside.
4. Spread the butter on the slices of bread and transfer to the air fryer oven, butter-side up. Brown for 3 minutes.
5. Remove the toast from the air fryer oven and top with goat cheese and vegetables. Serve warm.

Waffles with Chicken Wings

Prep time: 10 minutes | Cook time: 30 minutes | Serves 4

8 whole chicken wings
1 teaspoon garlic powder
Chicken seasoning or rub
Pepper

½ cup all-purpose flour
Cooking oil
8 frozen waffles
Maple syrup (optional)

1. In a medium bowl, season the chicken with the garlic powder and chicken seasoning and pepper to taste.
2. Transfer the chicken to a sealable plastic bag and add the flour. Shake to thoroughly coat the chicken.
3. Spray the air fryer basket with cooking oil.
4. Using tongs, transfer the chicken from the bag to the air fryer oven. It is okay to stack the chicken wings on top of each other. Spray them with cooking oil. Select the AIR FRY function and cook at 400ºF (205ºC) for 5 minutes.
5. Open the air fryer oven and shake the basket. Continue to cook the chicken. Repeat shaking every 5 minutes until 20 minutes has passed and the chicken is fully cooked.
6. Remove the cooked chicken from the air fryer oven and set aside.
7. Rinse the basket and base out with warm water. Return them to the air fryer oven.
8. Reduce the temperature to 370ºF (188ºC).
9. Place the frozen waffles in the air fryer oven. Do not stack. Depending on the size of your air fryer oven, you may need to work in batches. Spray the waffles with cooking oil. Air fry for 6 minutes.
10. If necessary, remove the cooked waffles from the air fryer oven, then repeat with the remaining waffles.
11. Serve the waffles with the chicken and a touch of maple syrup if desired.

Oat and Chia Seeds Porridge
Prep time: 10 minutes | Cook time: 5 minutes | Serves 4

2 tablespoons peanut butter
4 tablespoons honey
1 tablespoon butter, melted
4 cups milk
2 cups oats
1 cup chia seeds

1. Select the BAKE function and preheat MAXX to 390ºF (199ºC).
2. Put the peanut butter, honey, butter, and milk in a bowl and stir to mix. Add the oats and chia seeds and stir.
3. Transfer the mixture to a bowl and bake in the air fryer oven for 5 minutes. Give another stir before serving.

Bacon and Broccoli Cheese Bread Pudding
Prep time: 15 minutes | Cook time: 48 minutes | Serves 2 to 4

½ pound (227 g) thick cut bacon, cut into ¼-inch pieces
3 cups brioche bread, cut into ½-inch cubes
2 tablespoons butter, melted
3 eggs
1 cup milk
½ teaspoon salt
Freshly ground black pepper, to taste
1 cup frozen broccoli florets, thawed and chopped
1½ cups grated Swiss cheese

1. Select the AIR FRY function and cook the bacon at 400ºF (204ºC) for 8 minutes, or until crispy, shaking the basket a few times to help it air fry evenly. Remove the bacon and set it aside on a paper towel.
2. Air fry the brioche bread cubes for 2 minutes to dry and toast lightly.
3. Butter a cake pan. Combine all the remaining ingredients in a large bowl and toss well. Transfer the mixture to the buttered cake pan, cover with aluminum foil and refrigerate the bread pudding overnight, or for at least 8 hours.
4. Remove the cake pan from the refrigerator an hour before you plan to bake and let it sit on the countertop to come to room temperature.
5. Switch from AIR FRY to BAKE and preheat MAXX to 330ºF (166ºC). Transfer the covered cake pan to the air fryer basket, lowering the pan into the basket. Fold the ends of the aluminum foil over the top of the pan before returning the basket to the air fryer oven.
6. Bake for 20 minutes. Remove the foil and air fry for an additional 20 minutes. If the top browns a little too much before the custard has set, simply return the foil to the pan. The bread pudding has cooked through when a skewer inserted into the center comes out clean.
7. Serve warm.

Classic PB&J
Prep time: 5 minutes | Cook time: 6 minutes | Serves 4

½ cup cornflakes, crushed
¼ cup shredded coconut
8 slices oat nut bread or any whole-grain, oversize bread
6 tablespoons peanut butter
2 medium bananas, cut into ½-inch-thick slices
6 tablespoons pineapple preserves
1 egg, beaten
Cooking spray

1. In a shallow dish, mix the cornflake crumbs and coconut.
2. For each sandwich, spread one bread slice with 1½ tablespoons of peanut butter. Top with banana slices. Spread another bread slice with 1½ tablespoons of preserves. Combine to make a sandwich.
3. Using a pastry brush, brush top of sandwich lightly with beaten egg. Sprinkle with about 1½ tablespoons of crumb coating, pressing it in to make it stick. Spray with cooking spray.
4. Turn sandwich over and repeat to coat and spray the other side.
5. Air frying 2 at a time, place sandwiches in air fryer basket. Select the AIR FRY function and cook at 360ºF (182ºC) for 6 minutes, or until coating is golden brown and crispy.
6. Cut the cooked sandwiches in half and serve warm.

Ricotta Spinach Omelet
Prep time: 10 minutes | Cook time: 10 minutes | Serves 1

1 teaspoon olive oil
3 eggs
Salt and ground black pepper, to taste
1 tablespoon ricotta cheese
¼ cup chopped spinach
1 tablespoon chopped parsley

1. Grease the air fryer basket with olive oil. Select the BAKE function and preheat MAXX to 330ºF (166ºC).
2. In a bowl, beat the eggs with a fork and sprinkle salt and pepper.
3. Add the ricotta, spinach, and parsley and then transfer to the air fryer oven. Bake for 10 minutes or until the egg is set.
4. Serve warm.

Blueberry Yogurt Muffins
Prep time: 15 minutes | Cook time: 15 minutes | Serves 6

Cooking spray
1½ tablespoons unsalted butter, at room temperature
6 tablespoons sugar
1 large egg
1 large egg white
1 teaspoon vanilla extract
1 teaspoon fresh
lemon juice
Grated zest of 1 lemon
5 ounces (142 g) 0% Greek yogurt
¾ cup plus 2 tablespoons self-rising cake flour
¾ cup fresh or frozen blueberries

1. Spray 6 lined foil baking cups with cooking spray.
2. In a medium bowl, with an electric hand mixer, beat the butter and sugar on medium speed until well combined, about 2 minutes.
3. In a small bowl, whisk together the whole egg, egg white, and vanilla. Add to the butter and sugar mixture along with the lemon juice and zest and beat until combined, about 30 seconds. Beat in the yogurt, then the flour, mixing on low speed until combined, about 30 seconds. Using a spatula, fold in the blueberries. Using an ice cream scoop, evenly divide the mixture among the prepared baking cups, filling them three-quarters of the way full.

4. Select the BAKE function and preheat MAXX to 300ºF (150ºC).
5. Working in batches, place the muffins in the air fryer basket. Bake for 15 minutes, or until the tops are golden and a toothpick inserted in the center comes out clean. Let cool before eating.

Ham and Grit Fritters
Prep time: 15 minutes | Cook time: 20 minutes | Serves 6 to 8

4 cups water
1 cup quick-cooking grits
¼ teaspoon salt
2 tablespoons butter
2 cups grated Cheddar cheese, divided
1 cup finely diced ham
1 tablespoon chopped chives
Salt and freshly ground black pepper, to taste
1 egg, beaten
2 cups panko bread crumbs
Cooking spray

1. Bring the water to a boil in a saucepan. Whisk in the grits and ¼ teaspoon of salt, and cook for 7 minutes until the grits are soft. Remove the pan from the heat and stir in the butter and 1 cup of the grated Cheddar cheese. Transfer the grits to a bowl and let them cool for 10 to 15 minutes.
2. Stir the ham, chives and the rest of the cheese into the grits and season with salt and pepper to taste. Add the beaten egg and refrigerate the mixture for 30 minutes.
3. Put the panko bread crumbs in a shallow dish. Measure out ¼-cup portions of the grits mixture and shape them into patties. Coat all sides of the patties with the panko bread crumbs, patting them with the hands so the crumbs adhere to the patties. You should have about 16 patties. Spritz both sides of the patties with cooking spray.
4. In batches of 5 or 6, select the AIR FRY function and cook at 400ºF (204ºC) for 8 minutes. Using a flat spatula, flip the fritters over and air fry for another 4 minutes.
5. Serve hot.

Spinach and Tomato with Scrambled Eggs

Prep time: 10 minutes | Cook time: 10 minutes | Serves 2

2 tablespoons olive oil
4 eggs, whisked
5 ounces (142 g) fresh spinach, chopped
1 medium tomato, chopped
1 teaspoon fresh lemon juice
½ teaspoon coarse salt
½ teaspoon ground black pepper
½ cup of fresh basil, roughly chopped

1. Grease a baking pan with the oil, tilting it to spread the oil around. Select the BAKE function and preheat MAXX to 280ºF (138ºC).
2. Mix the remaining ingredients, apart from the basil leaves, whisking well until everything is completely combined.
3. Bake in the air fryer oven for 10 minutes.
4. Top with fresh basil leaves before serving.

Cinnamon Rolls with Cream Cheese Glaze

Prep time: 10 minutes | Cook time: 9 minutes | Serves 8

1 pound (454 g) frozen bread dough, thawed
¼ cup butter, melted
¾ cup brown sugar
1½ tablespoons ground cinnamon
Cream Cheese Glaze:
4 ounces (113 g)
cream cheese, softened
2 tablespoons butter, softened
1¼ cups powdered sugar
½ teaspoon vanilla extract

1. Let the bread dough come to room temperature on the counter. On a lightly floured surface, roll the dough into a 13-inch by 11-inch rectangle. Position the rectangle so the 13-inch side is facing you. Brush the melted butter all over the dough, leaving a 1-inch border uncovered along the edge farthest away from you.
2. Combine the brown sugar and cinnamon in a small bowl. Sprinkle the mixture evenly over the buttered dough, keeping the 1-inch border uncovered. Roll the dough into a log, starting with the edge closest to you. Roll the dough tightly, rolling evenly, and push out any air pockets. When you get to the uncovered edge of the dough, press the dough onto the roll to seal it together.
3. Cut the log into 8 pieces, slicing slowly with a sawing motion so you don't flatten the dough. Turn the slices on their sides and cover with a clean kitchen towel. Let the rolls sit in the warmest part of the kitchen for 1½ to 2 hours to rise.
4. To make the glaze, place the cream cheese and butter in a microwave-safe bowl. Soften the mixture in the microwave for 30 seconds at a time until it is easy to stir. Gradually add the powdered sugar and stir to combine. Add the vanilla extract and whisk until smooth. Set aside.
5. When the rolls have risen, transfer 4 of the rolls to the air fryer basket. Select the AIR FRY function and cook at 350ºF (177ºC) for 5 minutes. Turn the rolls over and air fry for another 4 minutes. Repeat with the remaining 4 rolls.
6. Let the rolls cool for two minutes before glazing. Spread large dollops of cream cheese glaze on top of the warm cinnamon rolls, allowing some glaze to drip down the side of the rolls. Serve warm.

Tomato and Mozzarella Cheese Bruschetta

Prep time: 5 minutes | Cook time: 4 minutes | Serves 1

6 small loaf slices
½ cup tomatoes, finely chopped
3 ounces (85 g) Mozzarella cheese,
grated
1 tablespoon fresh basil, chopped
1 tablespoon olive oil

1. Put the loaf slices inside the air fryer oven. Select the AIR FRY function and cook at 350ºF (177ºC) for 3 minutes.
2. Add the tomato, Mozzarella, basil, and olive oil on top.
3. Air fry for an additional minute before serving.

Bacon and Ham Cups

Prep time: 5 minutes | Cook time: 20 minutes | Serves 2

3 slices bacon, cooked, sliced in half
2 slices ham
1 slice tomato
2 eggs
2 teaspoons grated Parmesan cheese
Salt and ground black pepper, to taste

1. Select the BAKE function and preheat MAXX to 375ºF (191ºC). Line 2 greased muffin tins with 3 half-strips of bacon
2. Put one slice of ham and half slice of tomato in each muffin tin on top of the bacon
3. Crack one egg on top of the tomato in each muffin tin and sprinkle each with half a teaspoon of grated Parmesan cheese. Sprinkle with salt and ground black pepper, if desired.
4. Bake in the preheated air fryer oven for 20 minutes. Remove from the air fryer oven and let cool.
5. Serve warm.

Cheesy Italian Sausage Egg Muffins

Prep time: 5 minutes | Cook time: 20 minutes | Serves 4

6 ounces (170 g) Italian sausage, sliced
6 eggs
⅛ cup heavy cream
Salt and ground black
pepper, to taste
3 ounces (85 g) Parmesan cheese, grated
Cooking spray

1. Select the BAKE function and preheat MAXX to 350ºF (177ºC). Spritz a muffin pan with cooking spray.
2. Put the sliced sausage in the muffin pan.
3. Beat the eggs with the cream in a bowl and season with salt and pepper.
4. Pour half of the mixture over the sausages in the pan.
5. Sprinkle with cheese and the remaining egg mixture.
6. Bake in the preheated air fryer oven for 20 minutes or until set.
7. Serve immediately.

Egg and Chicken Sausage Burrito

Prep time: 5 minutes | Cook time: 30 minutes | Serves 6

6 eggs
Salt
Pepper
Cooking oil
½ cup chopped red bell pepper
½ cup chopped green bell pepper
8 ounces (227 g) ground chicken sausage
½ cup salsa
6 medium (8-inch) flour tortillas
½ cup shredded Cheddar cheese

1. In a medium bowl, whisk the eggs. Add salt and pepper to taste.
2. Place a skillet on medium-high heat. Spray with cooking oil. Add the eggs. Scramble for 2 to 3 minutes, until the eggs are fluffy. Remove the eggs from the skillet and set aside.
3. If needed, spray the skillet with more oil. Add the chopped red and green bell peppers. Select the AIR FRY function and cook at 400ºF (205ºC) for 2 to 3 minutes, until the peppers are soft.
4. Add the ground sausage to the skillet. Break the sausage into smaller pieces using a spatula or spoon. Air fry for 3 to 4 minutes, until the sausage is brown.
5. Add the salsa and scrambled eggs. Stir to combine. Remove the skillet from heat.
6. Spoon the mixture evenly onto the tortillas.
7. To form the burritos, fold the sides of each tortilla in toward the middle and then roll up from the bottom. You can secure each burrito with a toothpick. Or you can moisten the outside edge of the tortilla with a small amount of water. I prefer to use a cooking brush, but you can also dab with your fingers.
8. Spray the burritos with cooking oil and place them in the air fryer oven. Do not stack. Work in batches if they do not all fit in the basket. Air fry for 8 minutes.
9. Open the air fryer oven and flip the burritos. Air fry for an additional 2 minutes or until crisp.
10. If necessary, repeat with the remaining burritos.
11. Sprinkle the Cheddar cheese over the burritos. Cool before serving.

Mozzarella Pepperoni Pizza

Prep time: 10 minutes | Cook time: 6 minutes | Serves 1

1 teaspoon olive oil
1 tablespoon pizza sauce
1 pita bread
6 pepperoni slices
¼ cup grated

Mozzarella cheese
¼ teaspoon garlic powder
¼ teaspoon dried oregano

1. Select the BAKE function and preheat MAXX to 350ºF (177ºC). Grease the air fryer basket with olive oil.
2. Spread the pizza sauce on top of the pita bread. Put the pepperoni slices over the sauce, followed by the Mozzarella cheese.
3. Season with garlic powder and oregano.
4. Put the pita pizza inside the air fryer oven and place a trivet on top.
5. Bake in the preheated air fryer oven for 6 minutes and serve.

Nuts and Seeds Muffins

Prep time: 15 minutes | Cook time: 10 minutes | Makes 8 muffins

½ cup whole-wheat flour, plus 2 tablespoons
¼ cup oat bran
2 tablespoons flaxseed meal
¼ cup brown sugar
½ teaspoon baking soda
½ teaspoon baking powder
¼ teaspoon salt
½ teaspoon cinnamon
½ cup buttermilk

2 tablespoons melted butter
1 egg
½ teaspoon pure vanilla extract
½ cup grated carrots
¼ cup chopped pecans
¼ cup chopped walnuts
1 tablespoon pumpkin seeds
1 tablespoon sunflower seeds
Cooking spray

Special Equipment:
16 foil muffin cups, paper liners removed

1. Select the BAKE function and preheat MAXX to 330ºF (166ºC).
2. In a large bowl, stir together the flour, bran, flaxseed meal, sugar, baking soda, baking powder, salt, and cinnamon.
3. In a medium bowl, beat together the buttermilk, butter, egg, and vanilla. Pour into flour mixture and stir just until dry ingredients moisten. Do not beat.
4. Gently stir in carrots, nuts, and seeds.
5. Double up the foil cups so you have 8 total and spritz with cooking spray.
6. Put 4 foil cups in air fryer basket and divide half the batter among them.
7. Bake for 10 minutes or until a toothpick inserted in center comes out clean.
8. Repeat with the remaining 4 muffins.
9. Serve warm.

Potato Lyonnaise

Prep time: 10 minutes | Cook time: 31 minutes | Serves 4

1 Vidalia onion, sliced
1 teaspoon butter, melted
1 teaspoon brown sugar
2 large russet potatoes (about 1 pound / 454 g in

total), sliced ½-inch thick
1 tablespoon vegetable oil
Salt and freshly ground black pepper, to taste

1. Toss the sliced onions, melted butter and brown sugar together in the air fryer basket. Select the AIR FRY function and cook at 370ºF (188ºC) for 8 minutes, shaking the basket occasionally to help the onions cook evenly.
2. While the onions are cooking, bring a saucepan of salted water to a boil on the stovetop. Par-cook the potatoes in boiling water for 3 minutes. Drain the potatoes and pat them dry with a clean kitchen towel.
3. Add the potatoes to the onions in the air fryer basket and drizzle with vegetable oil. Toss to coat the potatoes with the oil and season with salt and freshly ground black pepper.
4. Increase the air fryer oven temperature to 400ºF (204ºC) and air fry for 20 minutes, tossing the vegetables a few times during the cooking time to help the potatoes brown evenly.
5. Season with salt and freshly ground black pepper and serve warm.

Ranch Risotto with Parmesan Cheese
Prep time: 10 minutes | Cook time: 30 minutes | Serves 2

1 tablespoon olive oil
1 clove garlic, minced
1 tablespoon unsalted butter
1 onion, diced
¾ cup Arborio rice
2 cups chicken stock, boiling
½ cup Parmesan cheese, grated

1. Select the BAKE function and preheat MAXX to 390ºF (199ºC).
2. Grease a round baking tin with olive oil and stir in the garlic, butter, and onion.
3. Transfer the tin to the air fryer oven and bake for 4 minutes. Add the rice and bake for 4 more minutes.
4. Turn the air fryer oven to 320ºF (160ºC) and pour in the chicken stock. Cover and bake for 22 minutes.
5. Scatter with cheese and serve.

Warm Sourdough Croutons
Prep time: 5 minutes | Cook time: 6 minutes | Makes 4 cups

4 cups cubed sourdough bread, 1-inch cubes
1 tablespoon olive oil
1 teaspoon fresh
thyme leaves
¼ teaspoon salt
Freshly ground black pepper, to taste

1. Combine all ingredients in a bowl.
2. Toss the bread cubes into the air fryer oven. Select the AIR FRY function and cook at 400ºF (204ºC) for 6 minutes, shaking the basket once or twice while they cook.
3. Serve warm.

Onion Cheese Omelet
Prep time: 10 minutes | Cook time: 12 minutes | Serves 2

3 eggs
Salt and ground black pepper, to taste
½ teaspoons soy sauce
1 large onion, chopped
2 tablespoons grated Cheddar cheese
Cooking spray

1. Select the BAKE function and preheat MAXX to 355ºF (179ºC).
2. In a bowl, whisk together the eggs, salt, pepper, and soy sauce.
3. Spritz a small pan with cooking spray. Spread the chopped onion across the bottom of the pan, then transfer the pan to the air fryer oven.
4. Bake in the preheated air fryer oven for 6 minutes or until the onion is translucent.
5. Add the egg mixture on top of the onions to coat well. Add the cheese on top, then continue baking for another 6 minutes.
6. Allow to cool before serving.

All-in-One Cheese Toast
Prep time: 10 minutes | Cook time: 10 minutes | Serves 1

1 strip bacon, diced
1 slice 1-inch thick bread
1 egg
Salt and freshly
ground black pepper, to taste
¼ cup grated Colby cheese

1. Select the AIR FRY function and cook the bacon at 400ºF (204ºC) for 3 minutes, shaking the basket once or twice while it cooks. Remove the bacon to a paper towel lined plate and set aside.
2. Use a sharp paring knife to score a large circle in the middle of the slice of bread, cutting halfway through, but not all the way through to the cutting board. Press down on the circle in the center of the bread slice to create an indentation.
3. Transfer the slice of bread, hole side up, to the air fryer basket. Crack the egg into the center of the bread, and season with salt and pepper.
4. Adjust the air fryer oven temperature to 380ºF (193ºC) and air fry for 5 minutes. Sprinkle the grated cheese around the edges of the bread, leaving the center of the yolk uncovered, and top with the cooked bacon. Press the cheese and bacon into the bread lightly to help anchor it to the bread and prevent it from blowing around in the air fryer oven.
5. Air fry for one or two more minutes, just to melt the cheese and finish cooking the egg. Serve immediately.

Easy Cinnamon Toasts

Prep time: 5 minutes | Cook time: 4 minutes | Serves 4

1 tablespoon salted butter
2 teaspoons ground cinnamon
4 tablespoons sugar
½ teaspoon vanilla extract
10 bread slices

1. Select the BAKE function and preheat MAXX to 380ºF (193ºC).
2. In a bowl, combine the butter, cinnamon, sugar, and vanilla extract. Spread onto the slices of bread.
3. Put the bread inside the air fryer oven and bake for 4 minutes or until golden brown.
4. Serve warm.

Warm Pretzels

Prep time: 10 minutes | Cook time: 6 minutes | Makes 24 pretzels

2 teaspoons yeast
1 cup water, warm
1 teaspoon sugar
1 teaspoon salt
2½ cups all-purpose flour
2 tablespoons butter,
melted, plus more as needed
1 cup boiling water
1 tablespoon baking soda
Coarse sea salt, to taste

1. Combine the yeast and water in a small bowl. Combine the sugar, salt and flour in the bowl of a stand mixer. With the mixer running and using the dough hook, drizzle in the yeast mixture and melted butter and knead dough until smooth and elastic, about 10 minutes. Shape into a ball and let the dough rise for 1 hour.
2. Punch the dough down to release any air and divide the dough into 24 portions.
3. Roll each portion into a skinny rope using both hands on the counter and rolling from the center to the ends of the rope. Spin the rope into a pretzel shape (or tie the rope into a knot) and place the tied pretzels on a parchment lined baking sheet.
4. Combine the boiling water and baking soda in a shallow bowl and whisk to dissolve. Let the water cool so you can put the hands in it. Working in batches,

dip the pretzels (top side down) into the baking soda mixture and let them soak for 30 seconds to a minute. Then remove the pretzels carefully and return them (top side up) to the baking sheet. Sprinkle the coarse salt on the top.
5. Select the AIR FRY function and cook at 350ºF (177ºC) for 6 minutes, flipping once halfway. When the pretzels are finished, brush them generously with the melted butter and enjoy them warm.

Perfect Soufflé

Prep time: 10 minutes | Cook time: 22 minutes | Serves 4

¹/₃ cup butter, melted
¼ cup flour
1 cup milk
1 ounce (28 g) sugar
4 egg yolks
1 teaspoon vanilla
extract
6 egg whites
1 teaspoon cream of tartar
Cooking spray

1. In a bowl, mix the butter and flour until a smooth consistency is achieved.
2. Pour the milk into a saucepan over medium-low heat. Add the sugar and allow to dissolve before raising the heat to boil the milk.
3. Pour in the flour and butter mixture and stir rigorously for 7 minutes to eliminate any lumps. Make sure the mixture thickens. Take off the heat and allow to cool for 15 minutes.
4. Select the BAKE function and preheat MAXX to 320ºF (160ºC). Spritz 6 soufflé dishes with cooking spray.
5. Put the egg yolks and vanilla extract in a separate bowl and beat them together with a fork. Pour in the milk and combine well to incorporate everything.
6. In a smaller bowl mix the egg whites and cream of tartar with a fork. Fold into the egg yolks-milk mixture before adding in the flour mixture. Transfer equal amounts to the 6 soufflé dishes.
7. Put the dishes in the air fryer oven and bake for 15 minutes.
8. Serve warm.

Breaded Avocado
Prep time: 5 minutes | Cook time: 6 minutes | Serves 4

2 large avocados, sliced
¼ teaspoon paprika
Salt and ground black

pepper, to taste
½ cup flour
2 eggs, beaten
1 cup bread crumbs

1. Sprinkle paprika, salt and pepper on the slices of avocado.
2. Lightly coat the avocados with flour. Dredge them in the eggs, before covering with bread crumbs.
3. Transfer to the air fryer oven. Select the AIR FRY function and cook at 400ºF (204ºC) for 6 minutes.
4. Serve warm.

Cheddar Buttermilk Biscuits
Prep time: 10 minutes | Cook time: 22 minutes | Makes 8 biscuits

2⅓ cups self-rising flour
2 tablespoons sugar
½ cup butter (1 stick), frozen for 15 minutes
½ cup grated

Cheddar cheese, plus more to melt on top
1⅓ cups buttermilk
1 cup all-purpose flour, for shaping
1 tablespoon butter, melted

1. Line a buttered 7-inch metal cake pan with parchment paper or a silicone liner.
2. Combine the flour and sugar in a large mixing bowl. Grate the butter into the flour. Add the grated cheese and stir to coat the cheese and butter with flour. Then add the buttermilk and stir just until you can no longer see streaks of flour. The dough should be quite wet.
3. Spread the all-purpose (not self-rising) flour out on a small cookie sheet. With a spoon, scoop 8 evenly sized balls of dough into the flour, making sure they don't touch each other. With floured hands, coat each dough ball with flour and toss them gently from hand to hand to shake off any excess flour. Put each floured dough ball into the prepared pan, right up next to the other. This will help the biscuits rise, rather than spreading out.
4. Transfer the cake pan to the air fryer basket. Let the ends of the aluminum foil sling hang across the cake pan before returning the basket to the air fryer oven.
5. Select the AIR FRY function and cook at 380ºF (193ºC) for 20 minutes. Check the biscuits twice to make sure they are not getting too brown on top. If they are, re-arrange the aluminum foil strips to cover any brown parts. After 20 minutes, check the biscuits by inserting a toothpick into the center of the biscuits. It should come out clean. If it needs a little more time, continue to air fry for two extra minutes. Brush the tops of the biscuits with some melted butter and sprinkle a little more grated cheese on top if desired. Pop the basket back into the air fryer oven for another 2 minutes.
6. Remove the cake pan from the air fryer oven. Let the biscuits cool for just a minute or two and then turn them out onto a plate and pull apart. Serve immediately.

Scotch Eggs
Prep time: 5 minutes | Cook time: 25 minutes | Serves 4

4 large hard boiled eggs
1 (12-ounce / 340-g) package pork

sausage
8 slices thick-cut bacon

Special Equipment:
4 wooden toothpicks, soaked in water for at least 30 minutes

1. Slice the sausage into four parts and place each part into a large circle.
2. Put an egg into each circle and wrap it in the sausage. Put in the refrigerator for 1 hour.
3. Make a cross with two pieces of thick-cut bacon. Put a wrapped egg in the center, fold the bacon over top of the egg, and secure with a toothpick.
4. Select the AIR FRY function and cook at 450ºF (235ºC) for 25 minutes.
5. Serve immediately.

Whole-Wheat Banana Churros with Oatmeal

Prep time: 15 minutes | Cook time: 15 minutes | Serves 2

For the Churros:

1 large yellow banana, peeled, cut in half lengthwise, then cut in half widthwise
2 tablespoons whole-wheat pastry flour
⅛ teaspoon sea salt
2 teaspoons oil
(sunflower or melted coconut)
1 teaspoon water
Cooking spray
1 tablespoon coconut sugar
½ teaspoon cinnamon

For the Oatmeal:

¾ cup rolled oats
1½ cups water

To make the churros

1. Put the 4 banana pieces in a medium-size bowl and add the flour and salt. Stir gently. Add the oil and water. Stir gently until evenly mixed. You may need to press some coating onto the banana pieces.
2. Spray the air fryer basket with the oil spray. Put the banana pieces in the air fryer basket. Select the AIR FRY function and cook at 340ºF (171ºC) for 5 minutes. Remove, gently turn over, and air fry for another 5 minutes or until browned.
3. In a medium bowl, add the coconut sugar and cinnamon and stir to combine. When the banana pieces are nicely browned, spray with the oil and place in the cinnamon-sugar bowl. Toss gently with a spatula to coat the banana pieces with the mixture.

To make the oatmeal

1. While the bananas are cooking, make the oatmeal. In a medium pot, bring the oats and water to a boil, then reduce to low heat. Simmer, stirring often, until all the water is absorbed, about 5 minutes. Put the oatmeal into two bowls.
2. Top the oatmeal with the coated banana pieces and serve immediately.

Posh Orange Glazed Rolls

Prep time: 15 minutes | Cook time: 8 minutes | Makes 8 rolls

3 ounces (85 g) low-fat cream cheese
1 tablespoon low-fat sour cream or plain yogurt
2 teaspoons sugar
¼ teaspoon pure vanilla extract
¼ teaspoon orange extract
1 can (8 count)
organic crescent roll dough
¼ cup chopped walnuts
¼ cup dried cranberries
¼ cup shredded, sweetened coconut
Butter-flavored cooking spray

Orange Glaze:

½ cup powdered sugar
1 tablespoon orange juice
¼ teaspoon orange extract
Dash of salt

1. Cut a circular piece of parchment paper slightly smaller than the bottom of the air fryer basket. Set aside.
2. In a small bowl, combine the cream cheese, sour cream or yogurt, sugar, and vanilla and orange extracts. Stir until smooth.
3. Separate crescent roll dough into 8 triangles and divide cream cheese mixture among them. Starting at wide end, spread cheese mixture to within 1 inch of point.
4. Sprinkle nuts and cranberries evenly over cheese mixture.
5. Starting at wide end, roll up triangles, then sprinkle with coconut, pressing in lightly to make it stick. Spray tops of rolls with butter-flavored cooking spray.
6. Put parchment paper in air fryer basket, and place 4 rolls on top, spaced evenly.
7. Select the AIR FRY function and cook at 300ºF (149ºC) for 8 minutes, until rolls are golden brown and cooked through.
8. Repeat with the remaining 4 rolls. You should be able to use the same piece of parchment paper twice.
9. In a small bowl, stir together ingredients for glaze and drizzle over warm rolls. Serve warm.

Brown Sugar-Pumpkin Bread

Prep time: 20 minutes | Cook time: 40 to 45 minutes | Serves 6

Cooking spray
1/3 cup unbleached all-purpose or gluten-free flour
1/4 cup white whole wheat or gluten-free flour
5 tablespoons loosely packed light brown sugar
1/4 teaspoon baking soda
1/4 teaspoon baking powder
1 teaspoon pumpkin pie spice
1/8 teaspoon ground cinnamon
1/8 teaspoon ground nutmeg
1/8 teaspoon kosher salt
3/4 cup canned unsweetened pumpkin puree
1 tablespoon coconut or vegetable oil
1 large egg
3/4 teaspoon vanilla extract

Crumb Topping:
2 tablespoons light brown sugar
1/2 tablespoon white whole wheat or gluten-free flour
1/8 teaspoon ground cinnamon
1/2 tablespoon cold unsalted butter

1. Spray a 6 × 3½ × 2-inch mini loaf pan with cooking spray.
2. In a medium bowl, whisk together the flours, brown sugar, baking soda, baking powder, pumpkin pie spice, cinnamon, nutmeg, and salt.
3. In a large bowl, combine the pumpkin puree, oil, egg, and vanilla. Beat with an electric hand mixer on medium speed, pausing to scrape down the sides of the bowl with a spatula, until thick.
4. Add the flour mixture to the pumpkin mixture and mix on low speed until combined. Pour the batter into the prepared pan.
5. For the crumb topping: In a small bowl, combine the brown sugar, flour, and cinnamon. Cut the butter in with a fork until the mixture resembles coarse crumbs. Evenly sprinkle over the batter.
6. Select the BAKE function and preheat MAXX to 300ºF (150ºC).
7. Place the pan in the air fryer basket. Bake for 40 to 45 minutes, until a toothpick inserted in the center comes out clean. Let cool for at least 30 minutes before cutting into 6 slices to serve.

Shakshuka with Tomato Sauce

Prep time: 15 minutes | Cook time: 30 minutes | Serves 2

Tomato Sauce:
3 tablespoons extra-virgin olive oil
1 small yellow onion, diced
1 jalapeño pepper, seeded and minced
1 red bell pepper, diced
2 cloves garlic, minced
1 teaspoon cumin
1 teaspoon sweet paprika
Pinch cayenne pepper
1 tablespoon tomato paste
1 (28-ounce / 794-g) can whole plum tomatoes with juice
2 teaspoons granulated sugar

Shakshuka:
4 eggs
1 tablespoon heavy cream
1 tablespoon chopped
cilantro
Kosher salt and pepper to taste

1. Heat the olive oil in a large, deep skillet over medium heat. Add the onion and peppers, season with salt, and sauté until softened, about 10 minutes. Add the garlic and spices and sauté a few additional minutes until fragrant. Add the tomato paste and stir to combine. Add the plum tomatoes along with their juice—breaking up the tomatoes with a spoon—and the sugar. Turn the heat to high and bring the mixture to a boil. Turn the heat down and simmer until the tomatoes are thickened, about 10 minutes. Turn off the heat.
2. Select the BAKE function and preheat MAXX to 300ºF (150ºC).
3. Crack the eggs into a 7-inch round cake pan insert for the air fryer oven. Remove 1 cup of the tomato sauce from the skillet and spoon it over the egg whites only, leaving the yolks exposed. Drizzle the cream over the yolks.
4. Place the cake pan in the air fryer oven. Bake for 10 to 12 minutes, until the egg whites are set and the yolks still runny. Remove the pan from the air fryer oven and garnish with chopped cilantro. Season with salt and pepper.
5. Serve immediately with crusty bread to mop up the sauce.

French Toast with Cinnamon Streusel
Prep time: 10 minutes | Cook time: 9 minutes | Serves 4

Streusel:

½ cup all-purpose flour

¼ cup granulated sugar

¼ cup light brown sugar

½ teaspoon cinnamon

Pinch kosher salt

4 tablespoons unsalted butter, melted

French Toast:

2 eggs

¼ cup milk

1 teaspoon vanilla extract

½ teaspoon cinnamon

Pinch nutmeg

4 slices brioche, challah, or white bread, preferably slightly stale

Maple syrup for serving

1. To make the streusel, combine the flour, sugars, cinnamon, and salt in a medium bowl. Pour the melted butter over the dry ingredients and stir with a fork to combine. Transfer the mixture to a plastic bag and place it in the freezer while you prepare the French toast.
2. Select the BAKE function and preheat MAXX to 375ºF (190ºC).
3. To make the French toast, whisk together the eggs, milk, vanilla, cinnamon, and nutmeg in a medium bowl. Line the air fryer basket with perforated parchment paper to prevent sticking. Dunk each slice of bread in the egg mixture, making sure both sides are coated. Hold the bread over the bowl for a moment to allow any excess liquid to slide off.
4. Place the bread in the air fryer basket. Bake for 5 minutes. Open the air fryer oven and turn the bread over. Top each slice of bread with 2 tablespoons of streusel. Bake for an additional 4 minutes until the bread is crispy and browned and the streusel is puffy and golden. Serve warm with maple syrup.

Potato and Mustard Seeds Bread Rolls
Prep time: 15 minutes | Cook time: 20 minutes | Serves 5

5 large potatoes, boiled and mashed

Salt and ground black pepper, to taste

½ teaspoon mustard seeds

1 tablespoon olive oil

2 small onions, chopped

2 sprigs curry leaves

½ teaspoon turmeric powder

2 green chilis, seeded and chopped

1 bunch coriander, chopped

8 slices bread, brown sides discarded

1. Put the mashed potatoes in a bowl and sprinkle on salt and pepper. Set to one side.
2. Fry the mustard seeds in olive oil over a medium-low heat in a skillet, stirring continuously, until they sputter.
3. Add the onions and cook until they turn translucent. Add the curry leaves and turmeric powder and stir. Cook for a further 2 minutes until fragrant.
4. Remove the pan from the heat and combine with the potatoes. Mix in the green chilies and coriander.
5. Wet the bread slightly and drain of any excess liquid.
6. Spoon a small amount of the potato mixture into the center of the bread and enclose the bread around the filling, sealing it entirely. Continue until the rest of the bread and filling is used up. Brush each bread roll with some oil and transfer to the air fryer basket.
7. Select the AIR FRY function and cook at 400ºF (204ºC) for 15 minutes, gently shaking the air fryer basket at the halfway point to ensure each roll is cooked evenly.
8. Serve immediately.

Chapter 3 Sauces, Dips, and Dressings

Nut-Lemon Dip
Prep time: 10 minutes | Cook time: 5 minutes | Makes 1 cup

1 slice hearty white sandwich bread, crusts removed, torn into 1-inch pieces
¾ cup water, plus extra as needed
1 cup blanched almonds, blanched hazelnuts, pine nuts, or walnuts, toasted
¼ cup extra-virgin olive oil
2 tablespoons lemon juice, plus extra as needed
1 small garlic clove, minced
Salt and pepper
Pinch cayenne pepper

1. With fork, mash bread and water together in bowl into paste. Process bread mixture, nuts, oil, lemon juice, garlic, ½ teaspoon salt, ⅛ teaspoon pepper, and cayenne in blender until smooth, about 2 minutes. Add extra water as needed until sauce is barely thicker than consistency of heavy cream.
2. Season with salt, pepper, and extra lemon juice to taste. Serve at room temperature. (Sauce can be refrigerated for up to 2 days; bring to room temperature before serving.)

Greek Cucumber Yogurt Sauce
Prep time: 5 minutes | Cook time: 0 minutes | Makes 2 cups

1 (12-ounce / 340-g) cucumber, peeled, halved lengthwise, seeded, and shredded
Salt and pepper
1 cup whole-milk
Greek yogurt
2 tablespoons extra-virgin olive oil
2 tablespoons minced fresh mint and/or dill
1 small garlic clove, minced

1. Toss cucumber with ½ teaspoon salt in colander and let drain for 15 minutes.
2. Whisk yogurt, oil, mint, and garlic together in bowl, then stir in drained cucumber. Cover and refrigerate until chilled, at least 1 hour or up to 2 days. Season with salt and pepper to taste before serving.

Avocado-Lemon Tahini
Prep time: 5 minutes | Cook time: 0 minutes | Makes 12 tablespoons

1 large avocado, pitted and peeled
½ cup water
2 tablespoons tahini
2 tablespoons freshly squeezed lemon juice
1 teaspoon dried basil
1 teaspoon white wine vinegar
1 garlic clove
¼ teaspoon pink Himalayan salt
¼ teaspoon freshly ground black pepper

1. Combine all the ingredients in a food processor and blend until smooth.

Balsamic Mustard Dressing
Prep time: 5 minutes | Cook time: 0 minutes | Makes 1 cup

2 tablespoons Dijon mustard
¼ cup balsamic
vinegar
¾ cup olive oil

1. Put all ingredients in a jar with a tight-fitting lid. Put on the lid and shake vigorously until thoroughly combined. Refrigerate until ready to use and shake well before serving.

Cashew Mayonnaise
Prep time: 5 minutes | Cook time: 0 minutes | Makes 18 tablespoons

1 cup cashews, soaked in hot water for at least 1 hour
¼ cup plus 3 tablespoons milk
1 tablespoon apple cider vinegar
1 tablespoon freshly
squeezed lemon juice
1 tablespoon Dijon mustard
1 tablespoon aquafaba
⅛ teaspoon pink Himalayan salt

1. In a food processor, combine all the ingredients and blend until creamy and smooth.

Barbecue Sauce
Prep time: 10 minutes | Cook time: 3 minutes | Makes 2½ cups

1 tablespoon vegetable oil	sugar
2 cloves garlic, minced	1 tablespoon unsalted butter
1¾ cups ketchup	2 teaspoons Worcestershire sauce
¼ cup apple cider vinegar	¼ teaspoon cayenne
¼ cup water	¼ teaspoon salt
¼ cup packed brown	¼ teaspoon ground black pepper

1. Heat the vegetable oil in a medium-size saucepan over medium heat. Add the minced garlic and cook for 30 seconds, until it becomes fragrant. Do not let the garlic burn or brown. This will cause it to become bitter and will ruin the sauce. Add the ketchup, vinegar, water, and brown sugar. Simmer over medium heat for 3 to 4 minutes, stirring often. Add the remaining ingredients, decrease the heat to low, and simmer for 5 more minutes.
2. Remove the sauce from the heat and let cool for 10 minutes before using as a baste. If making ahead of time, allow the sauce to cool for 30 minutes and place in an airtight container. Store in the refrigerator for up to 10 days. Reheat before using.

Cashew Marinara Sauce
Prep time: 15 minutes | Cook time: 5 minutes | Makes 3 cups

¾ cup raw cashews	1 tablespoon arrowroot powder
¼ cup boiling water	1 teaspoon salt
1 tablespoon olive oil	1 tablespoon nutritional yeast
4 garlic cloves, minced	1¼ cups marinara sauce
1½ cups unsweetened almond milk	

1. Put the cashews in a heatproof bowl and add boiling water to cover. Let soak for 10 minutes. Drain the cashews and place them in a blender. Add ¼ cup boiling water and blend for 1 to 2 minutes or until creamy. Set aside.
2. In a small saucepan, heat the olive oil over medium heat. Add the garlic and sauté for 2 minutes until golden. Whisk in the almond milk, arrowroot powder, and salt. Bring to a simmer. Continue to simmer, whisking frequently, for about 5 minutes or until the sauce thickens.
3. Carefully transfer the hot almond milk mixture to the blender with the cashews. Blend for 30 seconds to combine, then add the nutritional yeast and marinara sauce. Blend for 1 minute or until creamy.

Cashew-Lemon Ranch Dressing
Prep time: 15 minutes | Cook time: 0 minutes | Serves 12

1 cup cashews, soaked in warm water for at least 1 hour	1 tablespoon vinegar
	1 teaspoon garlic powder
½ cup water	1 teaspoon onion powder
2 tablespoons freshly squeezed lemon juice	2 teaspoons dried dill

1. In a food processor, combine the cashews, water, lemon juice, vinegar, garlic powder, and onion powder. Blend until creamy and smooth. Add the dill and pulse a few times until combined.

Cashew and Basil Pesto
Prep time: 10 minutes | Cook time: 0 minutes | Makes 1 cup

¼ cup raw cashews	1 tablespoon olive oil
Juice of 1 lemon	4 cups basil leaves, packed
2 garlic cloves	1 cup wheatgrass
1/3 red onion (about 2 ounces / 56 g in total)	¼ cup water
	¼ teaspoon salt

1. Put the cashews in a heatproof bowl and add boiling water to cover. Soak for 5 minutes and then drain.
2. Put all ingredients in a blender and blend for 2 to 3 minutes or until fully combined.

Cauliflower-Almond Alfredo Sauce
Prep time: 2 minutes | Cook time: 0 minutes | Makes 4 cups

2 tablespoons olive oil
6 garlic cloves, minced
3 cups unsweetened almond milk
1 (1-pound / 454-g) head cauliflower, cut

into florets
1 teaspoon salt
¼ teaspoon freshly ground black pepper
Juice of 1 lemon
4 tablespoons nutritional yeast

1. In a medium saucepan, heat the olive oil over medium-high heat. Add the garlic and sauté for 1 minute or until fragrant. Add the almond milk, stir, and bring to a boil.
2. Gently add the cauliflower. Stir in the salt and pepper and return to a boil. Continue cooking over medium-high heat for 5 minutes or until the cauliflower is soft. Stir frequently and reduce heat if needed to prevent the liquid from boiling over.
3. Carefully transfer the cauliflower and cooking liquid to a food processor, using a slotted spoon to scoop out the larger pieces of cauliflower before pouring in the liquid. Add the lemon and nutritional yeast and blend for 1 to 2 minutes until smooth.
4. Serve immediately.

Pico de Gallo
Prep time: 5 minutes | Cook time: 0 minutes | Serves 2

3 large tomatoes, chopped
½ small red onion, diced
⅛ cup chopped fresh cilantro
3 garlic cloves, chopped

2 tablespoons chopped pickled jalapeño pepper
1 tablespoon lime juice
¼ teaspoon pink Himalayan salt (optional)

1. In a medium bowl, combine all the ingredients and mix with a wooden spoon.

Anchovy Fillet-Almond Dip
Prep time: 10 minutes | Cook time: 20 minutes | Makes 1½ cups

¾ cup whole blanched almonds
20 (1½-ounce / 43-g) anchovy fillets, rinsed, patted dry, and minced
¼ cup water
2 tablespoons raisins
2 tablespoons lemon juice, plus extra for

serving
1 garlic clove, minced
1 teaspoon Dijon mustard
Salt and pepper
¼ cup extra-virgin olive oil, plus extra for serving
1 tablespoon minced fresh chives

1. Bring 4 cups water to boil in medium saucepan over medium-high heat. Add almonds and cook until softened, about 20 minutes. Drain and rinse well.
2. Process drained almonds, anchovies, water, raisins, lemon juice, garlic, mustard, ¼ teaspoon pepper, and ⅛ teaspoon salt in food processor to mostly smooth paste, about 2 minutes, scraping down sides of bowl as needed. With processor running, slowly add oil and process to smooth puree, about 2 minutes.
3. Transfer mixture to bowl, stir in 2 teaspoons chives, and season with salt and extra lemon juice to taste. (Dip can be refrigerated for up to 2 days; bring to room temperature before serving.) Sprinkle with remaining 1 teaspoon chives and drizzle with extra oil to taste before serving.

Homemade Hummus
Prep time: 5 minutes | Cook time: 0 minutes | Serves 2

1 (19-ounce / 539-g) can chickpeas, drained and rinsed
¼ cup tahini
3 tablespoons cold water
2 tablespoons freshly squeezed lemon juice

1 garlic clove
½ teaspoon turmeric powder
⅛ teaspoon black pepper
Pinch pink Himalayan salt, to taste

1. Combine all the ingredients in a food processor and blend until smooth.

Sweet Ginger Sauce

Prep time: 5 minutes | Cook time: 5 minutes | Makes ²/₃ cup

3 tablespoons ketchup
2 tablespoons water
2 tablespoons maple syrup
1 tablespoon rice vinegar
2 teaspoons peeled

minced fresh ginger root
2 teaspoons soy sauce (or tamari, which is a gluten-free option)
1 teaspoon cornstarch

1. In a small saucepan over medium heat, combine all the ingredients and stir continuously for 5 minutes, or until slightly thickened. Enjoy warm or cold.

Lemon Tahini

Prep time: 5 minutes | Cook time: 0 minutes | Serves 4

¾ cup water
½ cup tahini
3 garlic cloves, minced

Juice of 3 lemons
½ teaspoon pink Himalayan salt

1. In a bowl, whisk together all the ingredients until mixed well.

Spiced Mushroom Apple Gravy

Prep time: 5 minutes | Cook time: 10 minutes | Serves 4

2 cups vegetable broth
½ cup finely chopped mushrooms
2 tablespoons whole wheat flour
1 tablespoon unsweetened applesauce
1 teaspoon onion

powder
½ teaspoon dried thyme
¼ teaspoon dried rosemary
⅛ teaspoon pink Himalayan salt
Freshly ground black pepper, to taste

1. In a nonstick saucepan over medium-high heat, combine all the ingredients and mix well. Bring to a boil, stirring frequently, reduce the heat to low, and simmer, stirring constantly, until it thickens.

Hemp Seeds and Spices Dressing

Prep time: 5 minutes | Cook time: 0 minutes | Makes 12 tablespoons

½ cup white wine vinegar
¼ cup tahini
¼ cup water
1 tablespoon hemp seeds
½ tablespoon freshly squeezed lemon juice
1 teaspoon garlic powder
1 teaspoon dried

oregano
1 teaspoon dried basil
1 teaspoon red pepper flakes
½ teaspoon onion powder
½ teaspoon pink Himalayan salt
½ teaspoon freshly ground black pepper

1. In a bowl, combine all the ingredients and whisk until mixed well.

Buffalo Sauce

Prep time: 5 minutes | Cook time: 20 minutes | Makes 2 cups

¼ cup olive oil
4 garlic cloves, roughly chopped
1 (5-ounce / 142-g) small red onion, roughly chopped
6 red chiles, roughly chopped (about 2

ounces / 56 g in total)
1 cup water
½ cup apple cider vinegar
½ teaspoon salt
½ teaspoon freshly ground black pepper

1. In a large nonstick sauté pan, heat ¼ cup olive oil over medium-high heat. Once it's hot, add the garlic, onion, and chiles. Cook for 5 minutes, stirring occasionally, until onions are golden brown.
2. Add the water and bring to a boil. Cook for about 10 minutes or until the water has nearly evaporated.
3. Transfer the cooked onion and chile mixture to a food processor or blender and blend briefly to combine. Add the apple cider vinegar, salt, and pepper. Blend again for 30 seconds.
4. Using a mesh sieve, strain the sauce into a bowl. Use a spoon or spatula to scrape and press all the liquid from the pulp.

Dijon Mustard-Balsamic Vinaigrette
Prep time: 5 minutes | Cook time: 0 minutes | Makes 12 tablespoons

6 tablespoons water
4 tablespoons Dijon mustard
4 tablespoons balsamic vinegar
1 teaspoon maple syrup
½ teaspoon pink Himalayan salt
¼ teaspoon freshly ground black pepper

1. In a bowl, whisk together all the ingredients.

Potato-Yogurt Dip
Prep time: 10 minutes | Cook time: 15 to 20 minutes | Makes 2 cups

1 (10- to 12-ounce / 284- to 340-g) russet potato, peeled and cut into 1-inch chunks
3 garlic cloves, minced to paste
3 tablespoons lemon juice
2 slices hearty white sandwich bread, crusts removed, torn into 1-inch pieces
6 tablespoons warm water, plus extra as needed
Salt and pepper
¼ cup extra-virgin olive oil
¼ cup plain Greek yogurt

1. Place potato in small saucepan and add water to cover by 1 inch. Bring water to boil, then reduce to simmer and cook until potato is tender and paring knife can be inserted into potato with no resistance, 15 to 20 minutes. Drain potato in colander, tossing to remove any excess water.
2. Meanwhile, combine garlic and lemon juice in bowl and let sit for 10 minutes. In separate medium bowl, mash bread, ¼ cup warm water, and ½ teaspoon salt into paste with fork.
3. Transfer potato to ricer (food mill fitted with small disk) and process into bowl with bread mixture. Stir in lemon-garlic mixture, oil, yogurt, and remaining 2 tablespoons warm water until well combined. (Sauce can be refrigerated for up to 3 days; bring to room temperature before serving.) Season with salt and pepper to taste and adjust consistency with extra warm water as needed before serving.

Cannellini Bean Dip with Rosemary
Prep time: 5 minutes | Cook time: 0 minutes | Makes 1¼ cups

1 (15-ounce / 425-g) can cannellini beans, rinsed
¼ cup extra-virgin olive oil
2 tablespoons water
2 teaspoons lemon juice
1 teaspoon minced fresh rosemary
1 small garlic clove, minced
Salt and pepper
Pinch cayenne pepper

1. Process beans, 3 tablespoons oil, water, lemon juice, rosemary, garlic, ¼ teaspoon salt, ¼ teaspoon pepper, and cayenne in food processor until smooth, about 45 seconds, scraping down sides of bowl as needed.
2. Transfer to serving bowl, cover with plastic wrap, and let sit at room temperature until flavors meld, about 30 minutes. (Dip can be refrigerated for up to 24 hours; if necessary, loosen dip with 1 tablespoon warm water before serving.) Season with salt and pepper to taste and drizzle with remaining 1 tablespoon oil before serving.

Roasted Red Pepper and Walnut Dip
Prep time: 10 minutes | Cook time: 0 minutes | Makes 2 cups

1½ cups jarred roasted red peppers, rinsed and patted dry
1 cup walnuts, toasted
¼ cup plain wheat crackers, crumbled
3 tablespoons pomegranate molasses
2 tablespoons extra-virgin olive oil
¾ teaspoon salt
½ teaspoon ground cumin
⅛ teaspoon cayenne pepper
Lemon juice, as needed
1 tablespoon minced fresh parsley (optional)

1. Pulse all ingredients except parsley in food processor until smooth, about 10 pulses. Transfer to serving bowl, cover, and refrigerate for 15 minutes. (Dip can be refrigerated for up to 24 hours; bring to room temperature before serving.) Season with lemon juice, salt, and cayenne to taste and sprinkle with parsley, if using, before serving.

Chapter 4 Fish and Seafood

Crab Cake Sandwich with Cajun Mayo
Prep time: 15 minutes | Cook time: 10 minutes | Serves 4

Crab Cakes:

½ cup panko bread crumbs
1 large egg, beaten
1 large egg white
1 tablespoon mayonnaise
1 teaspoon Dijon mustard
¼ cup minced fresh parsley
1 tablespoon fresh lemon juice

½ teaspoon Old Bay seasoning
⅛ teaspoon sweet paprika
⅛ teaspoon kosher salt
Freshly ground black pepper, to taste
10 ounces (283 g) lump crab meat
Cooking spray

Cajun Mayo:

¼ cup mayonnaise
1 tablespoon minced dill pickle
1 teaspoon fresh

lemon juice
¾ teaspoon Cajun seasoning

For Serving:

4 Boston lettuce leaves
4 whole wheat potato

buns or gluten-free buns

1. For the crab cakes: In a large bowl, combine the panko, whole egg, egg white, mayonnaise, mustard, parsley, lemon juice, Old Bay, paprika, salt, and pepper to taste and mix well. Fold in the crab meat, being careful not to over mix. Gently shape into 4 round patties, about ½ cup each, ¾ inch thick. Spray both sides with oil.
2. Working in batches, place the crab cakes in the air fryer basket. Select the AIR FRY function and cook at 370ºF (188ºC) for 10 minutes, flipping halfway, until the edges are golden.
3. Meanwhile, for the Cajun mayo: In a small bowl, combine the mayonnaise, pickle, lemon juice, and Cajun seasoning.
4. To serve: Place a lettuce leaf on each bun bottom and top with a crab cake and a generous tablespoon of Cajun mayonnaise. Add the bun top and serve.

Shrimp Spring Rolls
Prep time: 10 minutes | Cook time: 17 to 22 minutes | Serves 4

2 teaspoons minced garlic
2 cups finely sliced cabbage
1 cup matchstick cut carrots
2 (4-ounce / 113-g) cans tiny shrimp, drained

4 teaspoons soy sauce
Salt and freshly ground black pepper, to taste
16 square spring roll wrappers
Cooking spray

1. Spray the air fryer basket lightly with cooking spray. Spray a medium sauté pan with cooking spray.
2. Add the garlic to the sauté pan and cook over medium heat until fragrant, 30 to 45 seconds. Add the cabbage and carrots and sauté until the vegetables are slightly tender, about 5 minutes.
3. Add the shrimp and soy sauce and season with salt and pepper, then stir to combine. Sauté until the moisture has evaporated, 2 more minutes. Set aside to cool.
4. Place a spring roll wrapper on a work surface so it looks like a diamond. Place 1 tablespoon of the shrimp mixture on the lower end of the wrapper.
5. Roll the wrapper away from you halfway, then fold in the right and left sides, like an envelope. Continue to roll to the very end, using a little water to seal the edge. Repeat with the remaining wrappers and filling.
6. Place the spring rolls in the air fryer basket in a single layer, leaving room between each roll. Lightly spray with cooking spray. You may need to cook them in batches.
7. Select the AIR FRY function and cook at 370ºF (188ºC) for 5 minutes. Turn the rolls over, lightly spray with cooking spray, and air fry until heated through and the rolls start to brown, 5 to 10 more minutes. Cool for 5 minutes before serving.

Shrimp, Chorizo Sausage, and Potatoes
Prep time: 10 minutes | Cook time: 16 minutes | Serves 4

½ red onion, chopped into 1-inch chunks
8 fingerling potatoes, sliced into 1-inch slices or halved lengthwise
1 teaspoon olive oil
Salt and freshly ground black pepper
8 ounces (227 g) raw chorizo sausage,
sliced into 1-inch chunks
16 raw large shrimp, peeled, deveined and tails removed
1 lime
¼ cup chopped fresh cilantro
Chopped orange zest (optional)

1. Combine the red onion and potato chunks in a bowl and toss with the olive oil, salt and freshly ground black pepper.
2. Transfer the vegetables to the air fryer basket. Select the AIR FRY function and cook at 380ºF (193ºC) for 6 minutes, shaking the basket a few times during the cooking process.
3. Add the chorizo chunks and continue to air fry for another 5 minutes.
4. Add the shrimp, season with salt and continue to air fry, shaking the basket every once in a while, for another 5 minutes.
5. Transfer the tossed shrimp, chorizo and potato to a bowl and squeeze some lime juice over the top to taste. Toss in the fresh cilantro, orange zest and a drizzle of olive oil, and season again to taste.
6. Serve with a fresh green salad.

Panko-Crusted Haddock Fillet
Prep time: 10 minutes | Cook time: 10 to 12 minutes | Serves 4

Salt and pepper, to taste
1½ pounds (680g) skinless haddock fillets, ¾ inch thick, sliced into 4-inch strips
2 cups panko bread crumbs
1 tablespoon vegetable oil
¼ cup all-purpose flour
¼ cup mayonnaise
2 large eggs
1 tablespoon Old Bay seasoning
Vegetable oil spray

1. Dissolve ¼ cup salt in 2 quarts cold water in a large container. Add the haddock, cover, and let sit for 15 minutes.
2. Toss the panko with the oil in a bowl until evenly coated. Microwave, stirring frequently, until light golden brown, 2 to 4 minutes; transfer to a shallow dish. Whisk the flour, mayonnaise, eggs, Old Bay, ⅛ teaspoon salt, and ⅛ teaspoon pepper together in a second shallow dish.
3. Set a wire rack in a rimmed baking sheet and spray with vegetable oil spray. Remove the haddock from the brine and thoroughly pat dry with paper towels. Working with 1 piece at a time, dredge the haddock in the egg mixture, letting excess drip off, then coat with the panko mixture, pressing gently to adhere. Transfer the fish sticks to the prepared rack and freeze until firm, about 1 hour.
4. Lightly spray the air fryer basket with vegetable oil spray. Arrange up to 5 fish sticks in the prepared basket, spaced evenly apart.
5. Select the AIR FRY function and cook at 400ºF (204ºC) for 10 to 12 minutes, or until fish sticks are golden and register 140ºF (60ºC), flipping and rotating fish sticks halfway through cooking.
6. Serve warm.

Fresh Cod with Sesame Seeds
Prep time: 5 minutes | Cook time: 7 to 9 minutes | Makes 1 fillet

1 tablespoon reduced-sodium soy sauce
2 teaspoons honey
Cooking spray
6 ounces (170 g) fresh cod fillet
1 teaspoon sesame seeds

1. Select the ROAST function and preheat MAXX to 360ºF (182ºC).
2. In a small bowl, combine the soy sauce and honey.
3. Spray the air fryer basket with cooking spray, then place the cod in the basket, brush with the soy mixture, and sprinkle sesame seeds on top. Roast for 7 to 9 minutes or until opaque.
4. Remove the fish and allow to cool on a wire rack for 5 minutes before serving.

Italian Salmon Patties

Prep time: 10 minutes | Cook time: 8 minutes | Serves 4

2 (5-ounce / 142 g) cans salmon, flaked
2 large eggs, beaten
1/3 cup minced onion
2/3 cup panko bread crumbs
1½ teaspoons Italian-Style seasoning
1 teaspoon garlic powder
Cooking spray

1. In a medium bowl, stir together the salmon, eggs, and onion.
2. In a small bowl, whisk the bread crumbs, Italian-Style seasoning, and garlic powder until blended. Add the bread crumb mixture to the salmon mixture and stir until blended. Shape the mixture into 8 patties.
3. Select the BAKE function and preheat MAXX to 350ºF (177ºC). Line the air fryer basket with parchment paper.
4. Working in batches as needed, place the patties on the parchment and spritz with oil.
5. Bake for 4 minutes. Flip, spritz the patties with oil, and bake for 4 to 8 minutes more, until browned and firm. Serve.

Horseradish Crusted Salmon Fillet

Prep time: 5 minutes | Cook time: 12 minutes | Serves 2

2 (5-ounce / 142-g) salmon fillets
Salt and freshly ground black pepper
2 teaspoons Dijon mustard
½ cup panko bread crumbs
2 tablespoons prepared horseradish
½ teaspoon finely chopped lemon zest
1 tablespoon olive oil
1 tablespoon chopped fresh parsley

1. Season the salmon with salt and freshly ground black pepper. Then spread the Dijon mustard on the salmon, coating the entire surface.
2. Combine the bread crumbs, horseradish, lemon zest and olive oil in a small bowl. Spread the mixture over the top of the salmon and press down lightly with your hands, adhering it to the salmon using the mustard as "glue".

3. Transfer the salmon to the air fryer basket. Select the AIR FRY function and cook at 360ºF (182ºC) for 12 to 14 minutes (depending on how thick your fillet is), or until the fish feels firm to the touch. Sprinkle with the parsley.

Tangy Coconut Shrimp

Prep time: 15 minutes | Cook time: 12 minutes | Serves 4

1 pound (454 g) large shrimp (about 16 to 20), peeled and deveined
½ cup flour
Salt and freshly ground black pepper
2 egg whites
½ cup fine bread crumbs
½ cup shredded
unsweetened coconut
Zest of one lime
½ teaspoon salt
1/8 to 1/4 teaspoon ground cayenne pepper
Vegetable or canola oil
Sweet chili sauce or duck sauce (for serving)

1. Set up a dredging station. Place the flour in a shallow dish and season well with salt and freshly ground black pepper. Whisk the egg whites in a second shallow dish. In a third shallow dish, combine the bread crumbs, coconut, lime zest, salt and cayenne pepper.
2. Dredge each shrimp first in the flour, then dip it in the egg mixture, and finally press it into the bread crumb-coconut mixture to coat all sides. Place the breaded shrimp on a plate or baking sheet and spray both sides with vegetable oil.
3. Work in two batches, being sure not to over-crowd the basket. Select the AIR FRY function and cook at 400ºF (205ºC) for 5 minutes, turning the shrimp over for the last minute or two. Repeat with the second batch of shrimp.
4. Reduce the temperature to 340ºF (171ºC). Return the first batch of shrimp to the air fryer basket with the second batch and air fry for an additional 1 to 2 minutes, just to reheat everything.
5. Serve with sweet chili sauce, duck sauce or just eat them plain!

Bacon-Wrapped Scallops with Salad

Prep time: 10 minutes | Cook time: 12 minutes | Serves 4

12 slices bacon
24 large sea scallops, tendons removed
1 teaspoon plus 2 tablespoons extra-virgin olive oil, divided
Salt and pepper, to taste
1 tablespoon cider vinegar
1 teaspoon Dijon mustard
5 ounces (142 g) baby spinach
1 fennel bulb, stalks discarded, bulb halved, cored, and sliced thin
5 ounces (142 g) raspberries

1. Select the BAKE function and preheat MAXX to 350ºF (177ºC).
2. Line large plate with 4 layers of paper towels and arrange 6 slices bacon over towels in a single layer. Top with 4 more layers of paper towels and remaining 6 slices bacon. Cover with 2 layers of paper towels, place a second large plate on top, and press gently to flatten. Microwave until fat begins to render but bacon is still pliable, about 5 minutes.
3. Pat scallops dry with paper towels and toss with 1 teaspoon oil, ⅛ teaspoon salt, and ⅛ teaspoon pepper in a bowl until evenly coated. Arrange 2 scallops side to side, flat side down, on the cutting board. Starting at narrow end, wrap 1 slice bacon tightly around sides of scallop bundle. (Bacon should overlap slightly; trim excess as needed.) Thread scallop bundle onto skewer through bacon. Repeat with remaining scallops and bacon, threading 2 bundles onto each skewer.
4. Arrange 3 skewers in air fryer basket, parallel to each other and spaced evenly apart. Arrange remaining 3 skewers on top, perpendicular to the bottom layer. Bake until bacon is crisp and scallops are firm and centers are opaque, 12 to 16 minutes, flipping and rotating skewers halfway through cooking.
5. Meanwhile, whisk remaining 2 tablespoons oil, vinegar, mustard, ⅛ teaspoon salt, and ⅛ teaspoon pepper in large serving bowl until combined. Add spinach, fennel, and raspberries and gently toss to coat. Serve skewers with salad.

Baja Tilapia Tacos

Prep time: 15 minutes | Cook time: 10 minutes | Serves 4

Fried Fish:
1 pound (454 g) tilapia fillets (or other mild white fish)
½ cup all-purpose flour
1 teaspoon garlic powder
1 teaspoon kosher salt
¼ teaspoon cayenne pepper
½ cup mayonnaise
3 tablespoons milk
1¾ cups panko bread crumbs
Vegetable oil, for spraying

Tacos:
8 corn tortillas
¼ head red or green cabbage, shredded
1 ripe avocado, halved and each half cut into 4 slices
12 ounces (340 g)
pico de gallo or other fresh salsa
Dollop of Mexican crema
1 lime, cut into wedges

1. To make the fish, cut the fish fillets into strips 3 to 4 inches long and 1 inch wide. Combine the flour, garlic powder, salt, and cayenne pepper on a plate and whisk to combine. In a shallow bowl, whisk the mayonnaise and milk together. Place the panko on a separate plate. Dredge the fish strips in the seasoned flour, shaking off any excess. Dip the strips in the mayonnaise mixture, coating them completely, then dredge in the panko, shaking off any excess. Place the fish strips on a plate or rack.
2. Working in batches, spray half the fish strips with oil and arrange them in the air fryer basket, taking care not to crowd them. Select the AIR FRY function and cook at 400ºF (204ºC) for 4 minutes, then flip and air fry for another 3 to 4 minutes until the outside is brown and crisp and the inside is opaque and flakes easily with a fork. Repeat with the remaining strips.
3. Heat the tortillas in the microwave or on the stovetop. To assemble the tacos, place 2 fish strips inside each tortilla. Top with shredded cabbage, a slice of avocado, pico de gallo, and a dollop of crema. Serve with a lime wedge on the side.

Blackened Tilapia Fillet
Prep time: 15 minutes | Cook time: 8 minutes | Serves 4

1 large egg, beaten
Blackened seasoning, as needed
2 tablespoons light

brown sugar
4 (4-ounce / 113- g) tilapia fillets
Cooking spray

1. In a shallow bowl, place the beaten egg. In a second shallow bowl, stir together the Blackened seasoning and the brown sugar.
2. One at a time, dip the fish fillets in the egg, then the brown sugar mixture, coating thoroughly.
3. Select the BAKE function and preheat MAXX to 300ºF (149ºC). Line the air fryer basket with parchment paper.
4. Place the coated fish on the parchment and spritz with oil.
5. Bake for 4 minutes. Flip the fish, spritz it with oil, and bake for 4 to 6 minutes more until the fish is white inside and flakes easily with a fork.
6. Serve immediately.

Almond-Bread Crusted Fish Fillet
Prep time: 15 minutes | Cook time: 10 minutes | Serves 4

4 (4-ounce / 113-g) fish fillets
¾ cup bread crumbs
¼ cup sliced almonds, crushed
2 tablespoons lemon juice

⅛ teaspoon cayenne
Salt and pepper
¾ cup flour
1 egg, beaten with 1 tablespoon water
Oil for misting or cooking spray

1. Split fish fillets lengthwise down the center to create 8 pieces.
2. Mix bread crumbs and almonds together and set aside.
3. Mix the lemon juice and cayenne together. Brush on all sides of fish.
4. Season fish to taste with salt and pepper.
5. Place the flour on a sheet of wax paper.
6. Roll fillets in flour, dip in egg wash, and roll in the crumb mixture.
7. Mist both sides of fish with oil or cooking spray.
8. Spray air fryer basket and lay fillets inside.

9. Select the AIR FRY function and cook at 390ºF (199ºC) for 5 minutes. Turn fish over and air fry for an additional 5 minutes or until fish is done and flakes easily.

Tilapia Fillet Sandwich with Tartar Sauce
Prep time: 10 minutes | Cook time: 17 minutes | Serves 2

Tartar Sauce:
½ cup mayonnaise
2 tablespoons dried minced onion
1 dill pickle spear, finely chopped
Fish:
2 tablespoons all-purpose flour
1 egg, lightly beaten
1 cup panko
2 teaspoons lemon

2 teaspoons pickle juice
¼ teaspoon salt
⅛ teaspoon ground black pepper

pepper
2 tilapia fillets
Cooking spray
2 hoagie rolls

1. In a small bowl, combine the mayonnaise, dried minced onion, pickle, pickle juice, salt, and pepper.
2. Whisk to combine and chill in the refrigerator while you make the fish.
3. Place a parchment liner in the air fryer basket.
4. Scoop the flour out onto a plate; set aside.
5. Put the beaten egg in a medium shallow bowl.
6. On another plate, mix to combine the panko and lemon pepper.
7. Dredge the tilapia fillets in the flour, then dip in the egg, and then press into the panko mixture.
8. Place the prepared fillets on the liner in the air fryer oven in a single layer.
9. Spray lightly with cooking spray. Select the AIR FRY function and cook at 400ºF (204ºC) for 8 minutes. Carefully flip the fillets, spray with more cooking spray, and air fry for an additional 9 minutes, until golden and crispy.
10. Place each cooked fillet in a hoagie roll, top with a little bit of tartar sauce, and serve.

Cod Croquettes with Lemon-Dill Aioli

Prep time: 15 minutes | Cook time: 10 minutes | Serves 4

Croquettes:

3 large eggs, divided
12 ounces (340 g) raw cod fillet, flaked apart with two forks
¼ cup 1% milk
½ cup boxed instant mashed potatoes
2 teaspoons olive oil
⅓ cup chopped fresh dill
1 shallot, minced
1 large garlic clove, minced

¾ cup plus 2 tablespoons bread crumbs, divided
1 teaspoon fresh lemon juice
1 teaspoon kosher salt
½ teaspoon dried thyme
¼ teaspoon freshly ground black pepper
Cooking spray

Lemon-Dill Aioli:

5 tablespoons mayonnaise
Juice of ½ lemon

1 tablespoon chopped fresh dill

1. For the croquettes: In a medium bowl, lightly beat 2 of the eggs. Add the fish, milk, instant mashed potatoes, olive oil, dill, shallot, garlic, 2 tablespoons of the bread crumbs, lemon juice, salt, thyme, and pepper. Mix to thoroughly combine. Place in the refrigerator for 30 minutes.
2. For the lemon-dill aioli: In a small bowl, combine the mayonnaise, lemon juice, and dill. Set aside.
3. Measure out about 3½ tablespoons of the fish mixture and gently roll in your hands to form a log about 3 inches long. Repeat to make a total of 12 logs.
4. Beat the remaining egg in a small bowl. Place the remaining ¾ cup bread crumbs in a separate bowl. Dip the croquettes in the egg, then coat in the bread crumbs, gently pressing to adhere. Place on a work surface and spray both sides with cooking spray.
5. Working in batches, arrange a single layer of the croquettes in the air fryer basket. Select the AIR FRY function and cook at 350ºF (177ºC) for 10 minutes, flipping halfway, until golden.
6. Serve with the aioli for dipping.

Salmon with Cucumber-Avocado Salsa

Prep time: 10 minutes | Cook time: 5 to 7 minutes | Serves 4

Salmon:

1 tablespoon sweet paprika
½ teaspoon cayenne pepper
1 teaspoon garlic powder
1 teaspoon dried oregano
1 teaspoon dried

thyme
¾ teaspoon kosher salt
⅛ teaspoon freshly ground black pepper
Cooking spray
4 (6 ounces / 170 g each) wild salmon fillets

Cucumber-Avocado Salsa:

2 tablespoons chopped red onion
1½ tablespoons fresh lemon juice
1 teaspoon extra-virgin olive oil
¼ teaspoon plus ⅛

teaspoon kosher salt
Freshly ground black pepper, to taste
4 Persian cucumbers, diced
6 ounces (170 g) Hass avocado, diced

1. For the salmon: In a small bowl, combine the paprika, cayenne, garlic powder, oregano, thyme, salt, and black pepper. Spray both sides of the fish with oil and rub all over. Coat the fish all over with the spices.
2. For the cucumber-avocado salsa: In a medium bowl, combine the red onion, lemon juice, olive oil, salt, and pepper. Let stand for 5 minutes, then add the cucumbers and avocado.
3. Working in batches, arrange the salmon fillets skin side down in the air fryer basket. Select the AIR FRY function and cook at 400ºF (204ºC) for 5 to 7 minutes, or until the fish flakes easily with a fork, depending on the thickness of the fish.
4. Serve topped with the salsa.

Lime Blackened Shrimp Tacos

Prep time: 10 minutes | Cook time: 10 to 15 minutes | Serves 4

12 ounces (340 g) medium shrimp, deveined, with tails off	8 corn tortillas, warmed
1 teaspoon olive oil	1 (14-ounce / 397-g) bag coleslaw mix
1 to 2 teaspoons Blackened seasoning	2 limes, cut in half
	Cooking spray

1. Spray the air fryer basket lightly with cooking spray.
2. Dry the shrimp with a paper towel to remove excess water.
3. In a medium bowl, toss the shrimp with olive oil and Blackened seasoning.
4. Place the shrimp in the air fryer basket. Select the AIR FRY function and cook at 400ºF (204ºC) for 5 minutes. Shake the basket, lightly spray with cooking spray, and cook until the shrimp are cooked through and starting to brown, 5 to 10 more minutes.
5. Fill each tortilla with the coleslaw mix and top with the blackened shrimp. Squeeze fresh lime juice over top and serve.

Cajun Catfish Fillet

Prep time: 15 minutes | Cook time: 6 minutes | Serves 4

¾ cup all-purpose flour	¼ cup Cajun seasoning
¼ cup yellow cornmeal	4 (4-ounce / 113-g) catfish fillets
1 large egg, beaten	Cooking spray

1. In a shallow bowl, whisk the flour and cornmeal until blended. Place the egg in a second shallow bowl and the Cajun seasoning in a third shallow bowl.
2. One at a time, dip the catfish fillets in the breading, the egg, and the Cajun seasoning, coating thoroughly.
3. Select the BAKE function and preheat MAXX to 300ºF (149ºC). Line the air fryer basket with parchment paper.
4. Place the coated fish on the parchment and spritz with oil.

5. Bake for 3 minutes. Flip the fish, spritz it with oil, and bake for 3 to 5 minutes more until the fish flakes easily with a fork and reaches an internal temperature of 145ºF (63ºC). Serve warm.

Golden Trout Fingers

Prep time: 15 minutes | Cook time: 6 minutes | Serves 2

½ cup yellow cornmeal, medium or finely ground (not coarse)	skinless trout fillets, cut into strips 1 inch wide and 3 inches long
⅓ cup all-purpose flour	3 large eggs, lightly beaten
1½ teaspoons baking powder	Cooking spray
1 teaspoon kosher salt, plus more as needed	½ cup mayonnaise
½ teaspoon freshly ground black pepper, plus more as needed	2 tablespoons capers, rinsed and finely chopped
⅛ teaspoon cayenne pepper	1 tablespoon fresh tarragon
¾ pound (340 g)	1 teaspoon fresh lemon juice, plus lemon wedges, for serving

1. In a large bowl, whisk together the cornmeal, flour, baking powder, salt, black pepper, and cayenne. Dip the trout strips in the egg, then toss them in the cornmeal mixture until fully coated. Transfer the trout to a rack set over a baking sheet and liberally spray all over with cooking spray.
2. Transfer half the fish to the air fryer oven. Select the AIR FRY function and cook at 400ºF (204ºC) for 6 minutes, or until the fish is cooked through and golden brown. Transfer the fish sticks to a plate and repeat with the remaining fish.
3. Meanwhile, in a bowl, whisk together the mayonnaise, capers, tarragon, and lemon juice. Season the tartar sauce with salt and black pepper.
4. Serve the trout fingers hot along with the tartar sauce and lemon wedges.

Tilapia Fillet Tacos

Prep time: 5 minutes | Cook time: 10 to 15 minutes | Serves 6

2 teaspoons avocado oil
1 tablespoon Cajun seasoning
4 tilapia fillets
1 (14-ounce / 397-g) package coleslaw mix
12 corn tortillas
2 limes, cut into wedges

1. Line the air fryer basket with parchment paper.
2. In a medium, shallow bowl, mix the avocado oil and the Cajun seasoning to make a marinade. Add the tilapia fillets and coat evenly.
3. Place the fillets in the basket in a single layer, leaving room between each fillet. You may need to cook in batches.
4. Select the AIR FRY function and cook at 380ºF (193ºC) for 10 to 15 minutes, or until the fish is cooked and easily flakes with a fork.
5. Assemble the tacos by placing some of the coleslaw mix in each tortilla. Add 1/3 of a tilapia fillet to each tortilla. Squeeze some lime juice over the top of each taco and serve.

Mayo Salmon Burgers

Prep time: 10 minutes | Cook time: 10 to 15 minutes | Serves 4

4 (5-ounce / 142-g) cans pink salmon in water, any skin and bones removed, drained
2 eggs, beaten
1 cup whole-wheat bread crumbs
4 tablespoons light mayonnaise
2 teaspoons Cajun seasoning
2 teaspoons dry mustard
4 whole-wheat buns
Cooking spray

1. In a medium bowl, mix the salmon, egg, bread crumbs, mayonnaise, Cajun seasoning, and dry mustard. Cover with plastic wrap and refrigerate for 30 minutes.
2. Spray the air fryer basket lightly with cooking spray.
3. Shape the mixture into four ½-inch-thick patties about the same size as the buns.
4. Place the salmon patties in the air fryer basket in a single layer and lightly spray the tops with cooking spray. You may need to cook them in batches.
5. Select the AIR FRY function and cook at 360ºF (182ºC) for 6 to 8 minutes. Turn the patties over and lightly spray with cooking spray. Air fry until crispy on the outside, 4 to 7 more minutes.
6. Serve on whole-wheat buns.

Crispy Shrimp Empanadas

Prep time: 10 minutes | Cook time: 8 minutes | Serves 5

½ pound (227g) raw shrimp, peeled, deveined and chopped
¼ cup chopped red onion
1 scallion, chopped
2 garlic cloves, minced
2 tablespoons minced red bell pepper
2 tablespoons chopped fresh cilantro
½ tablespoon fresh lime juice
¼ teaspoon sweet paprika
⅛ teaspoon kosher salt
⅛ teaspoon crushed red pepper flakes (optional)
1 large egg, beaten
10 frozen Goya Empanada Discos, thawed
Cooking spray

1. In a medium bowl, combine the shrimp, red onion, scallion, garlic, bell pepper, cilantro, lime juice, paprika, salt, and pepper flakes (if using).
2. In a small bowl, beat the egg with 1 teaspoon water until smooth.
3. Place an empanada disc on a work surface and put 2 tablespoons of the shrimp mixture in the center. Brush the outer edges of the disc with the egg wash. Fold the disc over and gently press the edges to seal. Use a fork and press around the edges to crimp and seal completely. Brush the tops of the empanadas with the egg wash.
4. Spray the bottom of the air fryer basket with cooking spray to prevent sticking. Working in batches, arrange a single layer of the empanadas in the air fryer basket. Select the AIR FRY function and cook at 380ºF (193ºC) for 8 minutes, flipping halfway, until golden brown and crispy.
5. Serve hot.

Confetti Salmon and Bell Pepper Burgers

Prep time: 10 minutes | Cook time: 12 minutes | Serves 4

14 ounces (397 g) cooked fresh or canned salmon, flaked with a fork
¼ cup minced scallion, white and light green parts only
¼ cup minced red bell pepper
¼ cup minced celery
2 small lemons
1 teaspoon crab boil

seasoning such as Old Bay
½ teaspoon kosher salt
½ teaspoon black pepper
1 egg, beaten
½ cup fresh bread crumbs
Vegetable oil, for spraying

1. In a large bowl, combine the salmon, vegetables, the zest and juice of 1 of the lemons, crab boil seasoning, salt, and pepper. Add the egg and bread crumbs and stir to combine. Form the mixture into 4 patties weighing approximately 5 ounces (142 g) each. Chill until firm, about 15 minutes.
2. Spray the salmon patties with oil on all sides and spray the air fryer basket to prevent sticking.
3. Select the AIR FRY function and cook at 400ºF (204ºC) for 12 minutes, flipping halfway through, until the burgers are browned and cooked through. Cut the remaining lemon into 4 wedges and serve with the burgers.

Cornmeal-Crusted Catfish Strips

Prep time: 5 minutes | Cook time: 16 to 18 minutes | Serves 4

1 cup buttermilk
5 catfish fillets, cut into 1½-inch strips
Cooking spray

1 cup cornmeal
1 tablespoon Creole, Cajun, or Old Bay seasoning

1. Pour the buttermilk into a shallow baking dish. Place the catfish in the dish and refrigerate for at least 1 hour to help remove any fishy taste.
2. Spray the air fryer basket lightly with cooking spray.
3. In a shallow bowl, combine cornmeal and Creole seasoning.

4. Shake any excess buttermilk off the catfish. Place each strip in the cornmeal mixture and coat completely. Press the cornmeal into the catfish gently to help it stick.
5. Place the strips in the air fryer basket in a single layer. Lightly spray the catfish with cooking spray. You may need to cook the catfish in more than one batch.
6. Select the AIR FRY function and cook at 400ºF (204ºC) for 8 minutes. Turn the catfish strips over and lightly spray with cooking spray. Air fry until golden brown and crispy, 8 to 10 more minutes.
7. Serve warm.

Sesame Glazed Salmon Fillet

Prep time: 5 minutes | Cook time: 12 to 16 minutes | Serves 4

3 tablespoons soy sauce
1 tablespoon rice wine or dry sherry
1 tablespoon brown sugar
1 tablespoon toasted sesame oil
1 teaspoon minced

garlic
¼ teaspoon minced ginger
4 (6-ounce / 170-g) salmon fillets, skin-on
½ tablespoon sesame seeds
Cooking spray

1. In a small bowl, mix the soy sauce, rice wine, brown sugar, toasted sesame oil, garlic, and ginger.
2. Place the salmon in a shallow baking dish and pour the marinade over the fillets. Cover and refrigerate for at least 1 hour, turning the fillets occasionally to coat in the marinade.
3. Spray the air fryer basket lightly with cooking spray.
4. Shake off as much marinade as possible and place the fillets, skin-side down, in the air fryer basket in a single layer. Reserve the marinade. You may need to cook them in batches.
5. Select the AIR FRY function and cook at 370ºF (188ºC) for 8 to 10 minutes. Brush the tops of the salmon fillets with the reserved marinade and sprinkle with sesame seeds.
6. Increase the temperature to 400ºF (204ºC) and air fry for 2 to 5 more minutes for medium, 1 to 3 minutes for medium rare, or 4 to 6 minutes for well done.
7. Serve warm.

Country Shrimp and Sausage

Prep time: 10 minutes | Cook time: 15 to 20 minutes | Serves 4

1 pound (454 g) large shrimp, deveined, with tails on	1 zucchini, cut into bite-sized pieces
1 pound (454 g) smoked turkey sausage, cut into thick slices	1 red bell pepper, cut into chunks
2 corn cobs, quartered	1 tablespoon Old Bay seasoning
	2 tablespoons olive oil
	Cooking spray

1. Spray the air fryer basket lightly with cooking spray.
2. In a large bowl, mix the shrimp, turkey sausage, corn, zucchini, bell pepper, and Old Bay seasoning, and toss to coat with the spices. Add the olive oil and toss again until evenly coated.
3. Spread the mixture in the air fryer basket in a single layer. You will need to cook in batches.
4. Select the AIR FRY function and cook at 400ºF (204ºC) for 15 to 20 minutes, or until cooked through, shaking the basket every 5 minutes for even cooking.
5. Serve immediately.

Panko-Cod Cakes with Salad Greens

Prep time: 15 minutes | Cook time: 12 minutes | Serves 4

1 pound (454 g) cod fillets, cut into chunks	¼ teaspoon salt
⅓ cup packed fresh basil leaves	¼ teaspoon pepper
	1 large egg, beaten
3 cloves garlic, crushed	1 cup panko bread crumbs
½ teaspoon smoked paprika	Cooking spray
	Salad greens, for serving

1. In a food processor, pulse cod, basil, garlic, smoked paprika, salt, and pepper until cod is finely chopped, stirring occasionally. Form into 8 patties, about 2 inches in diameter. Dip each first into the egg, then into the panko, patting to adhere. Spray with oil on one side.

2. Working in batches, place half the cakes in the basket, oil-side down; spray with oil. Select the AIR FRY function and cook at 400ºF (204ºC) for 12 minutes, until golden brown and cooked through.
3. Serve cod cakes with salad greens.

Sherry Shrimp Skewers

Prep time: 10 minutes | Cook time: 15 minutes | Serves 4

2 teaspoons sherry	1 teaspoon kosher salt
3 tablespoons unsalted butter, melted	Pinch of cayenne pepper
1 cup panko bread crumbs	1½ pounds (680 g) shrimp, peeled and deveined
3 cloves garlic, minced	Vegetable oil, for spraying
⅓ cup minced flat-leaf parsley, plus more for garnish	Lemon wedges, for serving

1. Stir the sherry and melted butter together in a shallow bowl or pie plate and whisk until combined. Set aside. Whisk together the panko, garlic, parsley, salt, and cayenne pepper on a large plate or shallow bowl.
2. Thread the shrimp onto metal skewers designed for the air fryer oven or bamboo skewers, 3 to 4 per skewer. Dip 1 shrimp skewer in the butter mixture, then dredge in the panko mixture until each shrimp is lightly coated. Place the skewer on a plate or rimmed baking sheet and repeat the process with the remaining skewers.
3. Arrange 4 skewers in the air fryer basket. Spray the skewers with oil. Select the AIR FRY function and cook at 350ºF (177ºC) for 8 minutes, until the bread crumbs are golden brown and the shrimp are cooked through. Transfer the cooked skewers to a serving plate and keep warm while cooking the remaining 4 skewers in the air fryer oven.
4. Sprinkle the cooked skewers with additional fresh parsley and serve with lemon wedges if desired.

Crab Cakes with Lush Salad

Prep time: 10 minutes | Cook time: 13 minutes | Serves 2

8 ounces (227 g) lump crab meat, picked over for shells
2 tablespoons panko bread crumbs
1 scallion, minced
1 large egg
1 tablespoon mayonnaise
1½ teaspoons Dijon mustard
Pinch of cayenne pepper
2 shallots, sliced thin
1 tablespoon extra-virgin olive oil, divided
1 teaspoon lemon juice, plus lemon wedges for serving
⅛ teaspoon salt
Pinch of pepper
½ (3-ounce / 85-g) small head Bibb lettuce, torn into bite-size pieces
½ apple, cored and sliced thin

1. Line large plate with triple layer of paper towels. Transfer crab meat to prepared plate and pat dry with additional paper towels. Combine panko, scallion, egg, mayonnaise, mustard, and cayenne in a bowl. Using a rubber spatula, gently fold in crab meat until combined; discard paper towels. Divide crab mixture into 4 tightly packed balls, then flatten each into 1-inch-thick cake (cakes will be delicate). Transfer cakes to plate and refrigerate until firm, about 10 minutes.
2. Toss shallots with ½ teaspoon oil in separate bowl; transfer to air fryer basket. Select the AIR FRY function and cook at 400ºF (204ºC) for 5 to 7 minutes, or until shallots are browned, tossing once halfway through cooking. Return shallots to now-empty bowl and set aside.
3. Arrange crab cakes in air fryer basket, spaced evenly apart. Return basket to air fryer oven and air fry until crab cakes are light golden brown on both sides, 8 to 10 minutes, flipping and rotating cakes halfway through cooking.
4. Meanwhile, whisk remaining 2½ teaspoons oil, lemon juice, salt, and pepper together in large bowl. Add lettuce, apple, and shallots and toss to coat. Serve crab cakes with salad, passing lemon wedges separately.

Hearty Crab Cakes with Mango Mayo

Prep time: 25 minutes | Cook time: 15 minutes | Serves 4

Crab Cakes:

½ cup chopped red onion
½ cup fresh cilantro leaves
1 small serrano chile or jalapeño, seeded and quartered
½ pound (227 g) lump crabmeat
1 large egg
1 tablespoon mayonnaise
1 tablespoon whole-grain mustard
2 teaspoons minced fresh ginger
½ teaspoon ground cumin
½ teaspoon ground coriander
¼ teaspoon kosher salt
2 tablespoons fresh lemon juice
1½ cups panko bread crumbs
Vegetable oil spray

Mango Mayo:

½ cup diced fresh mango
½ cup mayonnaise
½ teaspoon grated lime zest
2 teaspoons fresh lime juice
Pinch of cayenne pepper

1. For the crab cakes: Combine the onion, cilantro, and serrano in a food processor. Pulse until minced.
2. In a large bowl, combine the minced vegetable mixture with the crabmeat, egg, mayonnaise, mustard, ginger, cumin, coriander, and salt. Add the lemon juice and mix gently until thoroughly combined. Add 1 cup of the bread crumbs. Mix gently again until well blended.
3. Form into four evenly sized patties. Put the remaining ½ cup bread crumbs in a shallow bowl and press both sides of each patty into the bread crumbs.
4. Arrange the patties in the air fryer basket. Spray with vegetable oil spray. Select the AIR FRY function and cook at 375ºF (190ºC) for 15 minutes, turning and spraying other side of the patties with vegetable oil spray halfway through the cooking time, until the crab cakes are golden brown and crisp.
5. Meanwhile, for the mayonnaise: In a blender, combine the mango, mayonnaise, lime zest, lime juice, and cayenne. Blend until smooth.
6. Serve the crab cakes warm, with the mango mayo.

Crab Cakes with Sriracha Mayonnaise
Prep time: 15 minutes | Cook time: 10 minutes | Serves 4

Sriracha Mayonnaise:

1 cup mayonnaise	1½ teaspoons freshly
1 tablespoon sriracha	squeezed lemon juice

Crab Cakes:

1 teaspoon extra-virgin olive oil	seasoning
	1 egg
¼ cup finely diced red bell pepper	1½ teaspoons freshly squeezed lemon juice
¼ cup diced onion	1¾ cups panko bread
¼ cup diced celery	crumbs, divided
1 pound (454 g) lump crab meat	Vegetable oil, for spraying
1 teaspoon Old Bay	

1. Mix the mayonnaise, sriracha, and lemon juice in a small bowl. Place ²/₃ cup of the mixture in a separate bowl to form the base of the crab cakes. Cover the remaining sriracha mayonnaise and refrigerate. (This will become dipping sauce for the crab cakes once they are cooked.)
2. Heat the olive oil in a heavy-bottomed, medium skillet over medium-high heat. Add the bell pepper, onion, and celery and sauté for 3 minutes. Transfer the vegetables to the bowl with the reserved ²/₃ cup of sriracha mayonnaise. Mix in the crab, Old Bay seasoning, egg, and lemon juice. Add 1 cup of the panko. Form the crab mixture into 8 cakes. Dredge the cakes in the remaining ¾ cup of panko, turning to coat. Place on a baking sheet. Cover and refrigerate for at least 1 hour and up to 8 hours.
3. Select the BAKE function and preheat MAXX to 375ºF (191ºC). Spray the air fryer basket with oil. Working in batches as needed so as not to overcrowd the basket, place the chilled crab cakes in a single layer in the basket. Spray the crab cakes with oil. Bake until golden brown, 8 to 10 minutes, carefully turning halfway through cooking. Remove to a platter and keep warm. Repeat with the remaining crab cakes as needed. Serve the crab cakes immediately with sriracha mayonnaise dipping sauce.

Crunchy Cod Fillet
Prep time: 10 minutes | Cook time: 12 minutes | Serves 2

¹/₃ cup panko bread crumbs	fresh parsley
1 teaspoon vegetable oil	1 tablespoon mayonnaise
1 small shallot, minced	1 large egg yolk
1 small garlic clove, minced	¼ teaspoon grated lemon zest, plus lemon wedges for serving
½ teaspoon minced fresh thyme	2 (8-ounce / 227-g) skinless cod fillets, 1¼ inches thick
Salt and pepper, to taste	Vegetable oil spray
1 tablespoon minced	

1. Select the BAKE function and preheat MAXX to 300ºF (149ºC).
2. Make foil sling for air fryer basket by folding 1 long sheet of aluminum foil so it is 4 inches wide. Lay sheet of foil widthwise across basket, pressing foil into and up sides of basket. Fold excess foil as needed so that edges of foil are flush with top of basket. Lightly spray the foil and basket with vegetable oil spray.
3. Toss the panko with the oil in a bowl until evenly coated. Stir in the shallot, garlic, thyme, ¼ teaspoon salt, and ⅛ teaspoon pepper. Microwave, stirring frequently, until the panko is light golden brown, about 2 minutes. Transfer to a shallow dish and let cool slightly; stir in the parsley. Whisk the mayonnaise, egg yolk, lemon zest, and ⅛ teaspoon pepper together in another bowl.
4. Pat the cod dry with paper towels and season with salt and pepper. Arrange the fillets, skinned-side down, on plate and brush tops evenly with mayonnaise mixture. (Tuck thinner tail ends of fillets under themselves as needed to create uniform pieces.) Working with 1 fillet at a time, dredge the coated side in panko mixture, pressing gently to adhere. Arrange the fillets, crumb-side up, on sling in the prepared basket, spaced evenly apart.
5. Bake for 12 to 16 minutes, using a sling to rotate fillets halfway through cooking. Using a sling, carefully remove cod from air fryer oven. Serve with the lemon wedges.

Green Curry Jumbo Shrimp

Prep time: 15 minutes | Cook time: 5 minutes | Serves 4

1 to 2 tablespoons Thai green curry paste	fresh ginger
2 tablespoons coconut oil, melted	1 clove garlic, minced
1 tablespoon half-and-half or coconut milk	1 pound (454 g) jumbo raw shrimp, peeled and deveined
1 teaspoon fish sauce	¼ cup chopped fresh Thai basil or sweet basil
1 teaspoon soy sauce	¼ cup chopped fresh cilantro
1 teaspoon minced	

1. In a baking pan, combine the curry paste, coconut oil, half-and-half, fish sauce, soy sauce, ginger, and garlic. Whisk until well combined.
2. Add the shrimp and toss until well coated. Marinate at room temperature for 15 to 30 minutes.
3. Place the pan in the air fryer basket. Select the AIR FRY function and cook at 400ºF (204ºC) for 5 minutes, stirring halfway through the cooking time.
4. Transfer the shrimp to a serving bowl or platter. Garnish with the basil and cilantro. Serve immediately.

Crispy Fish Sticks

Prep time: 15 minutes | Cook time: 10 to 15 minutes | Serves 4

4 fish fillets	1½ cups whole-wheat panko bread crumbs
½ cup whole-wheat flour	
1 teaspoon seasoned salt	½ tablespoon dried parsley flakes
2 eggs	Cooking spray

1. Spray the air fryer basket lightly with cooking spray.
2. Cut the fish fillets lengthwise into "sticks."
3. In a shallow bowl, mix the whole-wheat flour and seasoned salt.
4. In a small bowl, whisk the eggs with 1 teaspoon of water.
5. In another shallow bowl, mix the panko bread crumbs and parsley flakes.
6. Coat each fish stick in the seasoned flour, then in the egg mixture, and dredge them in the panko bread crumbs.
7. Place the fish sticks in the air fryer basket in a single layer and lightly spray the fish sticks with cooking spray. You may need to cook them in batches.
8. Select the AIR FRY function and cook at 400ºF (204ºC) for 5 to 8 minutes. Flip the fish sticks over and lightly spray with the cooking spray. Air fry until golden brown and crispy, 5 to 7 more minutes.
9. Serve warm.

Italian Tuna Loin Roast

Prep time: 15 minutes | Cook time: 21 minutes | Serves 8

Cooking spray	juice
1 tablespoon Italian seasoning	1 tuna loin (approximately 2 pounds / 907 g, 3 to 4 inches thick, large enough to fill a 6 x 6-inch baking dish)
⅛ teaspoon ground black pepper	
1 tablespoon extra-light olive oil	
1 teaspoon lemon	

1. Spray a baking dish with cooking spray and place in the air fryer basket. Select the ROAST function and preheat MAXX to 390ºF (199ºC).
2. Mix together the Italian seasoning, pepper, oil, and lemon juice.
3. Using a dull table knife or butter knife, pierce top of tuna about every half inch: Insert knife into top of the tuna loin and pierce almost all the way to the bottom.
4. Spoon oil mixture into each of the holes and use the knife to push seasonings into the tuna as deeply as possible.
5. Spread any remaining oil mixture on all outer surfaces of tuna.
6. Place tuna in baking dish and roast for 20 minutes. Check temperature with a meat thermometer. Roast for an additional 1 to 4 minutes or until temperature reaches 145ºF (63ºC).
7. Remove basket from fryer and let tuna sit in basket for 10 minutes.

Jalapeño-Lime Fish Tacos
Prep time: 25 minutes | Cook time: 10 minutes | Serves 4

Fish Tacos:

1 pound (454 g) fish fillets
¼ teaspoon cumin
¼ teaspoon coriander
⅛ teaspoon ground red pepper
1 tablespoon lime zest
¼ teaspoon smoked paprika
1 teaspoon oil
Cooking spray

6 to 8 corn or flour tortillas (6-inch size)
Jalapeño-Lime Sauce
½ cup sour cream
1 tablespoon lime juice
¼ teaspoon grated lime zest
½ teaspoon minced jalapeño (flesh only)
¼ teaspoon cumin

Napa Cabbage Garnish:

1 cup shredded Napa cabbage
¼ cup slivered red or

green bell pepper
¼ cup slivered onion

1. Slice the fish fillets into strips approximately ½-inch thick.
2. Put the strips into a sealable plastic bag along with the cumin, coriander, red pepper, lime zest, smoked paprika, and oil. Massage seasonings into the fish until evenly distributed.
3. Spray air fryer basket with nonstick cooking spray and place seasoned fish inside.
4. Select the AIR FRY function and cook at 390°F (199°C) for approximately 5 minutes. Shake basket to distribute fish. Air fry for an additional 2 to 5 minutes, until fish flakes easily.
5. While the fish is cooking, prepare the Jalapeño-Lime Sauce by mixing the sour cream, lime juice, lime zest, jalapeño, and cumin together to make a smooth sauce. Set aside.
6. Mix the cabbage, bell pepper, and onion together and set aside.
7. To warm refrigerated tortillas, wrap in damp paper towels and microwave for 30 to 60 seconds.
8. To serve, spoon some of fish into a warm tortilla. Add one or two tablespoons Napa Cabbage Garnish and drizzle with Jalapeño-Lime Sauce.

Garlic Small Scallops
Prep time: 10 minutes | Cook time: 10 to 15 minutes | Serves 4

2 teaspoons olive oil
1 packet dry zesty Italian dressing mix
1 teaspoon minced garlic

16 ounces (454 g) small scallops, patted dry
Cooking spray

1. Spray the air fryer basket lightly with cooking spray.
2. In a large zip-top plastic bag, combine the olive oil, Italian dressing mix, and garlic.
3. Add the scallops, seal the zip-top bag, and coat the scallops in the seasoning mixture.
4. Place the scallops in the air fryer basket and lightly spray with cooking spray.
5. Select the AIR FRY function and cook at 400°F (204°C) for 5 minutes. Shake the basket, and air fry for 5 to 10 more minutes, or until the scallops reach an internal temperature of 120°F (49°C).
6. Serve immediately.

Chili-Lemon Tilapia Fillet
Prep time: 5 minutes | Cook time: 10 to 15 minutes | Serves 4

1 tablespoon lemon juice
1 tablespoon olive oil
1 teaspoon minced garlic

½ teaspoon chili powder
4 (6-ounce / 170-g) tilapia fillets

1. Line the air fryer basket with parchment paper.
2. In a large, shallow bowl, mix together the lemon juice, olive oil, garlic, and chili powder to make a marinade. Place the tilapia fillets in the bowl and coat evenly.
3. Place the fillets in the basket in a single layer, leaving space between each fillet. You may need to cook in more than one batch.
4. Select the AIR FRY function and cook at 380°F (193°C) for 10 to 15 minutes, or until the fish is cooked and flakes easily with a fork.
5. Serve hot.

Creole Crawfish Casserole

Prep time: 20 minutes | Cook time: 25 minutes | Serves 4

1½ cups crawfish meat
½ cup chopped celery
½ cup chopped onion
½ cup chopped green bell pepper
2 large eggs, beaten
1 cup half-and-half
1 tablespoon butter, melted
1 tablespoon cornstarch
1 teaspoon Creole seasoning
¾ teaspoon salt
½ teaspoon freshly ground black pepper
1 cup shredded Cheddar cheese
Cooking spray

1. In a medium bowl, stir together the crawfish, celery, onion, and green pepper.
2. In another medium bowl, whisk the eggs, half-and-half, butter, cornstarch, Creole seasoning, salt, and pepper until blended. Stir the egg mixture into the crawfish mixture. Add the cheese and stir to combine.
3. Select the BAKE function and preheat MAXX to 300ºF (149ºC). Spritz a baking pan with oil.
4. Transfer the crawfish mixture to the prepared pan and place it in the air fryer basket.
5. Bake for 25 minutes, stirring every 10 minutes, until a knife inserted into the center comes out clean.
6. Serve immediately.

Fried Breaded Shrimp

Prep time: 15 minutes | Cook time: 5 minutes | Serves 4

½ cup self-rising flour
1 teaspoon paprika
1 teaspoon salt
½ teaspoon freshly ground black pepper
1 large egg, beaten
1 cup finely crushed panko bread crumbs
20 frozen large shrimp (about 1-pound / 907-g), peeled and deveined
Cooking spray

1. In a shallow bowl, whisk the flour, paprika, salt, and pepper until blended. Add the beaten egg to a second shallow bowl and the bread crumbs to a third.

2. One at a time, dip the shrimp into the flour, the egg, and the bread crumbs, coating thoroughly.
3. Line the air fryer basket with parchment paper.
4. Place the shrimp on the parchment and spritz with oil.
5. Select the AIR FRY function and cook at 400ºF (204ºC) for 2 minutes. Shake the basket, spritz the shrimp with oil, and air fry for 3 minutes more until lightly browned and crispy. Serve hot.

Coconut Shrimp with Sweet Chili Mayo

Prep time: 15 minutes | Cook time: 8 minutes | Serves 4

Sweet Chili Mayo:
3 tablespoons mayonnaise
3 tablespoons Thai
sweet chili sauce
1 tablespoon Sriracha sauce
Shrimp:
²⁄₃ cup sweetened shredded coconut
²⁄₃ cup panko bread crumbs
Kosher salt, to taste
2 tablespoons all-purpose or gluten-
free flour
2 large eggs
24 extra-jumbo shrimp (about 1 pound / 454 g), peeled and deveined
Cooking spray

1. In a medium bowl, combine the mayonnaise, Thai sweet chili sauce, and Sriracha and mix well.
2. In a medium bowl, combine the coconut, panko, and ¼ teaspoon salt. Place the flour in a shallow bowl. Whisk the eggs in another shallow bowl.
3. Season the shrimp with ⅛ teaspoon salt. Dip the shrimp in the flour, shaking off any excess, then into the egg. Coat in the coconut-panko mixture, gently pressing to adhere, then transfer to a large plate. Spray both sides of the shrimp with oil.
4. Working in batches, arrange a single layer of the shrimp in the air fryer basket. Select the AIR FRY function and cook at 360ºF (182ºC) for 8 minutes, flipping halfway, until the crust is golden brown and the shrimp are cooked through.
5. Serve with the sweet chili mayo for dipping.

Fish Tacos with Sriracha Slaw

Prep time: 20 minutes | Cook time: 5 minutes | Serves 2 to 3

Sriracha Slaw:

½ cup mayonnaise
2 tablespoons rice vinegar
1 teaspoon sugar
2 tablespoons sriracha chili sauce
5 cups shredded

green cabbage
¼ cup shredded carrots
2 scallions, chopped
Salt and freshly ground black pepper

Tacos:

½ cup flour
1 teaspoon chili powder
½ teaspoon ground cumin
1 teaspoon salt
Freshly ground black pepper
½ teaspoon baking powder
1 egg, beaten

¼ cup milk
1 cup bread crumbs
1 pound (454 g) mahi-mahi or snapper fillets
1 tablespoon canola or vegetable oil
6 (6-inch) flour tortillas
1 lime, cut into wedges

1. Start by making the sriracha slaw. Combine the mayonnaise, rice vinegar, sugar, and sriracha sauce in a large bowl. Mix well and add the green cabbage, carrots, and scallions. Toss until all the vegetables are coated with the dressing and season with salt and pepper. Refrigerate the slaw until you are ready to serve the tacos.
2. Combine the flour, chili powder, cumin, salt, pepper and baking powder in a bowl. Add the egg and milk and mix until the batter is smooth. Place the bread crumbs in shallow dish.
3. Cut the fish fillets into 1-inch wide sticks, approximately 4-inches long. You should have about 12 fish sticks total. Dip the fish sticks into the batter, coating all sides. Let the excess batter drip off the fish and then roll them in the bread crumbs, patting the crumbs onto all sides of the fish sticks. Set the coated fish on a plate or baking sheet until all the fish has been coated.
4. Spray the coated fish sticks with oil on all sides. Spray or brush the inside of the air fryer basket with oil and transfer the fish to the basket. Place as many sticks as you can in one layer, leaving a little room

around each stick. Place any remaining sticks on top, perpendicular to the first layer.
5. Select the AIR FRY function and cook the fish at 400ºF (205ºC) for 3 minutes. Turn the fish sticks over and air fry for an additional 2 minutes.
6. While the fish is air frying, warm the tortilla shells either in a 350ºF (180ºC) oven wrapped in foil or in a skillet with a little oil over medium-high heat for a couple minutes. Fold the tortillas in half and keep them warm until the remaining tortillas and fish are ready.
7. To assemble the tacos, place two pieces of the fish in each tortilla shell and top with the sriracha slaw. Squeeze the lime wedge over top and dig in.

Shrimp, Black Beans, and Rice Bowl

Prep time: 10 minutes | Cook time: 10 to 15 minutes | Serves 4

2 teaspoons lime juice
1 teaspoon olive oil
1 teaspoon honey
1 teaspoon minced garlic
1 teaspoon chili powder
Salt, to taste
12 ounces (340 g) medium shrimp,

peeled and deveined
2 cups cooked brown rice
1 (15-ounce / 425-g) can seasoned black beans, warmed
1 large avocado, chopped
1 cup sliced cherry tomatoes
Cooking spray

1. Spray the air fryer basket lightly with cooking spray.
2. In a medium bowl, mix together the lime juice, olive oil, honey, garlic, chili powder, and salt to make a marinade.
3. Add the shrimp and toss to coat evenly in the marinade.
4. Place the shrimp in the air fryer basket. Select the AIR FRY function and cook at 400ºF (204ºC) for 5 minutes. Shake the basket and air fry until the shrimp are cooked through and starting to brown, an additional 5 to 10 minutes.
5. To assemble the bowls, spoon ¼ of the rice, black beans, avocado, and cherry tomatoes into each of four bowls. Top with the shrimp and serve.

Oregano Shrimp and Zucchini

Prep time: 15 minutes | Cook time: 7 to 8 minutes | Serves 4

1¼ pounds (567 g) extra-large raw shrimp, peeled and deveined
2 medium zucchini (about 8 ounces / 227 g each), halved lengthwise and cut into ½-inch-thick slices
1½ tablespoons olive oil
½ teaspoon garlic salt
1½ teaspoons dried oregano
⅛ teaspoon crushed red pepper flakes (optional)
Juice of ½ lemon
1 tablespoon chopped fresh mint
1 tablespoon chopped fresh dill

1. In a large bowl, combine the shrimp, zucchini, oil, garlic salt, oregano, and pepper flakes (if using) and toss to coat.
2. Working in batches, arrange a single layer of the shrimp and zucchini in the air fryer basket. Select the AIR FRY function and cook at 350ºF (177ºC) for 7 to 8 minutes, shaking the basket halfway, until the zucchini is golden and the shrimp are cooked through.
3. Transfer to a serving dish and tent with foil while you air fry the remaining shrimp and zucchini.
4. Top with the lemon juice, mint, and dill and serve.

Dijon Catfish Fillet

Prep time: 20 minutes | Cook time: 7 minutes | Serves 4

4 tablespoons butter, melted
2 teaspoons Worcestershire sauce, divided
1 teaspoon lemon pepper
1 cup panko bread crumbs
4 (4-ounce / 113-g) catfish fillets
Cooking spray
½ cup sour cream
1 tablespoon Dijon mustard

1. In a shallow bowl, stir together the melted butter, 1 teaspoon of Worcestershire sauce, and the lemon pepper. Place the bread crumbs in another shallow bowl.
2. One at a time, dip both sides of the fillets in the butter mixture, then the bread crumbs, coating thoroughly.
3. Select the BAKE function and preheat MAXX to 300ºF (149ºC). Line the air fryer basket with parchment paper.
4. Place the coated fish on the parchment and spritz with oil.
5. Bake for 4 minutes. Flip the fish, spritz it with oil, and bake for 3 to 6 minutes more, depending on the thickness of the fillets, until the fish flakes easily with a fork.
6. In a small bowl, stir together the sour cream, Dijon, and remaining 1 teaspoon of Worcestershire sauce. This sauce can be made 1 day in advance and refrigerated before serving. Serve with the fried fish.

New Orleans Crab Cakes

Prep time: 10 minutes | Cook time: 8 to 10 minutes | Serves 4

1¼ cups bread crumbs
2 teaspoons Creole Seasoning
1 teaspoon dry mustard
1 teaspoon salt
1 teaspoon freshly ground black pepper
1½ cups crab meat
2 large eggs, beaten
1 teaspoon butter, melted
⅓ cup minced onion
Cooking spray
Pecan Tartar Sauce, for serving

1. Line the air fryer basket with parchment paper.
2. In a medium bowl, whisk the bread crumbs, Creole Seasoning, dry mustard, salt, and pepper until blended. Add the crab meat, eggs, butter, and onion. Stir until blended. Shape the crab mixture into 8 patties.
3. Place the crab cakes on the parchment and spritz with oil.
4. Select the AIR FRY function and cook at 350ºF (177ºC) for 4 minutes. Flip the cakes, spritz them with oil, and air fry for 4 to 6 minutes more until the outsides are firm and a fork inserted into the center comes out clean. Serve with the Pecan Tartar Sauce.

Fried Seafood with Salsa Criolla
Prep time: 20 minutes | Cook time: 10 minutes | Serves 4

Salsa Criolla:
½ red onion, thinly sliced
2 tomatoes, diced
1 serrano or jalapeño pepper, deseeded and diced

1 clove garlic, minced
¼ cup chopped fresh cilantro
Pinch of kosher salt
3 limes

Fried Seafood:
1 pound (454 g) firm, white-fleshed fish such as cod (add an extra ½-pound /227-g fish if not using shrimp)
20 large or jumbo shrimp, shelled and deveined
¼ cup all-purpose flour
¼ cup cornstarch
1 teaspoon garlic powder

1 teaspoon kosher salt
¼ teaspoon cayenne pepper
2 cups panko bread crumbs
2 eggs, beaten with 2 tablespoons water
Vegetable oil, for spraying
Mayonnaise or tartar sauce, for serving (optional)

1. To make the Salsa Criolla, combine the red onion, tomatoes, pepper, garlic, cilantro, and salt in a medium bowl. Add the juice and zest of 2 of the limes. Refrigerate the salad while you make the fish.
2. To make the seafood, cut the fish fillets into strips approximately 2 inches long and 1 inch wide. Place the flour, cornstarch, garlic powder, salt, and cayenne pepper on a plate and whisk to combine. Place the panko on a separate plate. Dredge the fish strips in the seasoned flour mixture, shaking off any excess. Dip the strips in the egg mixture, coating them completely, then dredge in the panko, shaking off any excess. Place the fish strips on a plate or rack. Repeat with the shrimp, if using.
3. Spray the air fryer basket with oil. Working in 2 or 3 batches, arrange the fish and shrimp in a single layer in the basket, taking care not to crowd the basket. Spray with oil.
4. Select the AIR FRY function and cook at 400ºF (204ºC) for 5 minutes, then flip and air fry for another 4 to 5 minutes

until the outside is brown and crisp and the inside of the fish is opaque and flakes easily with a fork. Repeat with the remaining seafood.
5. Place the fried seafood on a platter. Use a slotted spoon to remove the salsa criolla from the bowl, leaving behind any liquid that has accumulated. Place the salsa criolla on top of the fried seafood. Serve immediately with the remaining lime, cut into wedges, and mayonnaise or tartar sauce as desired.

Marinated Salmon Fillet
Prep time: 10 minutes | Cook time: 15 to 20 minutes | Serves 4

¼ cup soy sauce
¼ cup rice wine vinegar
1 tablespoon brown sugar
1 tablespoon olive oil
1 teaspoon mustard powder
1 teaspoon ground

ginger
½ teaspoon freshly ground black pepper
½ teaspoon minced garlic
4 (6-ounce / 170-g) salmon fillets, skin-on
Cooking spray

1. In a small bowl, combine the soy sauce, rice wine vinegar, brown sugar, olive oil, mustard powder, ginger, black pepper, and garlic to make a marinade.
2. Place the fillets in a shallow baking dish and pour the marinade over them. Cover the baking dish and marinate for at least 1 hour in the refrigerator, turning the fillets occasionally to keep them coated in the marinade.
3. Spray the air fryer basket lightly with cooking spray.
4. Shake off as much marinade as possible from the fillets and place them, skin-side down, in the air fryer basket in a single layer. You may need to cook the fillets in batches.
5. Select the AIR FRY function and cook at 370ºF (188ºC) for 15 to 20 minutes. The minimum internal temperature should be 145ºF (63ºC) at the thickest part of the fillets.
6. Serve hot.

Moroccan Halibut Fillet with Chickpea Salad

Prep time: 15 minutes | Cook time: 12 minutes | Serves 2

¾ teaspoon ground coriander
½ teaspoon ground cumin
¼ teaspoon ground ginger
⅛ teaspoon ground cinnamon
Salt and pepper, to taste
2 (8-ounce / 227-g) skinless halibut fillets, 1¼ inches thick
4 teaspoons extra-virgin olive oil,
divided, plus extra for drizzling
1 (15-ounce / 425-g) can chickpeas, rinsed
1 tablespoon lemon juice, plus lemon wedges for serving
1 teaspoon harissa
½ teaspoon honey
2 carrots, peeled and shredded
2 tablespoons chopped fresh mint, divided
Vegetable oil spray

1. Select the BAKE function and preheat MAXX to 300ºF (149ºC).
2. Make foil sling for air fryer basket by folding 1 long sheet of aluminum foil so it is 4 inches wide. Lay sheet of foil widthwise across basket, pressing foil into and up sides of basket. Fold excess foil as needed so that edges of foil are flush with top of basket. Lightly spray foil and basket with vegetable oil spray.
3. Combine coriander, cumin, ginger, cinnamon, ⅛ teaspoon salt, and ⅛ teaspoon pepper in a small bowl. Pat halibut dry with paper towels, rub with 1 teaspoon oil, and sprinkle all over with spice mixture. Arrange fillets skinned side down on sling in prepared basket, spaced evenly apart. Bake until halibut flakes apart when gently prodded with a paring knife and registers 140ºF (60ºC), 12 to 16 minutes, using the sling to rotate fillets halfway through cooking.
4. Meanwhile, microwave chickpeas in medium bowl until heated through, about 2 minutes. Stir in remaining 1 tablespoon oil, lemon juice, harissa, honey, ⅛ teaspoon salt, and ⅛ teaspoon pepper. Add carrots and 1 tablespoon mint and toss to combine. Season with salt and pepper, to taste.
5. Using sling, carefully remove halibut from air fryer oven and transfer to individual plates. Sprinkle with remaining 1 tablespoon mint and drizzle with extra oil to taste. Serve with salad and lemon wedges.

Old Bay Crawfish

Prep time: 15 minutes | Cook time: 18 minutes | Serves 4

½ cup flour, plus 2 tablespoons
½ teaspoon garlic powder
1½ teaspoons Old Bay Seasoning
½ teaspoon onion powder
Coating:
1½ cups panko crumbs
1 teaspoon Old Bay
½ cup beer, plus 2 tablespoons
1 (12-ounce / 340-g) package frozen crawfish tail meat, thawed and drained
Oil for misting or cooking spray

Seasoning
½ teaspoon ground black pepper

1. In a large bowl, mix together the flour, garlic powder, Old Bay Seasoning, and onion powder. Stir in beer to blend.
2. Add crawfish meat to batter and stir to coat.
3. Combine the coating ingredients in food processor and pulse to finely crush the crumbs. Transfer crumbs to shallow dish.
4. Pour the crawfish and batter into a colander to drain. Stir with a spoon to drain excess batter.
5. Working with a handful of crawfish at a time, roll in crumbs and place on a cookie sheet. It's okay if some of the smaller pieces of crawfish meat stick together.
6. Spray breaded crawfish with oil or cooking spray and place all at once into air fryer basket.
7. Select the AIR FRY function and cook at 390ºF (199ºC) for 5 minutes. Shake basket or stir and mist again with olive oil or spray. Air fry for 5 more minutes, shake basket again, and mist lightly again. Continue cooking for 3 to 5 more minutes, until browned and crispy.

Remoulade Crab Cakes

Prep time: 15 minutes | Cook time: 10 minutes | Serves 4

Remoulade:

¾ cup mayonnaise
2 teaspoons Dijon mustard
1½ teaspoons yellow mustard
1 teaspoon vinegar
¼ teaspoon hot

sauce
1 teaspoon tiny capers, drained and chopped
¼ teaspoon salt
⅛ teaspoon ground black pepper

Crab Cakes:

1 cup bread crumbs, divided
2 tablespoons mayonnaise
1 scallion, finely chopped
6 ounces (170 g) crab meat
2 tablespoons pasteurized egg

product (liquid eggs in a carton)
2 teaspoons lemon juice
½ teaspoon red pepper flakes
½ teaspoon Old Bay seasoning
Cooking spray

1. In a small bowl, whisk to combine the mayonnaise, Dijon mustard, yellow mustard, vinegar, hot sauce, capers, salt, and pepper.
2. Refrigerate for at least 1 hour before serving.
3. Place a parchment liner in the air fryer basket.
4. In a large bowl, mix to combine ½ cup of bread crumbs with the mayonnaise and scallion. Set the other ½ cup of bread crumbs aside in a small bowl.
5. Add the crab meat, egg product, lemon juice, red pepper flakes, and Old Bay seasoning to the large bowl, and stir to combine.
6. Divide the crab mixture into 4 portions, and form into patties.
7. Dredge each patty in the remaining bread crumbs to coat.
8. Place the prepared patties on the liner in the air fryer oven in a single layer.
9. Spray lightly with cooking spray. Select the AIR FRY function and cook at 400ºF (204ºC) for 5 minutes. Flip the crab cakes over, air fry for another 5 minutes, until golden, and serve.

Salmon Puttanesca en Papillote

Prep time: 10 minutes | Cook time: 17 minutes | Serves 2

1 small zucchini, sliced into ¼-inch thick half moons
1 teaspoon olive oil
Salt and freshly ground black pepper
2 (5-ounce / 142-g) salmon fillets
1 beefsteak tomato, chopped

1 tablespoon capers, rinsed
10 black olives, pitted and sliced
2 tablespoons dry vermouth or white wine
2 tablespoons butter
¼ cup chopped fresh basil, chopped

1. Toss the zucchini with the olive oil, salt and freshly ground black pepper. Transfer the zucchini into the air fryer basket. Select the AIR FRY function and cook at 400ºF (205ºC) for 5 minutes, shaking the basket once or twice during the cooking process.
2. Cut out 2 large rectangles of parchment paper (about 13-inches by 15-inches each). Divide the air-fried zucchini between the two pieces of parchment paper, placing the vegetables in the center of each rectangle.
3. Place a fillet of salmon on each pile of zucchini. Season the fish very well with salt and pepper. Toss the tomato, capers, olives and vermouth (or white wine) together in a bowl. Divide the tomato mixture between the two fish packages, placing it on top of the fish fillets and pouring any juice out of the bowl onto the fish. Top each fillet with a tablespoon of butter.
4. Fold up each parchment square. Bring two edges together and fold them over a few times, leaving some space above the fish. Twist the open sides together and upwards so they can serve as handles for the packet, but don't let them extend beyond the top of the air fryer basket.
5. Place the two packages into the air fryer oven and air fry for 12 minutes. The packages should be puffed up and slightly browned when fully cooked. Once cooked, let the fish sit in the parchment for 2 minutes.
6. Serve the fish in the parchment paper, or if desired, remove the parchment paper before serving. Garnish with a little fresh basil.

Cod Fillet with Potatoes
Prep time: 10 minutes | Cook time: 28 minutes | Serves 2

3 tablespoons unsalted butter, softened, divided
2 garlic cloves, minced
1 lemon, grated to yield 2 teaspoons zest and sliced ¼ inch thick
Salt and pepper, to taste

1 large russet potato (12 ounce / 340-g), unpeeled, sliced ¼ inch thick
1 tablespoon minced fresh parsley, chives, or tarragon
2 (8-ounce / 227-g) skinless cod fillets, 1¼ inches thick
Vegetable oil spray

1. Make foil sling for air fryer basket by folding 1 long sheet of aluminum foil so it is 4 inches wide. Lay sheet of foil widthwise across basket, pressing foil into and up sides of basket. Fold excess foil as needed so that edges of foil are flush with top of basket. Lightly spray the foil and basket with vegetable oil spray.
2. Microwave 1 tablespoon butter, garlic, 1 teaspoon lemon zest, ¼ teaspoon salt, and ⅛ teaspoon pepper in a medium bowl, stirring once, until the butter is melted and the mixture is fragrant, about 30 seconds. Add the potato slices and toss to coat. Shingle the potato slices on sling in prepared basket to create 2 even layers.
3. Select the AIR FRY function and cook at 400ºF (204ºC) for 16 to 18 minutes, or until potato slices are spotty brown and just tender, using a sling to rotate potatoes halfway through cooking.
4. Combine the remaining 2 tablespoons butter, remaining 1 teaspoon lemon zest, and parsley in a small bowl. Pat the cod dry with paper towels and season with salt and pepper. Place the fillets, skinned-side down, on top of potato slices, spaced evenly apart. (Tuck thinner tail ends of fillets under themselves as needed to create uniform pieces.) Dot the fillets with the butter mixture and top with the lemon slices. Return the basket to the air fryer oven and air fry until the cod flakes apart when gently prodded with a paring knife and registers 140ºF (60ºC), 12 to 15 minutes, using a sling to rotate the potato slices and cod

halfway through cooking.
5. Using a sling, carefully remove potatoes and cod from air fryer oven. Cut the potato slices into 2 portions between fillets using fish spatula. Slide spatula along underside of potato slices and transfer with cod to individual plates. Serve.

Citrus-Mustard Glazed Salmon
Prep time: 10 minutes | Cook time: 10 minutes | Serves 2

1 tablespoon orange marmalade
¼ teaspoon grated orange zest plus 1 tablespoon juice
2 teaspoons whole-grain mustard

2 (8-ounce / 227-g) skin-on salmon fillets, 1½ inches thick
Salt and pepper, to taste
Vegetable oil spray

1. Make foil sling for air fryer basket by folding 1 long sheet of aluminum foil so it is 4 inches wide. Lay sheet of foil widthwise across basket, pressing foil into and up sides of basket. Fold excess foil as needed so that edges of foil are flush with top of basket. Lightly spray foil and basket with vegetable oil spray.
2. Combine marmalade, orange zest and juice, and mustard in bowl. Pat salmon dry with paper towels and season with salt and pepper. Brush tops and sides of fillets evenly with glaze. Arrange fillets skin side down on sling in prepared basket, spaced evenly apart.
3. Select the AIR FRY function and cook at 400ºF (204ºC) for 10 to 14 minutes, or until center is still translucent when checked with the tip of a paring knife and registers 125ºF (52ºC) (for medium-rare), using sling to rotate fillets halfway through cooking.
4. Using the sling, carefully remove salmon from air fryer oven. Slide fish spatula along underside of fillets and transfer to individual serving plates, leaving skin behind. Serve.

Pecan-Crusted Tilapia Fillet
Prep time: 10minutes | Cook time: 10 minutes | Serves 4

1¼ cups pecans
¾ cup panko bread crumbs
½ cup all-purpose flour
2 tablespoons Cajun seasoning
2 eggs, beaten with

2 tablespoons water
4 (6-ounce/ 170-g) tilapia fillets
Vegetable oil, for spraying
Lemon wedges, for serving

1. Grind the pecans in the food processor until they resemble coarse meal. Combine the ground pecans with the panko on a plate. On a second plate, combine the flour and Cajun seasoning. Dry the tilapia fillets using paper towels and dredge them in the flour mixture, shaking off any excess. Dip the fillets in the egg mixture and then dredge them in the pecan and panko mixture, pressing the coating onto the fillets. Place the breaded fillets on a plate or rack.
2. Spray both sides of the breaded fillets with oil. Carefully transfer 2 of the fillets to the air fryer basket. Select the AIR FRY function and cook at 375ºF (191ºC) for 9 to 10 minutes, flipping once halfway through, until the flesh is opaque and flaky. Repeat with the remaining fillets.
3. Serve immediately with lemon wedges.

Quick Salmon Fillets
Prep time: 5 minutes | Cook time: 10 minutes | Serves 2

2 (8-ounce / 227 -g) skin-on salmon fillets, 1½ inches thick
1 teaspoon vegetable

oil
Salt and pepper, to taste
Vegetable oil spray

1. Make foil sling for air fryer basket by folding 1 long sheet of aluminum foil so it is 4 inches wide. Lay sheet of foil widthwise across basket, pressing foil into and up sides of basket. Fold excess foil as needed so that edges of foil are flush with top of basket. Lightly spray foil and basket with vegetable oil spray.
2. Pat salmon dry with paper towels, rub with oil, and season with salt and pepper. Arrange fillets skin side down on sling in prepared basket, spaced evenly apart.
3. Select the AIR FRY function and cook at 400ºF (204ºC) for 10 to 14 minutes, or until center is still translucent when checked with the tip of a paring knife and registers 125ºF (52ºC) (for medium-rare), using sling to rotate fillets halfway through cooking.
4. Using the sling, carefully remove salmon from air fryer oven. Slide fish spatula along underside of fillets and transfer to individual serving plates, leaving skin behind. Serve.

Fried Oyster Po'Boy
Prep time: 20 minutes | Cook time: 5 minutes | Serves 4

¾ cup all-purpose flour
¼ cup yellow cornmeal
1 tablespoon Cajun seasoning
1 teaspoon salt
2 large eggs, beaten
1 teaspoon hot sauce
1 pound (454 g) pre-shucked oysters

1 (12-inch) French baguette, quartered and sliced horizontally
Tartar Sauce, as needed
2 cups shredded lettuce, divided
2 tomatoes, cut into slices
Cooking spray

1. In a shallow bowl, whisk the flour, cornmeal, Cajun seasoning, and salt until blended. In a second shallow bowl, whisk together the eggs and hot sauce.
2. One at a time, dip the oysters in the cornmeal mixture, the eggs, and again in the cornmeal, coating thoroughly.
3. Line the air fryer basket with parchment paper.
4. Place the oysters on the parchment and spritz with oil.
5. Select the AIR FRY function and cook at 400ºF (204ºC) for 2 minutes. Shake the basket, spritz the oysters with oil, and air fry for 3 minutes more until lightly browned and crispy.
6. Spread each sandwich half with Tartar Sauce. Assemble the po'boys by layering each sandwich with fried oysters, ½ cup shredded lettuce, and 2 tomato slices.
7. Serve immediately.

Salmon and Veggie Burgers
Prep time: 10 minutes | Cook time: 8 minutes | Serves 4

2 (6-ounce / 170-g) fillets of salmon, finely chopped by hand or in a food processor
1 cup fine bread crumbs
1 teaspoon freshly grated lemon zest
2 tablespoons chopped fresh dill
weed
1 teaspoon salt
Freshly ground black pepper
2 eggs, lightly beaten
4 brioche or hamburger buns
Lettuce, tomato, red onion, avocado, mayonnaise or mustard, for serving

1. Combine all the ingredients in a bowl. Mix together well and divide into four balls. Flatten the balls into patties, making an indentation in the center of each patty with your thumb (this will help the burger stay flat as it cooks) and flattening the sides of the burgers so that they fit nicely into the air fryer basket.
2. Transfer the burgers to the air fryer basket. Select the AIR FRY function and cook at 400ºF (205ºC) for 4 minutes. Flip the burgers over and air fry for another 3 to 4 minutes, until nicely browned and firm to the touch.
3. Serve on soft brioche buns with your choice of topping – lettuce, tomato, red onion, avocado, mayonnaise or mustard.

Old Bay Breaded Shrimp
Prep time: 15 minutes | Cook time: 10 to 15 minutes | Serves 4

2 teaspoons Old Bay seasoning, divided
½ teaspoon garlic powder
½ teaspoon onion powder
1 pound (454 g) large
shrimp, deveined, with tails on
2 large eggs
½ cup whole-wheat panko bread crumbs
Cooking spray

1. Spray the air fryer basket lightly with cooking spray.
2. In a medium bowl, mix together 1 teaspoon of Old Bay seasoning, garlic powder, and onion powder. Add the shrimp and toss with the seasoning mix to lightly coat.

3. In a separate small bowl, whisk the eggs with 1 teaspoon water.
4. In a shallow bowl, mix together the remaining 1 teaspoon Old Bay seasoning and the panko bread crumbs.
5. Dip each shrimp in the egg mixture and dredge in the bread crumb mixture to evenly coat.
6. Place the shrimp in the air fryer basket, in a single layer. Lightly spray the shrimp with cooking spray. You many need to cook the shrimp in batches.
7. Select the AIR FRY function and cook at 380ºF (193ºC) for 10 to 15 minutes, or until the shrimp is cooked through and crispy, shaking the basket at 5-minute intervals to redistribute and evenly cook.
8. Serve immediately.

Fish Fillet with Almond-Lemon Crumbs
Prep time: 10 minutes | Cook time: 7 to 8 minutes | Serves 4

½ cup raw whole almonds
1 scallion, finely chopped
Grated zest and juice of 1 lemon
½ tablespoon extra-virgin olive oil
¾ teaspoon kosher
salt, divided
Freshly ground black pepper, to taste
4 (6 ounces / 170 g each) skinless fish fillets
Cooking spray
1 teaspoon Dijon mustard

1. In a food processor, pulse the almonds to coarsely chop. Transfer to a small bowl and add the scallion, lemon zest, and olive oil. Season with ¼ teaspoon of the salt and pepper to taste and mix to combine.
2. Spray the top of the fish with oil and squeeze the lemon juice over the fish. Season with the remaining ½ teaspoon salt and pepper to taste. Spread the mustard on top of the fish. Dividing evenly, press the almond mixture onto the top of the fillets to adhere.
3. Working in batches, place the fillets in the air fryer basket in a single layer. Select the AIR FRY function and cook at 375ºF (191ºC) for 7 to 8 minutes, until the crumbs start to brown and the fish is cooked through.
4. Serve immediately.

Chapter 5 Poultry

Chicken and Bell Pepper Fajitas

Prep time: 15 minutes | Cook time: 10 to 15 minutes | Serves 4

4 (5-ounce / 142-g) low-sodium boneless, skinless chicken breasts, cut into 4-by-½-inch strips
1 tablespoon freshly squeezed lemon juice
2 teaspoons olive oil
2 teaspoons chili powder
2 red bell peppers, sliced
4 low-sodium whole-wheat tortillas
⅓ cup nonfat sour cream
1 cup grape tomatoes, sliced

1. Select the ROAST function and preheat MAXX to 380ºF (193ºC).
2. In a large bowl, mix the chicken, lemon juice, olive oil, and chili powder. Toss to coat. Transfer the chicken to the air fryer basket. Add the red bell peppers. Roast for 10 to 15 minutes, or until the chicken reaches an internal temperature of 165ºF (74ºC) on a meat thermometer.
3. Assemble the fajitas with the tortillas, chicken, bell peppers, sour cream, and tomatoes. Serve immediately.

Barbecued Chicken Breast with Coleslaw

Prep time: 10 minutes | Cook time: 20 minutes | Serves 2

3 cups shredded coleslaw mix
Salt and pepper
2 (12-ounce / 340-g) bone-in split chicken breasts, trimmed
1 teaspoon vegetable oil
2 tablespoons barbecue sauce, plus
extra for serving
2 tablespoons mayonnaise
2 tablespoons sour cream
1 teaspoon distilled white vinegar, plus extra for seasoning
¼ teaspoon sugar

1. Select the BAKE function and preheat MAXX to 350ºF (177ºC).
2. Toss coleslaw mix and ¼ teaspoon salt in a colander set over bowl. Let sit until wilted slightly, about 30 minutes. Rinse, drain, and dry well with a dish towel.
3. Meanwhile, pat chicken dry with paper towels, rub with oil, and season with salt and pepper. Arrange breasts skin-side down in air fryer basket, spaced evenly apart, alternating ends. Bake for 10 minutes. Flip breasts and brush skin side with barbecue sauce. Return basket to air fryer oven and bake until well browned and chicken registers 160ºF (71ºC), 10 to 15 minutes.
4. Transfer chicken to serving platter, tent loosely with aluminum foil, and let rest for 5 minutes. While chicken rests, whisk mayonnaise, sour cream, vinegar, sugar, and pinch pepper together in a large bowl. Stir in coleslaw mix and season with salt, pepper, and additional vinegar to taste. Serve chicken with coleslaw, passing extra barbecue sauce separately.

Apricot Glazed Turkey Breast Tenderloin

Prep time: 20 minutes | Cook time: 30 minutes | Serves 4

¼ cup sugar-free apricot preserves
½ tablespoon spicy brown mustard
1½ pounds (680 g) turkey breast
tenderloin
Salt and freshly ground black pepper, to taste
Olive oil spray

1. Spray the air fryer basket lightly with olive oil spray.
2. In a small bowl, combine the apricot preserves and mustard to make a paste.
3. Season the turkey with salt and pepper. Spread the apricot paste all over the turkey.
4. Place the turkey in the air fryer basket and lightly spray with olive oil spray.
5. Select the AIR FRY function and cook at 370ºF (188ºC) for 15 minutes. Flip the turkey over and lightly spray with olive oil spray. Air fry until the internal temperature reaches at least 170ºF (77ºC), an additional 10 to 15 minutes.
6. Let the turkey rest for 10 minutes before slicing and serving.

Apricot-Glazed Chicken Breasts

Prep time: 5 minutes | Cook time: 12 minutes | Serves 2

2 tablespoons apricot preserves
½ teaspoon minced fresh thyme or ⅛ teaspoon dried
2 (8-ounce / 227-g) boneless, skinless

chicken breasts, trimmed
1 teaspoon vegetable oil
Salt and pepper, to taste

1. Microwave apricot preserves and thyme in bowl until fluid, about 30 seconds; set aside. Pound chicken to uniform thickness as needed. Pat dry with paper towels, rub with oil, and season with salt and pepper.
2. Arrange breasts skin-side down in air fryer basket, spaced evenly apart, alternating ends.
3. Select the AIR FRY function and cook at 400ºF (204ºC) for 4 minutes. Flip chicken and brush skin side with apricot-thyme mixture. Air fry until chicken registers 160ºF (71ºC), 8 to 12 minutes more.
4. Transfer chicken to serving platter, tent loosely with aluminum foil, and let rest for 5 minutes. Serve.

Chili Chicken Breast Tenders

Prep time: 5 minutes | Cook time: 7 minutes | Serves 4

Seasoning:
1 teaspoon kosher salt
½ teaspoon garlic powder
½ teaspoon onion powder

½ teaspoon chili powder
¼ teaspoon sweet paprika
¼ teaspoon freshly ground black pepper

Chicken:
8 chicken breast tenders (1 pound / 454 g total)

2 tablespoons mayonnaise

1. For the seasoning: In a small bowl, combine the salt, garlic powder, onion powder, chili powder, paprika, and pepper.

2. For the chicken: Place the chicken in a medium bowl and add the mayonnaise. Mix well to coat all over, then sprinkle with the seasoning mix.
3. Working in batches, arrange a single layer of the chicken in the air fryer basket. Select the AIR FRY function and cook at 375ºF (191ºC) for 6 to 7 minutes, flipping halfway, until cooked through in the center. Serve immediately.

Balsamic Chicken Thighs and Broccoli

Prep time: 10 minutes | Cook time: 32 minutes | Serves 4

3 tablespoons low-sodium soy sauce
1 tablespoon balsamic vinegar
2 teaspoons peeled and grated fresh ginger
2 cloves garlic, crushed with press
2 tablespoons honey
4 bone-in chicken thighs (about 2

pounds / 907 g), fat and excess skin trimmed
1 pound (454 g) broccoli florets, cut in half if large
1 bunch green onions, cut into 2-inch lengths
1 tablespoon vegetable oil

1. Combine soy sauce, balsamic vinegar, ginger, garlic, and 1 tablespoon honey in a small dish. Place all but 1 tablespoon of the soy mixture in a food storage bag. Add chicken skin side up, push out air, and seal. Refrigerate for 1 hour. Stir the remaining 1 tablespoon of honey into the 1 tablespoon of marinade on the dish as a glaze. Set aside.
2. Place chicken in basket, skin side down. Select the AIR FRY function and cook at 375ºF (190ºC) for 12 minutes. Brush chicken with soy-honey glaze and flip over, using tongs. Air fry for 10 more minutes until chicken is cooked through (165ºF / 74ºC), brushing twice with glaze during the last 3 minutes of cooking. Place on plate and tent with foil.
3. Meanwhile, place broccoli in a microwavable bowl, cover with plastic wrap, and microwave 3 minutes on High. Toss in green onions and oil. Place in air fryer basket and air fry for 7 minutes, or until tender and lightly roasted, shaking basket once.
4. Serve broccoli with chicken.

Mustard Chicken Breast

Prep time: 10 minutes | Cook time: 18 to 20 minutes | Serves 4

⅓ cup no-salt-added tomato sauce	minced
2 tablespoons low-sodium grainy mustard	1 jalapeño pepper, minced
2 tablespoons apple cider vinegar	3 tablespoons minced onion
1 tablespoon honey	4 (5-ounce / 142-g) low-sodium boneless, skinless chicken breasts
2 garlic cloves,	

1. In a small bowl, stir together the tomato sauce, mustard, cider vinegar, honey, garlic, jalapeño, and onion.
2. Brush the chicken breasts with some sauce and transfer to the air fryer basket. Select the AIR FRY function and cook at 370°F (188°C) for 10 minutes.
3. Remove the air fryer basket and turn the chicken; brush with more sauce. Air fry for 5 minutes more.
4. Remove the air fryer basket and turn the chicken again; brush with more sauce. Air fry for 3 to 5 minutes more, or until the chicken reaches an internal temperature of 165°F (74°C) on a meat thermometer. Discard any remaining sauce.
5. Serve immediately.

Blackened Chicken Breast

Prep time: 10 minutes | Cook time: 20 minutes | Serves 4

1 large egg, beaten	breasts (about 1 pound / 454 g each), halved
¾ cup Blackened seasoning	
2 whole boneless, skinless chicken	Cooking spray

1. Line the air fryer basket with parchment paper.
2. Place the beaten egg in one shallow bowl and the Blackened seasoning in another shallow bowl.
3. One at a time, dip the chicken pieces in the beaten egg and the Blackened seasoning, coating thoroughly.
4. Place the chicken pieces on the parchment and spritz with cooking spray.

5. Select the AIR FRY function and cook at 360°F (182°C) for 10 minutes. Flip the chicken, spritz it with cooking spray, and air fry for 10 minutes more until the internal temperature reaches 165°F (74°C) and the chicken is no longer pink inside. Let sit for 5 minutes before serving.

Low-Fat Buttermilk Chicken Drumettes

Prep time: 10 minutes | Cook time: 20 minutes | Serves 4

16 chicken drumettes (party wings)	Pepper
1 teaspoon garlic powder	½ cup all-purpose flour
Chicken seasoning or rub	¼ cup low-fat buttermilk
	Cooking oil

1. Place the chicken in a sealable plastic bag. Add the garlic powder, then add chicken seasoning or rub and pepper to taste. Seal the bag. Shake the bag thoroughly to combine the seasonings and coat the chicken.
2. Pour the flour into a second sealable plastic bag.
3. Pour the buttermilk into a bowl large enough to dunk the chicken. One at a time, dunk the drumettes in the buttermilk, then place them in the bag of flour. Seal and shake to thoroughly coat the chicken.
4. Spray the air fryer basket with cooking oil.
5. Using tongs, transfer the chicken from the bag to the air fryer basket. It is okay to stack the drumettes on top of each other. Spray the chicken with cooking oil, being sure to cover the bottom layer. Select the AIR FRY function and cook at 400°F (205°C) for 5 minutes.
6. Remove the basket and shake it to ensure all of the chicken pieces will cook fully.
7. Return the basket to the air fryer oven and continue to cook the chicken. Repeat shaking every 5 minutes until 20 minutes has passed.
8. Cool before serving.

Golden Chicken Nuggets

Prep time: 10 minutes | Cook time: 10 to 13 minutes | Serves 4

1 egg white
1 tablespoon freshly squeezed lemon juice
½ teaspoon dried basil
½ teaspoon ground paprika
1 pound (454 g) low-sodium boneless,

skinless chicken breasts, cut into 1½-inch cubes
½ cup ground almonds
2 slices low-sodium whole-wheat bread, crumbled

1. Select the BAKE function and preheat MAXX to 400ºF (204ºC).
2. In a shallow bowl, beat the egg white, lemon juice, basil, and paprika with a fork until foamy.
3. Add the chicken and stir to coat.
4. On a plate, mix the almonds and bread crumbs.
5. Toss the chicken cubes in the almond and bread crumb mixture until coated.
6. Bake the nuggets in the air fryer oven, in two batches, for 10 to 13 minutes, or until the chicken reaches an internal temperature of 165ºF (74ºC) on a meat thermometer. Serve immediately.

Paprika Chicken Breast

Prep time: 7 minutes | Cook time: 17 to 23 minutes | Serves 4

4 (5-ounce / 142-g) low-sodium boneless, skinless chicken breasts, pounded to about ½ inch thick
½ cup buttermilk
½ cup all-purpose flour

2 tablespoons cornstarch
1 teaspoon dried thyme
1 teaspoon ground paprika
1 egg white
1 tablespoon olive oil

1. In a shallow bowl, mix the chicken and buttermilk. Let stand for 10 minutes.
2. Meanwhile, in another shallow bowl, mix the flour, cornstarch, thyme, and paprika.
3. In a small bowl, whisk the egg white and olive oil. Quickly stir this egg mixture into the flour mixture so the dry ingredients are evenly moistened.

4. Remove the chicken from the buttermilk and shake off any excess liquid. Dip each piece of chicken into the flour mixture to coat. Transfer to the air fryer basket.
5. Select the AIR FRY function and cook at 390ºF (199ºC) for 17 to 23 minutes minutes, or until the chicken reaches an internal temperature of 165ºF (74ºC) on a meat thermometer. Serve immediately.

Buttermilk Chicken Breast

Prep time: 10 minutes | Cook time: 16 minutes | Serves 2

Vegetable oil spray
2 (12-ounce / 340-g) bone-in split chicken breasts, trimmed
Salt and pepper
⅓ cup buttermilk
½ teaspoon dry mustard
½ teaspoon garlic powder

¼ cup all-purpose flour
2 cups cornflakes, finely crushed
1½ teaspoons poultry seasoning
½ teaspoon paprika
⅛ teaspoon cayenne pepper

1. Lightly spray base of air fryer basket with oil spray. Remove skin from chicken and trim any excess fat. Halve each breast crosswise, pat dry with paper towels, and season with salt and pepper. Whisk buttermilk, mustard, garlic powder, ½ teaspoon salt, and ¼ teaspoon pepper together in medium bowl. Spread flour in shallow dish. Combine cornflakes, poultry seasoning, paprika, ¼ teaspoon salt, and cayenne in second shallow dish.
2. Working with 1 piece of chicken at a time, dredge in flour, dip in buttermilk mixture, letting excess drip off, then coat with cornflake mixture, pressing gently to adhere; transfer to large plate. Lightly spray chicken with oil spray.
3. Arrange chicken pieces in prepared basket, spaced evenly apart. Place basket in air fryer oven. Select the AIR FRY function and cook at 400ºF (205ºC) for 16 to 24 minutes, or until chicken is crisp and registers 160ºF (70ºC), flipping and rotating pieces halfway through cooking. Serve.

Chicken with Celery and Bell Pepper
Prep time: 10 minutes | Cook time: 15 minutes | Serves 4

½ cup soy sauce
2 tablespoons hoisin sauce
4 teaspoons minced garlic
1 teaspoon freshly ground black pepper
8 boneless, skinless chicken tenderloins
1 cup chopped celery
1 medium red bell pepper, diced
Olive oil spray

1. Spray the air fryer basket lightly with olive oil spray.
2. In a large bowl, mix together the soy sauce, hoisin sauce, garlic, and black pepper to make a marinade. Add the chicken, celery, and bell pepper and toss to coat.
3. Shake the excess marinade off the chicken, place it and the vegetables in the air fryer basket, and lightly spray with olive oil spray. You may need to cook them in batches. Reserve the remaining marinade.
4. Select the AIR FRY function and cook at 375ºF (191ºC) for 8 minutes. Turn the chicken over and brush with some of the remaining marinade. Air fry for an additional 5 to 7 minutes, or until the chicken reaches an internal temperature of at least 165ºF (74ºC). Serve.

Cheddar Chicken Tacos
Prep time: 10 minutes | Cook time: 12 to 16 minutes | Serves 2 to 4

1 teaspoon chili powder
½ teaspoon ground cumin
½ teaspoon garlic powder
Salt and pepper, to taste
Pinch cayenne pepper
1 pound (454 g) boneless, skinless chicken thighs, trimmed
1 teaspoon vegetable oil
1 tomato, cored and chopped
2 tablespoons finely chopped red onion
2 teaspoons minced jalapeño chile
1½ teaspoons lime juice
6 to 12 (6-inch) corn tortillas, warmed
1 cup shredded iceberg lettuce
3 ounces (85 g) cheddar cheese, shredded (¾ cup)

1. Combine chili powder, cumin, garlic powder, ½ teaspoon salt, ¼ teaspoon pepper, and cayenne in bowl. Pat chicken dry with paper towels, rub with oil, and sprinkle evenly with spice mixture. Place chicken in air fryer basket.
2. Select the AIR FRY function and cook at 400ºF (204ºC) for 12 to 16 minutes, or until chicken registers 165ºF (74ºC), flipping chicken halfway through cooking.
3. Meanwhile, combine tomato, onion, jalapeño, and lime juice in a bowl; season with salt and pepper to taste and set aside until ready to serve.
4. Transfer chicken to a cutting board, let cool slightly, then shred into bite-size pieces using 2 forks. Serve chicken on warm tortillas, topped with salsa, lettuce, and cheddar.

Chicken Satay Skewers with Peanut Sauce
Prep time: 12 minutes | Cook time: 12 to 18 minutes | Serves 4

½ cup crunchy peanut butter
⅓ cup chicken broth
3 tablespoons low-sodium soy sauce
2 tablespoons lemon juice
2 cloves garlic,
minced
2 tablespoons olive oil
1 teaspoon curry powder
1 pound (454 g) chicken tenders

1. In a medium bowl, combine the peanut butter, chicken broth, soy sauce, lemon juice, garlic, olive oil, and curry powder, and mix well with a wire whisk until smooth. Remove 2 tablespoons of this mixture to a small bowl. Put remaining sauce into a serving bowl and set aside.
2. Add the chicken tenders to the bowl with the 2 tablespoons sauce and stir to coat. Let stand for a few minutes to marinate, then run a bamboo skewer through each chicken tender lengthwise.
3. Put the chicken in the air fryer basket. You may need to work in batches.
4. Select the AIR FRY function and cook at 390ºF (199ºC) for 6 to 9 minutes, or until the chicken reaches 165ºF (74ºC) on a meat thermometer. Serve the chicken with the reserved sauce.

Chicken Tenderloins with Parmesan
Prep time: 5 minutes | Cook time: 8 minutes | Serves 4

1 pound (454 g) chicken tenderloins
3 large egg whites
½ cup Italian-style
bread crumbs
¼ cup grated Parmesan cheese

1. Select the BAKE function and preheat MAXX to 370ºF (188ºC). Spray the air fryer basket with olive oil.
2. Trim off any white fat from the chicken tenders.
3. In a small bowl, beat the egg whites until frothy.
4. In a separate small mixing bowl, combine the bread crumbs and Parmesan cheese. Mix well.
5. Dip the chicken tenders into the egg mixture, then into the Parmesan and bread crumbs. Shake off any excess breading.
6. Place the chicken tenders in the greased air fryer basket in a single layer. Generously spray the chicken with olive oil to avoid powdery, uncooked breading.
7. Bake for 4 minutes. Using tongs, flip the chicken tenders and bake for 4 minutes more.
8. Check that the chicken has reached an internal temperature of 165ºF (74ºC). Add cooking time if needed.
9. Once the chicken is fully cooked, plate, serve, and enjoy!

Chicken Wings with Hot Sauce
Prep time: 10 minutes | Cook time: 24 minutes | Serves 4

8 tablespoons (1 stick) unsalted butter, melted
½ cup hot sauce
2 tablespoons white vinegar
2 teaspoons
Worcestershire sauce
1 teaspoon garlic powder
½ cup all-purpose flour
16 frozen chicken wings

1. In a small saucepan over low heat, combine the butter, hot sauce, vinegar, Worcestershire sauce, and garlic. Mix well and bring to a simmer.
2. Pour the flour into a medium mixing bowl. Dredge the chicken wings in the flour.
3. Place the flour-coated wings into the air fryer basket.
4. Select the AIR FRY function and cook at 370ºF (188ºC) for 12 minutes.
5. Using tongs, flip the wings. Air fry for 12 minutes more.
6. Remove the air fryer basket from the oven. Transfer the chicken wings into a large mixing bowl, then pour the sauce over them.
7. Serve and enjoy!

Baked Chicken with Pineapple and Peach
Prep time: 10 minutes | Cook time: 14 to 15 minutes | Serves 4

1 pound (454 g) low-sodium boneless, skinless chicken breasts, cut into 1-inch pieces
1 medium red onion, chopped
1 (8-ounce / 227-g) can pineapple chunks, drained, ¼ cup juice reserved
1 tablespoon peanut
oil or safflower oil
1 peach, peeled, pitted, and cubed
1 tablespoon cornstarch
½ teaspoon ground ginger
¼ teaspoon ground allspice
Brown rice, cooked (optional)

1. Select the BAKE function and preheat MAXX to 380ºF (193ºC).
2. In a medium metal bowl, mix the chicken, red onion, pineapple, and peanut oil. Bake in the air fryer oven for 9 minutes. Remove and stir.
3. Add the peach and return the bowl to the air fryer oven. Bake for 3 minutes more. Remove and stir again.
4. In a small bowl, whisk the reserved pineapple juice, the cornstarch, ginger, and allspice well. Add to the chicken mixture and stir to combine.
5. Bake for 2 to 3 minutes more, or until the chicken reaches an internal temperature of 165ºF (74ºC) on a meat thermometer and the sauce is slightly thickened.
6. Serve immediately over hot cooked brown rice, if desired.

Chicken Burgers with Ham and Cheese
Prep time: 12 minutes | Cook time: 13 to 16 minutes | Serves 4

⅓ cup soft bread crumbs	pepper, to taste
3 tablespoons milk	1¼ pounds (567 g) ground chicken
1 egg, beaten	¼ cup finely chopped ham
½ teaspoon dried thyme	⅓ cup grated Havarti cheese
Pinch salt	Olive oil for misting
Freshly ground black	

1. Select the BAKE function and preheat MAXX to 350ºF (177ºC).
2. In a medium bowl, combine the bread crumbs, milk, egg, thyme, salt, and pepper. Add the chicken and mix gently but thoroughly with clean hands.
3. Form the chicken into eight thin patties and place on waxed paper.
4. Top four of the patties with the ham and cheese. Top with remaining four patties and gently press the edges together to seal, so the ham and cheese mixture is in the middle of the burger.
5. Place the burgers in the basket and mist with olive oil. Bake for 13 to 16 minutes or until the chicken is thoroughly cooked to 165ºF (74ºC) as measured with a meat thermometer. Serve immediately.

Chicken and Bell Peppers Fajitas
Prep time: 10 minutes | Cook time: 14 minutes | Serves 4

1 pound (454 g) chicken tenders	1 orange bell pepper, diced
1 onion, sliced	2 tablespoons olive oil
1 yellow bell pepper, diced	1 tablespoon fajita seasoning mix
1 red bell pepper, diced	

1. Slice the chicken into thin strips.
2. In a large mixing bowl, combine the chicken, onion, and peppers.
3. Add the olive oil and fajita seasoning and mix well, so that the chicken and vegetables are thoroughly covered with oil.

4. Place the chicken and vegetable mixture into the air fryer basket in a single layer.
5. Select the AIR FRY function and cook at 350ºF (180ºC) for 7 minutes.
6. Shake the basket and use tongs to flip the chicken. Air fry for 7 minutes more, or until the chicken is cooked through and the juices run clear.
7. Once the chicken is fully cooked, transfer it to a platter and serve.

Chicken and Vegetable Fajitas Tacos
Prep time: 15 minutes | Cook time: 23 minutes | Serves 6

Chicken:

1 pound (454 g) boneless, skinless chicken thighs, cut crosswise into thirds	1 cup sliced bell pepper
1 tablespoon vegetable oil	1 or 2 jalapeños, quartered lengthwise
4½ teaspoons taco seasoning	1 tablespoon vegetable oil
Vegetables	½ teaspoon kosher salt
1 cup sliced onion	½ teaspoon ground cumin

For Serving:

Tortillas	Guacamole
Sour cream	Salsa
Shredded cheese	

1. For the chicken: In a medium bowl, toss together the chicken, vegetable oil, and taco seasoning to coat.
2. For the vegetables: In a separate bowl, toss together the onion, bell pepper, jalapeño (s), vegetable oil, salt, and cumin to coat.
3. Place the chicken in the air fryer basket.
4. Select the AIR FRY function and cook at 375ºF (191ºC) for 10 minutes. Add the vegetables to the basket, toss everything together to blend the seasonings, and air fry for 13 minutes more. Use a meat thermometer to ensure the chicken has reached an internal temperature of 165ºF (74ºC).
5. Transfer the chicken and vegetables to a serving platter. Serve with tortillas and the desired fajita fixings.

Chicken with Pickle Brine
Prep time: 15 minutes | Cook time: 47 minutes | Serves 4

4 bone-in, skin-on chicken legs, cut into drumsticks and thighs (about 3½ pounds / 1.5 kg)
Pickle juice from 1 (24-ounce / 680-g) jar kosher dill pickles
½ cup flour
Salt and freshly ground black pepper
2 eggs

1 cup fine bread crumbs
1 teaspoon salt
1 teaspoon freshly ground black pepper
½ teaspoon ground paprika
⅛ teaspoon ground cayenne pepper
Vegetable or canola oil in a spray bottle

1. Place the chicken in a shallow dish and pour the pickle juice over the top. Cover and transfer the chicken to the refrigerator to brine in the pickle juice for 3 to 8 hours.
2. When you are ready to cook, remove the chicken from the refrigerator to let it come to room temperature while you set up a dredging station. Place the flour in a shallow dish and season well with salt and freshly ground black pepper. Whisk the eggs in a second shallow dish. In a third shallow dish, combine the bread crumbs, salt, pepper, paprika and cayenne pepper.
3. Remove the chicken from the pickle brine and gently dry it with a clean kitchen towel. Dredge each piece of chicken in the flour, then dip it into the egg mixture, and finally press it into the bread crumb mixture to coat all sides of the chicken. Place the breaded chicken on a plate or baking sheet and spray each piece all over with vegetable oil.
4. Work in two batches. Place two chicken thighs and two drumsticks into the air fryer basket. Select the AIR FRY function and cook at 370ºF (188ºC) for 10 minutes. Then, gently turn the chicken pieces over and air fry for another 10 minutes. Remove the chicken pieces and let them rest on plate – do not cover. Repeat with the second batch of chicken, air frying for 20 minutes, turning the chicken over halfway through.

5. Reduce the temperature to 340ºF (171ºC). Place the first batch of chicken on top of the second batch already in the basket and air fry for an additional 7 minutes. Serve warm and enjoy.

Chicken Breast Wraps with Ranch Seasoning
Prep time: 10 minutes | Cook time: 25 minutes | Serves 4

2 (4-ounce / 113-g) boneless, skinless breasts
½ (1-ounce / 28-g) packet Hidden Valley Ranch seasoning mix
Chicken seasoning or rub
1 cup all-purpose flour

1 egg
½ cup bread crumbs
Cooking oil
4 medium (8-inch) flour tortillas
1½ cups shredded lettuce
3 tablespoons ranch dressing

1. With your knife blade parallel to the cutting board, slice the chicken breasts in half horizontally to create 4 thin cutlets.
2. Season the chicken cutlets with the ranch seasoning and chicken seasoning to taste.
3. In a bowl large enough to dip a chicken cutlet, beat the egg. In another bowl, place the flour. Put the bread crumbs in a third bowl.
4. Spray the air fryer basket with cooking oil.
5. Dip each chicken cutlet in the flour, then the egg, and then the bread crumbs.
6. Place the chicken in the air fryer oven. Do not stack. Work in batches. Spray the chicken with cooking oil. Select the AIR FRY function and cook at 370ºF (188ºC) for 7 minutes.
7. Open the air fryer oven and flip the chicken. Air fry for an additional 3 to 4 minutes, until crisp.
8. Remove the cooked chicken from the air fryer oven and allow to cool for 2 to 3 minutes.
9. Repeat with the remaining chicken.
10. Cut the chicken into strips. Divide the chicken strips, shredded lettuce, and ranch dressing evenly among the tortillas and serve.

Coconut Chicken Drumettes with Mango Salsa

Prep time: 10 minutes | Cook time: 20 minutes | Serves 4

Coconut Chicken:

16 chicken drumettes (party wings)
¼ cup full-fat coconut milk
1 tablespoon Sriracha
1 teaspoon onion powder
1 teaspoon garlic powder
Salt
Pepper
⅓ cup shredded unsweetened coconut
½ cup all-purpose flour
Cooking oil

Mango Salsa:

1 cup mango sliced into ½ inch chunks
¼ cup cilantro, chopped
½ cup red onion, chopped
2 garlic cloves, minced
Juice of ½ lime

Make the Coconut Chicken

1. Place the drumettes in a sealable plastic bag.
2. In a small bowl, combine the coconut milk and Sriracha. Whisk until fully combined.
3. Drizzle the drumettes with the spicy coconut milk mixture. Season the drumettes with the onion powder, garlic powder, and salt and pepper to taste.
4. Seal the bag. Shake it thoroughly to combine the seasonings and coat the chicken. Marinate for at least 30 minutes, preferably overnight, in the refrigerator.
5. When the drumettes are almost done marinating, combine the shredded coconut and flour in a large bowl. Stir.
6. Spray the air fryer basket with cooking oil.
7. Dip the drumettes in the coconut and flour mixture. Place the drumettes in the air fryer oven. It is okay to stack them on top of each other. Spray the drumettes with cooking oil, being sure to cover the bottom layer. Select the AIR FRY function and cook at 400ºF (205ºC) for 5 minutes.
8. Remove the basket and shake it to ensure all of the pieces will cook fully.
9. Return the basket to the air fryer oven and continue to cook the chicken. Repeat shaking every 5 minutes until a total of 20 minutes has passed.

10. Cool before serving.

Make the Mango Salsa

11. While the chicken cooks, combine the mango, cilantro, red onion, garlic, and lime juice in a small bowl. Mix well until fully combined.

Herb Chicken Breast

Prep time: 5 minutes | Cook time: 40 minutes | Serves 2

1 large bone-in, skin-on chicken breast
1 cup buttermilk
1½ teaspoons dried parsley
1½ teaspoons dried chives
¾ teaspoon kosher salt
½ teaspoon dried dill
½ teaspoon onion powder
¼ teaspoon garlic powder
¼ teaspoon dried tarragon
Cooking spray

1. Place the chicken breast in a bowl and pour over the buttermilk, turning the chicken in it to make sure it's completely covered. Let the chicken stand at room temperature for at least 20 minutes or in the refrigerator for up to 4 hours.
2. Meanwhile, in a bowl, stir together the parsley, chives, salt, dill, onion powder, garlic powder, and tarragon.
3. Select the BAKE function and preheat MAXX to 300ºF (149ºC).
4. Remove the chicken from the buttermilk, letting the excess drip off, then place the chicken skin-side up directly in the air fryer oven. Sprinkle the seasoning mix all over the top of the chicken breast, then let stand until the herb mix soaks into the buttermilk, at least 5 minutes.
5. Spray the top of the chicken with cooking spray. Bake for 10 minutes, then increase the temperature to 350ºF (177ºC) and bake until an instant-read thermometer inserted into the thickest part of the breast reads 160ºF (71ºC) and the chicken is deep golden brown, 30 to 35 minutes.
6. Transfer the chicken breast to a cutting board, let rest for 10 minutes, then cut the meat off the bone and cut into thick slices for serving.

Tangy Chicken Thighs
Prep time: 10 minutes | Cook time: 16 to 19 minutes | Serves 4

¾ pound (340 g) boneless, skinless chicken thighs, cut into 1-inch pieces	Olive oil for misting
1 yellow bell pepper, cut into 1½-inch pieces	¼ cup chicken stock
	2 tablespoons honey
	¼ cup orange juice
	1 tablespoon cornstarch
1 small red onion, sliced	2 to 3 teaspoons curry powder

1. Select the ROAST function and preheat MAXX to 370ºF (188ºC).
2. Put the chicken thighs, pepper, and red onion in the air fryer basket and mist with olive oil.
3. Roast for 12 to 14 minutes or until the chicken is cooked to 165ºF (74ºC), shaking the basket halfway through cooking time.
4. Remove the chicken and vegetables from the air fryer basket and set aside.
5. In a metal bowl, combine the stock, honey, orange juice, cornstarch, and curry powder, and mix well. Add the chicken and vegetables, stir, and put the bowl in the basket.
6. Return the basket to the air fryer oven and roast for 2 minutes. Remove and stir, then roast for 2 to 3 minutes or until the sauce is thickened and bubbly.
7. Serve warm.

Itanlian Dill Chicken Strips
Prep time: 15 minutes | Cook time: 10 minutes | Serves 4

2 whole boneless, skinless chicken breasts, halved lengthwise	1 tablespoon dried dill weed
1 cup Italian dressing	1 tablespoon garlic powder
3 cups finely crushed potato chips	1 large egg, beaten
	Cooking spray

1. In a large resealable bag, combine the chicken and Italian dressing. Seal the bag and refrigerate to marinate at least 1 hour.

2. In a shallow dish, stir together the potato chips, dill, and garlic powder. Place the beaten egg in a second shallow dish.
3. Remove the chicken from the marinade. Roll the chicken pieces in the egg and the potato chip mixture, coating thoroughly.
4. Select the BAKE function and preheat MAXX to 325ºF (163ºC). Line the air fryer basket with parchment paper.
5. Place the coated chicken on the parchment and spritz with cooking spray.
6. Bake for 5 minutes. Flip the chicken, spritz it with cooking spray, and bake for 5 minutes more until the outsides are crispy and the insides are no longer pink. Serve immediately.

Asian Turkey Meatballs
Prep time: 10 minutes | Cook time: 11 to 14 minutes | Serves 4

2 tablespoons peanut oil, divided	2 tablespoons low-sodium soy sauce
1 small onion, minced	¼ cup panko bread crumbs
¼ cup water chestnuts, finely chopped	1 egg, beaten
½ teaspoon ground ginger	1 pound (454 g) ground turkey

1. Select the BAKE function and preheat MAXX to 400ºF (204ºC).
2. In a round metal pan, combine 1 tablespoon of peanut oil and onion. Bake for 1 to 2 minutes or until crisp and tender. Transfer the onion to a medium bowl.
3. Add the water chestnuts, ground ginger, soy sauce, and bread crumbs to the onion and mix well. Add egg and stir well. Mix in the ground turkey until combined.
4. Form the mixture into 1-inch meatballs. Drizzle the remaining 1 tablespoon of oil over the meatballs.
5. Bake the meatballs in the pan in batches for 10 to 12 minutes or until they are 165ºF (74ºC) on a meat thermometer. Rest for 5 minutes before serving.

Cranberry Curry Chicken Breast
Prep time: 12 minutes | Cook time: 18 minutes | Serves 4

3 (5-ounce / 142-g) low-sodium boneless, skinless chicken breasts, cut into 1½-inch cubes
2 teaspoons olive oil
2 tablespoons cornstarch
1 tablespoon curry powder
1 tart apple, chopped
½ cup low-sodium chicken broth
⅓ cup dried cranberries
2 tablespoons freshly squeezed orange juice
Brown rice, cooked (optional)

1. Select the BAKE function and preheat MAXX to 380ºF (193ºC).
2. In a medium bowl, mix the chicken and olive oil. Sprinkle with the cornstarch and curry powder. Toss to coat. Stir in the apple and transfer to a metal pan. Bake in the air fryer oven for 8 minutes, stirring once during cooking.
3. Add the chicken broth, cranberries, and orange juice. Bake for about 10 minutes more, or until the sauce is slightly thickened and the chicken reaches an internal temperature of 165ºF (74ºC) on a meat thermometer. Serve over hot cooked brown rice, if desired.

Paprika Breaded Chicken Wings
Prep time: 15 minutes | Cook time: 20 minutes | Serves 4

1 pound (454 g) chicken wings
3 tablespoons vegetable oil
½ cup all-purpose flour
½ teaspoon smoked paprika
½ teaspoon garlic powder
½ teaspoon kosher salt
1½ teaspoons freshly cracked black pepper

1. Place the chicken wings in a large bowl. Drizzle the vegetable oil over wings and toss to coat.
2. In a separate bowl, whisk together the flour, paprika, garlic powder, salt, and pepper until combined.
3. Dredge the wings in the flour mixture one at a time, coating them well, and place in the air fryer basket.
4. Select the AIR FRY function and cook at 400ºF (204ºC) for 20 minutes, turning the wings halfway through the cooking time, until the breading is browned and crunchy.
5. Serve hot.

Hawaiian Chicken with Pineapple
Prep time: 10 minutes | Cook time: 15 minutes | Serves 4

4 boneless, skinless chicken thighs (about 1½ pounds / 680 g)
1 (8-ounce / 227-g) can pineapple chunks in juice, drained, ¼ cup juice reserved
¼ cup soy sauce
¼ cup sugar
2 tablespoons ketchup
1 tablespoon minced fresh ginger
1 tablespoon minced garlic
¼ cup chopped scallions

1. Use a fork to pierce the chicken all over to allow the marinade to penetrate better. Place the chicken in a large bowl or large resealable plastic bag.
2. Set the drained pineapple chunks aside. In a small microwave-safe bowl, combine the pineapple juice, soy sauce, sugar, ketchup, ginger, and garlic. Pour half the sauce over the chicken; toss to coat. Reserve the remaining sauce. Marinate the chicken at room temperature for 30 minutes, or cover and refrigerate for up to 24 hours.
3. Select the BAKE function and preheat MAXX to 350ºF (177ºC).
4. Place the chicken in the air fryer basket, discarding marinade. Bake for 15 minutes, turning halfway through the cooking time.
5. Meanwhile, microwave the reserved sauce on high for 45 to 60 seconds, stirring every 15 seconds, until the sauce has the consistency of a thick glaze.
6. At the end of the cooking time, use a meat thermometer to ensure the chicken has reached an internal temperature of 165ºF (74ºC).
7. Transfer the chicken to a serving platter. Pour the sauce over the chicken. Garnish with the pineapple chunks and scallions before serving.

Paprika Chicken Drumsticks
Prep time: 5 minutes | Cook time: 22 minutes | Serves 2

2 teaspoons paprika
1 teaspoon packed brown sugar
1 teaspoon garlic powder
½ teaspoon dry mustard
½ teaspoon salt
Pinch pepper

4 (5-ounce / 142-g) chicken drumsticks, trimmed
1 teaspoon vegetable oil
1 scallion, green part only, sliced thin on bias

1. Combine paprika, sugar, garlic powder, mustard, salt, and pepper in a bowl. Pat drumsticks dry with paper towels. Using metal skewer, poke 10 to 15 holes in skin of each drumstick. Rub with oil and sprinkle evenly with spice mixture.
2. Arrange drumsticks in air fryer basket, spaced evenly apart, alternating ends. Select the AIR FRY function and cook at 400ºF (204ºC) for 22 to 25 minutes, or until chicken is crisp and registers 195ºF (91ºC), flipping chicken halfway through cooking.
3. Transfer chicken to serving platter, tent loosely with aluminum foil, and let rest for 5 minutes. Sprinkle with scallion and serve.

Chicken Cordon Bleu
Prep time: 15 minutes | Cook time: 13 to 15 minutes | Serves 4

4 chicken breast fillets
¼ cup chopped ham
1/3 cup grated Swiss or Gruyère cheese
¼ cup flour
Pinch salt
Freshly ground black

pepper, to taste
½ teaspoon dried marjoram
1 egg
1 cup panko bread crumbs
Olive oil for misting

1. Select the BAKE function and preheat MAXX to 380ºF (193ºC).
2. Put the chicken breast fillets on a work surface and gently press them with the palm of your hand to make them a bit thinner. Don't tear the meat.
3. In a small bowl, combine the ham and cheese. Divide this mixture among the chicken fillets. Wrap the chicken around the filling to enclose it, using toothpicks to hold the chicken together.
4. In a shallow bowl, mix the flour, salt, pepper, and marjoram. In another bowl, beat the egg. Spread the bread crumbs out on a plate.
5. Dip the chicken into the flour mixture, then into the egg, then into the bread crumbs to coat thoroughly.
6. Put the chicken in the air fryer basket and mist with olive oil.
7. Bake for 13 to 15 minutes or until the chicken is thoroughly cooked to 165ºF (74ºC). Carefully remove the toothpicks and serve.

Fried Chicken Strips
Prep time: 15 minutes | Cook time: 20 minutes | Serves 4

1 tablespoon olive oil
1 pound (454 g) boneless, skinless chicken tenderloins
1 teaspoon salt
½ teaspoon freshly ground black pepper
½ teaspoon paprika

½ teaspoon garlic powder
½ cup whole-wheat seasoned bread crumbs
1 teaspoon dried parsley
Cooking spray

1. Spray the air fryer basket lightly with cooking spray.
2. In a medium bowl, toss the chicken with the salt, pepper, paprika, and garlic powder until evenly coated.
3. Add the olive oil and toss to coat the chicken evenly.
4. In a separate, shallow bowl, mix together the bread crumbs and parsley.
5. Coat each piece of chicken evenly in the bread crumb mixture.
6. Place the chicken in the air fryer basket in a single layer and spray it lightly with cooking spray. You may need to cook them in batches.
7. Select the AIR FRY function and cook at 370ºF (188ºC) for 10 minutes. Flip the chicken over, lightly spray it with cooking spray, and air fry for an additional 8 to 10 minutes, until golden brown. Serve.

Rosemary Chicken Breast

Prep time: 10 minutes | Cook time: 20 minutes | Serves 4

¼ cup balsamic vinegar
¼ cup honey
2 tablespoons olive oil
1 tablespoon dried rosemary leaves
1 teaspoon salt

½ teaspoon freshly ground black pepper
2 whole boneless, skinless chicken breasts (about 1 pound / 454 g each), halved
Cooking spray

1. In a large resealable bag, combine the vinegar, honey, olive oil, rosemary, salt, and pepper. Add the chicken pieces, seal the bag, and refrigerate to marinate for at least 2 hours.
2. Select the BAKE function and preheat MAXX to 325ºF (163ºC). Line the air fryer basket with parchment paper.
3. Remove the chicken from the marinade and place it on the parchment. Spritz with cooking spray.
4. Bake for 10 minutes. Flip the chicken, spritz it with cooking spray, and bake for 10 minutes more until the internal temperature reaches 165ºF (74ºC) and the chicken is no longer pink inside. Let sit for 5 minutes before serving.

Turkey Breast with Herb

Prep time: 20 minutes | Cook time: 45 minutes | Serves 6

1 tablespoon olive oil
Cooking spray
2 garlic cloves, minced
2 teaspoons Dijon mustard
1½ teaspoons rosemary

1½ teaspoons sage
1½ teaspoons thyme
1 teaspoon salt
½ teaspoon freshly ground black pepper
3 pounds (1.4 kg) turkey breast, thawed if frozen

1. Spray the air fryer basket lightly with cooking spray.
2. In a small bowl, mix together the garlic, olive oil, Dijon mustard, rosemary, sage, thyme, salt, and pepper to make a paste. Smear the paste all over the turkey breast.

3. Place the turkey breast in the air fryer basket. Select the AIR FRY function and cook at 370ºF (188ºC) for 20 minutes. Flip turkey breast over and baste it with any drippings that have collected in the bottom drawer of the air fryer oven. Air fry until the internal temperature of the meat reaches at least 170ºF (77ºC), 20 more minutes.
4. If desired, increase the temperature to 400ºF (204ºC), flip the turkey breast over one last time, and air fry for 5 minutes to get a crispy exterior.
5. Let the turkey rest for 10 minutes before slicing and serving.

Jamaican Jerk Chicken

Prep time: 8 minutes | Cook time: 27 minutes | Serves 2

1 tablespoon packed brown sugar
1 teaspoon ground allspice
1 teaspoon pepper
1 teaspoon garlic powder
¾ teaspoon dry mustard
¾ teaspoon dried thyme

½ teaspoon salt
¼ teaspoon cayenne pepper
2 (10-ounce / 284-g) chicken leg quarters, trimmed
1 teaspoon vegetable oil
1 scallion, green part only, sliced thin
Lime wedges

1. Combine sugar, allspice, pepper, garlic powder, mustard, thyme, salt, and cayenne in a bowl. Pat chicken dry with paper towels. Using metal skewer, poke 10 to 15 holes in skin of each chicken leg. Rub with oil and sprinkle evenly with spice mixture.
2. Arrange chicken skin-side up in the air fryer basket, spaced evenly apart. Select the AIR FRY function and cook at 400ºF (204ºC) for 27 to 30 minutes, or until chicken is well browned and crisp, rotating chicken halfway through cooking (do not flip).
3. Transfer chicken to plate, tent loosely with aluminum foil, and let rest for 5 minutes. Sprinkle with scallion. Serve with lime wedges.

Tandoori Chicken Breast

Prep time: 5 minutes | Cook time: 18 to 23 minutes | Serves 4

⅔ cup plain low-fat yogurt
2 tablespoons freshly squeezed lemon juice
2 teaspoons curry powder
½ teaspoon ground cinnamon

2 garlic cloves, minced
2 teaspoons olive oil
4 (5-ounce / 142-g) low-sodium boneless, skinless chicken breasts

1. In a medium bowl, whisk the yogurt, lemon juice, curry powder, cinnamon, garlic, and olive oil.
2. With a sharp knife, cut thin slashes into the chicken. Add it to the yogurt mixture and turn to coat. Let stand for 10 minutes at room temperature. You can also prepare this ahead of time and marinate the chicken in the refrigerator for up to 24 hours.
3. Select the ROAST function and preheat MAXX to 360ºF (182ºC).
4. Remove the chicken from the marinade and shake off any excess liquid. Discard any remaining marinade.
5. Roast the chicken for 10 minutes. With tongs, carefully turn each piece. Roast for 8 to 13 minutes more, or until the chicken reaches an internal temperature of 165ºF (74ºC) on a meat thermometer. Serve immediately.

Fajita Chicken Strips with Veggie

Prep time: 10 minutes | Cook time: 15 minutes | Serves 4

1 pound (454 g) boneless, skinless chicken tenderloins, cut into strips
3 bell peppers, any color, cut into chunks

1 onion, cut into chunks
1 tablespoon olive oil
1 tablespoon fajita seasoning mix
Cooking spray

1. In a large bowl, mix together the chicken, bell peppers, onion, olive oil, and fajita seasoning mix until completely coated.
2. Spray the air fryer basket lightly with cooking spray.
3. Place the chicken and vegetables in the air fryer basket and lightly spray with cooking spray.
4. Select the AIR FRY function and cook at 370ºF (188ºC) for 7 minutes. Shake the basket and air fry for an additional 5 to 8 minutes, until the chicken is cooked through and the veggies are starting to char.
5. Serve warm.

Ginger Chicken Thighs Bake

Prep time: 10 minutes | Cook time: 10 minutes | Serves 4

¼ cup julienned peeled fresh ginger
2 tablespoons vegetable oil
1 tablespoon honey
1 tablespoon soy sauce
1 tablespoon ketchup
1 teaspoon garam masala
1 teaspoon ground turmeric

¼ teaspoon kosher salt
½ teaspoon cayenne pepper
Vegetable oil spray
1 pound (454 g) boneless, skinless chicken thighs, cut crosswise into thirds
¼ cup chopped fresh cilantro, for garnish

1. In a small bowl, combine the ginger, oil, honey, soy sauce, ketchup, garam masala, turmeric, salt, and cayenne. Whisk until well combined. Place the chicken in a resealable plastic bag and pour the marinade over. Seal the bag and massage to cover all of the chicken with the marinade. Marinate at room temperature for 30 minutes or in the refrigerator for up to 24 hours.
2. Select the BAKE function and preheat MAXX to 350ºF (177ºC).
3. Spray the air fryer basket with vegetable oil spray and add the chicken and as much of the marinade and julienned ginger as possible. Bake for 10 minutes. Use a meat thermometer to ensure the chicken has reached an internal temperature of 165ºF (74ºC).
4. To serve, garnish with cilantro.

Parmesan Chicken Breast

Prep time: 10 minutes | Cook time: 20 minutes | Serves 4

1 egg	4 boneless, skinless
2 tablespoons lemon	chicken breasts, thin
juice	cut
2 teaspoons minced	Olive oil spray
garlic	½ cup whole-wheat
½ teaspoon salt	bread crumbs
½ teaspoon freshly	¼ cup grated
ground black pepper	Parmesan cheese

1. In a medium bowl, whisk together the egg, lemon juice, garlic, salt, and pepper. Add the chicken breasts, cover, and refrigerate for up to 1 hour.
2. In a shallow bowl, combine the bread crumbs and Parmesan cheese.
3. Spray the air fryer basket lightly with olive oil spray.
4. Remove the chicken breasts from the egg mixture, then dredge them in the bread crumb mixture, and place in the air fryer basket in a single layer. Lightly spray the chicken breasts with olive oil spray. You may need to cook the chicken in batches.
5. Select the AIR FRY function and cook at 360ºF (182ºC) for 8 minutes. Flip the chicken over, lightly spray with olive oil spray, and air fry until the chicken reaches an internal temperature of 165ºF (74ºC), for an additional 7 to 12 minutes.
6. Serve warm.

Mayo-Mustard Chicken

Prep time: 10 minutes | Cook time: 15 minutes | Serves 4

6 tablespoons	powder
mayonnaise	1 teaspoon kosher
2 tablespoons	salt
coarse-ground	1 teaspoon cayenne
mustard	pepper
2 teaspoons honey	1 pound (454 g)
(optional)	chicken tenders
2 teaspoons curry	

1. Select the BAKE function and preheat MAXX to 350ºF (177ºC).

2. In a large bowl, whisk together the mayonnaise, mustard, honey (if using), curry powder, salt, and cayenne. Transfer half of the mixture to a serving bowl to serve as a dipping sauce. Add the chicken tenders to the large bowl and toss until well coated.
3. Place the tenders in the air fryer basket and bake for 15 minutes. Use a meat thermometer to ensure the chicken has reached an internal temperature of 165ºF (74ºC).
4. Serve the chicken with the dipping sauce.

Flavorful Chicken Manchurian

Prep time: 10 minutes | Cook time: 20 minutes | Serves 2

1 pound (454 g)	vegetable oil
boneless, skinless	1 teaspoon hot
chicken breasts, cut	sauce, such as
into 1-inch pieces	Tabasco
¼ cup ketchup	½ teaspoon garlic
1 tablespoon tomato-	powder
based chili sauce,	¼ teaspoon cayenne
such as Heinz	pepper
1 tablespoon soy	2 scallions, thinly
sauce	sliced
1 tablespoon rice	Cooked white rice,
vinegar	for serving
2 teaspoons	

1. Select the BAKE function and preheat MAXX to 350ºF (177ºC).
2. In a bowl, combine the chicken, ketchup, chili sauce, soy sauce, vinegar, oil, hot sauce, garlic powder, cayenne, and three-quarters of the scallions and toss until evenly coated.
3. Scrape the chicken and sauce into a metal cake pan and place the pan in the air fryer oven. Bake until the chicken is cooked through and the sauce is reduced to a thick glaze, about 20 minutes, flipping the chicken pieces halfway through.
4. Remove the pan from the air fryer oven. Spoon the chicken and sauce over rice and top with the remaining scallions. Serve immediately.

Buffalo Chicken Taquitos
Prep time: 15 minutes | Cook time: 5 to 10 minutes | Serves 6

8 ounces (227 g) fat-free cream cheese, softened
⅛ cup Buffalo sauce
2 cups shredded

cooked chicken
12 (7-inch) low-carb flour tortillas
Olive oil spray

1. Spray the air fryer basket lightly with olive oil spray.
2. In a large bowl, mix together the cream cheese and Buffalo sauce until well combined. Add the chicken and stir until combined.
3. Place the tortillas on a clean workspace. Spoon 2 to 3 tablespoons of the chicken mixture in a thin line down the center of each tortilla. Roll up the tortillas.
4. Place the tortillas in the air fryer basket, seam-side down. Spray each tortilla lightly with olive oil spray. You may need to cook the taquitos in batches.
5. Select the AIR FRY function and cook at 360ºF (182ºC) for 5 to 10 minutes, or until golden brown. Serve hot.

Coconut Chicken Meatballs
Prep time: 10 minutes | Cook time: 14 minutes | Serves 4

1 pound (454 g) ground chicken
2 scallions, finely chopped
1 cup chopped fresh cilantro leaves
¼ cup unsweetened shredded coconut
1 tablespoon hoisin sauce

1 tablespoon soy sauce
2 teaspoons sriracha or other hot sauce
1 teaspoon toasted sesame oil
½ teaspoon kosher salt
1 teaspoon black pepper

1. In a large bowl, gently mix the chicken, scallions, cilantro, coconut, hoisin, soy sauce, sriracha, sesame oil, salt, and pepper until thoroughly combined (the mixture will be wet and sticky).
2. Place a sheet of parchment paper in the air fryer basket. Using a small scoop or teaspoon, drop rounds of the mixture in a single layer onto the parchment paper.

3. Select the AIR FRY function and cook at 350ºF (177ºC) for 10 minutes, turning the meatballs halfway through the cooking time. Increase the temperature to 400ºF (204ºC) and air fry for 4 minutes more to brown the outsides of the meatballs. Use a meat thermometer to ensure the meatballs have reached an internal temperature of 165ºF (74ºC).
4. Transfer the meatballs to a serving platter. Repeat with any remaining chicken mixture. Serve.

Soy Garlic-Glazed Chicken Thighs
Prep time: 10 minutes | Cook time: 30 minutes | Serves 1 to 2

2 tablespoons chicken stock
2 tablespoons reduced-sodium soy sauce
1½ tablespoons sugar
4 garlic cloves, smashed and peeled

2 large scallions, cut into 2- to 3-inch batons, plus more, thinly sliced, for garnish
2 bone-in, skin-on chicken thighs (7 to 8 ounces / 198 to 227 g each)

1. Select the BAKE function and preheat MAXX to 375ºF (191ºC).
2. In a metal cake pan, combine the chicken stock, soy sauce, and sugar and stir until the sugar dissolves. Add the garlic cloves, scallions, and chicken thighs, turning the thighs to coat them in the marinade, then resting them skin-side up. Place the pan in the air fryer oven and bake, flipping the thighs every 5 minutes after the first 10 minutes, until the chicken is cooked through and the marinade is reduced to a sticky glaze over the chicken, about 30 minutes.
3. Remove the pan from the air fryer oven and serve the chicken thighs warm, with any remaining glaze spooned over top and sprinkled with more sliced scallions.

Brown Sugar-Glazed Chicken Drumsticks

Prep time: 5 minutes | Cook time: 20 minutes | Serves 2

4 chicken drumsticks
3 tablespoons soy sauce
2 tablespoons brown sugar
1 teaspoon minced garlic
1 teaspoon minced fresh ginger
1 teaspoon toasted sesame oil
½ teaspoon red pepper flakes
½ teaspoon kosher salt
½ teaspoon black pepper

1. Line a round baking pan with aluminum foil. (If you don't do this, you'll either end up scrubbing forever or throwing out the pan.) Arrange the drumsticks in the prepared pan.
2. In a medium bowl, stir together the soy sauce, brown sugar, garlic, ginger, sesame oil, red pepper flakes, salt, and black pepper. Pour the sauce over the drumsticks and toss to coat.
3. Place the pan in the air fryer basket.
4. Select the AIR FRY function and cook at 400ºF (204ºC) for 20 minutes, turning the drumsticks halfway through the cooking time. Use a meat thermometer to ensure the chicken has reached an internal temperature of 165ºF (74ºC). Serve immediately.

Chicken Wings with Parmesan

Prep time: 15 minutes | Cook time: 16 to 18 minutes | Serves 4

1¼ cups grated Parmesan cheese
1 tablespoon garlic powder
1 teaspoon salt
½ teaspoon freshly ground black pepper
¾ cup all-purpose flour
1 large egg, beaten
12 chicken wings (about 1 pound / 454 g)
Cooking spray

1. Line the air fryer basket with parchment paper.
2. In a shallow bowl, whisk the Parmesan cheese, garlic powder, salt, and pepper until blended. Place the flour in a second shallow bowl and the beaten egg in a third shallow bowl.
3. One at a time, dip the chicken wings into the flour, the beaten egg, and the Parmesan cheese mixture, coating thoroughly.
4. Place the chicken wings on the parchment and spritz with cooking spray.
5. Select the AIR FRY function and cook at 390ºF (199ºC) for 8 minutes. Flip the chicken, spritz it with cooking spray, and air fry for 8 to 10 minutes more until the internal temperature reaches 165ºF (74ºC) and the insides are no longer pink. Let sit for 5 minutes before serving.

Chicken Breast and Vegetable Salad

Prep time: 10 minutes | Cook time: 16 to 20 minutes | Serves 4

3 (5-ounce / 142-g) low-sodium boneless, skinless chicken breasts, cut into 1-inch cubes
5 teaspoons olive oil
½ teaspoon dried thyme
1 medium red onion, sliced
1 red bell pepper, sliced
1 small zucchini, cut into strips
3 tablespoons freshly squeezed lemon juice
6 cups fresh baby spinach

1. Select the ROAST function and preheat MAXX to 400ºF (204ºC).
2. In a large bowl, mix the chicken with the olive oil and thyme. Toss to coat. Transfer to a medium metal bowl and roast for 8 minutes in the air fryer oven.
3. Add the red onion, red bell pepper, and zucchini. Roast for 8 to 12 minutes more, stirring once during cooking, or until the chicken reaches an internal temperature of 165ºF (74ºC) on a meat thermometer.
4. Remove the bowl from the air fryer oven and stir in the lemon juice.
5. Put the spinach in a serving bowl and top with the chicken mixture. Toss to combine and serve immediately.

Turkey and Almond Meatloaves
Prep time: 6 minutes | Cook time: 20 to 24 minutes | Serves 4

⅓ cup minced onion	2 teaspoons olive oil
¼ cup grated carrot	1 teaspoon dried
2 garlic cloves,	marjoram
minced	1 egg white
2 tablespoons ground	¾ pound (340 g)
almonds	ground turkey breast

1. Select the BAKE function and preheat MAXX to 400ºF (204ºC).
2. In a medium bowl, stir together the onion, carrot, garlic, almonds, olive oil, marjoram, and egg white.
3. Add the ground turkey. With your hands, gently but thoroughly mix until combined.
4. Double 16 foil muffin cup liners to make 8 cups. Divide the turkey mixture evenly among the liners.
5. Bake for 20 to 24 minutes, or until the meatloaves reach an internal temperature of 165ºF (74ºC) on a meat thermometer. Serve immediately.

Pecan-Crusted Chicken Tenders
Prep time: 5 minutes | Cook time: 12 minutes | Serves 4

1 pound (454 g)	paprika
chicken tenders	¼ cup coarse
1 teaspoon kosher	mustard
salt	2 tablespoons honey
1 teaspoon black	1 cup finely crushed
pepper	pecans
½ teaspoon smoked	

1. Select the BAKE function and preheat MAXX to 350ºF (177ºC).
2. Place the chicken in a large bowl. Sprinkle with the salt, pepper, and paprika. Toss until the chicken is coated with the spices. Add the mustard and honey and toss until the chicken is coated.
3. Place the pecans on a plate. Working with one piece of chicken at a time, roll the chicken in the pecans until both sides are coated. Lightly brush off any loose pecans. Place the chicken in the air fryer basket.
4. Bake for 12 minutes, or until the chicken is cooked through and the pecans are golden brown.
5. Serve warm.

Duck Breasts with Apples
Prep time: 5 minutes | Cook time: 15 minutes | Serves 2 to 3

1 pound (454 g)	orange
duck breasts (2 to 3	¼ cup honey
breasts)	2 sprigs thyme, plus
Kosher salt and	more for garnish
pepper, to taste	2 firm tart apples,
Juice and zest of 1	such as Fuji

1. Select the ROAST function and preheat MAXX to 400ºF (204ºC).
2. Pat the duck breasts dry and, using a sharp knife, make 3 to 4 shallow, diagonal slashes in the skin. Turn the breasts and score the skin on the diagonal in the opposite direction to create a cross-hatch pattern. Season well with salt and pepper.
3. Place the duck breasts skin-side up in the air fryer basket. Roast for 8 minutes, then flip and roast for 4 more minutes on the second side.
4. While the duck is cooking, prepare the sauce. Combine the orange juice and zest, honey, and thyme in a small saucepan. Bring to a boil, stirring to dissolve the honey, then reduce the heat and simmer until thickened. Core the apples and cut into quarters. Cut each quarter into 3 or 4 slices depending on the size.
5. After the duck has cooked on both sides, turn it and brush the skin with the orange-honey glaze. Roast for 1 more minute. Remove the duck breasts to a cutting board and allow to rest.
6. Toss the apple slices with the remaining orange-honey sauce in a medium bowl. Arrange the apples in a single layer in the air fryer basket. Switch from ROAST to AIR FRY. Air fry for 10 minutes while the duck breast rests. Slice the duck breasts on the bias and divide them and the apples among 2 or 3 plates.
7. Serve warm, garnished with additional thyme.

Chicken Parmesan with Marinara and Basil

Prep time: 15 minutes | Cook time: 13 minutes | Serves 2

¾ cup panko bread crumbs
2 tablespoons extra-virgin olive oil
¼ cup grated Parmesan cheese
1 large egg
1 tablespoon all-purpose flour
¾ teaspoon garlic powder
½ teaspoon dried oregano
Salt and pepper

2 (8-ounce / 227-g) boneless, skinless chicken breasts, trimmed
2 ounces (57 g) whole-milk Mozzarella cheese, shredded
¼ cup jarred marinara sauce, warmed
2 tablespoons chopped fresh basil

1. Toss panko with oil in bowl until evenly coated. Microwave, stirring frequently, until light golden brown, 1 to 3 minutes. Transfer to shallow dish, let cool slightly, then stir in Parmesan. Whisk egg, flour, garlic powder, oregano, ⅛ teaspoon salt, and ⅛ teaspoon pepper together in second shallow dish.
2. Pound chicken to uniform thickness as needed. Pat dry with paper towels and season with salt and pepper. Working with 1 breast at a time, dredge in egg mixture, letting excess drip off, then coat with panko mixture, pressing gently to adhere.
3. Lightly spray base of air fryer basket with vegetable oil spray. Arrange breasts in prepared basket, spaced evenly apart, alternating ends. Place basket in air fryer oven. Select the AIR FRY function and cook at 400ºF (205ºC) for 12 to 16 minutes, or until chicken is crisp and registers 160ºF (70ºC), flipping and rotating breasts halfway through cooking.
4. Sprinkle chicken with Mozzarella. Return basket to air fryer oven and air fry until cheese is melted, about 1 minute. Transfer chicken to individual serving plates. Top each breast with 2 tablespoons warm marinara sauce and sprinkle with basil. Serve.

Indian Fennel Chicken

Prep time: 10 minutes | Cook time: 15 minutes | Serves 4

1 pound (454 g) boneless, skinless chicken thighs, cut crosswise into thirds
1 yellow onion, cut into 1½-inch-thick slices
1 tablespoon coconut oil, melted
2 teaspoons minced fresh ginger
2 teaspoons minced garlic
1 teaspoon smoked paprika

1 teaspoon ground fennel
1 teaspoon garam masala
1 teaspoon ground turmeric
1 teaspoon kosher salt
½ to 1 teaspoon cayenne pepper
Vegetable oil spray
2 teaspoons fresh lemon juice
¼ cup chopped fresh cilantro or parsley

1. Use a fork to pierce the chicken all over to allow the marinade to penetrate better.
2. In a large bowl, combine the onion, coconut oil, ginger, garlic, paprika, fennel, garam masala, turmeric, salt, and cayenne. Add the chicken, toss to combine, and marinate at room temperature for 30 minutes, or cover and refrigerate for up to 24 hours.
3. Place the chicken and onion in the air fryer basket. (Discard remaining marinade.) Spray with some vegetable oil spray.
4. Select the AIR FRY function and cook at 350ºF (177ºC) for 15 minutes. Halfway through the cooking time, remove the basket, spray the chicken and onion with more vegetable oil spray, and toss gently to coat. At the end of the cooking time, use a meat thermometer to ensure the chicken has reached an internal temperature of 165ºF (74ºC).
5. Transfer the chicken and onion to a serving platter. Sprinkle with the lemon juice and cilantro and serve.

Israeli-Style Chicken Schnitzel
Prep time: 5 minutes | Cook time: 10 minutes | Serves 4

2 large boneless, skinless chicken breasts, each weighing about 1 pound (454 g)
1 cup all-purpose flour
2 teaspoons garlic powder
2 teaspoons kosher salt
1 teaspoon black pepper
1 teaspoon paprika
2 eggs beaten with 2 tablespoons water
2 cups panko bread crumbs
Vegetable oil spray
Lemon juice, for serving

1. Place 1 chicken breast between 2 pieces of plastic wrap. Use a mallet or a rolling pin to pound the chicken until it is ¼ inch thick. Set aside. Repeat with the second breast. Whisk together the flour, garlic powder, salt, pepper, and paprika on a large plate. Place the panko in a separate shallow bowl or pie plate.
2. Dredge 1 chicken breast in the flour, shaking off any excess, then dip it in the egg mixture. Dredge the chicken breast in the panko, making sure to coat it completely. Shake off any excess panko. Place the battered chicken breast on a plate. Repeat with the second chicken breast.
3. Spray the air fryer basket with oil spray. Place 1 of the battered chicken breasts in the basket and spray the top with oil spray. Select the AIR FRY function and cook at 375ºF (191ºC) for 5 minutes, or until the top is browned. Flip the chicken and spray the second side with oil spray. Air fry until the second side is browned and crispy and the internal temperature reaches 165ºF (74ºC). Remove the first chicken breast from the air fryer oven and repeat with the second chicken breast.
4. Serve hot with lemon juice.

Ham-Wrapped Swiss Chicken Breast
Prep time: 10 minutes | Cook time: 13 minutes | Serves 2

2 (8-ounce / 227-g) boneless, skinless chicken breasts, trimmed
Salt and pepper
4 thick slices ham (4 ounces / 113 g)
2 slices Swiss cheese
(2 ounces / 57 g)
2 tablespoons mayonnaise
1 tablespoon Dijon mustard
1 teaspoon water
1 tablespoon minced fresh chives

1. Pound chicken to uniform thickness as needed. Pat dry with paper towels and season with salt and pepper. For each chicken breast, shingle 2 slices of ham on counter, overlapping edges slightly, and lay chicken, skinned side down, in center. Fold ham around chicken and secure overlapping ends by threading toothpick through ham and chicken. Flip chicken and thread toothpick through ham and chicken on second side.
2. Lightly spray base of air fryer basket with vegetable oil spray. Arrange breasts skinned side down in prepared basket, spaced evenly apart, alternating ends. Place basket in air fryer oven. Select the AIR FRY function and cook at 400ºF (205ºC) for 12 to 16 minutes, or until edges of ham begin to brown and chicken registers 160ºF (70ºC), flipping and rotating breasts halfway through cooking. Top each breast with 1 slice Swiss, folding cheese as needed. Return basket to air fryer oven and cook until cheese is melted, about 1 minute.
3. Transfer chicken to serving platter and discard toothpicks. Tent loosely with aluminum foil and let rest for 5 minutes. Meanwhile, combine mayonnaise, mustard, and water in small bowl. Drizzle chicken with 1 tablespoon sauce and sprinkle with chives. Serve, passing remaining sauce separately.

Panko-Crusted Chicken Nuggets
Prep time: 10 minutes | Cook time: 12 minutes | Serves 4

4 (8-ounce / 227-g) boneless, skinless chicken breasts, trimmed
Salt and pepper
3 tablespoons sugar
3 cups panko bread crumbs
¼ cup extra-virgin
olive oil
3 large eggs
3 tablespoons all-purpose flour
1 tablespoon onion powder
¾ teaspoon garlic powder

1. Pound chicken to uniform thickness as needed. Cut each breast diagonally into thirds, then cut each piece into thirds. Dissolve 3 tablespoons salt and sugar in 2 quarts cold water in large container. Add chicken, cover, and let sit for 15 minutes.
2. Meanwhile, toss panko with oil in bowl until evenly coated. Microwave, stirring frequently, until light golden brown, about 5 minutes. Transfer to shallow dish and let cool slightly. Whisk eggs, flour, onion powder, garlic powder, 1 teaspoon salt, and ¼ teaspoon pepper together in second shallow dish.
3. Set wire rack in rimmed baking sheet. Remove chicken from brine and pat dry with paper towels. Working with several chicken pieces at a time, dredge in egg mixture, letting excess drip off, then coat with panko mixture, pressing gently to adhere; transfer to prepared rack. Freeze until firm, about 4 hours. (Frozen nuggets can be transferred to zipper-lock bag and stored in freezer for up to 1 month.)
4. Lightly spray base of air fryer basket with vegetable oil spray. Place up to 18 nuggets in prepared basket. Place basket in air fryer oven. Select the AIR FRY function and cook at 400ºF (205ºC) for 6 minutes. Transfer nuggets to clean bowl and gently toss to redistribute. Return nuggets to air fryer oven and air fry until chicken is crisp and registers 160ºF (70ºC), 6 to 10 minutes. Serve.

Chicken Breast and Lettuce Sandwich
Prep time: 15 minutes | Cook time: 12 minutes | Serves 4

1 cup panko bread crumbs
2 tablespoons extra-virgin olive oil
1 large egg
3 tablespoons hot sauce
1 tablespoon all-purpose flour
½ teaspoon garlic powder
Salt and pepper
2 (8-ounce / 227-g) boneless, skinless chicken breasts, trimmed
¼ cup mayonnaise
4 hamburger buns, toasted if desired
2 cups shredded iceberg lettuce
¼ cup jarred sliced jalapeños

1. Toss panko with oil in bowl until evenly coated. Microwave, stirring frequently, until light golden brown, 1 to 3 minutes. Transfer to shallow dish and set aside to cool slightly. Whisk egg, 2 tablespoons hot sauce, flour, garlic powder, ⅛ teaspoon salt, and ⅛ teaspoon pepper together in second shallow dish.
2. Pound chicken to uniform thickness as needed. Halve each breast crosswise, pat dry with paper towels, and season with salt and pepper. Working with 1 piece of chicken at a time, dredge in egg mixture, letting excess drip off, then coat with panko mixture, pressing gently to adhere.
3. Lightly spray base of air fryer basket with vegetable oil spray. Arrange chicken pieces in prepared basket, spaced evenly apart. Place basket in air fryer oven. Select the AIR FRY function and cook at 400ºF (205ºC) for 12 to 16 minutes, or until chicken is crisp and registers 160ºF (70ºC), flipping and rotating chicken pieces halfway through cooking.
4. Combine mayonnaise and remaining 1 tablespoon hot sauce in small bowl. Spread mayonnaise mixture evenly over bun bottoms, then top with 1 piece chicken, lettuce, jalapeños, and bun tops. Serve.

Chicken Merguez Meatballs

Prep time: 10 minutes | Cook time: 10 minutes | Serves 4

1 pound (454 g) ground chicken
2 garlic cloves, finely minced
1 tablespoon sweet Hungarian paprika
1 teaspoon kosher salt
1 teaspoon sugar
1 teaspoon ground cumin

½ teaspoon black pepper
½ teaspoon ground fennel
½ teaspoon ground coriander
½ teaspoon cayenne pepper
¼ teaspoon ground allspice

1. In a large bowl, gently mix the chicken, garlic, paprika, salt, sugar, cumin, black pepper, fennel, coriander, cayenne, and allspice until all the ingredients are incorporated. Let stand for 30 minutes at room temperature, or cover and refrigerate for up to 24 hours.
2. Form the mixture into 16 meatballs. Arrange them in a single layer in the air fryer basket.
3. Select the AIR FRY function and cook at 400ºF (204ºC) for 10 minutes, turning the meatballs halfway through the cooking time. Use a meat thermometer to ensure the meatballs have reached an internal temperature of 165ºF (74ºC).
4. Serve warm.

Lemony Chicken Breast

Prep time: 10 minutes | Cook time: 16 to 19 minutes | Serves 4

4 (5-ounce / 142-g) low-sodium boneless, skinless chicken breasts, cut into 4-by-½-inch strips
2 teaspoons olive oil
2 tablespoons cornstarch
3 garlic cloves, minced

½ cup low-sodium chicken broth
¼ cup freshly squeezed lemon juice
1 tablespoon honey
½ teaspoon dried thyme
Brown rice, cooked (optional)

1. Select the BAKE function and preheat MAXX to 400ºF (204ºC).
2. In a large bowl, mix the chicken and olive oil. Sprinkle with the cornstarch. Toss to coat.
3. Add the garlic and transfer to a metal pan. Bake in the air fryer oven for 10 minutes, stirring once during cooking.
4. Add the chicken broth, lemon juice, honey, and thyme to the chicken mixture. Bake for 6 to 9 minutes more, or until the sauce is slightly thickened and the chicken reaches an internal temperature of 165ºF (74ºC) on a meat thermometer. Serve over hot cooked brown rice, if desired.

Chapter 6 Meats

Peppery Baby Back Ribs

Prep time: 5 minutes | Cook time: 30 minutes | Serves 2

2 teaspoons red pepper flakes	garlic
¾ ground ginger	Salt and ground black pepper, to taste
3 cloves minced	2 baby back ribs

1. Combine the red pepper flakes, ginger, garlic, salt and pepper in a bowl, making sure to mix well. Massage the mixture into the baby back ribs. Transfer to the air fryer basket.
2. Select the AIR FRY function and cook at 350ºF (177ºC) for 30 minutes.
3. Take care when taking the rubs out of the air fryer oven. Put them on a serving dish and serve.

Chuck and Pork Sausage Meatloaf

Prep time: 20 minutes | Cook time: 25 minutes | Serves 4

¾ pound (340 g) ground chuck	½ teaspoon cumin powder
4 ounces (113 g) ground pork sausage	1 teaspoon garlic paste
1 cup shallots, finely chopped	1 tablespoon fresh parsley
2 eggs, well beaten	Salt and crushed red pepper flakes, to taste
3 tablespoons plain milk	1 cup crushed saltines
1 tablespoon oyster sauce	Cooking spray
1 teaspoon porcini mushrooms	

1. Select the BAKE function and preheat MAXX to 360ºF (182ºC). Spritz a baking dish with cooking spray.
2. Mix all the ingredients in a large bowl, combining everything well.
3. Transfer to the baking dish and bake in the air fryer oven for 25 minutes.
4. Serve hot.

Lamb Satay Skewers

Prep time: 5 minutes | Cook time: 8 minutes | Serves 2

¼ teaspoon cumin	pepper, to taste
1 teaspoon ginger	2 boneless lamb steaks
½ teaspoons nutmeg	Cooking spray
Salt and ground black	

1. Combine the cumin, ginger, nutmeg, salt and pepper in a bowl.
2. Cube the lamb steaks and massage the spice mixture into each one.
3. Leave to marinate for 10 minutes, then transfer onto metal skewers.
4. Spritz the skewers with the cooking spray and place in the air fryer basket.
5. Select the AIR FRY function and cook at 400ºF (204ºC) for 8 minutes.
6. Take care when removing them from the air fryer oven and serve.

Apple Cider Beef Ribs

Prep time: 20 minutes | Cook time: 8 minutes | Serves 4

1 pound (454 g) meaty beef ribs, rinsed and drained	chopped
	1 chipotle powder
3 tablespoons apple cider vinegar	1 teaspoon fennel seeds
1 cup coriander, finely chopped	1 teaspoon hot paprika
1 tablespoon fresh basil leaves, chopped	Kosher salt and black pepper, to taste
2 garlic cloves, finely	½ cup vegetable oil

1. Coat the ribs with the remaining ingredients and refrigerate for at least 3 hours.
2. Separate the ribs from the marinade and put them in the air fryer basket.
3. Select the AIR FRY function and cook at 360ºF (182ºC) for 8 minutes.
4. Pour the remaining marinade over the ribs before serving.

Beef, Vegetable, and Egg Rolls
Prep time: 15 minutes | Cook time: 8 minutes | Makes 6 egg rolls

8 ounces (227 g) raw lean ground beef
½ cup chopped onion
½ cup chopped bell pepper
¼ teaspoon onion powder
¼ teaspoon garlic powder
3 tablespoons cream cheese
1 tablespoon yellow mustard
3 tablespoons shredded Cheddar cheese
6 chopped dill pickle chips
6 egg roll wrappers

1. In a skillet, add the beef, onion, bell pepper, onion powder, and garlic powder. Stir and crumble beef until fully cooked, and vegetables are soft.
2. Take skillet off the heat and add cream cheese, mustard, and Cheddar cheese, stirring until melted.
3. Pour beef mixture into a bowl and fold in pickles.
4. Lay out egg wrappers and divide the beef mixture into each one. Moisten egg roll wrapper edges with water. Fold sides to the middle and seal with water.
5. Repeat with all other egg rolls.
6. Put rolls into air fryer oven, one batch at a time. Select the AIR FRY function and cook at 392ºF (200ºC) for 8 minutes.
7. Serve immediately.

Beef Chimichangas
Prep time: 10 minutes | Cook time: 20 minutes | Serves 4

Cooking oil
½ cup chopped onion
2 garlic cloves, minced
1 pound (454 g) 93% lean ground beef
2 tablespoons taco seasoning
Salt
Pepper
1 (15-ounce / 425-g) can diced tomatoes with chiles
4 medium (8-inch) flour tortillas
1 cup shredded Cheddar cheese

1. Spray a skillet with cooking oil and place over medium-high heat. Add the chopped onion and garlic. Cook for 2 to 3 minutes, until fragrant.
2. Add the ground beef, taco seasoning, and salt and pepper to taste. Use a large spoon or spatula to break up the beef. Cook for 2 to 4 minutes, until browned.
3. Add the diced tomatoes with chiles. Stir to combine.
4. Mound ½ cup of the ground beef mixture on each of the tortillas.
5. To form the chimichangas, fold the sides of the tortilla in toward the middle and then roll up from the bottom. You can secure the chimichanga with a toothpick. Or you can moisten the upper edge of the tortilla with a small amount of water before sealing. I prefer to use a cooking brush, but you can dab with your fingers.
6. Spray the chimichangas with cooking oil.
7. Place the chimichangas in the air fryer basket. Do not stack. Work in batches. Select the AIR FRY function and cook at 400ºF (205ºC) for 8 minutes.
8. Remove the cooked chimichangas from the air fryer oven and top them with the shredded cheese. The heat from the chimichangas will melt the cheese.
9. Repeat with the remaining chimichangas, and serve.

Beef Cheeseburgers
Prep time: 10 minutes | Cook time: 15 minutes | Serves 4

¾ pound (340 g) ground beef chuck
1 envelope onion soup mix
Kosher salt and freshly ground black
pepper, to taste
1 teaspoon paprika
4 slices Monterey Jack cheese
4 ciabatta rolls

1. In a bowl, stir together the ground chuck, onion soup mix, salt, black pepper, and paprika to combine well.
2. Take four equal portions of the mixture and mold each one into a patty. Transfer to the air fryer oven. Select the AIR FRY function and cook at 385ºF (196ºC) for 10 minutes.
3. Put the slices of cheese on the top of the burgers.
4. Air fry for another minute before serving on ciabatta rolls.

Shoulder Steak with Brussels Sprouts
Prep time: 20 minutes | Cook time: 15 minutes | Serves 4

1 pound (454 g) beef chuck shoulder steak
2 tablespoons vegetable oil
1 tablespoon red wine vinegar
1 teaspoon fine sea salt
½ teaspoon ground black pepper
1 teaspoon smoked paprika
1 teaspoon onion powder
½ teaspoon garlic powder
½ pound (227 g) Brussels sprouts, cleaned and halved
½ teaspoon fennel seeds
1 teaspoon dried basil
1 teaspoon dried sage

1. Massage the beef with the vegetable oil, wine vinegar, salt, black pepper, paprika, onion powder, and garlic powder, coating it well.
2. Allow to marinate for a minimum of 3 hours.
3. Remove the beef from the marinade and put in the air fryer oven. Select the AIR FRY function and cook at 390ºF (199ºC) for 10 minutes. Flip the beef halfway through.
4. Put the prepared Brussels sprouts in the air fryer oven along with the fennel seeds, basil, and sage.
5. Lower the heat to 380ºF (193ºC) and air fry everything for another 5 minutes.
6. Give them a good stir. Air fry for an additional 10 minutes.
7. Serve immediately.

Beef Egg Rolls with Mexican Cheese
Prep time: 15 minutes | Cook time: 12 minutes | Makes 8 egg rolls

½ chopped onion
2 garlic cloves, chopped
½ packet taco seasoning
Salt and ground black pepper, to taste
1 pound (454 g) lean ground beef
½ can cilantro lime rotel
16 egg roll wrappers
1 cup shredded Mexican cheese
1 tablespoon olive oil
1 teaspoon cilantro

1. Add onions and garlic to a skillet, cooking until fragrant. Then add taco seasoning, pepper, salt, and beef, cooking until beef is broke up into tiny pieces and cooked thoroughly.
2. Add rotel and stir well.
3. Lay out egg wrappers and brush with a touch of water to soften a bit.
4. Load wrappers with beef filling and add cheese to each.
5. Fold diagonally to close and use water to secure edges.
6. Brush filled egg wrappers with olive oil and add to the air fryer oven.
7. Select the AIR FRY function and cook at 400ºF (205ºC) for 8 minutes. Flip, and air fry for another 4 minutes.
8. Serve sprinkled with cilantro.

Sausage and Bell Pepper Rolls
Prep time: 5 minutes | Cook time: 15 minutes | Serves 5

5 Italian sausages
1 green bell pepper, seeded and cut into strips
1 red bell pepper, seeded and cut into strips
½ onion, cut into strips
1 teaspoon dried oregano
½ teaspoon garlic powder
5 Italian rolls or buns

1. Place the sausages in the air fryer oven. No cooking oil is needed as the sausages will produce oil during the cooking process. The sausages should fit in the basket without stacking. If not, stacking is okay.
2. Select the AIR FRY function and cook at 360ºF (182ºC) for 10 minutes.
3. Season the green and red bell peppers and the onion with the oregano and garlic powder.
4. Open the air fryer oven and flip the sausages. Add the peppers and onion to the basket. Air fry for an additional 3 to 5 minutes, until the vegetables are soft and the sausages are no longer pink on the inside.
5. Serve the sausages (sliced or whole) on buns with the peppers and onion.

Lamb Ribs with Mint Yogurt
Prep time: 5 minutes | Cook time: 18 minutes | Serves 4

2 tablespoons mustard
1 pound (454 g) lamb ribs
1 teaspoon rosemary, chopped
Salt and ground black pepper, to taste
¼ cup mint leaves, chopped
1 cup Greek yogurt

1. Use a brush to apply the mustard to the lamb ribs, and season with rosemary, salt, and pepper. Transfer to the air fryer basket.
2. Select the AIR FRY function and cook at 350°F (177°C) for 18 minutes.
3. Meanwhile, combine the mint leaves and yogurt in a bowl.
4. Remove the lamb ribs from the air fryer oven when cooked and serve with the mint yogurt.

Steak and Vegetable Cubes
Prep time: 15 minutes | Cook time: 17 minutes | Serves 4

2 tablespoons olive oil
1 tablespoon apple cider vinegar
1 teaspoon fine sea salt
½ teaspoons ground black pepper
1 teaspoon shallot powder
¾ teaspoon smoked cayenne pepper
½ teaspoons garlic powder
¼ teaspoon ground cumin
1 pound (454 g) top round steak, cut into cubes
4 ounces (113 g) broccoli, cut into florets
4 ounces (113 g) mushrooms, sliced
1 teaspoon dried basil
1 teaspoon celery seeds

1. Massage the olive oil, vinegar, salt, black pepper, shallot powder, cayenne pepper, garlic powder, and cumin into the cubed steak, ensuring to coat each piece evenly.
2. Allow to marinate for a minimum of 3 hours.
3. Put the beef cubes in the air fryer basket.
4. Select the AIR FRY function and cook at 365°F (185°C) for 12 minutes.
5. When the steak is cooked through, place it in a bowl.
6. Wipe the grease from the basket and pour in the vegetables. Season them with basil and celery seeds.
7. Increase the temperature of the air fryer oven to 400°F (204°C) and air fry for 5 to 6 minutes. When the vegetables are hot, serve them with the steak.

American Beef Cheeseburgers
Prep time: 10 minutes | Cook time: 19 minutes | Serves 2

½ slice hearty white sandwich bread, crust removed, torn into ¼-inch pieces
1 tablespoon milk
½ teaspoon garlic powder
½ teaspoon onion powder
12 ounces (340 g) 85% lean ground beef
Salt and pepper
2 slices American cheese (2 ounces / 57 g)
2 hamburger buns, toasted if desired

1. Mash bread, milk, garlic powder, and onion powder into paste in medium bowl using fork. Break up ground beef into small pieces over bread mixture in bowl and lightly knead with hands until well combined. Divide mixture into 2 lightly packed balls, then gently flatten each into 1-inch-thick patty. Press center of each patty with fingertips to create ¼-inch-deep depression. Season with salt and pepper.
2. Arrange patties in air fryer basket, spaced evenly apart. Place basket in air fryer oven. Select the AIR FRY function and cook at 350°F (180°C) for 18 to 21 minutes, or until burgers are lightly browned and register 140°F (60°C) to 145°F (63°C) (for medium-well) or 150°F (66°C) to 155°F (68°C) (for well-done), flipping and rotating burgers halfway through cooking.
3. Top each burger with 1 slice cheese. Return basket to air fryer oven and cook until cheese is melted, about 30 seconds. Serve burgers on buns.

Double Cheese Beef Meatballs

Prep time: 5 minutes | Cook time: 18 minutes | Serves 6

1 pound (454 g) ground beef	garlic
½ cup grated Parmesan cheese	½ cup Mozzarella cheese
1 tablespoon minced	1 teaspoon freshly ground pepper

1. In a bowl, mix all the ingredients together.
2. Roll the meat mixture into 5 generous meatballs. Arrange in the air fryer basket.
3. Select the AIR FRY function and cook at 400ºF (204ºC) for 18 minutes.
4. Serve immediately.

Chicken Fried Steak with Gravy

Prep time: 15 minutes | Cook time: 10 minutes | Serves 4

½ cup flour	For the Gravy:
2 teaspoons salt, divided	2 tablespoons butter or bacon drippings
Freshly ground black pepper, to taste	¼ onion, minced
¼ teaspoon garlic powder	1 clove garlic, smashed
1 cup buttermilk	¼ teaspoon dried thyme
1 cup fine bread crumbs	3 tablespoons flour
4 (6-ounce / 170-g) tenderized top round steaks, ½-inch thick	1 cup milk
	Salt and freshly ground black pepper, to taste
Vegetable or canola oil	Dashes of Worcestershire sauce

1. Set up a dredging station. Combine the flour, 1 teaspoon of salt, black pepper and garlic powder in a shallow bowl. Pour the buttermilk into a second shallow bowl. Finally, put the bread crumbs and 1 teaspoon of salt in a third shallow bowl.
2. Dip the tenderized steaks into the flour, then the buttermilk, and then the bread crumb mixture, pressing the crumbs onto the steak. Put them on a baking sheet and spray both sides generously with vegetable or canola oil.

3. Transfer the steaks to the air fryer basket, two at a time. Select the AIR FRY function and cook at 400ºF (204ºC) for 10 minutes, flipping the steaks over halfway through the cooking time. Hold the first batch of steaks warm in a 170ºF (77ºC) oven while you air fry the second batch.
4. While the steaks are cooking, make the gravy. Melt the butter in a small saucepan over medium heat on the stovetop. Add the onion, garlic and thyme and cook for five minutes, until the onion is soft and just starting to brown. Stir in the flour and cook for another five minutes, stirring regularly, until the mixture starts to brown. Whisk in the milk and bring the mixture to a boil to thicken. Season to taste with salt, lots of freshly ground black pepper, and a few dashes of Worcestershire sauce.
5. Pour the gravy over the chicken fried steaks and serve.

Citrus-Mustard Pork Loin Roast

Prep time: 10 minutes | Cook time: 45 minutes | Serves 8

1 tablespoon lime juice	1 teaspoon dried lemongrass
1 tablespoon orange marmalade	2 pound (907 g) boneless pork loin roast
1 teaspoon coarse brown mustard	
1 teaspoon curry powder	Salt and ground black pepper, to taste
	Cooking spray

1. Mix the lime juice, marmalade, mustard, curry powder, and lemongrass.
2. Rub mixture all over the surface of the pork loin. Season with salt and pepper.
3. Spray air fryer basket with cooking spray and place pork roast diagonally in the basket.
4. Select the AIR FRY function and cook at 360ºF (182ºC) for 45 minutes, until the internal temperature reaches at least 145ºF (63ºC).
5. Wrap roast in foil and let rest for 10 minutes before slicing.
6. Serve immediately.

Dijon Bacon Wrapped Pork with Apple Gravy

Prep time: 10 minutes | Cook time: 25 minutes | Serves 4

Pork:

1 tablespoons Dijon mustard

1 pork tenderloin
3 strips bacon

Apple Gravy:

3 tablespoons ghee, divided
1 small shallot, chopped
2 apples
1 tablespoon almond

flour
1 cup vegetable broth
½ teaspoon Dijon mustard

1. Spread Dijon mustard all over tenderloin and wrap with strips of bacon.
2. Put into air fryer oven. Select the AIR FRY function and cook at 360ºF (182ºC) for 12 minutes. Use a meat thermometer to check for doneness.
3. To make sauce, heat 1 tablespoons of ghee in a pan and add shallots. Cook for 1 minute.
4. Then add apples, cooking for 4 minutes until softened.
5. Add flour and 2 tablespoons of ghee to make a roux. Add broth and mustard, stirring well to combine.
6. When sauce starts to bubble, add 1 cup of sautéed apples, cooking until sauce thickens.
7. Once pork tenderloin is cooked, allow to sit 8 minutes to rest before slicing.
8. Serve topped with apple gravy.

Savory London Broil

Prep time: 15 minutes | Cook time: 25 minutes | Serves 8

2 pounds (907 g) London broil
3 large garlic cloves, minced
3 tablespoons balsamic vinegar
3 tablespoons whole-

grain mustard
2 tablespoons olive oil
Sea salt and ground black pepper, to taste
½ teaspoons dried hot red pepper flakes

1. Wash and dry the London broil. Score its sides with a knife.

2. Mix the remaining ingredients. Rub this mixture into the broil, coating it well. Allow to marinate for a minimum of 3 hours.
3. Transfer the broil to the air fryer basket.
4. Select the AIR FRY function and cook at 400ºF (204ºC) for 15 minutes. Turn it over and air fry for an additional 10 minutes before serving.

Greek-Style Lamb Pita Pockets

Prep time: 15 minutes | Cook time: 6 minutes | Serves 4

Dressing:

1 cup plain yogurt
1 tablespoon lemon juice
1 teaspoon dried dill

weed, crushed
1 teaspoon ground oregano
½ teaspoon salt

Meatballs:

½ pound (227 g) ground lamb
1 tablespoon diced onion
1 teaspoon dried parsley
1 teaspoon dried dill weed, crushed
¼ teaspoon oregano
¼ teaspoon coriander
¼ teaspoon ground cumin

¼ teaspoon salt
4 pita halves
Suggested Toppings:
1 red onion, slivered
1 medium cucumber, deseeded, thinly sliced
Crumbled feta cheese
Sliced black olives
Chopped fresh peppers

1. Stir the dressing ingredients together in a small bowl and refrigerate while preparing lamb.
2. Combine all meatball ingredients in a large bowl and stir to distribute seasonings.
3. Shape meat mixture into 12 small meatballs, rounded or slightly flattened if you prefer.
4. Transfer the meatballs to the air fryer oven. Select the AIR FRY function and cook at 390ºF (199ºC) for 6 minutes, until well done. Remove and drain on paper towels.
5. To serve, pile meatballs and the choice of toppings in pita pockets and drizzle with dressing.

Cantonese Char Siew

Prep time: 10 minutes | Cook time: 20 minutes | Serves 4 to 6

1 strip of pork shoulder butt with a good amount of fat	marbling
Olive oil, for brushing the pan

Marinade:

1 teaspoon sesame oil	1 teaspoon light soy sauce
4 tablespoons raw honey	1 tablespoon rose wine
1 teaspoon low-sodium dark soy sauce	2 tablespoons Hoisin sauce

1. Combine all the marinade ingredients together in a Ziploc bag. Put pork in bag, making sure all sections of pork strip are engulfed in the marinade. Chill for 3 to 24 hours.
2. Take out the strip 30 minutes before planning to roast.
3. Select the ROAST function and preheat MAXX to 350ºF (177ºC).
4. Put foil on small pan and brush with olive oil. Put marinated pork strip onto prepared pan.
5. Roast in the preheated air fryer oven for 20 minutes.
6. Glaze with marinade every 5 to 10 minutes.
7. Remove strip and leave to cool a few minutes before slicing.
8. Serve immediately.

Chimichurri Flank Steak

Prep time: 5 minutes | Cook time: 12 minutes | Serves 1

1 flank steak	2 tablespoons butter, melted
Salt and ground black pepper, to taste	½ cup chimichurri sauce
2 avocados	

1. Rub the flank steak with salt and pepper to taste and leave to sit for 20 minutes.
2. Halve the avocados and take out the pits. Spoon the flesh into a bowl and mash with a fork. Mix in the melted butter and chimichurri sauce, making sure everything is well combined.

3. Put the steak in the air fryer basket. Select the AIR FRY function and cook at 400ºF (204ºC) for 6 minutes. Flip over and allow to air fry for another 6 minutes.
4. Serve the steak with the avocado butter.

Beef and Mushrooms Calzones

Prep time: 10 minutes | Cook time: 20 minutes | Serves 6

Cooking oil	Salt
½ cup chopped onion	Pepper
2 garlic cloves, minced	1½ cups pizza sauce
¼ cup chopped mushrooms	1 teaspoon all-purpose flour
1 pound (454 g) 93% lean ground beef	1 (13-ounce / 369-g) can refrigerated pizza dough
1 tablespoon Italian seasoning	1 cup shredded Cheddar cheese

1. Spray a skillet with cooking oil and place over medium-high heat. Add the chopped onion, garlic, and mushrooms. Cook for 2 to 3 minutes, until fragrant.
2. Add the ground beef, Italian seasoning, and salt and pepper to taste. Use a large spoon or spatula to break up the beef into small pieces. Cook for 2 to 4 minutes, until browned.
3. Add the pizza sauce. Stir to combine.
4. Sprinkle the flour on a flat work surface. Roll out the pizza dough. Cut the dough into 6 equal-sized rectangles.
5. Mound ½ cup of the ground beef mixture on each of the rectangles. Sprinkle 1 tablespoon of shredded cheese over the beef mixture.
6. Fold each crust up to close the calzones. Using the back of a fork, press along the open edges of each calzone to seal.
7. Place the calzones in the air fryer oven. Do not stack. Work in batches. Spray the calzones with cooking oil. Select the AIR FRY function and cook at 400ºF (205ºC) for 10 minutes.
8. Remove the cooked calzones from the air fryer oven, then repeat with the remaining calzones.
9. Cool before serving.

Bacon in Pear Stuffed Pork Chops

Prep time: 20 minutes | Cook time: 24 minutes | Serves 3

4 slices bacon, chopped
1 tablespoon butter
½ cup finely diced onion
⅓ cup chicken stock
1½ cups seasoned stuffing cubes
1 egg, beaten
½ teaspoon dried thyme
½ teaspoon salt
⅛ teaspoon freshly ground black pepper
1 pear, finely diced
⅓ cup crumbled blue cheese
3 boneless center-cut pork chops (2-inch thick)
Olive oil, for greasing
Salt and freshly ground black pepper, to taste

1. Put the bacon into the air fryer basket. Select the AIR FRY function and cook at 400°F (204°C) for 6 minutes, stirring halfway through the cooking time. Remove the bacon and set it aside on a paper towel. Pour out the grease from the bottom of the air fryer oven.
2. To make the stuffing, melt the butter in a medium saucepan over medium heat on the stovetop. Add the onion and sauté for a few minutes until it starts to soften. Add the chicken stock and simmer for 1 minute. Remove the pan from the heat and add the stuffing cubes. Stir until the stock has been absorbed. Add the egg, dried thyme, salt and freshly ground black pepper, and stir until combined. Fold in the diced pear and crumbled blue cheese.
3. Put the pork chops on a cutting board. Using the palm of the hand to hold the chop flat and steady, slice into the side of the pork chop to make a pocket in the center of the chop. Leave about an inch of chop uncut and make sure you don't cut all the way through the pork chop. Brush both sides of the pork chops with olive oil and season with salt and freshly ground black pepper. Stuff each pork chop with a third of the stuffing, packing the stuffing tightly inside the pocket.
4. Adjust the temperature to 360°F (182°C).
5. Spray or brush the sides of the air fryer basket with oil. Put the pork chops in the air fryer basket with the open, stuffed edge of the pork chop facing the outside edges of the basket.
6. Air fry the pork chops for 18 minutes, turning the pork chops over halfway through the cooking time. When the chops are done, let them rest for 5 minutes and then transfer to a serving platter.

Chili Pork Chops with Parmesan

Prep time: 10 minutes | Cook time: 12 minutes | Serves 4 to 6

¼ teaspoon pepper
½ teaspoons salt
4 to 6 thick boneless pork chops
1 cup pork rind crumbs
¼ teaspoon chili powder
½ teaspoons onion powder
1 teaspoon smoked paprika
2 beaten eggs
3 tablespoons grated Parmesan cheese
Cooking spray

1. Rub the pepper and salt on both sides of pork chops.
2. In a food processor, pulse pork rinds into crumbs. Mix crumbs with chili powder, onion powder, and paprika in a bowl.
3. Beat eggs in another bowl.
4. Dip pork chops into eggs then into pork rind crumb mixture.
5. Spritz the air fryer basket with cooking spray and add pork chops to the basket.
6. Select the AIR FRY function and cook at 400°F (205°C) for 12 minutes.
7. Serve garnished with the Parmesan cheese.

BBQ-Cajun Pork Steaks

Prep time: 5 minutes | Cook time: 15 minutes | Serves 4

4 pork steaks
1 tablespoon Cajun seasoning
2 tablespoons BBQ sauce
1 tablespoon vinegar
1 teaspoon soy sauce
½ cup brown sugar
½ cup ketchup

1. Sprinkle pork steaks with Cajun seasoning.
2. Combine remaining ingredients and brush onto steaks.
3. Add coated steaks to air fryer oven. Select the AIR FRY function and cook at 290°F (143°C) for 15 minutes, or until just browned.
4. Serve immediately.

Beef and Baby Spinach Rolls

Prep time: 10 minutes | Cook time: 14 minutes | Serves 2

3 teaspoons pesto	roasted red bell
2 pounds (907 g)	peppers
beef flank steak	¾ cup baby spinach
6 slices provolone	1 teaspoon sea salt
cheese	1 teaspoon black
3 ounces (85 g)	pepper

1. Spoon equal amounts of the pesto onto each flank steak and spread it across evenly.
2. Put the cheese, roasted red peppers and spinach on top of the meat, about three-quarters of the way down.
3. Roll the steak up, holding it in place with toothpicks. Sprinkle with the sea salt and pepper.
4. Put inside the air fryer oven. Select the AIR FRY function and cook at 400ºF (204ºC) for 14 minutes, turning halfway through the cooking time.
5. Allow the beef to rest for 10 minutes before slicing up and serving.

Panko-Crusted Pork Chops

Prep time: 5 minutes | Cook time: 15 minutes | Serves 5

5 (3½- to 5-ounce /	¼ cup all-purpose
99- to 142-g) pork	flour
chops (bone-in or	2 tablespoons panko
boneless)	bread crumbs
Seasoning salt	Cooking oil
Pepper	

1. Season the pork chops with the seasoning salt and pepper to taste.
2. Sprinkle the flour on both sides of the pork chops, then coat both sides with panko bread crumbs.
3. Place the pork chops in the air fryer oven. Spray the pork chops with cooking oil. Select the AIR FRY function and cook at 380ºF (193ºC) for 6 minutes.
4. Open the air fryer oven and flip the pork chops. Air fry for an additional 6 minutes
5. Cool before serving.

Pork Ribs with Barbecue Dry Rub

Prep time: 5 minutes | Cook time: 30 minutes | Serves 4

1 tablespoon	1 teaspoon sesame
barbecue dry rub	oil
1 teaspoon mustard	1 pound (454 g) pork
1 tablespoon apple	ribs, chopped
cider vinegar	

1. Combine the dry rub, mustard, apple cider vinegar, and sesame oil, then coat the ribs with this mixture. Refrigerate the ribs for 20 minutes.
2. When the ribs are ready, place them in the air fryer oven. Select the AIR FRY function and cook at 360ºF (182ºC) for 15 minutes. Flip them and air fry on the other side for a further 15 minutes.
3. Serve immediately.

Carne Asada Tacos

Prep time: 5 minutes | Cook time: 14 minutes | Serves 4

$1/_3$ cup olive oil	½ cup chopped fresh
1½ pounds (680 g)	cilantro
flank steak	4 teaspoons minced
Salt and freshly	garlic
ground black pepper,	1 teaspoon ground
to taste	cumin
$1/_3$ cup freshly	1 teaspoon chili
squeezed lime juice	powder

1. Brush the air fryer basket with olive oil.
2. Put the flank steak in a large mixing bowl. Season with salt and pepper.
3. Add the lime juice, cilantro, garlic, cumin, and chili powder and toss to coat the steak.
4. For the best flavor, let the steak marinate in the refrigerator for about 1 hour.
5. Put the steak in the air fryer basket. Select the AIR FRY function and cook at 400ºF (204ºC) for 7 minutes. Flip the steak. Air fry for 7 minutes more or until an internal temperature reaches at least 145ºF (63ºC).
6. Let the steak rest for about 5 minutes, then cut into strips to serve.

Beef Spring Rolls

Prep time: 10 minutes | Cook time: 8 minutes | Serves 20

1/3 cup noodles	1 small onion, diced
1 cup ground beef	1 tablespoon sesame oil
1 teaspoon soy sauce	
1 cup fresh mix vegetables	1 packet spring roll sheets
3 garlic cloves, minced	2 tablespoons cold water

1. Cook the noodle in enough hot water to soften them up, drain them and snip them to make them shorter.
2. In a frying pan over medium heat, cook the beef, soy sauce, mixed vegetables, garlic, and onion in sesame oil until the beef is cooked through. Take the pan off the heat and throw in the noodles. Mix well to incorporate everything.
3. Unroll a spring roll sheet and lay it flat. Scatter the filling diagonally across it and roll it up, brushing the edges lightly with water to act as an adhesive. Repeat until you have used up all the sheets and the filling.
4. Coat each spring roll with a light brushing of oil and transfer to the air fryer oven.
5. Select the AIR FRY function and cook at 350ºF (177ºC) for 8 minutes.
6. Serve hot.

Golden Filet Mignon

Prep time: 15 minutes | Cook time: 12 minutes | Serves 4

½ pound (227 g) filet mignon	1 teaspoon dried rosemary
Sea salt and ground black pepper, to taste	1 teaspoon dried thyme
½ teaspoon cayenne pepper	1 tablespoon sesame oil
1 teaspoon dried basil	1 small egg, whisked
	½ cup bread crumbs

1. Cover the filet mignon with the salt, black pepper, cayenne pepper, basil, rosemary, and thyme. Coat with sesame oil.
2. Put the egg in a shallow plate.
3. Pour the bread crumbs in another plate.

4. Dip the filet mignon into the egg. Roll it into the crumbs.
5. Transfer the steak to the air fryer oven. Select the AIR FRY function and cook at 360ºF (182ºC) for 12 minutes, or until it turns golden.
6. Serve immediately.

New York Strip Steak with Bell Peppers

Prep time: 10 minutes | Cook time: 30 minutes | Serves 4

2 tablespoons cornstarch	ground black pepper
1 tablespoon sugar	1½ pounds (680 g) boneless New York strip steaks, sliced into ½-inch strips
¾ cup beef broth	
¼ cup hoisin sauce	
3 tablespoons soy sauce	1 onion, sliced
1 teaspoon sesame oil	3 small bell peppers, red, yellow and green, sliced
½ teaspoon freshly	

1. Whisk the cornstarch and sugar together in a large bowl to break up any lumps in the cornstarch. Add the beef broth and whisk until combined and smooth. Stir in the hoisin sauce, soy sauce, sesame oil and freshly ground black pepper. Add the beef, onion and peppers, and toss to coat. Marinate the beef and vegetables at room temperature for 30 minutes, stirring a few times to keep meat and vegetables coated.
2. Transfer the beef, onion, and peppers to the air fryer basket with tongs, reserving the marinade. Select the AIR FRY function and cook at 350ºF (180ºC) for 30 minutes, stirring well two or three times during the cooking process.
3. While the beef is air frying, bring the reserved marinade to a simmer in a small saucepan over medium heat on the stovetop. Simmer for 5 minutes until the sauce thickens.
4. When the steak and vegetables have finished cooking, transfer them to a serving platter. Pour the hot sauce over the pepper steak and serve with white rice.

Sirloin Steak and Veggie Kebabs
Prep time: 20 minutes | Cook time: 18 minutes | Serves 2

2 tablespoons vegetable oil
1 teaspoon grated fresh ginger
1 garlic clove, minced
¼ teaspoon red pepper flakes
1 tablespoon toasted sesame oil
2 teaspoons soy sauce
1½ teaspoons honey
½ teaspoon grated orange zest plus 1 tablespoon juice
12 ounces (340 g) sirloin steak tips,
trimmed and cut into 1½-inch pieces
1 small red onion, halved and cut through root end into 6 equal wedges
4 ounces (113 g) shiitake mushrooms, stemmed and halved if large
1 zucchini, sliced into ½-inch-thick rounds
¼ teaspoon salt
¼ teaspoon pepper
5 (6-inch) wooden skewers

1. Microwave 4 teaspoons vegetable oil, ginger, garlic, and pepper flakes in large bowl until fragrant, about 30 seconds, stirring once halfway through. Whisk in sesame oil, soy sauce, honey, and orange zest and juice until combined. Measure out and reserve 3 tablespoons oil mixture. Add beef to remaining oil mixture and toss to coat; set aside.
2. Meanwhile, toss red onion, mushrooms, and zucchini with remaining 2 teaspoons vegetable oil, salt, and pepper in bowl. Thread 1 piece of onion onto wooden skewer. Thread one-third of zucchini and mushrooms onto skewer, followed by second piece of onion. Repeat skewering remaining vegetables with 2 more skewers. Arrange skewers in air fryer basket, parallel to each other and spaced evenly apart. Place basket in air fryer oven. Select the AIR FRY function and cook at 400ºF (205ºC) for 8 minutes, or until vegetables are beginning to brown.
3. While vegetable skewers cook, thread beef evenly onto remaining 2 skewers. Flip and rotate vegetable skewers, then arrange beef skewers on top, perpendicular to vegetable skewers. Return basket to air fryer oven and air fry until beef registers 130ºF (54ºC) to 135ºF (57ºC) (for medium) and vegetables are crisp-tender, 10 to 14 minutes, flipping and rotating beef skewers halfway through cooking.
4. Transfer skewers to serving platter, tent with aluminum foil, and let rest for 5 minutes. Whisk reserved oil mixture to recombine. Using fork, push beef and vegetables off skewers onto platter and drizzle with oil mixture. Serve.

Kielbasa and Onions with Pierogies
Prep time: 15 minutes | Cook time: 30 minutes | Serves 3 to 4

1 sweet onion, sliced
1 teaspoon olive oil
Salt and freshly ground black pepper, to taste
2 tablespoons butter, cut into small cubes
1 teaspoon sugar
1 pound (454 g) light Polish kielbasa
sausage, cut into 2-inch chunks
1 (13-ounce / 369-g) package frozen mini pierogies
2 teaspoons vegetable or olive oil
Chopped scallions, for garnish

1. Toss the sliced onions with olive oil, salt and pepper and transfer them to the air fryer basket. Dot the onions with pieces of butter. Select the AIR FRY function and cook at 400ºF (204ºC) for 2 minutes. Then sprinkle the sugar over the onions and stir. Pour any melted butter from the bottom of the air fryer oven drawer over the onions. Continue to air fry for another 13 minutes, stirring or shaking the basket every few minutes to air fry the onions evenly.
2. Add the kielbasa chunks to the onions and toss. Air fry for another 5 minutes, shaking the basket halfway through the cooking time. Transfer the kielbasa and onions to a bowl and cover with aluminum foil to keep warm.
3. Toss the frozen pierogies with the vegetable or olive oil and transfer them to the air fryer basket. Air fry for 8 minutes, shaking the basket twice during the cooking time.
4. When the pierogies have finished cooking, return the kielbasa and onions to the air fryer oven and gently toss with the pierogies. Air fry for 2 more minutes and then transfer everything to a serving platter. Garnish with the chopped scallions and serve hot.

Beef and Raisins Empanadas

Prep time: 20 minutes | Cook time: 21 minutes | Serves 4

2 tablespoons unsalted butter
1 yellow onion, diced
1 red bell pepper, diced
1 pound (454 g) ground beef
1½ tablespoons cumin
1 tablespoon paprika
1 teaspoon oregano
1 teaspoon kosher salt, plus more for seasoning
⅓ cup raisins
½ cup green olives, sliced
2 hard-boiled eggs, sliced
Juice of 1 lime
1 (12-ounce / 340-g) package frozen empanada discs, thawed
Vegetable oil for spraying

1. To make the empanada filling, heat the butter in a large, deep skillet over medium heat. When the butter is foamy, add the onion, season with salt, and sauté for 5 minutes. Add the bell pepper and sauté an additional 3 minutes. Add the ground beef and spices and cook, stirring, until the meat is no longer pink. Remove from the heat. Drain any accumulated fat from the pan. Add the raisins, green olives, and eggs, stir to combine, and allow to cool to room temperature. Add the lime juice and stir to combine. Taste and adjust the seasoning, adding more salt as necessary.
2. Remove 1 of the empanada wrappers from the package and place it on a board. Using a rolling pin, roll the wrapper out in each direction so that it is slightly larger. Place a heaping ¼ cup of the beef filling on 1 side of the empanada wrapper. Moisten the edges of the wrapper with a little water and fold the wrapper in half to form a half-moon shape. Press the dough closed around the filling and then crimp the edges of the dough with a fork to seal them shut. Place the filled empanada on a baking tray lined with parchment paper. Repeat with the remaing wrappers and filling.
3. Select the BAKE function and preheat MAXX to 375ºF (190ºC). Spray the air fryer basket and the empanadas with oil. Working in 2 batches, place 5 empanadas in the air fryer basket. Bake for 8 minutes, then turn the empanadas over. Bake until the second side is firm and baked, another 5 to 7 minutes. Repeat with the second batch of empanadas. Serve immediately.

Teriyaki Glazed Baby Back Ribs

Prep time: 10 minutes | Cook time: 1 hour | Serves 4

1 teaspoon Chinese five-spice powder
½ teaspoon garlic powder
1 teaspoon kosher salt
1 teaspoon black pepper
2½ to 3 pounds (1.1 to 1.4 kg) rack baby back ribs, cut into 4 pieces
¼ cup soy sauce, preferably low-sodium
1 tablespoon brown sugar
1 tablespoon vegetable oil
½ tablespoon grated fresh ginger
1 clove garlic, minced
3 teaspoons rice vinegar
1 teaspoon toasted sesame oil

1. Select the ROAST function and preheat MAXX to 250ºF (121ºC).
2. Combine the Chinese five-spice powder, garlic powder, salt, and pepper in a small bowl and whisk to combine. Place each rib section on a large piece of foil and sprinkle all over with the spice mixture. Wrap the foil tightly around each rib section.
3. Arrange the foil-wrapped ribs in the air fryer basket. Roast for 50 minutes. While the ribs are cooking, combine the soy sauce, brown sugar, oil, ginger, garlic, rice vinegar, and sesame oil in a small bowl and whisk until combined.
4. After 50 minutes, use tongs to remove the ribs from the air fryer oven and place on a rimmed baking sheet. Allow the ribs to cool slightly, then carefully remove from the foil.
5. Brush the ribs evenly with the sauce mixture and return to the air fryer oven. Select the AIR FRY function and cook at 400ºF (205ºC) for 10 minutes, occasionally basting the ribs with additional sauce. The ribs should be crispy, tender, and slightly charred when cooked. Brush the cooked ribs with any remaining sauce and serve immediately.

Lean Beef Meatballs with Zucchini Noodles

Prep time: 15 minutes | Cook time: 35 minutes | Serves 2

1 slice hearty white sandwich bread, crust removed, torn into ½-inch pieces
1 large egg
3 tablespoons milk
1 shallot, minced
1 ounce (28 g) Parmesan cheese, grated (½ cup), plus extra for serving
¼ cup chopped fresh basil
1 teaspoon garlic powder
Salt and pepper
1 pound (454 g) 93% lean ground beef
1 pound (454 g) zucchini noodles
2 teaspoons extra-virgin olive oil
¾ cup jarred marinara sauce, warmed

1. Select the ROAST function and preheat MAXX to 250ºF (121ºC).
2. Mash bread, egg, and milk into paste in large bowl using fork. Stir in shallot, Parmesan, 2 tablespoons basil, garlic powder, ¼ teaspoon salt, and ¼ teaspoon pepper. Break up ground beef into small pieces over bread mixture in bowl and lightly knead with hands until well combined. Pinch off and roll mixture into four meatballs.
3. Arrange meatballs in air fryer basket, spaced evenly apart. Place basket in air fryer oven. Roast for 20 minutes. Flip and rotate meatballs and continue to roast until well browned and register 160ºF (70ºC), 10 to 15 minutes. Transfer meatballs to serving platter, tent with aluminum foil, and let rest while preparing noodles.
4. Toss zucchini noodles in clean bowl with oil and season with salt and pepper. Arrange noodles in even layer in now-empty air fryer basket. Return basket to air fryer oven. Select the AIR FRY function and cook at 400ºF (205ºC) for 5 to 7 minutes, or until noodles are just tender. Divide zucchini noodles and meatballs between individual serving bowls and top with warm marinara sauce. Sprinkle with remaining 2 tablespoons basil and serve, passing extra Parmesan separately.

Steak Fingers

Prep time: 5 minutes | Cook time: 8 minutes | Serves 4

4 small beef cube steaks
Salt and ground black
pepper, to taste
½ cup flour
Cooking spray

1. Cut cube steaks into 1-inch-wide strips.
2. Sprinkle lightly with salt and pepper to taste.
3. Roll in flour to coat all sides.
4. Spritz air fryer basket with cooking spray.
5. Put steak strips in air fryer basket in a single layer. Spritz top of steak strips with cooking spray.
6. Select the AIR FRY function and cook at 390ºF (199ºC) for 4 minutes. Turn strips over, and spritz with cooking spray.
7. Air fry 4 more minutes and test with fork for doneness. Steak fingers should be crispy outside with no red juices inside.
8. Repeat with the remaining strips.
9. Serve immediately.

Chipotle Bacon Burst with Spinach

Prep time: 5 minutes | Cook time: 60 minutes | Serves 8

30 slices bacon
1 tablespoon Chipotle seasoning
2 teaspoons Italian
seasoning
2½ cups Cheddar cheese
4 cups raw spinach

1. Select the BAKE function and preheat MAXX to 375ºF (191ºC).
2. Weave the bacon into 15 vertical pieces and 12 horizontal pieces. Cut the extra 3 in half to fill in the rest, horizontally.
3. Season the bacon with Chipotle seasoning and Italian seasoning.
4. Add the cheese to the bacon.
5. Add the spinach and press down to compress.
6. Tightly roll up the woven bacon.
7. Line a baking sheet with kitchen foil and add plenty of salt to it.
8. Put the bacon on top of a cooling rack and put that on top of the baking sheet.
9. Bake for 60 minutes.
10. Let cool for 15 minutes before slicing and serving.

Beef Satay Skewers
Prep time: 25 minutes | Cook time: 6 minutes | Serves 2

1 tablespoon packed light brown sugar
2 teaspoons vegetable oil
1 teaspoon ground coriander
¼ teaspoon salt
⅛ teaspoon cayenne pepper
1 (12-ounce / 340-g) flank steak, ½ to ¾ inch thick, trimmed
10 (6-inch) wooden skewers
4 ounces (113 g) rice vermicelli
½ cup canned coconut milk
2 teaspoons Thai red curry paste
1 tablespoon lime juice, plus extra for seasoning
2 teaspoons fish sauce, plus extra for seasoning
1 small red bell pepper, stemmed, seeded, and cut into 2-inch-long matchsticks
4 ounces (113 g) snow peas, strings removed and sliced lengthwise into matchsticks
½ cup chopped fresh basil

1. Combine 1 teaspoon sugar, oil, coriander, salt, and cayenne in bowl. Slice steak against grain into ½-inch-thick slices (you should have at least 10 slices) and pat dry with paper towels. Add beef to sugar mixture and toss to coat. Weave beef evenly onto skewers, leaving 1 inch at bottom of skewer exposed.
2. Arrange half of beef skewers in air fryer basket, parallel to each other and spaced evenly apart. Arrange remaining skewers on top, perpendicular to bottom layer. Place basket in air fryer oven.
3. Select the AIR FRY function and cook at 400ºF (205ºC) for 6 to 8 minutes, or until beef is lightly browned, flipping and rotating skewers twice during cooking. Transfer skewers to serving platter, tent with aluminum foil, and let rest while preparing noodles.
4. Place noodles in large bowl and pour 6 cups boiling water over top. Stir noodles briefly to ensure they are completely submerged, then let soak, stirring occasionally, until tender, about 2 minutes. Drain noodles and set aside.
5. Whisk coconut milk, red curry paste, and remaining 2 teaspoons sugar together in now-empty bowl and microwave until fragrant, about 1 minute. Whisk in lime juice and fish sauce. Add noodles, bell pepper, snow peas, and basil and gently toss to coat. Season with extra lime juice and fish sauce to taste. Adjust consistency with hot water as needed. Serve beef skewers with noodles.

Mexican-Flavored Pork Chops
Prep time: 5 minutes | Cook time: 15 minutes | Serves 2

¼ teaspoon dried oregano
1½ teaspoons taco seasoning mix
2 (4-ounce / 113-g)
boneless pork chops
2 tablespoons unsalted butter, divided

1. Combine the dried oregano and taco seasoning in a small bowl and rub the mixture into the pork chops. Brush the chops with 1 tablespoon butter. Transfer to the air fryer basket.
2. Select the AIR FRY function and cook at 400ºF (204ºC) for 15 minutes, turning them over halfway through to air fry on the other side.
3. When the chops are a brown color, check the internal temperature has reached 145ºF (63ºC) and remove from the air fryer oven. Serve with a garnish of remaining butter.

Buttery Beef Loin with Thyme
Prep time: 5 minutes | Cook time: 15 minutes | Serves 4

1 tablespoon butter, melted
¼ dried thyme
1 teaspoon garlic salt
¼ teaspoon dried parsley
1 pound (454 g) beef loin

1. In a bowl, combine the melted butter, thyme, garlic salt, and parsley.
2. Cut the beef loin into slices and generously apply the seasoned butter using a brush. Transfer to the air fryer basket.
3. Select the AIR FRY function and cook at 400ºF (204ºC) for 15 minutes.
4. Take care when removing it and serve hot.

Sweet and Sour Pork
Prep time: 20 minutes | Cook time: 14 minutes | Serves 2 to 4

¹/₃ cup all-purpose flour
¹/₃ cup cornstarch
2 teaspoons Chinese five-spice powder
1 teaspoon salt
Freshly ground black pepper,to taste
1 egg
2 tablespoons milk
¾ pound (340 g) boneless pork, cut into 1-inch cubes
Vegetable or canola oil
1½ cups large chunks of red and green peppers
½ cup ketchup
2 tablespoons rice wine vinegar or apple cider vinegar
2 tablespoons brown sugar
¼ cup orange juice
1 tablespoon soy sauce
1 clove garlic, minced
1 cup cubed pineapple
Chopped scallions, for garnish

1. Set up a dredging station with two bowls. Combine the flour, cornstarch, Chinese five-spice powder, salt and pepper in one large bowl. Whisk the egg and milk together in a second bowl. Dredge the pork cubes in the flour mixture first, then dip them into the egg and then back into the flour to coat on all sides. Spray the coated pork cubes with vegetable or canola oil.
2. Toss the pepper chunks with a little oil and transfer to the air fryer basket. Select the AIR FRY function and cook at 400°F (204°C) for 5 minutes, shaking the basket halfway through the cooking time.
3. While the peppers are cooking, start making the sauce. Combine the ketchup, rice wine vinegar, brown sugar, orange juice, soy sauce, and garlic in a medium saucepan and bring the mixture to a boil on the stovetop. Reduce the heat and simmer for 5 minutes. When the peppers have finished air frying, add them to the saucepan along with the pineapple chunks. Simmer the peppers and pineapple in the sauce for an additional 2 minutes. Set aside and keep warm.
4. Add the dredged pork cubes to the air fryer basket and air fry for 6 minutes, shaking the basket to turn the cubes over for the last minute of the cooking process.
5. When ready to serve, toss the cooked pork with the pineapple, peppers and sauce. Serve garnished with chopped scallions.

Beef Steak with Dried Herb
Prep time: 5 minutes | Cook time: 22 minutes | Serves 6

1 teaspoon dried dill
1 teaspoon dried thyme
1 teaspoon garlic powder
2 pounds (907 g) beef steak
3 tablespoons butter

1. Combine the dill, thyme, and garlic powder in a small bowl, and massage into the steak. Transfer the steak to the air fryer basket.
2. Select the AIR FRY function and cook at 360°F (182°C) for 20 minutes. Then remove, shred, and return to the air fryer oven.
3. Add the butter and air fry the shredded steak for a further 2 minutes at 365°F (185°C). Make sure the beef is coated in the butter before serving.

Lamb Chops with Avocado Mayonnaise
Prep time: 5 minutes | Cook time: 12 minutes | Serves 2

2 lamp chops
2 teaspoons Italian herbs
2 avocados
½ cup mayonnaise
1 tablespoon lemon juice

1. Season the lamb chops with the Italian herbs, then set aside for 5 minutes.
2. Place the rack in the air fryer basket. Select the AIR FRY function and cook at 400°F (204°C) for 12 minutes.
3. In the meantime, halve the avocados and open to remove the pits. Spoon the flesh into a blender.
4. Add the mayonnaise and lemon juice and pulse until a smooth consistency is achieved.
5. Take care when removing the chops from the air fryer oven, then plate up and serve with the avocado mayo.

Beef and Kale Omelet
Prep time: 15 minutes | Cook time: 16 minutes | Serves 4

½ pound (227 g) leftover beef, coarsely chopped
2 garlic cloves, pressed
1 cup kale, torn into pieces and wilted
1 tomato, chopped
¼ teaspoon sugar
4 eggs, beaten
4 tablespoons heavy cream
½ teaspoon turmeric powder
Salt and ground black pepper, to taste
⅛ teaspoon ground allspice
Cooking spray

1. Spritz four ramekins with cooking spray.
2. Put equal amounts of each of the ingredients into each ramekin and mix well. Transfer to the air fryer oven.
3. Select the AIR FRY function and cook at 360ºF (182ºC) for 16 minutes.
4. Serve immediately.

Dijon Beef Burgers
Prep time: 15 minutes | Cook time: 18 minutes | Serves 3 to 4

1 pound (454 g) lean ground beef
⅓ cup panko bread crumbs
¼ cup finely chopped onion
3 tablespoons Dijon mustard
1 tablespoon chopped fresh thyme
4 teaspoons Worcestershire sauce
1 teaspoon salt
Freshly ground black pepper
Topping (optional):
2 tablespoons Dijon mustard
1 tablespoon dark brown sugar
1 teaspoon Worcestershire sauce
4 ounces (113 g) sliced Swiss cheese, optional

1. Combine all the burger ingredients together in a large bowl and mix well. Divide the meat into 4 equal portions and then form the burgers, being careful not to over-handle the meat. One good way to do this is to throw the meat back and forth from one hand to another, packing the meat each time you catch it. Flatten the balls into patties, making an indentation in the center of each patty with your thumb (this will help it stay flat as it cooks) and flattening the sides of the burgers so that they will fit nicely into the air fryer basket.
2. Select the AIR FRY function and cook at 370ºF (188ºC). If you don't have room for all four burgers, air fry two or three burgers at a time for 8 minutes. Flip the burgers over and air fry for another 6 minutes.
3. While the burgers are cooking combine the Dijon mustard, dark brown sugar, and Worcestershire sauce in a small bowl and mix well. This optional topping to the burgers really adds a boost of flavor at the end. Spread the Dijon topping evenly on each burger. If you cooked the burgers in batches, return the first batch to the cooker at this time – it's ok to place the fourth burger on top of the others in the center of the basket. Air fry the burgers for another 3 minutes.
4. Finally, if desired, top each burger with a slice of Swiss cheese. Reduce the temperature to 330ºF (166ºC) and air fry for another minute to melt the cheese. Serve the burgers on toasted brioche buns, dressed the way you like them.

Rosemary Lamb Chops
Prep time: 5 minutes | Cook time: 15 minutes | Serves 4

8 (3-ounce / 85-g) lamb chops
2 teaspoons extra-virgin olive oil
1½ teaspoons
chopped fresh rosemary
1 garlic clove, minced
Salt
Pepper

1. Select the ROAST function and preheat MAXX to 390ºF (199ºC).
2. Drizzle the lamb chops with olive oil.
3. In a small bowl, combine the rosemary, garlic, and salt and pepper to taste. Rub the seasoning onto the front and back of each lamb chop.
4. Place the lamb chops in the air fryer oven. It is okay to stack them. Roast for 10 minutes.
5. Open the air fryer oven. Flip the lamb chops. Roast for an additional 5 minutes.
6. Cool before serving.

Simple Beef Schnitzel
Prep time: 5 minutes | Cook time: 12 minutes | Serves 1

½ cup friendly bread crumbs	Pepper and salt, to taste
2 tablespoons olive oil	1 egg, beaten
	1 thin beef schnitzel

1. In a shallow dish, combine the bread crumbs, oil, pepper, and salt.
2. In a second shallow dish, place the beaten egg.
3. Dredge the schnitzel in the egg before rolling it in the bread crumbs.
4. Put the coated schnitzel in the air fryer basket. Select the AIR FRY function and cook at 350ºF (177ºC) for 12 minutes. Flip the schnitzel halfway through.
5. Serve immediately.

Feta Lamb Burger
Prep time: 15 minutes | Cook time: 16 minutes | Serves 3 to 4

2 teaspoons olive oil	oregano, finely chopped
⅓ onion, finely chopped	½ cup black olives, finely chopped
1 clove garlic, minced	⅓ cup crumbled feta cheese
1 pound (454 g) ground lamb	½ teaspoon salt
2 tablespoons fresh parsley, finely chopped	Freshly ground black pepper, to taste
1½ teaspoons fresh	4 thick pita breads

1. Preheat a medium skillet over medium-high heat on the stovetop. Add the olive oil and cook the onion until tender, but not browned about 4 to 5 minutes. Add the garlic and cook for another minute. Transfer the onion and garlic to a mixing bowl and add the ground lamb, parsley, oregano, olives, feta cheese, salt and pepper. Gently mix the ingredients together.
2. Divide the mixture into 3 or 4 equal portions and then form the hamburgers, being careful not to over-handle the meat. One good way to do this is to throw the meat back and forth between the hands like a baseball, packing the meat each time you catch it. Flatten the balls into patties, making an indentation in the center of each patty. Flatten the sides of the patties as well to make it easier to fit them into the air fryer basket.
3. Select the AIR FRY function and cook at 370ºF (188ºC) for 8 minutes. Flip the burgers over and air fry for another 8 minutes. If you cooked the burgers in batches, return the first batch of burgers to the air fryer oven for the last two minutes of cooking to re-heat. This should give you a medium-well burger. If you'd prefer a medium-rare burger, shorten the cooking time to about 13 minutes. Remove the burgers to a resting plate and let the burgers rest for a few minutes before dressing and serving.
4. While the burgers are resting, switch from AIR FRY to BAKE and bake the pita breads in the air fryer oven for 2 minutes. Tuck the burgers into the toasted pita breads, or wrap the pitas around the burgers and serve with a tzatziki sauce or some mayonnaise.

Miso Marinated Flank Steak
Prep time: 5 minutes | Cook time: 12 minutes | Serves 4

¾ pound (340 g) flank steak	1 teaspoon honey
1½ tablespoons sake	2 cloves garlic, pressed
1 tablespoon brown miso paste	1 tablespoon olive oil

1. Put all the ingredients in a Ziploc bag. Shake to cover the steak well with the seasonings and refrigerate for at least 1 hour.
2. Coat all sides of the steak with cooking spray. Put the steak in the baking pan.
3. Select the AIR FRY function and cook at 400ºF (204ºC) for 12 minutes, turning the steak twice during the cooking time, then serve immediately.

Lamb Meatballs with Tomato Sauce

Prep time: 20 minutes | Cook time: 8 minutes | Serves 4

Meatballs:

½ small onion, finely diced	oregano, finely chopped
1 clove garlic, minced	2 tablespoons milk
1 pound (454 g) ground lamb	1 egg yolk
2 tablespoons fresh parsley, finely chopped (plus more for garnish)	Salt and freshly ground black pepper, to taste
2 teaspoons fresh	½ cup crumbled feta cheese, for garnish

Tomato Sauce:

2 tablespoons butter	cinnamon
1 clove garlic, smashed	1 (28-ounce / 794-g) can crushed tomatoes
Pinch crushed red pepper flakes	Salt, to taste
¼ teaspoon ground	Olive oil, for greasing

1. Combine all ingredients for the meatballs in a large bowl and mix just until everything is combined. Shape the mixture into 1½-inch balls or shape the meat between two spoons to make quenelles.
2. While the air fryer oven is preheating, start the quick tomato sauce. Put the butter, garlic and red pepper flakes in a sauté pan and heat over medium heat on the stovetop. Let the garlic sizzle a little, but before the butter browns, add the cinnamon and tomatoes. Bring to a simmer and simmer for 15 minutes. Season with salt.
3. Grease the bottom of the air fryer basket with olive oil and transfer the meatballs to the air fryer basket in one layer, air frying in batches if necessary.
4. Select the AIR FRY function and cook at 400ºF (204ºC) for 8 minutes, giving the basket a shake once during the cooking process to turn the meatballs over.
5. To serve, spoon a pool of the tomato sauce onto plates and add the meatballs. Sprinkle the feta cheese on top and garnish with more fresh parsley.

Mongolian-Style Flank Steak

Prep time: 20 minutes | Cook time: 15 minutes | Serves 4

1½ pounds (680 g) flank steak, thinly	sliced on the bias into ¼-inch strips

Marinade:

2 tablespoons soy sauce	smashed
1 clove garlic,	Pinch crushed red pepper flakes

Sauce:

1 tablespoon vegetable oil	¾ cup chicken stock
2 cloves garlic, minced	5 to 6 tablespoons brown sugar
1 tablespoon finely grated fresh ginger	½ cup cornstarch, divided
3 dried red chili peppers	1 bunch scallions, sliced into 2-inch pieces
¾ cup soy sauce	

1. Marinate the beef in the soy sauce, garlic and red pepper flakes for one hour.
2. In the meantime, make the sauce. Preheat a small saucepan over medium heat on the stovetop. Add the oil, garlic, ginger and dried chili peppers and sauté for just a minute or two. Add the soy sauce, chicken stock and brown sugar and continue to simmer for a few minutes. Dissolve 3 tablespoons of cornstarch in 3 tablespoons of water and stir this into the saucepan. Stir the sauce over medium heat until it thickens. Set this aside.
3. Remove the beef from the marinade and transfer it to a zipper sealable plastic bag with the remaining cornstarch. Shake it around to completely coat the beef and transfer the coated strips of beef to a baking sheet or plate, shaking off any excess cornstarch. Spray the strips with vegetable oil on all sides and transfer them to the air fryer basket.
4. Select the AIR FRY function and cook at 400ºF (204ºC) for 15 minutes, shaking the basket to toss and rotate the beef strips throughout the cooking process. Add the scallions for the last 4 minutes of the cooking. Transfer the hot beef strips and scallions to a bowl and toss with the sauce, coating all the beef strips with the sauce. Serve warm.

Beef and Cheese Hand Pies

Prep time: 10 minutes | Cook time: 12 minutes | Makes 8 pies

8 ounces (227 g) 93% lean ground beef
3 garlic cloves, minced
2 teaspoons chili powder
1 teaspoon ground cumin
1 teaspoon minced fresh oregano or ¼ teaspoon dried
4 ounces (113 g) Monterey Jack cheese, shredded
1 cup mild tomato salsa, drained
2 tablespoons chopped fresh cilantro
1 package store-bought pie dough
1 large egg, lightly beaten

1. Microwave beef, garlic, chili powder, cumin, and oregano in bowl, stirring occasionally and breaking up meat with wooden spoon, until beef is no longer pink, about 3 minutes. Transfer beef mixture to fine-mesh strainer set over large bowl and let drain for 10 minutes; discard juices. Return drained beef mixture to now-empty bowl and stir in Monterey Jack, salsa, and cilantro.
2. Roll 1 dough round into 12-inch circle on lightly floured counter. Using 5-inch round biscuit cutter, stamp out 4 rounds; discard dough scraps. Repeat with remaining dough round. Mound beef mixture evenly in center of each stamped round. Fold dough over filling and crimp edges with fork to seal. Transfer hand pies to parchment paper–lined rimmed baking sheet, brush with egg, and freeze until firm, about 1 hour. (Hand pies can be transferred to zipper-lock bag and stored in freezer for up to 2 weeks; do not thaw before cooking.)
3. Select the BAKE function and preheat MAXX to 350ºF (180ºC).
4. Lightly spray base of air fryer basket with vegetable oil spray. Arrange up to 2 hand pies in prepared basket, spaced evenly apart. Place basket in air fryer oven.
5. Bake for 12 to 15 minutes, or until hand pies are golden brown. Transfer to wire rack and let cool slightly. Serve.

Beef Cheeseburgers with Taco Seasoning

Prep time: 10 minutes | Cook time: 22 minutes | Serves 4

1¼ pounds (567 g) ground beef
¼ cup finely chopped onion
½ cup crushed yellow corn tortilla chips
1 (1¼-ounce / 35-g) packet taco seasoning
¼ cup canned diced green chilies
1 egg, lightly beaten
4 ounces (113 g) Pepper Jack cheese, grated
4 (12-inch) flour tortillas
Shredded lettuce, sour cream, guacamole, salsa (for topping)

1. Combine the ground beef, minced onion, crushed tortilla chips, taco seasoning, green chilies, and egg in a large bowl. Mix thoroughly until combined – your hands are good tools for this. Divide the meat into four equal portions and shape each portion into an oval-shaped burger. Transfer to the air fryer basket.
2. Select the AIR FRY function and cook at 370ºF (188ºC) for 18 minutes, turning them over halfway through the cooking time.
3. Divide the cheese between the burgers. Reduce the temperature to 340ºF (171ºC) and air fry for an additional 4 minutes to melt the cheese.
4. While the burgers are cooking, warm the tortillas wrapped in aluminum foil in a 350ºF (180ºC) oven, or in a skillet with a little oil over medium-high heat for a couple of minutes. Keep the tortillas warm until the burgers are ready.
5. To assemble the burgers, spread sour cream over three quarters of the tortillas and top each with some shredded lettuce and salsa. Place the Mexican cheeseburgers on the lettuce and top with guacamole. Fold the tortillas around the burger, starting with the bottom and then folding the sides in over the top. (A little sour cream can help hold the seam of the tortilla together.) Serve immediately.

Marinated Pork Tenderloin Roast
Prep time: 10 minutes | Cook time: 30 minutes | Serves 4 to 6

¼ cup olive oil
¼ cup soy sauce
¼ cup freshly squeezed lemon juice
1 garlic clove, minced
1 tablespoon Dijon mustard
1 teaspoon salt
½ teaspoon freshly ground black pepper
2 pounds (907 g) pork tenderloin

1. In a large mixing bowl, make the marinade: Mix the olive oil, soy sauce, lemon juice, minced garlic, Dijon mustard, salt, and pepper. Reserve ¼ cup of the marinade.
2. Put the tenderloin in a large bowl and pour the remaining marinade over the meat. Cover and marinate in the refrigerator for about 1 hour.
3. Select the ROAST function and preheat MAXX to 400ºF (204ºC).
4. Put the marinated pork tenderloin into the air fryer basket. Roast for 10 minutes. Flip the pork and baste it with half of the reserved marinade. Roast for 10 minutes more.
5. Flip the pork, then baste with the remaining marinade. Roast for another 10 minutes, for a total cooking time of 30 minutes.
6. Serve immediately.

Lollipop Lamb Chops with Mint Pesto
Prep time: 15 minutes | Cook time: 7 minutes | Serves 4

½ small clove garlic
¼ cup packed fresh parsley
¾ cup packed fresh mint
½ teaspoon lemon juice
¼ cup grated Parmesan cheese
⅓ cup shelled pistachios
¼ teaspoon salt
½ cup olive oil
8 lamb chops (1 rack)
2 tablespoons vegetable oil
Salt and freshly ground black pepper, to taste
1 tablespoon dried rosemary, chopped
1 tablespoon dried thyme

1. Make the pesto by combining the garlic, parsley and mint in a food processor and process until finely chopped. Add the lemon juice, Parmesan cheese, pistachios and salt. Process until all the ingredients have turned into a paste. With the processor running, slowly pour the olive oil in. Scrape the sides of the processor with a spatula and process for another 30 seconds.
2. Rub both sides of the lamb chops with vegetable oil and season with salt, pepper, rosemary and thyme, pressing the herbs into the meat gently with the fingers. Transfer the lamb chops to the air fryer basket.
3. Select the AIR FRY function and cook at 400ºF (204ºC) for 5 minutes. Flip the chops over and air fry for an additional 2 minutes.
4. Serve the lamb chops with mint pesto drizzled on top.

Greek Lamb Rib Rack
Prep time: 5 minutes | Cook time: 10 minutes | Serves 4

¼ cup freshly squeezed lemon juice
1 teaspoon oregano
2 teaspoons minced fresh rosemary
1 teaspoon minced fresh thyme
2 tablespoons minced garlic
Salt and freshly ground black pepper, to taste
2 to 4 tablespoons olive oil
1 lamb rib rack (7 to 8 ribs)

1. Select the ROAST function and preheat MAXX to 360ºF (182ºC).
2. In a small mixing bowl, combine the lemon juice, oregano, rosemary, thyme, garlic, salt, pepper, and olive oil and mix well.
3. Rub the mixture over the lamb, covering all the meat. Put the rack of lamb in the air fryer oven. Roast for 10 minutes. Flip the rack halfway through.
4. After 10 minutes, measure the internal temperature of the rack of lamb reaches at least 145ºF (63ºC).
5. Serve immediately.

Ham and Cheese Stromboli

Prep time: 10 minutes | Cook time: 20 minutes | Serves 6

1 teaspoon all-purpose flour
1 (13-ounce / 369-g) can refrigerated pizza dough
6 slices provolone cheese
½ cup shredded Mozzarella cheese
12 slices deli ham

½ red bell pepper, seeded and sliced
½ teaspoon dried basil
½ teaspoon oregano
Pepper
Cooking oil

1. Sprinkle the flour on a flat work surface. Roll out the pizza dough. Cut the dough into 6 equal-sized rectangles.
2. Add 1 slice of provolone, 1 tablespoon of Mozzarella, 2 slices of ham, and a few slices of red bell pepper to each of the rectangles.
3. Season each with dried basil, oregano, and pepper to taste.
4. Fold up each crust to close the stromboli. Using the back of a fork, press along the open edges to seal.
5. Place the stromboli in the air fryer oven. Do not stack. Work in batches. Spray the stromboli with cooking oil. Select the AIR FRY function and cook at 400ºF (205ºC) for 10 minutes.
6. Remove the cooked stromboli from the air fryer oven, then repeat with the remaining stromboli.
7. Cool before serving.

Beef and Mushroom Meatloaf

Prep time: 10 minutes | Cook time: 25 minutes | Serves 4

1 pound (454 g) ground beef
1 egg, beaten
1 mushrooms, sliced
1 tablespoon thyme

1 small onion, chopped
3 tablespoons bread crumbs
Ground black pepper, to taste

1. Select the BAKE function and preheat MAXX to 400ºF (204ºC).
2. Put all the ingredients into a large bowl and combine entirely.
3. Transfer the meatloaf mixture into the loaf pan and move it to the air fryer basket.
4. Bake for 25 minutes. Slice up before serving.

Chapter 7 Vegan and Vegetarian

Falafel Balls with Tomato Salad

Prep time: 20 minutes | Cook time: 10 minutes | Serves 4

1 cup dried chickpeas
½ onion, chopped
1 clove garlic
¼ cup fresh parsley leaves
1 teaspoon salt
¼ teaspoon crushed red pepper flakes

1 teaspoon ground cumin
½ teaspoon ground coriander
1 to 2 tablespoons flour
Olive oil

Tomato Salad:

2 tomatoes, seeds removed and diced
½ cucumber, finely diced
¼ red onion, finely diced and rinsed with water
1 teaspoon red wine

vinegar
1 tablespoon olive oil
Salt and freshly ground black pepper
2 tablespoons chopped fresh parsley

1. Cover the chickpeas with water and let them soak overnight on the counter. Then drain the chickpeas and put them in a food processor, along with the onion, garlic, parsley, spices and 1 tablespoon of flour. Pulse in the food processor until the mixture has broken down into a coarse paste consistency. The mixture should hold together when you pinch it. Add more flour as needed, until you get this consistency.
2. Scoop portions of the mixture (about 2 tablespoons in size) and shape into balls. Place the balls on a plate and refrigerate for at least 30 minutes. You should have between 12 and 14 balls.
3. Spray the falafel balls with oil and place them in the air fryer basket. Select the AIR FRY function and cook at 380°F (193°C) for 10 minutes, rolling them over and spraying them with oil again halfway through the cooking time so that they cook and brown evenly.
4. Serve with pita bread, hummus, cucumbers, hot peppers, tomatoes or any other fillings you might like.

Mediterranean Fried Vegetable

Prep time: 10 minutes | Cook time: 6 minutes | Serves 4

1 large zucchini, sliced
1 cup cherry tomatoes, halved
1 parsnip, sliced
1 green pepper, sliced
1 carrot, sliced
1 teaspoon mixed

herbs
1 teaspoon mustard
1 teaspoon garlic purée
6 tablespoons olive oil
Salt and ground black pepper, to taste

1. Combine all the ingredients in a bowl, making sure to coat the vegetables well.
2. Transfer to the air fryer oven. Select the AIR FRY function and cook at 400°F (204°C) for 6 minutes, ensuring the vegetables are tender and browned.
3. Serve immediately.

Tomato and Black Bean Chili

Prep time: 15 minutes | Cook time: 23 minutes | Serves 6

1 tablespoon olive oil
1 medium onion, diced
3 garlic cloves, minced
1 cup vegetable broth
3 cans black beans, drained and rinsed
2 cans diced

tomatoes
2 chipotle peppers, chopped
2 teaspoons cumin
2 teaspoons chili powder
1 teaspoon dried oregano
½ teaspoon salt

1. Over a medium heat, fry the garlic and onions in the olive oil for 3 minutes.
2. Add the remaining ingredients, stirring constantly and scraping the bottom to prevent sticking.
3. Select the BAKE function and preheat MAXX to 400°F (204°C).
4. Take a dish and place the mixture inside. Put a sheet of aluminum foil on top.
5. Transfer to the air fryer oven and bake for 20 minutes.
6. When ready, plate up and serve immediately.

Maple Brussels Sprouts

Prep time: 5 minutes | Cook time: 13 minutes | Serves 2

2 cups Brussels sprouts, halved
1 tablespoon olive oil
1 tablespoon
balsamic vinegar
1 tablespoon maple syrup
¼ teaspoon sea salt

1. Evenly coat the Brussels sprouts with the olive oil, balsamic vinegar, maple syrup, and salt.
2. Transfer to the air fryer basket. Select the AIR FRY function and cook at 375ºF (191ºC) for 5 minutes.
3. Give the basket a good shake, turn the heat to 400ºF (204ºC) and continue to air fry for another 8 minutes.
4. Serve hot.

Arugula, Fig, and Chickpea Salad

Prep time: 15 minutes | Cook time: 20 minutes | Serves 4

8 fresh figs, halved
1½ cups cooked chickpeas
1 teaspoon crushed roasted cumin seeds
4 tablespoons balsamic vinegar
2 tablespoons extra-
virgin olive oil, plus more for greasing
Salt and ground black pepper, to taste
3 cups arugula rocket, washed and dried

1. Cover the air fryer basket with aluminum foil and grease lightly with oil. Put the figs in the air fryer basket. Select the AIR FRY function and cook at 375ºF (191ºC) for 10 minutes.
2. In a bowl, combine the chickpeas and cumin seeds.
3. Remove the air fried figs from the air fryer oven and replace with the chickpeas. Air fry for 10 minutes. Leave to cool.
4. In the meantime, prepare the dressing. Mix the balsamic vinegar, olive oil, salt and pepper.
5. In a salad bowl, combine the arugula rocket with the cooled figs and chickpeas.
6. Toss with the sauce and serve.

Basmati Rice Risotto

Prep time: 10 minutes | Cook time: 30 minutes | Serves 2

1 onion, diced
1 small carrot, diced
2 cups vegetable broth, boiling
½ cup grated Cheddar cheese
1 clove garlic, minced
¾ cup long-grain basmati rice
1 tablespoon olive oil
1 tablespoon unsalted butter

1. Select the BAKE function and preheat MAXX to 390ºF (199ºC).
2. Grease a baking tin with oil and stir in the butter, garlic, carrot, and onion.
3. Put the tin in the air fryer oven and bake for 4 minutes.
4. Pour in the rice and bake for a further 4 minutes, stirring three times throughout the baking time.
5. Turn the temperature down to 320ºF (160ºC).
6. Add the vegetable broth and give the dish a gentle stir. Bake for 22 minutes, leaving the air fryer oven uncovered.
7. Pour in the cheese, stir once more and serve.

Cauliflower and Chickpea Flatbread with Avocado

Prep time: 10 minutes | Cook time: 25 minutes | Serves 4

1 medium head cauliflower, cut into florets
1 can chickpeas, drained and rinsed
1 tablespoon extra-virgin olive oil
2 tablespoons lemon juice
Salt and ground black pepper, to taste
4 flatbreads, toasted
2 ripe avocados, mashed

1. In a bowl, mix the chickpeas, cauliflower, lemon juice and olive oil. Sprinkle salt and pepper as desired.
2. Put inside the air fryer basket. Select the AIR FRY function and cook at 425ºF (218ºC) for 25 minutes.
3. Spread on top of the flatbread along with the mashed avocado. Sprinkle with more pepper and salt and serve.

Blistered Shishito Peppers with Lemony Cream

Prep time: 10 minutes | Cook time: 6 minutes | Serves 4

Dipping Sauce:

1 cup sour cream
2 tablespoons fresh lemon juice
1 clove garlic, minced

1 green onion (white and green parts), finely chopped

Peppers:

8 ounces (227 g) shishito peppers
1 tablespoon vegetable oil
1 teaspoon toasted sesame oil

Kosher salt and black pepper, to taste
¼ to ½ teaspoon red pepper flakes
½ teaspoon toasted sesame seeds

1. In a small bowl, stir all the ingredients for the dipping sauce to combine. Cover and refrigerate until serving time.
2. In a medium bowl, toss the peppers with the vegetable oil. Put the peppers in the air fryer basket. Select the AIR FRY function and cook at 400ºF (204ºC) for 6 minutes, or until peppers are lightly charred in spots, stirring the peppers halfway through the cooking time.
3. Transfer the peppers to a serving bowl. Drizzle with the sesame oil and toss to coat. Season with salt and pepper. Sprinkle with the red pepper and sesame seeds and toss again.
4. Serve immediately with the dipping sauce.

Parmesan Spinach

Prep time: 10 minutes | Cook time: 15 minutes | Serves 4

Vegetable oil spray
1 (10-ounce / 283-g) package frozen spinach, thawed and squeezed dry
½ cup chopped onion
2 cloves garlic, minced
4 ounces (113 g)

cream cheese, diced
½ teaspoon ground nutmeg
1 teaspoon kosher salt
1 teaspoon black pepper
½ cup grated Parmesan cheese

1. Select the BAKE function and preheat MAXX to 350ºF (177ºC). Spray a heatproof pan with vegetable oil spray.

2. In a medium bowl, combine the spinach, onion, garlic, cream cheese, nutmeg, salt, and pepper. Transfer to the prepared pan.
3. Put the pan in the air fryer basket. Bake for 10 minutes. Open and stir to thoroughly combine the cream cheese and spinach.
4. Sprinkle the Parmesan cheese on top. Bake for 5 minutes, or until the cheese has melted and browned.
5. Serve hot.

Cauliflower Faux Rice in Omelet

Prep time: 15 minutes | Cook time: 40 minutes | Serves 8

1 large head cauliflower, rinsed and drained, cut into florets
½ lemon, juiced
2 garlic cloves, minced
2 (8-ounce / 227-g) cans mushrooms
1 (8-ounce / 227-g) can water chestnuts

¾ cup peas
1 egg, beaten
4 tablespoons soy sauce
1 tablespoon peanut oil
1 tablespoon sesame oil
1 tablespoon minced fresh ginger
Cooking spray

1. Mix the peanut oil, soy sauce, sesame oil, minced ginger, lemon juice, and minced garlic to combine well.
2. In a food processor, pulse the florets in small batches to break them down to resemble rice grains. Pour into the air fryer basket.
3. Drain the chestnuts and roughly chop them. Pour into the basket. Select the AIR FRY function and cook at 350ºF (177ºC) for 20 minutes.
4. In the meantime, drain the mushrooms. Add the mushrooms and the peas to the air fryer oven and continue to air fry for another 15 minutes.
5. Lightly spritz a frying pan with cooking spray. Prepare an omelet with the beaten egg, ensuring it is firm. Lay on a cutting board and slice it up.
6. When the cauliflower is ready, throw in the omelet. Switch from AIR FRY to BAKE and bake for an additional 5 minutes. Serve hot.

Maple Glazed Brussels Sprouts

Prep time: 10 minutes | Cook time: 20 to 27 minutes | Serves 4

1½ pounds (680 g) Brussels sprouts, trimmed and, if large, halved
1 tablespoon extra-virgin olive oil
½ teaspoon kosher salt

3 tablespoons soy sauce
2 tablespoons maple syrup
Juice and zest of 1 lime
1 clove garlic, minced
1 tablespoon Sriracha

1. Toss the Brussels sprouts with the olive oil and salt. Working in batches if necessary, arrange the sprouts in a single layer in the air fryer basket. Select the AIR FRY function and cook at 375ºF (190ºC) for 15 to 20 minutes, or until browned, crispy, and fork-tender.
2. While the Brussels sprouts are cooking, combine the soy sauce, maple syrup, lime zest and juice, garlic, and sriracha in a small saucepan. Bring to a boil over medium heat. Reduce the heat and simmer until thickened and slightly syrupy, 5 to 7 minutes.
3. Remove the Brussels sprouts from the air fryer oven. (If you were not able to fit all the Brussels sprouts in the air fryer oven, cook the remaining Brussels sprouts in the same manner.) Place the Brussels sprouts in a serving bowl and drizzle the maple-soy sauce over them. Stir to coat the sprouts with the sauce and serve warm.

Chermoula Beet Roast

Prep time: 15 minutes | Cook time: 25 minutes | Serves 4

Chermoula:

1 cup packed fresh cilantro leaves
½ cup packed fresh parsley leaves
6 cloves garlic, peeled
2 teaspoons smoked paprika
2 teaspoons ground cumin

1 teaspoon ground coriander
½ to 1 teaspoon cayenne pepper
Pinch of crushed saffron (optional)
½ cup extra-virgin olive oil
Kosher salt, to taste

Beets:

3 medium beets, trimmed, peeled, and cut into 1-inch chunks
2 tablespoons

chopped fresh cilantro
2 tablespoons chopped fresh parsley

1. In a food processor, combine the cilantro, parsley, garlic, paprika, cumin, coriander, and cayenne. Pulse until coarsely chopped. Add the saffron, if using, and process until combined. With the food processor running, slowly add the olive oil in a steady stream; process until the sauce is uniform. Season with salt.
2. Select the ROAST function and preheat MAXX to 375ºF (191ºC).
3. In a large bowl, drizzle the beets with ½ cup of the chermoula to coat. Arrange the beets in the air fryer basket. Roast for 25 to minutes, or until the beets are tender.
4. Transfer the beets to a serving platter. Sprinkle with the chopped cilantro and parsley and serve.

Super Veggie Rolls

Prep time: 20 minutes | Cook time: 10 minutes | Serves 6

2 potatoes, mashed
¼ cup peas
¼ cup mashed carrots
1 small cabbage, sliced
¼ cups beans
2 tablespoons

sweetcorn
1 small onion, chopped
½ cup bread crumbs
1 packet spring roll sheets
½ cup cornstarch slurry

1. Boil all the vegetables in water over a low heat. Rinse and allow to dry.
2. Unroll the spring roll sheets and spoon equal amounts of vegetable onto the center of each one. Fold into spring rolls and coat each one with the slurry and bread crumbs.
3. Select the AIR FRY function and cook the rolls in the air fryer oven at 390ºF (199ºC) for 10 minutes.
4. Serve warm.

Red Potatoes with Chives

Prep time: 5 minutes | Cook time: 20 minutes | Serves 4

6 red potatoes, cut into 1-inch cubes
3 garlic cloves, minced
Salt
Pepper
1 teaspoon chopped chives
1 tablespoon extra-virgin olive oil

1. Select the BAKE function and preheat MAXX to 370ºF (188ºC).
2. In a sealable plastic bag, combine the potatoes, garlic, salt and pepper to taste, chives, and olive oil. Seal the bag and shake to coat the potatoes.
3. Transfer the potatoes to the air fryer basket. Bake for 10 minutes.
4. Open the air fryer oven and shake the basket. Bake for an additional 10 minutes.
5. Cool before serving.

Summer Veggie Rolls

Prep time: 15 minutes | Cook time: 15 minutes | Serves 4

1 cup shiitake mushroom, sliced thinly
1 celery stalk, chopped
1 medium carrot, shredded
½ teaspoon finely chopped ginger
1 teaspoon sugar
1 tablespoon soy sauce
1 teaspoon nutritional yeast
8 spring roll sheets
1 teaspoon corn starch
2 tablespoons water

1. In a bowl, combine the ginger, soy sauce, nutritional yeast, carrots, celery, mushroom, and sugar.
2. Mix the cornstarch and water to create an adhesive for the spring rolls.
3. Scoop a tablespoonful of the vegetable mixture into the middle of the spring roll sheets. Brush the edges of the sheets with the cornstarch adhesive and enclose around the filling to make spring rolls.
4. Place the rolls in the air fryer basket. Select the AIR FRY function and cook at 400ºF (204ºC) for 15 minutes, or until crisp.
5. Serve hot.

Mushroom and Bell Pepper Pizza Squares

Prep time: 10 minutes | Cook time: 10 minutes | Serves 10

1 pizza dough, cut into squares
1 cup chopped oyster mushrooms
1 shallot, chopped
¼ red bell pepper, chopped
2 tablespoons parsley
Salt and ground black pepper, to taste

1. Select the BAKE function and preheat MAXX to 400ºF (204ºC).
2. In a bowl, combine the oyster mushrooms, shallot, bell pepper and parsley. Sprinkle some salt and pepper as desired.
3. Spread this mixture on top of the pizza squares.
4. Bake in the air fryer oven for 10 minutes.
5. Serve warm.

Golden Ravioli

Prep time: 10 minutes | Cook time: 6 minutes | Serves 4

½ cup panko bread crumbs
2 teaspoons nutritional yeast
1 teaspoon dried basil
1 teaspoon dried oregano
1 teaspoon garlic powder
Salt and ground black pepper, to taste
¼ cup aquafaba
8 ounces (227 g) ravioli
Cooking spray

1. Cover the air fryer basket with aluminum foil and coat with a light brushing of oil.
2. Combine the panko bread crumbs, nutritional yeast, basil, oregano, and garlic powder. Sprinkle with salt and pepper to taste.
3. Put the aquafaba in a separate bowl. Dip the ravioli in the aquafaba before coating it in the panko mixture. Spritz with cooking spray and transfer to the air fryer oven.
4. Select the AIR FRY function and cook at 400ºF (204ºC) for 6 minutes. Shake the air fryer basket halfway.
5. Serve hot.

Russet Potato Gratin with Cheese
Prep time: 10 minutes | Cook time: 35 minutes | Serves 6

½ cup milk
7 medium russet potatoes, peeled
Salt, to taste
1 teaspoon black pepper
½ cup heavy whipping cream
½ cup grated semi-mature cheese
½ teaspoon nutmeg

1. Select the BAKE function and preheat MAXX to 390ºF (199ºC).
2. Cut the potatoes into wafer-thin slices.
3. In a bowl, combine the milk and cream and sprinkle with salt, pepper, and nutmeg.
4. Use the milk mixture to coat the slices of potatoes. Put in a baking dish. Top the potatoes with the rest of the milk mixture.
5. Put the baking dish into the air fryer basket and bake for 25 minutes.
6. Pour the cheese over the potatoes.
7. Bake for an additional 10 minutes, ensuring the top is nicely browned before serving.

Butternut Squash, Parsnips, and Celery Roast
Prep time: 15 minutes | Cook time: 20 minutes | Serves 6

1⅓ cups small parsnips, peeled and cubed
1⅓ cups celery
2 red onions, sliced
1⅓ cups small butternut squash, cut
in half, deseeded and cubed
1 tablespoon fresh thyme needles
1 tablespoon olive oil
Salt and ground black pepper, to taste

1. Select the ROAST function and preheat MAXX to 390ºF (199ºC).
2. Combine the cut vegetables with the thyme, olive oil, salt and pepper.
3. Put the vegetables in the basket and transfer the basket to the air fryer oven.
4. Roast for 20 minutes, stirring once throughout the roasting time, until the vegetables are nicely browned and cooked through.
5. Serve warm.

Asparagus and Mushroom Soufflés with Cheese
Prep time: 10 minutes | Cook time: 21 minutes | Serves 3

Butter
Grated Parmesan cheese
3 button mushrooms, thinly sliced
8 spears asparagus, sliced ½-inch long
1 teaspoon olive oil
1 tablespoon butter
4½ teaspoons flour
Pinch paprika
Pinch ground nutmeg
Salt and freshly ground black pepper
½ cup milk
½ cup grated Gruyère cheese or other Swiss cheese
2 eggs, separated

1. Butter 3 ramekins and dust with grated Parmesan cheese. (Butter the ramekins and then coat the butter with Parmesan by shaking it around in the ramekin and dumping out any excess.)
2. Toss the mushrooms and asparagus in a bowl with the olive oil. Transfer the vegetables to the air fryer basket. Select the AIR FRY function and cook at 400ºF (205ºC) for 7 minutes, shaking the basket once or twice to redistribute the ingredients while they cook.
3. While the vegetables are cooking, make the soufflé base. Melt the butter in a saucepan on the stovetop over medium heat. Add the flour, stir and cook for a minute or two. Add the paprika, nutmeg, salt and pepper. Whisk in the milk and bring the mixture to a simmer to thicken. Remove the pan from the heat and add the cheese, stirring to melt. Let the mixture cool for just a few minutes and then whisk the egg yolks in, one at a time. Stir in the cooked mushrooms and asparagus. Let this soufflé base cool.
4. In a separate bowl, whisk the egg whites to soft peak stage (the point at which the whites can almost stand up on the end of your whisk). Fold the whipped egg whites into the soufflé base, adding a little at a time.
5. Transfer the batter carefully to the buttered ramekins, leaving about ½-inch at the top. Place the ramekins into the air fryer basket. Select the AIR FRY function and cook at 330ºF (166ºC) for 14 minutes. The soufflés should have risen nicely and be brown on top. Serve immediately.

Lush Vegetable Bake

Prep time: 10 minutes | Cook time: 45 minutes | Serves 4

2 potatoes, peeled and cubed
4 carrots, cut into chunks
1 head broccoli, cut into florets
4 zucchinis, sliced thickly
Salt and ground black pepper, to taste
¼ cup olive oil
1 tablespoon dry onion powder

1. Select the BAKE function and preheat MAXX to 400ºF (204ºC).
2. In a baking dish, add all the ingredients and combine well.
3. Bake for 45 minutes in the air fryer oven, ensuring the vegetables are soft and the sides have browned before serving.

Vegetable and Potato Turnovers

Prep time: 20 minutes | Cook time: 40 minutes | Serves 4

Dough:
2 cups all-purpose flour
½ teaspoon baking powder
1 teaspoon salt
Freshly ground black pepper
¼ teaspoon dried thyme
¼ cup canola oil
½ to ²⁄₃ cup water

Turnover Filling:
1 tablespoon canola or vegetable oil
1 onion, finely chopped
1 clove garlic, minced
1 tablespoon grated fresh ginger
½ teaspoon cumin seeds
½ teaspoon fennel seeds
1 teaspoon curry powder
2 russet potatoes, diced
2 cups cauliflower florets
½ cup frozen peas
2 tablespoons chopped fresh cilantro
Salt and freshly ground black pepper
2 tablespoons butter, melted
Mango chutney, for serving

1. Start by making the dough. Combine the flour, baking powder, salt, pepper and dried thyme in a mixing bowl or the bowl of a stand mixer. Drizzle in the canola oil and pinch it together with your fingers to turn the flour into a crumby mixture. Stir in the water (enough to bring the dough together). Knead the dough for 5 minutes or so until it is smooth. Add a little more water or flour as needed. Let the dough rest while you make the turnover filling.
2. Preheat a large skillet on the stovetop over medium-high heat. Add the oil and sauté the onion until it starts to become tender – about 4 minutes. Add the garlic and ginger and continue to cook for another minute. Add the dried spices and toss everything to coat. Add the potatoes and cauliflower to the skillet and pour in 1½ cups of water. Simmer everything together for 20 to 25 minutes, or until the potatoes are soft and most of the water has evaporated. If the water has evaporated and the vegetables still need more time, just add a little water and continue to simmer until everything is tender. Stir well, crushing the potatoes and cauliflower a little as you do so. Stir in the peas and cilantro, season to taste with salt and freshly ground black pepper and set aside to cool.
3. Divide the dough into 4 balls. Roll the dough balls out into ¼-inch thick circles. Divide the cooled potato filling between the dough circles, placing a mound of the filling on one side of each piece of dough, leaving an empty border around the edge of the dough. Brush the edges of the dough with a little water and fold one edge of circle over the filling to meet the other edge of the circle, creating a half moon. Pinch the edges together with your fingers and then press the edge with the tines of a fork to decorate and seal.
4. Spray or brush the air fryer basket with oil. Brush the turnovers with the melted butter and place 2 turnovers into the air fryer basket. Select the AIR FRY function and cook at 380ºF (193ºC) for 15 minutes. Flip the turnovers over and air fry for another 5 minutes. Repeat with the remaining 2 turnovers.
5. These will be very hot when they come out of the air fryer oven. Let them cool for at least 20 minutes before serving warm with mango chutney.

Zucchini, Black Bean, and Mushroom Burgers

Prep time: 15 minutes | Cook time: 30 minutes | Serves 4

1 cup diced zucchini, (about ½ medium zucchini)	1 tablespoon chopped fresh cilantro
1 tablespoon olive oil	½ cup plain bread crumbs
Salt and freshly ground black pepper	1 egg, beaten
1 cup chopped brown mushrooms	½ teaspoon salt
1 small clove garlic	Freshly ground black pepper
1 (15-ounce / 425-g) can black beans, drained and rinsed	Whole-wheat pita bread, burger buns or brioche buns
1 teaspoon lemon zest	Mayonnaise, tomato, avocado and lettuce, for serving

1. Toss the zucchini with the olive oil, season with salt and freshly ground black pepper. Select the AIR FRY function and cook the zucchini in the air fryer oven at 400ºF (205ºC) for 6 minutes, shaking the basket once or twice while it cooks.
2. Transfer the zucchini to a food processor with the mushrooms, garlic and black beans and process until still a little chunky but broken down and pasty. Transfer the mixture to a bowl. Add the lemon zest, cilantro, bread crumbs and egg and mix well. Season again with salt and freshly ground black pepper. Shape the mixture into four burger patties and refrigerate for at least 15 minutes.
3. Transfer two of the veggie burgers to the air fryer basket. Select the AIR FRY function and cook at 370ºF (188ºC) for 12 minutes, flipping the burgers gently halfway through the cooking time. Keep the burgers warm by loosely tenting them with foil while you cook the remaining two burgers. Return the first batch of burgers back into the air fryer oven with the second batch for the last two minutes of cooking to reheat.
4. Serve on toasted whole-wheat pita bread, burger buns or brioche buns with some mayonnaise, tomato, avocado and lettuce.

Korean BBQ Fried Cauliflower

Prep time: 20 minutes | Cook time: 12 minutes | Serves 4

Korean BBQ Sauce:

3 tablespoons soy sauce	2 cloves garlic, minced
2 tablespoons gochujang	1 tablespoon minced fresh ginger
2 tablespoons rice vinegar	1 tablespoon sesame or vegetable oil
2 tablespoons brown sugar	½ cup warm water

Fried Cauliflower:

1 cup all-purpose flour	cut into florets
½ cup cornstarch	Vegetable oil for spraying
2 teaspoons baking soda	1 teaspoon sesame seeds
1 teaspoon kosher salt	2 scallions, white and light green parts only, sliced
1 cup water	
1 head cauliflower,	

1. To make the sauce, whisk together the soy sauce, gochujang, vinegar, brown sugar, garlic, and ginger in a large bowl. While whisking, slowly pour in the oil in a steady stream and continue whisking until emulsified. Gradually whisk in the warm water until you reach a thin sauce-like consistency; you may not need the entire ½ cup of water depending on how thick your gochujang is. Set aside.
2. To make the batter for the cauliflower, whisk together the flour, cornstarch, baking soda, and salt in a large bowl. Slowly whisk in the water until you have created a thick batter. Place a cooling rack over a board lined with wax or parchment paper. Dip the cauliflower florets in the batter and then place them on the rack to allow the excess batter to drip off.
3. Spray the air fryer basket lightly with oil. Working in batches, arrange the battered florets in a single layer in the air fryer basket. Select the AIR FRY function and cook at 350ºF (180ºC) for 12 minutes, or until the florets are browned on the outside and tender on the inside.
4. Place the cooked florets in the bowl with the sauce and toss to coat. Garnish with sesame seeds and scallions. Repeat with the remaining florets. Serve warm.

Eggplant Parmesan

Prep time: 15 minutes | Cook time: 50 minutes | Serves 4 to 6

1 medium eggplant (about 1 pound / 454 g), cut into ½-inch slices	½ teaspoon salt
Kosher salt	Freshly ground black pepper
½ cup bread crumbs	2 tablespoons milk
2 teaspoons dried parsley	½ cup mayonnaise
½ teaspoon Italian seasoning	1 cup tomato sauce
½ teaspoon garlic powder	1 (14-ounce / 397-g) can diced tomatoes
½ teaspoon onion powder	1 teaspoon Italian seasoning
	2 cups grated Mozzarella cheese
	½ cup grated Parmesan cheese

1. Lay the eggplant slices on a baking sheet and sprinkle kosher salt generously over the top. Let the eggplant sit for 15 minutes while you prepare the rest of the ingredients.
2. Prepare a dredging station. Combine the bread crumbs, parsley, Italian seasoning, garlic powder, onion powder, salt and black pepper in a shallow dish. Whisk the milk and mayonnaise together in a small bowl until smooth.
3. Brush the excess salt from the eggplant slices and then coat both sides of each slice with the mayonnaise mixture. Dip the eggplant into the bread crumbs, pressing the crumbs on to coat both sides of each slice. Place all the coated eggplant slices on a plate or baking sheet and spray both sides with olive oil. Select the AIR FRY function and cook the eggplant slices in batches in the air fryer oven at 400ºF (205ºC) for 15 minutes, turning them over halfway through the cooking time.
4. While the eggplant is cooking, prepare the components of the eggplant Parmesan. Mix the tomato sauce, diced tomatoes and Italian seasoning in a bowl. Combine the Mozzarella and Parmesan cheeses in a second bowl.
5. Once all of the eggplant has been browned, build the dish with all the ingredient components. Cover the bottom of a 1½-quart round baking dish (6-inches in diameter) with a few tablespoons of the tomato sauce mixture. Top with one third of the eggplant slices, one third of the tomato sauce and then one third of the cheese. Repeat these layers two more times, finishing with cheese on top. Cover the dish with aluminum foil and transfer the dish to the air fryer basket, lowering the dish into the basket using a sling made of aluminum foil (fold a piece of aluminum foil into a strip about 2-inches wide by 24-inches long). Fold the ends of the aluminum foil over the top of the dish before returning the basket to the air fryer oven.
6. Select the BAKE function and set the temperature to 350ºF (180ºC). Bake for 30 minutes. Remove the foil and bake for an additional 5 minutes to brown the cheese on top. Let the eggplant Parmesan rest for a few minutes to set up and cool to an edible temperature before serving.

Beans Oatmeal in Bell Peppers

Prep time: 15 minutes | Cook time: 6 minutes | Serves 2 to 4

2 large bell peppers, halved lengthwise, deseeded	1 teaspoon ground cumin
2 tablespoons cooked kidney beans	½ teaspoon paprika
2 tablespoons cooked chick peas	½ teaspoon salt or to taste
2 cups cooked oatmeal	¼ teaspoon black pepper powder
	¼ cup yogurt

1. Put the bell peppers, cut-side down, in the air fryer basket. Select the AIR FRY function and cook at 355ºF (179ºC) for 2 minutes.
2. Take the peppers out of the air fryer oven and let cool.
3. In a bowl, combine the rest of the ingredients.
4. Divide the mixture evenly and use each portion to stuff a pepper.
5. Return the stuffed peppers to the air fryer oven and continue to air fry for 4 minutes.
6. Serve hot.

Mascarpone Mushrooms with Pasta
Prep time: 10 minutes | Cook time: 15 minutes | Serves 4

Vegetable oil spray
4 cups sliced mushrooms
1 medium yellow onion, chopped
2 cloves garlic, minced
¼ cup heavy whipping cream or half-and-half
8 ounces (227 g) mascarpone cheese

1 teaspoon dried thyme
1 teaspoon kosher salt
1 teaspoon black pepper
½ teaspoon red pepper flakes
4 cups cooked konjac noodles, for serving
½ cup grated Parmesan cheese

1. Select the BAKE function and preheat MAXX to 350°F (177°C). Spray a heatproof pan with vegetable oil spray.
2. In a medium bowl, combine the mushrooms, onion, garlic, cream, mascarpone, thyme, salt, black pepper, and red pepper flakes. Stir to combine. Transfer the mixture to the prepared pan.
3. Put the pan in the air fryer basket. Bake for 15 minutes, stirring halfway through the baking time.
4. Divide the pasta among four shallow bowls. Spoon the mushroom mixture evenly over the pasta. Sprinkle with Parmesan cheese and serve.

Spinach Cheese Calzone
Prep time: 10 minutes | Cook time: 20 minutes | Serves 2

⅔ cup frozen chopped spinach, thawed
1 cup grated Mozzarella cheese
1 cup ricotta cheese
½ teaspoon Italian seasoning
½ teaspoon salt
Freshly ground black

pepper
1 store-bought or homemade pizza dough (about 12 to 16 ounces / 340 to 454 g)
2 tablespoons olive oil
Pizza or marinara sauce (optional)

1. Drain and squeeze all the water out of the thawed spinach and set it aside. Mix the Mozzarella cheese, ricotta cheese,

Italian seasoning, salt and freshly ground black pepper together in a bowl. Stir in the chopped spinach.
2. Divide the dough in half. With floured hands or on a floured surface, stretch or roll one half of the dough into a 10-inch circle. Spread half of the cheese and spinach mixture on half of the dough, leaving about one inch of dough empty around the edge.
3. Fold the other half of the dough over the cheese mixture, almost to the edge of the bottom dough to form a half moon. Fold the bottom edge of dough up over the top edge and crimp the dough around the edges in order to make the crust and seal the calzone. Brush the dough with olive oil. Repeat with the second half of dough to make the second calzone.
4. Brush or spray the air fryer basket with olive oil. Select the AIR FRY function and cook at 360°F (182°C) for 10 minutes, flipping the calzone over half way through. Serve with warm pizza or marinara sauce if desired.

Mozzarella Pepperoni Mushroom Pizza
Prep time: 5 minutes | Cook time: 18 minutes | Serves 4

4 large portobello mushrooms, stems removed
4 teaspoons olive oil
1 cup marinara sauce

1 cup shredded Mozzarella cheese
10 slices sugar-free pepperoni

1. Select the BAKE function and preheat MAXX to 375°F (191°C).
2. Brush each mushroom cap with the olive oil, one teaspoon for each cap.
3. Put on a baking sheet and bake, stem-side down, for 8 minutes.
4. Take out of the air fryer oven and divide the marinara sauce, Mozzarella cheese and pepperoni evenly among the caps.
5. Switch from BAKE to AIR FRY. Air fry for another 10 minutes until browned.
6. Serve hot.

Mushrooms with Horseradish Mayonnaise
Prep time: 15 minutes | Cook time: 10 minutes | Serves 5

½ cup bread crumbs
2 cloves garlic, pressed
2 tablespoons chopped fresh coriander
⅓ teaspoon kosher salt
½ teaspoon crushed red pepper flakes
1½ tablespoons olive oil
20 medium

mushrooms, stems removed
½ cup grated Gorgonzola cheese
¼ cup low-fat mayonnaise
1 teaspoon prepared horseradish, well-drained
1 tablespoon finely chopped fresh parsley

1. Combine the bread crumbs together with the garlic, coriander, salt, red pepper, and olive oil.
2. Take equal-sized amounts of the bread crumb mixture and use them to stuff the mushroom caps. Add the grated Gorgonzola on top of each.
3. Put the mushrooms in a baking pan and transfer to the air fryer oven.
4. Select the AIR FRY function and cook at 380ºF (193ºC) for 10 minutes, ensuring the stuffing is warm throughout.
5. In the meantime, prepare the horseradish mayo. Mix the mayonnaise, horseradish and parsley.
6. When the mushrooms are ready, serve with the mayo.

Stuffed Potatoes with Cheese
Prep time: 15 minutes | Cook time: 15 minutes | Serves 4

4 potatoes
2 tablespoons olive oil
½ cup Ricotta cheese, at room temperature
2 tablespoons chopped scallions
1 tablespoon roughly chopped fresh parsley

1 tablespoon minced coriander
2 ounces (57 g) Cheddar cheese, preferably freshly grated
1 teaspoon celery seeds
½ teaspoon salt
½ teaspoon garlic pepper

1. Pierce the skin of the potatoes with a knife. Transfer to the air fryer basket.
2. Select the AIR FRY function and cook at 350ºF (177ºC) for 13 minutes. If they are not cooked through by this time, leave for 2 to 3 minutes longer.
3. In the meantime, make the stuffing by combining all the other ingredients.
4. Cut halfway into the cooked potatoes to open them.
5. Spoon equal amounts of the stuffing into each potato and serve hot.

Paneer Tikka with Cumin
Prep time: 15 minutes | Cook time: 10 minutes | Serves 4

14 ounces (397 g) paneer
½ cup plain yogurt
2 limes
2 cloves garlic, minced
1 tablespoon melted unsalted butter or vegetable oil
1 tablespoon grated fresh ginger
1 teaspoon garam masala

1 teaspoon kosher salt
½ teaspoon cumin
¼ teaspoon turmeric
¼ teaspoon cayenne pepper
2 bell peppers, cored and cut into 1-inch squares
1 red onion, cut into wedges
Vegetable oil for spraying

1. Cut the paneer into 1-inch cubes. In a large bowl, whisk together the yogurt, zest and juice from 1 of the limes, garlic, butter, ginger, and spices. Add the paneer cubes to the yogurt mixture and toss gently to coat. Allow the paneer to marinate for 30 minutes.
2. Thread the paneer cubes, bell pepper pieces, and onion wedges onto metal skewers designed for the air fryer oven or bamboo skewers cut to fit an air fryer oven. (If using bamboo skewers, soak them in water for 30 minutes prior to use.)
3. Spray the air fryer basket with oil. Working in batches, place 4 of the skewers in the air fryer basket and spray with oil. Select the AIR FRY function and cook at 375ºF (190ºC) for 10 minutes, turning the skewers once. Repeat with the remaining skewers. Serve the paneer tikka hot with rice and lime wedges for spritzing.

Red Potato with Tofu Scramble
Prep time: 15 minutes | Cook time: 30 minutes | Serves 3

2½ cups chopped red potato
2 tablespoons olive oil, divided
1 block tofu, chopped finely
2 tablespoons tamari
1 teaspoon turmeric
powder
½ teaspoon onion powder
½ teaspoon garlic powder
½ cup chopped onion
4 cups broccoli florets

1. Toss together the potatoes and 1 tablespoon of the olive oil.
2. Select the AIR FRY function and cook the potatoes in a baking dish at 400ºF (204ºC) for 15 minutes, shaking once during the cooking time to ensure they fry evenly.
3. Combine the tofu, the remaining 1 tablespoon of the olive oil, turmeric, onion powder, tamari, and garlic powder together, stirring in the onions, followed by the broccoli.
4. Top the potatoes with the tofu mixture and air fry for an additional 15 minutes. Serve warm.

Red Potato Mash with Thyme
Prep time: 5 minutes | Cook time: 40 minutes | Serves 2 to 4

1½ pounds (680 g) small red potatoes, unpeeled
2 tablespoons extra-
virgin olive oil
1 teaspoon chopped fresh thyme
Salt and pepper

1. Arrange potatoes in center of large sheet of aluminum foil and lift sides to form bowl. Pour ¾ cup water over potatoes and crimp foil tightly to seal. Place foil packet in air fryer basket and place basket in air fryer oven.
2. Select the AIR FRY function and cook at 400ºF (205ºC) for 25 to 30 minutes, or until paring knife inserted into potatoes meets little resistance (poke through foil to test).
3. Carefully open foil packet, allowing steam to escape away from you, and let cool slightly. Arrange potatoes in single

layer on cutting board; discard foil. Place baking sheet on top of potatoes and press down firmly on baking sheet, flattening potatoes to ½-inch thickness. Transfer mashed potatoes to large bowl; drizzle with oil and sprinkle with thyme, ½ teaspoon salt, and ⅛ teaspoon pepper. Toss until well combined and most potatoes have broken apart into chunks.
4. Return potatoes to air fryer oven and air fry until well browned and crispy (do not stir or shake during cooking), 15 to 20 minutes. Season with salt and pepper to taste. Serve.

Cauliflower Roast with Chili Sauce
Prep time: 15 minutes | Cook time: 20 minutes | Serves 4

Cauliflower:
5 cups cauliflower florets
3 tablespoons vegetable oil
½ teaspoon ground
cumin
½ teaspoon ground coriander
½ teaspoon kosher salt
Sauce:
½ cup Greek yogurt or sour cream
¼ cup chopped fresh cilantro
1 jalapeño, coarsely chopped
4 cloves garlic, peeled
½ teaspoon kosher salt
2 tablespoons water

1. Select the ROAST function and preheat MAXX to 400ºF (204ºC).
2. In a large bowl, combine the cauliflower, oil, cumin, coriander, and salt. Toss to coat.
3. Put the cauliflower in the air fryer basket. Roast for 20 minutes, stirring halfway through the roasting time.
4. Meanwhile, in a blender, combine the yogurt, cilantro, jalapeño, garlic, and salt. Blend, adding the water as needed to keep the blades moving and to thin the sauce.
5. At the end of roasting time, transfer the cauliflower to a large serving bowl. Pour the sauce over and toss gently to coat. Serve immediately.

Breaded Parmesan Eggplant Balls

Prep time: 10 minutes | Cook time: 40 minutes | Serves 4

1 medium eggplant (about 1 pound / 454 g)	2 tablespoons chopped fresh parsley
Olive oil	2 tablespoons chopped fresh basil
Salt and freshly ground black pepper	1 clove garlic, minced
1 cup grated Parmesan cheese	1 egg, lightly beaten
2 cups fresh bread crumbs	½ cup fine dried bread crumbs

1. Quarter the eggplant by cutting it in half both lengthwise and horizontally. Make a few slashes in the flesh of the eggplant but not through the skin. Brush the cut surface of the eggplant generously with olive oil and transfer to the air fryer basket, cut side up.
2. Select the AIR FRY function and cook at 400ºF (205ºC) for 10 minutes. Turn the eggplant quarters cut side down and air fry for another 15 minutes or until the eggplant is soft all the way through. You may need to rotate the pieces in the air fryer oven so that they cook evenly. Transfer the eggplant to a cutting board to cool.
3. Place the Parmesan cheese, the fresh bread crumbs, fresh herbs, garlic and egg in a food processor. Scoop the flesh out of the eggplant, discarding the skin and any pieces that are tough. You should have about 1 to 1½ cups of eggplant. Add the eggplant to the food processor and process everything together until smooth. Season with salt and pepper. Refrigerate the mixture for at least 30 minutes.
4. Place the dried bread crumbs into a shallow dish or onto a plate. Scoop heaping tablespoons of the eggplant mixture into the dried bread crumbs. Roll the dollops of eggplant in the bread crumbs and then shape into small balls. You should have 16 to 18 eggplant balls at the end. Refrigerate until you are ready to air fry.
5. Spray the eggplant balls and the air fryer basket with olive oil. Select the AIR FRY function and cook the eggplant balls at 350ºF (180ºC) for 15 minutes, rotating the balls during the cooking process to brown evenly.

Cheddar-Parmesan Potatoes with Thyme

Prep time: 5 minutes | Cook time: 32 minutes | Serves 2

2 ounces (57 g) Cheddar cheese, shredded	1 teaspoon minced fresh thyme or ¼ teaspoon dried
¼ cup shredded Parmesan cheese	Salt and pepper
1 tablespoon unsalted butter	1 pound (454 g) russet potatoes, unpeeled, sliced ¼ inch thick
1 garlic clove, minced	

1. Make foil sling for air fryer basket by folding 1 long sheet of aluminum foil so it is 4 inches wide. Lay sheet of foil widthwise across basket, pressing foil into and up sides of basket. Fold excess foil as needed so that edges of foil are flush with top of basket. Lightly spray foil and basket with vegetable oil spray.
2. Combine Cheddar and Parmesan in bowl; set aside. Microwave butter, garlic, thyme, ¼ teaspoon salt, and ⅛ teaspoon pepper in large bowl at 50 percent power, stirring occasionally, until butter is melted, about 1 minute. Add potatoes and toss to coat. Shingle half of potatoes in single layer in prepared basket, covering center of foil. Sprinkle potatoes with half of cheese mixture. Shingle remaining potatoes in single layer over top.
3. Place basket in air fryer oven. Select the AIR FRY function and cook the potatoes at 400ºF (205ºC) for 30 to 35 minutes, or until tender and crispy at edges, using sling to rotate potatoes halfway through cooking. Sprinkle potatoes with remaining cheese mixture. Return basket to air fryer oven and air fry until cheese is bubbly and golden brown, about 2 minutes.
4. Using foil sling, carefully remove potatoes from basket and transfer to serving dish. Season with salt and pepper to taste. Serve.

Stuffed Potatoes with Broccoli
Prep time: 15 minutes | Cook time: 55 minutes | Serves 4

4 cups small broccoli florets (from about 2 stalks)
2 tablespoons vegetable oil plus more for spraying
4 russet potatoes
Cheddar Cheese Sauce:
4 tablespoons unsalted butter
¼ cup all-purpose flour
2 cups milk, warmed
1 teaspoon dry mustard
Dash Worcestershire sauce
Kosher salt and pepper to taste
12 ounces (340 g) sharp Cheddar cheese, grated
4 tablespoons unsalted butter (optional)

1. Toss the broccoli florets with 2 tablespoons of oil in a bowl and set aside. Rub the skins of the potatoes with a small amount of oil and prick them all over with a fork. Place the potatoes in the air fryer basket. Select the AIR FRY function and cook at 400°F (205°C) for 40 to 50 minutes, or until you can easily pierce the potato with a knife.
2. While the potatoes are cooking, make the cheese sauce. Melt the butter in a large, heavy saucepan. Whisk in the flour and continue to cook over low heat, whisking constantly, for 4 to 5 minutes to cook the flour. Gradually add the milk to the saucepan, whisking constantly. Raise the heat to medium and cook until the sauce begins to thicken, about 3 to 5 minutes. Remove the saucepan from the heat and add the mustard, Worcestershire sauce, salt, and pepper. Gradually add the grated Cheddar in handfuls and stir to combine. Stir until the sauce is completely smooth. Keep warm while the potatoes continue to cook.
3. When the potatoes are cooked, remove them from the air fryer basket. Add the broccoli florets to the basket and air fry until tender and the edges begin to brown, 8 to 10 minutes.
4. To serve, split open the top of each potato and squeeze the sides to open up the inside. If desired, add a pat of butter to each potato and season with salt and pepper. Divide the broccoli florets evenly among the 4 potatoes. Spoon cheese sauce over the broccoli and potatoes and serve immediately.

Parsnip with Romesco Sauce
Prep time: 20 minutes | Cook time: 24 minutes | Serves 2

3 parsnips, peeled and cut into long strips
2 teaspoons olive oil
Salt and freshly ground black pepper
Romesco Sauce:
1 red bell pepper, halved and seeded
1 (1-inch) thick slice of Italian bread, torn into pieces (about 1 to 1½ cups)
1 cup almonds, toasted
Olive oil
½ jalapeño pepper, seeded
1 tablespoon fresh parsley leaves
1 clove garlic
2 Roma tomatoes, peeled and seeded (or ⅓ cup canned crushed tomatoes)
1 tablespoon red wine vinegar
¼ teaspoon smoked paprika
½ teaspoon salt
¾ cup olive oil

1. Select the ROAST function and preheat MAXX to 400°F (205°C).
2. Place the red pepper halves, cut side down, in the air fryer basket. Roast for 8 to 10 minutes, or until the skin turns black all over. Remove the pepper from the air fryer oven and let it cool. When it is cool enough to handle, peel the pepper.
3. Toss the torn bread and almonds with a little olive oil and transfer to the basket. Switch from ROAST to TOAST. Toast for 4 minutes, shaking the basket a couple times throughout the cooking time. When the bread and almonds are nicely toasted, remove them from the air fryer oven and let them cool for just a minute or two.
4. Combine the toasted bread, almonds, roasted red pepper, Jalapeño pepper, parsley, garlic, tomatoes, vinegar, smoked paprika and salt in a food processor or blender. Process until smooth. With the processor running, add the olive oil through the feed tube until the sauce comes together in a smooth paste that is barely pourable.
5. Toss the parsnip strips with the olive oil, salt and freshly ground black pepper. Transfer to the basket. Switch from TOAST to AIR FRY. Air fry for 10 minutes, shaking the basket a couple times during the cooking process so they brown and cook evenly. Serve the parsnip fries warm with the Romesco sauce.

Kale and Mushroom Empanadas
Prep time: 10 minutes | Cook time: 25 minutes | Serves 4

4 tablespoons unsalted butter, divided
1 pound (454 g) mushrooms, sliced, divided
Kosher salt to taste
1 bunch kale, destemmed and cut into ribbons
3 cloves garlic, minced
Pinch red pepper flakes
Juice of 1 lemon
8 frozen empanada discs, thawed
Vegetable oil for spraying

1. Melt 2 tablespoons of butter in a large, deep skillet over medium-high heat. When the butter is foamy, add half the mushrooms and season with salt. Cook undisturbed for 2 minutes, then stir and cook for another minute or so. Turn the heat down to medium and sauté the mushrooms, stirring occasionally, until the liquid has evaporated and the mushrooms are browned, another 5 minutes. Remove the mushrooms to a paper towel–lined plate. Add the remaining butter and repeat with the remaining mushrooms. Set the mushrooms aside.
2. Add the kale to the same skillet and sauté until it begins to wilt, 2 to 3 minutes. Add the garlic and red pepper flakes and sauté for an additional minute. Add the lemon juice and season to taste with salt. Return the mushrooms to the skillet and stir to combine. Remove from the heat and allow the mixture to cool.
3. Remove 1 of the empanada wrappers and place it on a board. Place a heaping ¼ cup of the mushroom-kale filling on 1 side of the empanada wrapper. Moisten the edges of the wrapper with a little water and fold the wrapper in half to form a half-moon shape. Press the dough closed around the filling and then crimp the edges of the dough with a fork to seal them shut. Place the filled empanada on a baking tray lined with parchment paper. (May be refrigerated, covered, at this point for up to several hours.)
4. Select the BAKE function and preheat MAXX to 375ºF (190ºC). Spray the air fryer basket and the empanadas with oil.
5. Working in 2 batches, place 4 empanadas in the air fryer basket. Bake for 8 minutes, then turn over the empanadas. Bake until the second side is firm and baked, another 5 to 7 minutes. Repeat with the second batch of empanadas. Serve immediately.

Ratatouille with Herb Purée
Prep time: 20 minutes | Cook time: 25 minutes | Serves 4

1 sprig basil
1 sprig flat-leaf parsley
1 sprig mint
1 tablespoon coriander powder
1 teaspoon capers
½ lemon, juiced
Salt and ground black pepper, to taste
2 eggplants, sliced crosswise
2 red onions, chopped
4 cloves garlic, minced
2 red peppers, sliced crosswise
1 fennel bulb, sliced crosswise
3 large zucchinis, sliced crosswise
5 tablespoons olive oil
4 large tomatoes, chopped
2 teaspoons herbs de Provence

1. Blend the basil, parsley, coriander, mint, lemon juice and capers, with a little salt and pepper. Make sure all ingredients are well-incorporated.
2. Coat the eggplant, onions, garlic, peppers, fennel, and zucchini with olive oil.
3. Transfer the vegetables into a baking dish and top with the tomatoes and herb purée. Sprinkle with more salt and pepper, and the herbs de Provence.
4. Select the AIR FRY function and cook at 400ºF (204ºC) for 25 minutes.
5. Serve immediately.

Eggplant and Rice Bowl

Prep time: 15 minutes | Cook time: 10 minutes | Serves 4

¼ cup sliced cucumber
1 teaspoon salt
1 tablespoon sugar
7 tablespoons Japanese rice vinegar
3 medium eggplants, sliced
3 tablespoons sweet

white miso paste
1 tablespoon mirin rice wine
4 cups cooked sushi rice
4 spring onions
1 tablespoon toasted sesame seeds

1. Coat the cucumber slices with the rice wine vinegar, salt, and sugar.
2. Put a dish on top of the bowl to weight it down completely.
3. In a bowl, mix the eggplants, mirin rice wine, and miso paste. Allow to marinate for half an hour.
4. Put the eggplant slices in the air fryer oven. Select the AIR FRY function and cook at 400ºF (204ºC) for 10 minutes.
5. Fill the bottom of a serving bowl with rice and top with the eggplants and pickled cucumbers.
6. Add the spring onions and sesame seeds for garnish. Serve immediately.

Stuffed Zucchini Boats with Couscous

Prep time: 15 minutes | Cook time: 20 minutes | Serves 2

Olive oil
½ cup onion, finely chopped
1 clove garlic, finely minced
½ teaspoon dried oregano
¼ teaspoon dried thyme
¾ cup couscous
1½ cups chicken stock, divided
1 tomato, seeds removed and finely chopped
½ cup coarsely

chopped Kalamata olives
½ cup grated Romano cheese
¼ cup pine nuts, toasted
1 tablespoon chopped fresh parsley
1 teaspoon salt
Freshly ground black pepper
1 egg, beaten
1 cup grated Mozzarella cheese, divided
2 thick zucchini

1. Preheat a sauté pan on the stovetop over medium-high heat. Add the olive oil and sauté the onion until it just starts to soften–about 4 minutes. Stir in the garlic, dried oregano and thyme. Add the couscous and sauté for just a minute. Add 1¼ cups of the chicken stock and simmer over low heat for 3 to 5 minutes, until liquid has been absorbed and the couscous is soft. Remove the pan from heat and set it aside to cool slightly.
2. Fluff the couscous and add the tomato, Kalamata olives, Romano cheese, pine nuts, parsley, salt and pepper. Mix well. Add the remaining chicken stock, the egg and ½ cup of the Mozzarella cheese. Stir to ensure everything is combined.
3. Cut each zucchini in half lengthwise. Then, trim each half of the zucchini into four 5-inch lengths. (Save the trimmed ends of the zucchini for another use.) Use a spoon to scoop out the center of the zucchini, leaving some flesh around the sides. Brush both sides of the zucchini with olive oil and season the cut side with salt and pepper.
4. Divide the couscous filling between the four zucchini boats. Use your hands to press the filling together and fill the inside of the zucchini. The filling should be mounded into the boats and rounded on top.
5. Transfer the zucchini boats to the air fryer basket and drizzle the stuffed zucchini boats with olive oil. Select the AIR FRY function and cook at 380ºF (193ºC) for 19 minutes. Then, sprinkle the remaining Mozzarella cheese on top of the zucchini, pressing it down onto the filling lightly to prevent it from blowing around in the air fryer oven. Air fry for one more minute to melt the cheese. Transfer the finished zucchini boats to a serving platter and garnish with the chopped parsley.

French Green Beans with Shallot

Prep time: 10 minutes | Cook time: 10 minutes | Serves 4

1½ pounds (680 g) French green beans, stems removed and blanched
1 tablespoon salt
½ pound (227 g) shallots, peeled and cut

into quarters
½ teaspoon ground white pepper
2 tablespoons olive oil

1. Coat the vegetables with the rest of the ingredients in a bowl.
2. Transfer to the air fryer basket. Select the AIR FRY function and cook at 400ºF (204ºC) for 10 minutes, making sure the green beans achieve a light brown color.
3. Serve hot.

Green Tomatoes with Rëmoulade Sauce

Prep time: 20 minutes | Cook time: 10 minutes | Serves 4

Rëmoulade:
1 cup mayonnaise
3 tablespoons mustard
1 tablespoon freshly squeezed lemon juice
1 tablespoon capers
1 tablespoon chopped fresh flat-leaf parsley
2 scallions, white and light green part only,

sliced
2 teaspoons Louisiana-style hot sauce
1½ teaspoons Cajun seasoning
½ teaspoon garlic powder
½ teaspoon black pepper

Fried Green Tomatoes:
3 green tomatoes
¾ cup all-purpose flour
¾ cup cornmeal, preferably finely ground
1½ teaspoons kosher salt
1 teaspoon black pepper

½ teaspoon cayenne pepper
2 eggs
¼ cup buttermilk (regular milk is an acceptable substitute)
Vegetable oil for spraying

1. Combine all the rémoulade ingredients in a medium-size bowl. Cover and chill for at least 1 hour to allow the flavors to develop.
2. To make the fried green tomatoes, trim the ends off each tomato and slice into ¼-inch-thick slices. Place the slices on a paper towel–lined plate to absorb excess liquid.
3. Place the flour, cornmeal, salt, black pepper, and cayenne pepper on a second plate, stirring with a fork to combine. Whisk the eggs and buttermilk together in a shallow bowl.
4. Dip a third of the tomato slices in the egg mixture then dredge them in the flour-cornmeal mixture, shaking off any excess. (Do not coat the tomato slices until right before you cook them.) Spray both sides with oil, making sure to coat the slices well. Place the slices in the air fryer basket.
5. Select the AIR FRY function and cook at 400ºF (205ºC) for 10 minutes, flipping the slices once halfway through. (If you see spots that look like dry flour, spray those with additional oil.) While the first batch of tomatoes is cooking, batter the next batch. Repeat the process with the remaining slices.
6. Serve the fried green tomatoes hot out of the air fryer oven with rémoulade sauce.

Chapter 8 Vegetable Sides

Fresh Asparagus
Prep time: 5 minutes | Cook time: 5 minutes | Serves 4

1 pound (454 g) fresh asparagus spears, trimmed	1 tablespoon olive oil Salt and ground black pepper, to taste

1. Combine all the ingredients and transfer to the air fryer basket.
2. Select the AIR FRY function and cook at 375ºF (191ºC) for 5 minutes, or until soft.
3. Serve hot.

Air-Fried Brussels Sprouts
Prep time: 5 minutes | Cook time: 10 minutes | Serves 1

1 pound (454 g) Brussels sprouts 1 tablespoon coconut	oil, melted 1 tablespoon unsalted butter, melted

1. Prepare the Brussels sprouts by halving them, discarding any loose leaves.
2. Combine with the melted coconut oil and transfer to the air fryer oven.
3. Select the AIR FRY function and cook at 400ºF (204ºC) for 10 minutes, giving the basket a good shake throughout the air frying time to brown them up if desired.
4. The sprouts are ready when they are partially caramelized. Remove them from the air fryer oven and serve with a topping of melted butter before serving.

Potatoes with Olives and Chives
Prep time: 15 minutes | Cook time: 40 minutes | Serves 1

1 medium russet potatoes, scrubbed and peeled 1 teaspoon olive oil ¼ teaspoon onion powder ⅛ teaspoon salt	Dollop of butter Dollop of cream cheese 1 tablespoon Kalamata olives 1 tablespoon chopped chives

1. In a bowl, coat the potatoes with the onion powder, salt, olive oil, and butter.
2. Transfer to the air fryer oven. Select the AIR FRY function and cook at 400ºF (204ºC) for 40 minutes, turning the potatoes over at the halfway point.
3. Take care when removing the potatoes from the air fryer oven and serve with the cream cheese, Kalamata olives and chives on top.

Nice Chickpeas
Prep time: 5 minutes | Cook time: 15 minutes | Serves 4

1 (15-ounces / 425-g) can chickpeas, drained but not rinsed 2 tablespoons olive	oil 1 teaspoon salt 2 tablespoons lemon juice

1. Add all the ingredients together in a bowl and mix. Transfer this mixture to the air fryer basket.
2. Select the AIR FRY function and cook at 400ºF (204ºC) for 15 minutes, ensuring the chickpeas become nice and crispy.
3. Serve immediately.

Rosemary Green Beans
Prep time: 5 minutes | Cook time: 5 minutes | Serves 1

1 tablespoon butter, melted 2 tablespoons rosemary ½ teaspoon salt	3 cloves garlic, minced ¾ cup chopped green beans

1. Combine the melted butter with the rosemary, salt, and minced garlic. Toss in the green beans, coating them well.
2. Select the AIR FRY function and cook at 390ºF (199ºC) for 5 minutes.
3. Serve immediately.

Beef Stuffed Green Bell Peppers

Prep time: 10 minutes | Cook time: 30 minutes | Serves 4

1 pound (454 g) ground beef	and green chilis
1 tablespoon taco seasoning mix	4 green bell peppers
1 can diced tomatoes	1 cup shredded Monterey jack cheese, divided

1. Set a skillet over a high heat and cook the ground beef for 8 minutes. Make sure it is cooked through and browned all over. Drain the fat.
2. Stir in the taco seasoning mix, and the diced tomatoes and green chilis. Allow the mixture to cook for a further 4 minutes.
3. In the meantime, slice the tops off the green peppers and remove the seeds and membranes.
4. When the meat mixture is fully cooked, spoon equal amounts of it into the peppers and top with the Monterey jack cheese. Then place the peppers into the air fryer oven. Select the AIR FRY function and cook at 350ºF (177ºC) for 15 minutes.
5. The peppers are ready when they are soft, and the cheese is bubbling and brown. Serve warm.

Roasted Eggplant Slices

Prep time: 5 minutes | Cook time: 15 minutes | Serves 1

1 large eggplant, sliced	¼ teaspoon salt
2 tablespoons olive oil	½ teaspoon garlic powder

1. Select the ROAST function and preheat MAXX to 390ºF (199ºC).
2. Apply the olive oil to the slices with a brush, coating both sides. Season each side with sprinklings of salt and garlic powder.
3. Put the slices in the air fryer oven and roast for 15 minutes.
4. Serve immediately.

Roasted Cheesy Potatoes and Asparagus

Prep time: 5 minutes | Cook time: 23 minutes | Serves 4

4 medium potatoes	1 tablespoon wholegrain mustard
1 bunch asparagus	Salt and pepper, to taste
⅓ cup cottage cheese	Cooking spray
⅓ cup low-fat crème fraiche	

1. Spritz the air fryer basket with cooking spray.
2. Place the potatoes in the basket. Select the AIR FRY function and cook at 390ºF (199ºC) for 20 minutes.
3. Boil the asparagus in salted water for 3 minutes.
4. Remove the potatoes and mash them with rest of ingredients. Sprinkle with salt and pepper.
5. Serve immediately.

Thai-Style Tofu

Prep time: 5 minutes | Cook time: 25 minutes | Serves 4

1 block firm tofu, pressed and cut into 1-inch thick cubes	sesame seeds
2 tablespoons soy sauce	1 teaspoon rice vinegar
2 teaspoons toasted	1 tablespoon cornstarch

1. Add the tofu, soy sauce, sesame seeds, and rice vinegar in a bowl together and mix well to coat the tofu cubes. Then cover the tofu in cornstarch and put it in the air fryer basket.
2. Select the AIR FRY function and cook at 400ºF (204ºC) for 25 minutes, giving the basket a shake at five-minute intervals to ensure the tofu cooks evenly.
3. Serve immediately.

Stuffed Mushrooms with Cashew
Prep time: 10 minutes | Cook time: 15 minutes | Serves 6

1 cup basil
½ cup cashew, soaked overnight
½ cup nutritional yeast
1 tablespoon lemon juice

2 cloves garlic
1 tablespoon olive oil
Salt, to taste
1 pound (454 g) baby Bella mushroom, stems removed

1. Prepare the pesto. In a food processor, blend the basil, cashew nuts, nutritional yeast, lemon juice, garlic and olive oil to combine well. Sprinkle with salt as desired.
2. Turn the mushrooms cap-side down and spread the pesto on the underside of each cap.
3. Transfer to the air fryer oven. Select the AIR FRY function and cook at 400ºF (204ºC) for 15 minutes.
4. Serve warm.

Croquettes
Prep time: 15 minutes | Cook time: 15 minutes | Serves 10

¼ cup nutritional yeast
2 cups boiled potatoes, mashed
1 flax egg
1 tablespoon flour
2 tablespoons

chopped chives
Salt and ground black pepper, to taste
2 tablespoons vegetable oil
¼ cup bread crumbs

1. In a bowl, combine the nutritional yeast, potatoes, flax egg, flour, and chives. Sprinkle with salt and pepper as desired.
2. In a separate bowl, mix the vegetable oil and bread crumbs to achieve a crumbly consistency.
3. Shape the potato mixture into small balls and dip each one into the bread crumb mixture.
4. Put the croquettes inside the air fryer oven. Select the AIR FRY function and cook at 400ºF (204ºC) for 15 minutes, ensuring the croquettes turn golden brown.
5. Serve immediately.

Small Jicama Fries
Prep time: 5 minutes | Cook time: 20 minutes | Serves 1

1 small jicama, peeled
¼ teaspoon onion powder
¾ teaspoon chili

powder
¼ teaspoon garlic powder
¼ teaspoon ground black pepper

1. To make the fries, cut the jicama into matchsticks of the desired thickness.
2. In a bowl, toss them with the onion powder, chili powder, garlic powder, and black pepper to coat. Transfer the fries into the air fryer basket.
3. Select the AIR FRY function and cook at 350ºF (177ºC) for 20 minutes, giving the basket an occasional shake throughout the cooking process. The fries are ready when they are hot and golden.
4. Serve immediately.

Smoky Wax Beans
Prep time: 10 minutes | Cook time: 7 minutes | Serves 4

½ cup flour
1 teaspoon smoky chipotle powder
½ teaspoon ground black pepper
1 teaspoon sea salt flakes

2 eggs, beaten
½ cup crushed saltines
10 ounces (283 g) wax beans
Cooking spray

1. Combine the flour, chipotle powder, black pepper, and salt in a bowl. Put the eggs in a second bowl. Put the crushed saltines in a third bowl.
2. Wash the beans with cold water and discard any tough strings.
3. Coat the beans with the flour mixture, before dipping them into the beaten egg. Cover them with the crushed saltines.
4. Spritz the beans with cooking spray.
5. Select the AIR FRY function and cook at 360ºF (182ºC) for 4 minutes. Give the air fryer basket a good shake and continue to air fry for 3 minutes. Serve hot.

Paprika Vegetable Salad
Prep time: 15 minutes | Cook time: 10 minutes | Serves 4

6 plum tomatoes, halved
2 large red onions, sliced
4 long red pepper, sliced
2 yellow pepper, sliced
6 cloves garlic, crushed
1 tablespoon extra-virgin olive oil
1 teaspoon paprika
½ lemon, juiced
Salt and ground black pepper, to taste
1 tablespoon baby capers

1. Put the tomatoes, onions, peppers, and garlic in a large bowl and cover with the extra-virgin olive oil, paprika, and lemon juice. Sprinkle with salt and pepper as desired.
2. Line the inside of the air fryer basket with aluminum foil. Put the vegetables inside. Select the AIR FRY function and cook at 420ºF (216ºC) for 10 minutes, ensuring the edges turn brown.
3. Serve in a salad bowl with the baby capers.

Roasted Broccoli
Prep time: 5 minutes | Cook time: 15 minutes | Serves 6

2 heads broccoli, cut into florets
2 teaspoons extra-virgin olive oil, plus more for coating
1 teaspoon salt
½ teaspoon black pepper
1 clove garlic, minced
½ teaspoon lemon juice

1. Cover the air fryer basket with aluminum foil and coat with a light brushing of oil.
2. Select the ROAST function and preheat MAXX to 375ºF (191ºC).
3. In a bowl, combine all ingredients, save for the lemon juice, and transfer to the air fryer basket. Roast for 15 minutes.
4. Serve with the lemon juice.

Oregano Radishes
Prep time: 5 minutes | Cook time: 10 minutes | Serves 2

1 pound (454 g) radishes
2 tablespoons unsalted butter, melted
¼ teaspoon dried oregano
½ teaspoon dried parsley
½ teaspoon garlic powder

1. Prepare the radishes by cutting off their tops and bottoms and quartering them.
2. In a bowl, combine the butter, dried oregano, dried parsley, and garlic powder. Toss with the radishes to coat.
3. Transfer the radishes to the air fryer oven. Select the AIR FRY function and cook at 350ºF (177ºC) for 10 minutes, shaking the basket at the halfway point to ensure the radishes air fry evenly through. The radishes are ready when they turn brown.
4. Serve immediately.

Ranch Buffalo Cauliflower
Prep time: 5 minutes | Cook time: 5 minutes | Serves 1

½ packet dry ranch seasoning
2 tablespoons salted butter, melted
1 cup cauliflower florets
¼ cup buffalo sauce

1. Select the ROAST function and preheat MAXX to 400ºF (204ºC).
2. In a bowl, combine the dry ranch seasoning and butter. Toss with the cauliflower florets to coat and transfer them to the air fryer oven.
3. Roast for 5 minutes, shaking the basket occasionally to ensure the florets roast evenly.
4. Remove the cauliflower from the air fryer oven, pour the buffalo sauce over it, and serve.

Corn Pakodas
Prep time: 10 minutes | Cook time: 8 minutes | Serves 5

1 cup flour
¼ teaspoon baking soda
¼ teaspoon salt
½ teaspoon curry powder
½ teaspoon red chili powder
¼ teaspoon turmeric powder
¼ cup water
10 cobs baby corn, blanched
Cooking spray

1. Cover the air fryer basket with aluminum foil and spritz with the cooking spray.
2. In a bowl, combine all the ingredients, save for the corn. Stir with a whisk until well combined.
3. Coat the corn in the batter and put inside the air fryer oven.
4. Select the AIR FRY function and cook at 425ºF (218ºC) for 8 minutes, or until a golden brown color is achieved.
5. Serve hot.

Cheddar Macaroni Balls
Prep time: 10 minutes | Cook time: 10 minutes | Serves 2

2 cups leftover macaroni
1 cup shredded Cheddar cheese
½ cup flour
1 cup bread crumbs
3 large eggs
1 cup milk
½ teaspoon salt
¼ teaspoon black pepper

1. In a bowl, combine the leftover macaroni and shredded cheese.
2. Pour the flour in a separate bowl. Put the bread crumbs in a third bowl. Finally, in a fourth bowl, mix the eggs and milk with a whisk.
3. With an ice-cream scoop, create balls from the macaroni mixture. Coat them the flour, then in the egg mixture, and lastly in the bread crumbs.
4. Arrange the balls in the air fryer basket. Select the AIR FRY function and cook at 365ºF (185ºC) for 10 minutes, giving them an occasional stir. Ensure they crisp up nicely.
5. Serve hot.

Chili Potatoes
Prep time: 10 minutes | Cook time: 16 minutes | Serves 4

1 pound (454 g) fingerling potatoes, rinsed and cut into wedges
1 teaspoon olive oil
1 teaspoon salt
1 teaspoon black pepper
1 teaspoon cayenne pepper
1 teaspoon nutritional yeast
½ teaspoon garlic powder

1. Coat the potatoes with the rest of the ingredients.
2. Transfer to the air fryer basket. Select the AIR FRY function and cook at 400ºF (204ºC) for 16 minutes, shaking the basket at the halfway point.
3. Serve immediately.

Cauliflower Tater Tots
Prep time: 15 minutes | Cook time: 16 minutes | Serves 12

1 pound (454 g) cauliflower, steamed and chopped
½ cup nutritional yeast
1 tablespoon oats
1 tablespoon desiccated coconuts
3 tablespoons flaxseed meal
3 tablespoons water
1 onion, chopped
1 teaspoon minced garlic
1 teaspoon chopped parsley
1 teaspoon chopped oregano
1 teaspoon chopped chives
Salt and ground black pepper, to taste
½ cup bread crumbs

1. Drain any excess water out of the cauliflower by wringing it with a paper towel.
2. In a bowl, combine the cauliflower with the remaining ingredients, save the bread crumbs. Using the hands, shape the mixture into several small balls.
3. Coat the balls in the bread crumbs and transfer to the air fryer basket. Select the AIR FRY function and cook at 390ºF (199ºC) for 6 minutes. Then raise the temperature to 400ºF (204ºC) and then air fry for an additional 10 minutes.
4. Serve immediately.

Garlicky Breaded Mushrooms

Prep time: 10 minutes | Cook time: 10 minutes | Serves 4

6 small mushrooms
1 tablespoon bread crumbs
1 tablespoon olive oil
1 ounce (28 g) onion, peeled and diced
1 teaspoon parsley
1 teaspoon garlic purée
Salt and ground black pepper, to taste

1. Combine the bread crumbs, oil, onion, parsley, salt, pepper and garlic in a bowl. Cut out the mushrooms' stalks and stuff each cap with the crumb mixture.
2. Select the AIR FRY function and cook the mushrooms in the air fryer oven at 350°F (177°C) for 10 minutes.
3. Serve hot.

Dill Pickles

Prep time: 10 minutes | Cook time: 15 minutes | Serves 4

14 dill pickles, sliced
¼ cup flour
⅛ teaspoon baking powder
Pinch of salt
2 tablespoons
cornstarch plus 3 tablespoons water
6 tablespoons panko bread crumbs
½ teaspoon paprika
Cooking spray

1. Drain any excess moisture out of the dill pickles on a paper towel.
2. In a bowl, combine the flour, baking powder and salt.
3. Throw in the cornstarch and water mixture and combine well with a whisk.
4. Put the panko bread crumbs in a shallow dish along with the paprika. Mix thoroughly.
5. Dip the pickles in the flour batter, before coating in the bread crumbs. Spritz all the pickles with the cooking spray.
6. Transfer to the air fryer basket. Select the AIR FRY function and cook at 400°F (204°C) for 15 minutes, or until golden brown.
7. Serve immediately.

Falafel

Prep time: 15 minutes | Cook time: 15 minutes | Serves 8

1 teaspoon cumin seeds
½ teaspoon coriander seeds
2 cups chickpeas, drained and rinsed
½ teaspoon red pepper flakes
3 cloves garlic
¼ cup chopped
parsley
¼ cup chopped coriander
½ onion, diced
1 tablespoon juice from freshly squeezed lemon
3 tablespoons flour
½ teaspoon salt
Cooking spray

1. Fry the cumin and coriander seeds over medium heat until fragrant.
2. Grind using a mortar and pestle.
3. Put all of ingredients, except for the cooking spray, in a food processor and blend until a fine consistency is achieved.
4. Use the hands to mold the mixture into falafels and spritz with the cooking spray.
5. Transfer the falafels to the air fryer basket in one layer.
6. Select the AIR FRY function and cook at 400°F (204°C) for 15 minutes, serving when they turn golden brown.

Potato with Sour Cream and Parmesan

Prep time: 5 minutes | Cook time: 15 minutes | Serves 2

2 medium potatoes
1 teaspoon butter
3 tablespoons sour cream
1 teaspoon chives
1½ tablespoons grated Parmesan cheese

1. Pierce the potatoes with a fork and boil them in water until they are cooked.
2. Transfer to the air fryer oven. Select the AIR FRY function and cook at 350°F (177°C) for 15 minutes.
3. In the meantime, combine the sour cream, cheese and chives in a bowl. Cut the potatoes halfway to open them up and fill with the butter and sour cream mixture.
4. Serve immediately.

Chapter 9 Wraps and Sandwiches

Spicy Bacon and Bell Peppers Sandwich

Prep time: 10 minutes | Cook time: 6 minutes | Serves 4

⅓ cup spicy barbecue sauce
2 tablespoons honey
8 slices cooked bacon, cut into thirds
1 red bell pepper, sliced
1 yellow bell pepper, sliced
3 pita pockets, cut in half
1¼ cups torn butter lettuce leaves
2 tomatoes, sliced

1. Select the ROAST function and preheat MAXX to 350ºF (177ºC).
2. In a small bowl, combine the barbecue sauce and the honey. Brush this mixture lightly onto the bacon slices and the red and yellow pepper slices.
3. Put the peppers into the air fryer basket and roast for 4 minutes. Then shake the basket, add the bacon, and roast for 2 minutes or until the bacon is browned and the peppers are tender.
4. Fill the pita halves with the bacon, peppers, any remaining barbecue sauce, lettuce, and tomatoes, and serve immediately.

Vegetable Salsa Wraps

Prep time: 5 minutes | Cook time: 7 minutes | Serves 4

1 cup red onion, sliced
1 zucchini, chopped
1 poblano pepper, deseeded and finely chopped
1 head lettuce
½ cup salsa
8 ounces (227 g) Mozzarella cheese

1. Place the red onion, zucchini, and poblano pepper in the air fryer basket. Select the AIR FRY function and cook at 390ºF (199ºC) for 7 minutes, or until they are tender and fragrant.
2. Divide the veggie mixture among the lettuce leaves and spoon the salsa over the top. Finish off with Mozzarella cheese. Wrap the lettuce leaves around the filling.
3. Serve immediately.

Smoky Chicken Breast Sandwich

Prep time: 10 minutes | Cook time: 11 minutes | Serves 2

2 boneless, skinless chicken breasts (8 ounces / 227 g each), sliced horizontally in half and separated into 4 thinner cutlets
Kosher salt and freshly ground black pepper, to taste
½ cup all-purpose flour
3 large eggs, lightly beaten
½ cup dried bread crumbs
1 tablespoon smoked paprika
Cooking spray
½ cup marinara sauce
6 ounces (170 g) smoked Mozzarella cheese, grated
2 store-bought soft, sesame-seed hamburger or Italian buns, split

1. Season the chicken cutlets all over with salt and pepper. Set up three shallow bowls: Place the flour in the first bowl, the eggs in the second, and stir together the bread crumbs and smoked paprika in the third. Coat the chicken pieces in the flour, then dip fully in the egg. Dredge in the paprika bread crumbs, then transfer to a wire rack set over a baking sheet and spray both sides liberally with cooking spray.
2. Transfer 2 of the chicken cutlets to the air fryer oven. Select the AIR FRY function and cook at 350ºF (177ºC) for 6 minutes, or until beginning to brown. Spread each cutlet with 2 tablespoons of the marinara sauce and sprinkle with one-quarter of the smoked Mozzarella.
3. Increase the temperature to 400ºF (204ºC) and air fry for 5 minutes more, or until the chicken is cooked through and crisp and the cheese is melted and golden brown.
4. Transfer the cutlets to a plate, stack on top of each other, and place inside a bun. Repeat with the remaining chicken cutlets, marinara, smoked Mozzarella, and bun.
5. Serve the sandwiches warm.

Mozzarella Chicken Sandwich
Prep time: 10 minutes | Cook time: 5 to 7 minutes | Serves 1

¹/₃ cup chicken, cooked and shredded
2 Mozzarella slices
1 hamburger bun
¼ cup shredded cabbage
1 teaspoon mayonnaise
2 teaspoons butter, melted

1 teaspoon olive oil
½ teaspoon balsamic vinegar
¼ teaspoon smoked paprika
¼ teaspoon black pepper
¼ teaspoon garlic powder
Pinch of salt

1. Select the BAKE function and preheat MAXX to 370ºF (188ºC).
2. Brush some butter onto the outside of the hamburger bun.
3. In a bowl, coat the chicken with the garlic powder, salt, pepper, and paprika.
4. In a separate bowl, stir together the mayonnaise, olive oil, cabbage, and balsamic vinegar to make coleslaw.
5. Slice the bun in two. Start building the sandwich, starting with the chicken, followed by the Mozzarella, the coleslaw, and finally the top bun.
6. Transfer the sandwich to the air fryer oven and bake for 5 to 7 minutes.
7. Serve immediately.

Best Sloppy Joes
Prep time: 10 minutes | Cook time: 17 to 19 minutes | Makes 4 large sandwiches or 8 sliders

1 pound (454 g) very lean ground beef
1 teaspoon onion powder
¹/₃ cup ketchup
¼ cup water
½ teaspoon celery seed
1 tablespoon lemon juice
1½ teaspoons brown sugar

1¼ teaspoons low-sodium Worcestershire sauce
½ teaspoon salt (optional)
½ teaspoon vinegar
⅛ teaspoon dry mustard
Hamburger or slider buns, for serving
Cooking spray

1. Select the ROAST function and preheat MAXX to 390ºF (199ºC). Spray the air fryer basket with cooking spray.

2. Break raw ground beef into small chunks and pile into the basket. Roast for 5 minutes. Stir to break apart and roast for 3 minutes. Stir and roast for 2 to 4 minutes longer, or until meat is well done.
3. Remove the meat from the air fryer oven, drain, and use a knife and fork to crumble into small pieces.
4. Give your air fryer basket a quick rinse to remove any bits of meat.
5. Place all the remaining ingredients, except for the buns, in a baking pan and mix together. Add the meat and stir well.
6. Switch from ROAST to BAKE. Bake at 330ºF (166ºC) for 5 minutes. Stir and bake for 2 minutes.
7. Scoop onto buns. Serve hot.

Vegetable Pita Sandwich
Prep time: 10 minutes | Cook time: 9 to 12 minutes | Serves 4

1 baby eggplant, peeled and chopped
1 red bell pepper, sliced
½ cup diced red onion
½ cup shredded carrot

1 teaspoon olive oil
¹/₃ cup low-fat Greek yogurt
½ teaspoon dried tarragon
2 low-sodium whole-wheat pita breads, halved crosswise

1. Select the ROAST function and preheat MAXX to 390ºF (199ºC).
2. In a baking pan, stir together the eggplant, red bell pepper, red onion, carrot, and olive oil. Put the vegetable mixture into the air fryer basket and roast for 7 to 9 minutes, stirring once, until the vegetables are tender. Drain if necessary.
3. In a small bowl, thoroughly mix the yogurt and tarragon until well combined.
4. Stir the yogurt mixture into the vegetables. Stuff one-fourth of this mixture into each pita pocket.
5. Place the sandwiches in the air fryer oven. Switch from ROAST to BAKE and bake for 2 to 3 minutes, or until the bread is toasted.
6. Serve immediately.

Greens and Swiss Cheese Sandwich

Prep time: 15 minutes | Cook time: 10 to 13 minutes | Serves 4

1½ cups chopped mixed greens
2 garlic cloves, thinly sliced
2 teaspoons olive oil
2 slices low-sodium low-fat Swiss cheese
4 slices low-sodium whole-wheat bread
Cooking spray

1. Select the BAKE function and preheat MAXX to 400ºF (204ºC).
2. In a baking pan, mix the greens, garlic, and olive oil. Bake for 4 to 5 minutes, stirring once, until the vegetables are tender. Drain, if necessary.
3. Make 2 sandwiches, dividing half of the greens and 1 slice of Swiss cheese between 2 slices of bread. Lightly spray the outsides of the sandwiches with cooking spray.
4. Bake the sandwiches in the air fryer oven for 6 to 8 minutes, turning with tongs halfway through, until the bread is toasted and the cheese melts.
5. Cut each sandwich in half and serve.

Cheesy Shrimp and Green Onion Sandwich

Prep time: 10 minutes | Cook time: 5 to 7 minutes | Serves 4

1¼ cups shredded Colby, Cheddar, or Havarti cheese
1 (6-ounce / 170-g) can tiny shrimp, drained
3 tablespoons
mayonnaise
2 tablespoons minced green onion
4 slices whole grain or whole-wheat bread
2 tablespoons softened butter

1. In a medium bowl, combine the cheese, shrimp, mayonnaise, and green onion, and mix well.
2. Spread this mixture on two of the slices of bread. Top with the other slices of bread to make two sandwiches. Spread the sandwiches lightly with butter.
3. Select the AIR FRY function and cook at 400ºF (204ºC) for 5 to 7 minutes, or until the bread is browned and crisp and the cheese is melted.
4. Cut in half and serve warm.

Tuna Steak and Lettuce Wraps

Prep time: 10 minutes | Cook time: 4 to 7 minutes | Serves 4

1 pound (454 g) fresh tuna steak, cut into 1-inch cubes
1 tablespoon grated fresh ginger
2 garlic cloves, minced
½ teaspoon toasted sesame oil
4 low-sodium whole-wheat tortillas
¼ cup low-fat mayonnaise
2 cups shredded romaine lettuce
1 red bell pepper, thinly sliced

1. In a medium bowl, mix the tuna, ginger, garlic, and sesame oil. Let it stand for 10 minutes.
2. Transfer the tuna to the air fryer basket.
3. Select the AIR FRY function and cook at 390ºF (199ºC) for 4 to 7 minutes, or until lightly browned.
4. Make the wraps with the tuna, tortillas, mayonnaise, lettuce, and bell pepper.
5. Serve immediately.

Vegan Nugget and Veggie Taco Wraps

Prep time: 5 minutes | Cook time: 15 minutes | Serves 4

1 tablespoon water
4 pieces commercial vegan nuggets, chopped
1 small yellow onion, diced
1 small red bell
pepper, chopped
2 cobs grilled corn kernels
4 large corn tortillas
Mixed greens, for garnish

1. Over a medium heat, sauté the nuggets in the water with the onion, corn kernels and bell pepper in a skillet, then remove from the heat.
2. Fill the tortillas with the nuggets and vegetables and fold them up. Transfer to the air fryer basket. Select the AIR FRY function and cook at 400ºF (204ºC) for 15 minutes.
3. Once crispy, serve immediately, garnished with the mixed greens.

Chicken Breast Pita Sandwich

Prep time: 10 minutes | Cook time: 9 to 11 minutes | Serves 4

2 boneless, skinless chicken breasts, cut into 1-inch cubes
1 small red onion, sliced
1 red bell pepper, sliced
⅓ cup Italian salad dressing, divided
½ teaspoon dried thyme
4 pita pockets, split
2 cups torn butter lettuce
1 cup chopped cherry tomatoes

1. Select the BAKE function and preheat MAXX to 380ºF (193ºC).
2. Place the chicken, onion, and bell pepper in the air fryer basket. Drizzle with 1 tablespoon of the Italian salad dressing, add the thyme, and toss.
3. Bake for 9 to 11 minutes, or until the chicken is 165ºF (74ºC) on a food thermometer, stirring once during cooking time.
4. Transfer the chicken and vegetables to a bowl and toss with the remaining salad dressing.
5. Assemble sandwiches with the pita pockets, butter lettuce, and cherry tomatoes. Serve immediately.

Chicken Thighs-Lettuce Wraps

Prep time: 15 minutes | Cook time: 12 to 16 minutes | Serves 2 to 4

1 pound (454 g) boneless, skinless chicken thighs, trimmed
1 teaspoon vegetable oil
2 tablespoons lime juice
1 shallot, minced
1 tablespoon fish sauce, plus extra for serving
2 teaspoons packed brown sugar
1 garlic clove, minced
⅛ teaspoon red pepper flakes
1 mango, peeled, pitted, and cut into ¼-inch pieces
⅓ cup chopped fresh mint
⅓ cup chopped fresh cilantro
⅓ cup chopped fresh Thai basil
1 head Bibb lettuce, leaves separated (8 ounces / 227 g)
¼ cup chopped dry-roasted peanuts
2 Thai chiles, stemmed and sliced thin

1. Pat the chicken dry with paper towels and rub with oil. Place the chicken in air fryer basket. Select the AIR FRY function and cook at 400ºF (204ºC) for 12 to 16 minutes, or until the chicken registers 175ºF (79ºC), flipping and rotating chicken halfway through cooking.
2. Meanwhile, whisk lime juice, shallot, fish sauce, sugar, garlic, and pepper flakes together in large bowl; set aside.
3. Transfer chicken to cutting board, let cool slightly, then shred into bite-size pieces using 2 forks. Add the shredded chicken, mango, mint, cilantro, and basil to bowl with dressing and toss to coat.
4. Serve the chicken in the lettuce leaves, passing peanuts, Thai chiles, and extra fish sauce separately.

Fajita Lettuce Meatball Wraps

Prep time: 10 minutes | Cook time: 10 minutes | Serves 4

1 pound (454 g) 85% lean ground beef
½ cup salsa, plus more for serving
¼ cup chopped onions
¼ cup diced green or red bell peppers
1 large egg, beaten
1 teaspoon fine sea salt
½ teaspoon chili powder
½ teaspoon ground cumin
1 clove garlic, minced
Cooking spray
For Serving:
8 leaves Boston lettuce
Pico de gallo or salsa
Lime slices

1. Spray the air fryer basket with cooking spray.
2. In a large bowl, mix together all the ingredients until well combined.
3. Shape the meat mixture into eight 1-inch balls. Place the meatballs in the air fryer basket, leaving a little space between them.
4. Select the AIR FRY function and cook at 350ºF (177ºC) for 10 minutes, or until cooked through and no longer pink inside and the internal temperature reaches 145ºF (63ºC).
5. Serve each meatball on a lettuce leaf, topped with pico de gallo or salsa. Serve with lime slices.

Chapter 10 Appetizers and Snacks

Crispy Green Olives

Prep time: 5 minutes | Cook time: 8 minutes | Serves 4

1 (5½-ounce / 156-g) jar pitted green olives	Salt and pepper, to taste
½ cup all-purpose flour	½ cup bread crumbs
	1 egg
	Cooking spray

1. Remove the olives from the jar and dry thoroughly with paper towels.
2. In a small bowl, combine the flour with salt and pepper to taste. Place the bread crumbs in another small bowl. In a third small bowl, beat the egg.
3. Spritz the air fryer basket with cooking spray.
4. Dip the olives in the flour, then the egg, and then the bread crumbs.
5. Place the breaded olives in the air fryer oven. It is okay to stack them. Spray the olives with cooking spray.
6. Select the AIR FRY function and cook at 400ºF (204ºC) for 6 minutes. Flip the olives and air fry for an additional 2 minutes, or until brown and crisp.
7. Cool before serving.

Ricotta and Parmesan Cheese Bake

Prep time: 10 minutes | Cook time: 15 minutes | Makes 2 cups

1 (15-ounce / 425-g) container whole milk Ricotta cheese	1 teaspoon grated lemon zest
3 tablespoons grated Parmesan cheese, divided	1 clove garlic, crushed with press
2 tablespoons extra-virgin olive oil	¼ teaspoon salt
1 teaspoon chopped fresh thyme leaves	¼ teaspoon pepper
	Toasted baguette slices or crackers, for serving

1. Select the BAKE function and preheat MAXX to 380ºF (193ºC).
2. To get the baking dish in and out of the air fryer oven, create a sling using a 24-inch length of foil, folded lengthwise into thirds.
3. Whisk together the Ricotta, 2 tablespoons of the Parmesan, oil, thyme, lemon zest, garlic, salt, and pepper. Pour into a baking dish. Cover the dish tightly with foil.
4. Place the sling under dish and lift by the ends into the air fryer oven, tucking the ends of the sling around the dish. Bake for 10 minutes. Remove the foil cover and sprinkle with the remaining 1 tablespoon of the Parmesan. Switch from BAKE to AIR FRY and air fry for 5 more minutes, or until bubbly at edges and the top is browned.
5. Serve warm with toasted baguette slices or crackers.

Veggie Pot Stickers

Prep time: 10 minutes | Cook time: 18 to 20 minutes | Makes 30 pot stickers

½ cup finely chopped cabbage	cocktail sauce
¼ cup finely chopped red bell pepper	2 teaspoons low-sodium soy sauce
2 green onions, finely chopped	30 wonton wrappers
1 egg, beaten	1 tablespoon water, for brushing the wrappers
2 tablespoons	

1. In a small bowl, combine the cabbage, pepper, green onions, egg, cocktail sauce, and soy sauce, and mix well.
2. Put about 1 teaspoon of the mixture in the center of each wonton wrapper. Fold the wrapper in half, covering the filling; dampen the edges with water, and seal. You can crimp the edges of the wrapper with your fingers so they look like the pot stickers you get in restaurants. Brush them with water.
3. Place the pot stickers in the air fryer basket. Select the AIR FRY function and cook at 360ºF (182ºC) for 9 to 10 minutes, or until the pot stickers are hot and the bottoms are lightly browned.
4. Serve hot.

BBQ Bacon-Wrapped Shrimp and Jalapeño

Prep time: 20 minutes | Cook time: 26 minutes | Serves 8

24 large shrimp, peeled and deveined, about ¾ pound (340 g)
5 tablespoons barbecue sauce, divided
12 strips bacon, cut in half
24 small pickled jalapeño slices

1. Toss together the shrimp and 3 tablespoons of the barbecue sauce. Let stand for 15 minutes. Soak 24 wooden toothpicks in water for 10 minutes. Wrap 1 piece bacon around the shrimp and jalapeño slice, then secure with a toothpick.
2. Working in batches, place half of the shrimp in the air fryer basket, spacing them ½ inch apart.
3. Select the AIR FRY function and cook at 350°F (177°C) for 10 minutes. Turn shrimp over with tongs and air fry for 3 minutes more, or until bacon is golden brown and shrimp are cooked through.
4. Brush with the remaining barbecue sauce and serve.

Apple Chips

Prep time: 5 minutes | Cook time: 25 to 35 minutes | Serves 1

1 Honeycrisp or Pink Lady apple

1. Core the apple with an apple corer, leaving apple whole. Cut the apple into ⅛-inch-thick slices.
2. Arrange the apple slices in the basket, staggering slices as much as possible.
3. Select the AIR FRY function and cook at 300°F (149°C) for 25 to 35 minutes, or until the chips are dry and some are lightly browned, turning 4 times with tongs to separate and rotate them from top to bottom.
4. Place the chips in a single layer on a wire rack to cool. Apples will become crisper as they cool. Serve immediately.

Spinach and Artichoke Dip

Prep time: 10 minutes | Cook time: 10 minutes | Makes 3 cups

1 (14-ounce / 397-g) can artichoke hearts packed in water, drained and chopped
1 (10-ounce / 284-g) package frozen spinach, thawed and drained
1 teaspoon minced garlic
2 tablespoons
mayonnaise
¼ cup nonfat plain Greek yogurt
¼ cup shredded part-skim Mozzarella cheese
¼ cup grated Parmesan cheese
¼ teaspoon freshly ground black pepper
Cooking spray

1. Wrap the artichoke hearts and spinach in a paper towel and squeeze out any excess liquid, then transfer the vegetables to a large bowl.
2. Add the minced garlic, mayonnaise, plain Greek yogurt, Mozzarella, Parmesan, and black pepper to the large bowl, stirring well to combine.
3. Spray a baking pan with cooking spray, then transfer the dip mixture to the pan. Select the AIR FRY function and cook at 360°F (182°C) for 10 minutes.
4. Remove the dip from the air fryer oven and allow to cool in the pan on a wire rack for 10 minutes before serving.

Bacon-Wrapped Chinese Date

Prep time: 10 minutes | Cook time: 10 to 14 minutes | Serves 6

12 dates, pitted
6 slices high-quality
bacon, cut in half
Cooking spray

1. Select the BAKE function and preheat MAXX to 360°F (182°C).
2. Wrap each date with half a bacon slice and secure with a toothpick.
3. Spray the air fryer basket with cooking spray, then place 6 bacon-wrapped dates in the basket and bake for 5 to 7 minutes or until the bacon is crispy. Repeat this process with the remaining dates.
4. Remove the dates and allow to cool on a wire rack for 5 minutes before serving.

Savory Pork Ribs

Prep time: 5 minutes | Cook time: 35 minutes | Serves 2

1 tablespoon kosher salt
1 tablespoon dark brown sugar
1 tablespoon sweet paprika
1 teaspoon garlic powder
1 teaspoon onion powder

1 teaspoon poultry seasoning
½ teaspoon mustard powder
½ teaspoon freshly ground black pepper
2¼ pounds (1 kg) individually cut St. Louis–style pork spareribs

1. Select the ROAST function and preheat MAXX to 350ºF (177ºC).
2. In a large bowl, whisk together the salt, brown sugar, paprika, garlic powder, onion powder, poultry seasoning, mustard powder, and pepper. Add the ribs and toss. Rub the seasonings into them with your hands until they're fully coated.
3. Arrange the ribs in the air fryer basket, standing up on their ends and leaned up against the wall of the basket and each other. Roast for 35 minutes, or until the ribs are tender inside and golden brown and crisp on the outside. Transfer the ribs to plates and serve hot.

Artichoke Phyllo Triangles

Prep time: 15 minutes | Cook time: 9 to 12 minutes | Makes 18 triangles

¼ cup Ricotta cheese
1 egg white
⅓ cup minced and drained artichoke hearts
3 tablespoons grated Mozzarella cheese

½ teaspoon dried thyme
6 sheets frozen phyllo dough, thawed
2 tablespoons melted butter

1. Select the BAKE function and preheat MAXX to 400ºF (204ºC).
2. In a small bowl, combine the Ricotta cheese, egg white, artichoke hearts, Mozzarella cheese, and thyme, and mix well.

3. Cover the phyllo dough with a damp kitchen towel while you work so it doesn't dry out. Using one sheet at a time, place on the work surface and cut into thirds lengthwise.
4. Put about 1½ teaspoons of the filling on each strip at the base. Fold the bottom right-hand tip of phyllo over the filling to meet the other side in a triangle, then continue folding in a triangle. Brush each triangle with butter to seal the edges. Repeat with the remaining phyllo dough and filling.
5. Place the triangles in the air fryer basket. Bake, 6 at a time, for about 3 to 4 minutes, or until the phyllo is golden brown and crisp.
6. Serve hot.

Balsamic Beef and Mango Skewers

Prep time: 10 minutes | Cook time: 4 to 7 minutes | Serves 4

¾ pound (340 g) beef sirloin tip, cut into 1-inch cubes
2 tablespoons balsamic vinegar
1 tablespoon olive oil
1 tablespoon honey

½ teaspoon dried marjoram
Pinch of salt
Freshly ground black pepper, to taste
1 mango

1. Select the ROAST function and preheat MAXX to 390ºF (199ºC).
2. Put the beef cubes in a medium bowl and add the balsamic vinegar, olive oil, honey, marjoram, salt, and pepper. Mix well, then massage the marinade into the beef with your hands. Set aside.
3. To prepare the mango, stand it on end and cut the skin off, using a sharp knife. Then carefully cut around the oval pit to remove the flesh. Cut the mango into 1-inch cubes.
4. Thread metal skewers alternating with three beef cubes and two mango cubes.
5. Roast the skewers in the air fryer basket for 4 to 7 minutes, or until the beef is browned and at least 145ºF (63ºC).
6. Serve hot.

Stuffed Mushrooms with Cheese
Prep time: 10 minutes | Cook time: 8 to 12 minutes | Serves 4

16 medium button mushrooms, rinsed and patted dry
⅓ cup low-sodium salsa
3 garlic cloves, minced
1 medium onion, finely chopped

1 jalapeño pepper, minced
⅛ teaspoon cayenne pepper
3 tablespoons shredded Pepper Jack cheese
2 teaspoons olive oil

1. Remove the stems from the mushrooms and finely chop them, reserving the whole caps.
2. In a medium bowl, mix the salsa, garlic, onion, jalapeño, cayenne, and Pepper Jack cheese. Stir in the chopped mushroom stems.
3. Stuff this mixture into the mushroom caps, mounding the filling. Drizzle the olive oil on the mushrooms. Transfer to the air fryer basket.
4. Select the AIR FRY function and cook at 350ºF (177ºC) for 8 to 12 minutes, or until the filling is hot and the mushrooms are tender.
5. Serve immediately.

Whole Artichoke Hearts
Prep time: 5 minutes | Cook time: 8 minutes | Serves 14

14 whole artichoke hearts, packed in water
1 egg
½ cup all-purpose flour

⅓ cup panko bread crumbs
1 teaspoon Italian seasoning
Cooking spray

1. Squeeze excess water from the artichoke hearts and place them on paper towels to dry.
2. In a small bowl, beat the egg. In another small bowl, place the flour. In a third small bowl, combine the bread crumbs and Italian seasoning, and stir.
3. Spritz the air fryer basket with cooking spray.
4. Dip the artichoke hearts in the flour, then the egg, and then the bread crumb mixture.
5. Place the breaded artichoke hearts in the air fryer basket. Spray them with cooking spray.
6. Select the AIR FRY function and cook at 380ºF (193ºC) for 8 minutes, or until the artichoke hearts have browned and are crisp, flipping once halfway through.
7. Let cool for 5 minutes before serving.

Coconut Shrimp with Cucumber Yogurt
Prep time: 10 minutes | Cook time: 4 minutes | Serves 2 to 4

½ pound (227 g) medium shrimp, peeled and deveined (tails intact)
1 cup canned coconut milk
Finely grated zest of 1 lime
Kosher salt, to taste
½ cup panko bread crumbs

½ cup unsweetened shredded coconut
Freshly ground black pepper, to taste
Cooking spray
1 small or ½ medium cucumber, halved and deseeded
1 cup coconut yogurt
1 serrano chile, deseeded and minced

1. In a bowl, combine the shrimp, coconut milk, lime zest, and ½ teaspoon kosher salt. Let the shrimp stand for 10 minutes.
2. Meanwhile, in a separate bowl, stir together the bread crumbs and shredded coconut and season with salt and pepper.
3. A few at a time, add the shrimp to the bread crumb mixture and toss to coat completely. Transfer the shrimp to a wire rack set over a baking sheet. Spray the shrimp all over with cooking spray.
4. Transfer the shrimp to the air fryer oven. Select the AIR FRY function and cook at 400ºF (204ºC) for 4 minutes, or until golden brown and cooked through. Transfer the shrimp to a serving platter and season with more salt.
5. Grate the cucumber into a small bowl. Stir in the coconut yogurt and chile and season with salt and pepper. Serve alongside the shrimp while they're warm.

Zucchini Fries with Roasted Garlic Aïoli

Prep time: 10 minutes | Cook time: 12 minutes | Serves 4

Roasted Garlic Aïoli:

1 teaspoon roasted garlic
½ cup mayonnaise
2 tablespoons olive

oil
Juice of ½ lemon
Salt and pepper

Zucchini Fries:

½ cup flour
2 eggs, beaten
1 cup seasoned bread crumbs
Salt and pepper

1 large zucchini, cut into ½-inch sticks
Olive oil in a spray bottle, can or mister

1. To make the aïoli, combine the roasted garlic, mayonnaise, olive oil and lemon juice in a bowl and whisk well. Season the aïoli with salt and pepper to taste.
2. Prepare the zucchini fries. Create a dredging station with three shallow dishes. Place the flour in the first shallow dish and season well with salt and freshly ground black pepper. Put the beaten eggs in the second shallow dish. In the third shallow dish, combine the bread crumbs, salt and pepper. Dredge the zucchini sticks, coating with flour first, then dipping them into the eggs to coat, and finally tossing in bread crumbs. Shake the dish with the bread crumbs and pat the crumbs onto the zucchini sticks gently with your hands so they stick evenly.
3. Place the zucchini fries on a flat surface and let them sit at least 10 minutes before air frying to let them dry out a little.
4. Spray the zucchini sticks with olive oil, and place them into the air fryer basket. You can air fry the zucchini in two layers, placing the second layer in the opposite direction to the first.
5. Select the AIR FRY function and cook at 400ºF (205ºC) for 12 minutes, turning and rotating the fries halfway through the cooking time. Spray with additional oil when you turn them over.
6. Serve zucchini fries warm with the roasted garlic aïoli.

Spicy Sesame Nut Mix

Prep time: 10 minutes | Cook time: 2 minutes | Makes 4 cups

1 tablespoon buttery spread, melted
2 teaspoons honey
¼ teaspoon cayenne pepper
2 teaspoons sesame seeds
¼ teaspoon kosher salt

¼ teaspoon freshly ground black pepper
1 cup cashews
1 cup almonds
1 cup mini pretzels
1 cup rice squares cereal
Cooking spray

1. Select the BAKE function and preheat MAXX to 360ºF (182ºC).
2. In a large bowl, combine the buttery spread, honey, cayenne pepper, sesame seeds, kosher salt, and black pepper, then add the cashews, almonds, pretzels, and rice squares, tossing to coat.
3. Spray a baking pan with cooking spray, then pour the mixture into the pan and bake for 2 minutes.
4. Remove the sesame mix from the air fryer oven and allow to cool in the pan on a wire rack for 5 minutes before serving.

Cajun Seasoned Zucchini Chips

Prep time: 5 minutes | Cook time: 15 to 16 minutes | Serves 4

2 large zucchini, cut into ⅛-inch-thick slices

2 teaspoons Cajun seasoning
Cooking spray

1. Spray the air fryer basket lightly with cooking spray.
2. Put the zucchini slices in a medium bowl and spray them generously with cooking spray.
3. Sprinkle the Cajun seasoning over the zucchini and stir to make sure they are evenly coated with oil and seasoning.
4. Place the slices in a single layer in the air fryer basket, making sure not to overcrowd. You will need to cook these in several batches.
5. Select the AIR FRY function and cook at 370ºF (188ºC) for 8 minutes. Flip the slices over and air fry for an additional 7 to 8 minutes, or until they are as crisp and brown as you prefer.
6. Serve immediately.

Apple Rolls with Colby Jack Cheese

Prep time: 5 minutes | Cook time: 4 to 5 minutes | Makes 8 roll-ups

8 slices whole wheat sandwich bread	½ small apple, chopped
4 ounces (113 g) Colby Jack cheese, grated	2 tablespoons butter, melted

1. Remove the crusts from the bread and flatten the slices with a rolling pin. Don't be gentle. Press hard so that bread will be very thin.
2. Top bread slices with cheese and chopped apple, dividing the ingredients evenly.
3. Roll up each slice tightly and secure each with one or two toothpicks.
4. Brush outside of rolls with melted butter.
5. Place in air fryer basket. Select the AIR FRY function and cook at 390ºF (199ºC) for 4 to 5 minutes, or until outside is crisp and nicely browned.
6. Serve hot.

Super Cheesy Hash Brown Bruschetta

Prep time: 5 minutes | Cook time: 6 to 8 minutes | Serves 4

4 frozen hash brown patties	2 tablespoons grated Parmesan cheese
1 tablespoon olive oil	1 tablespoon balsamic vinegar
1/3 cup chopped cherry tomatoes	1 tablespoon minced fresh basil
3 tablespoons diced fresh Mozzarella	

1. Place the hash brown patties in the air fryer basket in a single layer. Select the AIR FRY function and cook at 400ºF (204ºC) for 6 to 8 minutes, or until the potatoes are crisp, hot, and golden brown.
2. Meanwhile, combine the olive oil, tomatoes, Mozzarella, Parmesan, vinegar, and basil in a small bowl.
3. When the potatoes are done, carefully remove from the basket and arrange on a serving plate. Top with the tomato mixture and serve.

Creamy-Cheesy Jalapeño Poppers

Prep time: 5 minutes | Cook time: 10 minutes | Serves 4

8 jalapeño peppers	¼ cup shredded Cheddar cheese
½ cup whipped cream cheese	

1. Use a paring knife to carefully cut off the jalapeño tops, then scoop out the ribs and seeds. Set aside.
2. In a medium bowl, combine the whipped cream cheese and shredded Cheddar cheese. Place the mixture in a sealable plastic bag, and using a pair of scissors, cut off one corner from the bag. Gently squeeze some cream cheese mixture into each pepper until almost full.
3. Place a piece of parchment paper on the bottom of the air fryer basket and place the poppers on top, distributing evenly. Select the AIR FRY function and cook at 360ºF (182ºC) for 10 minutes.
4. Allow the poppers to cool for 5 to 10 minutes before serving.

Steak Fries with Mozzarella

Prep time: 5 minutes | Cook time: 20 minutes | Serves 5

1 (28-ounce / 794-g) bag frozen steak fries	½ cup beef gravy
Cooking spray	1 cup shredded Mozzarella cheese
Salt and pepper, to taste	2 scallions, green parts only, chopped

1. Place the frozen steak fries in the air fryer oven. Select the AIR FRY function and cook at 400ºF (204ºC) for 10 minutes. Shake the basket and spritz the fries with cooking spray. Sprinkle with salt and pepper. Air fry for an additional 8 minutes.
2. Pour the beef gravy into a medium, microwave-safe bowl. Microwave for 30 seconds, or until the gravy is warm.
3. Sprinkle the fries with the cheese. Air fry for an additional 2 minutes, until the cheese is melted.
4. Transfer the fries to a serving dish. Drizzle the fries with gravy and sprinkle the scallions on top for a green garnish. Serve.

Mozzarella Bruschetta with Basil Pesto
Prep time: 10 minutes | Cook time: 5 to 11 minutes | Serves 4

8 slices French bread, ½ inch thick
2 tablespoons softened butter
1 cup shredded Mozzarella cheese
½ cup basil pesto
1 cup chopped grape tomatoes
2 green onions, thinly sliced

1. Select the BAKE function and preheat MAXX to 350ºF (177ºC).
2. Spread the bread with the butter and place butter-side up in the air fryer basket. Bake for 3 to 5 minutes, or until the bread is light golden brown.
3. Remove the bread from the basket and top each piece with some of the cheese. Return to the basket in 2 batches and bake for 1 to 3 minutes, or until the cheese melts.
4. Meanwhile, combine the pesto, tomatoes, and green onions in a small bowl.
5. When the cheese has melted, remove the bread from the air fryer oven and place on a serving plate. Top each slice with some of the pesto mixture and serve.

Cauliflower with Sour Dip
Prep time: 10 minutes | Cook time: 10 to 14 minutes | Serves 6

1 large head cauliflower, separated into small florets
1 tablespoon olive oil
½ teaspoon garlic powder
$\frac{1}{3}$ cup low-sodium hot wing sauce, divided
$\frac{2}{3}$ cup nonfat Greek yogurt
½ teaspoons Tabasco sauce
1 celery stalk, chopped
1 tablespoon crumbled blue cheese

1. In a large bowl, toss the cauliflower florets with the olive oil. Sprinkle with the garlic powder and toss again to coat. Put half of the cauliflower in the air fryer basket.
2. Select the AIR FRY function and cook at 380ºF (193ºC) for 5 to 7 minutes, or until the cauliflower is browned, shaking the basket once during cooking.
3. Transfer to a serving bowl and toss with half of the wing sauce. Repeat with the remaining cauliflower and wing sauce.
4. In a small bowl, stir together the yogurt, Tabasco sauce, celery, and blue cheese. Serve the cauliflower with the dip.

French Fries with Cheddar Cheese Sauce
Prep time: 10 minutes | Cook time: 30 minutes | Serves 2 to 3

2 to 3 large russet potatoes, peeled and cut into ½-inch sticks
2 tablespoons vegetable oil
2 tablespoons butter
2 tablespoons flour
1 to 1½ cups milk
½ cup grated white Cheddar cheese
Pinch of nutmeg
½ teaspoon salt
Freshly ground black pepper
1 tablespoon Old Bay Seasoning

1. Bring a large saucepan of salted water to a boil on the stovetop while you peel and cut the potatoes. Blanch the potatoes in the boiling salted water for 4 minutes. Strain the potatoes and rinse them with cold water. Dry them well with a clean kitchen towel.
2. Toss the dried potato sticks gently with the oil and place them in the air fryer basket. Select the AIR FRY function and cook at 400ºF (205ºC) for 25 minutes, shaking the basket a few times while the fries cook to help them brown evenly.
3. While the fries are cooking, melt the butter in a medium saucepan. Whisk in the flour and cook for one minute. Slowly add 1 cup of milk, whisking constantly. Bring the mixture to a simmer and continue to whisk until it thickens. Remove the pan from the heat and stir in the Cheddar cheese. Add a pinch of nutmeg and season with salt and freshly ground black pepper. Transfer the warm cheese sauce to a serving dish. Thin with more milk if you want the sauce a little thinner.
4. As soon as the French fries have finished air frying transfer them to a large bowl and season them with the Old Bay Seasoning. Return the fries to the air fryer basket and air fry for an additional 3 to 5 minutes. Serve immediately with the warm white Cheddar cheese sauce.

Cajun Dill Pickle Chips

Prep time: 5 minutes | Cook time: 10 minutes | Makes 16 slices

¼ cup all-purpose flour
½ cup panko bread crumbs
1 large egg, beaten
2 teaspoons Cajun seasoning
2 large dill pickles, sliced into 8 rounds each
Cooking spray

1. Place the all-purpose flour, panko bread crumbs, and egg into 3 separate shallow bowls, then stir the Cajun seasoning into the flour.
2. Dredge each pickle chip in the flour mixture, then the egg, and finally the bread crumbs. Shake off any excess, then place each coated pickle chip on a plate.
3. Spritz the air fryer basket with cooking spray, then place 8 pickle chips in the basket. Select the AIR FRY function and cook at 390ºF (199ºC) for 5 minutes, or until crispy and golden brown. Repeat this process with the remaining pickle chips.
4. Remove the chips and allow to slightly cool on a wire rack before serving.

Herbed-Spiced Chickpeas

Prep time: 5 minutes | Cook time: 6 to 12 minutes | Makes 1½ cups

1 can (15-ounce / 425-g) chickpeas, rinsed and dried with paper towels
1 tablespoon olive oil
½ teaspoon dried rosemary
½ teaspoon dried parsley
½ teaspoon dried
chives
¼ teaspoon mustard powder
¼ teaspoon sweet paprika
¼ teaspoon cayenne pepper
Kosher salt and freshly ground black pepper, to taste

1. In a large bowl, combine all the ingredients, except for the kosher salt and black pepper, and toss until the chickpeas are evenly coated in the herbs and spices.

2. Scrape the chickpeas and seasonings into the air fryer oven. Select the AIR FRY function and cook at 350ºF (177ºC) for 6 to 12 minutes, or until browned and crisp, shaking the basket halfway through.
3. Transfer the crispy chickpeas to a bowl, sprinkle with kosher salt and black pepper, and serve warm.

Mozzarella Cheese Sticks

Prep time: 5 minutes | Cook time: 6 to 7 minutes | Serves 4 to 8

1 egg
1 tablespoon water
8 eggroll wraps
8 Mozzarella string cheese "sticks"

1. Beat together egg and water in a small bowl.
2. Lay out eggroll wraps and moisten edges with egg wash.
3. Place one piece of string cheese on each wrap near one end.
4. Fold in sides of eggroll wrap over ends of cheese, and then roll up.
5. Brush outside of wrap with egg wash and press gently to seal well.
6. Place in air fryer basket in a single layer. Select the AIR FRY function and cook at 390ºF (199ºC) for 5 minutes. Air fry for an additional 1 or 2 minutes, if necessary, or until they are golden brown and crispy.
7. Serve immediately.

Corn Tortilla Chips

Prep time: 5 minutes | Cook time: 3 minutes | Serves 2

8 corn tortillas
1 tablespoon olive oil
Salt, to taste

1. Slice the corn tortillas into triangles. Coat with a light brushing of olive oil.
2. Put the tortilla pieces in the air fryer basket. Select the AIR FRY function and cook at 390ºF (199ºC) for 3 minutes. You may need to do this in batches.
3. Season with salt before serving.

Herb Pita Chips

Prep time: 5 minutes | Cook time: 5 to 6 minutes | Serves 4

¼ teaspoon dried basil
¼ teaspoon marjoram
¼ teaspoon ground oregano
¼ teaspoon garlic powder
¼ teaspoon ground thyme
¼ teaspoon salt
2 whole 6-inch pitas, whole grain or white
Cooking spray

1. Select the BAKE function and preheat MAXX to 330ºF (166ºC).
2. Mix all the seasonings together.
3. Cut each pita half into 4 wedges. Break apart wedges at the fold.
4. Mist one side of pita wedges with oil. Sprinkle with half of seasoning mix.
5. Turn pita wedges over, mist the other side with oil, and sprinkle with remaining seasonings.
6. Place pita wedges in air fryer basket and bake for 2 minutes.
7. Shake the basket and bake for 2 minutes longer. Shake again, and if needed, bake for 1 or 2 more minutes, or until crisp. Watch carefully because at this point they will cook very quickly.
8. Serve hot.

Sriracha Chicken

Prep time: 5 minutes | Cook time: 30 minutes | Serves 4

1 tablespoon Sriracha hot sauce
1 tablespoon honey
1 garlic clove, minced
½ teaspoon kosher salt
16 chicken wings and drumettes
Cooking spray

1. In a large bowl, whisk together the Sriracha hot sauce, honey, minced garlic, and kosher salt, then add the chicken and toss to coat.
2. Spray the air fryer basket with cooking spray, then place 8 wings in the basket.
3. Select the AIR FRY function and cook at 360ºF (182ºC) for 15 minutes, turning halfway through. Repeat with the remaining wings.
4. Remove the wings and allow to cool on a wire rack for 10 minutes before serving.

Chicken Drumsticks with Lemon

Prep time: 5 minutes | Cook time: 30 minutes | Serves 2

2 teaspoons freshly ground coarse black pepper
1 teaspoon baking powder
½ teaspoon garlic powder
4 chicken drumsticks (4 ounces / 113 g each)
Kosher salt, to taste
1 lemon

1. In a small bowl, stir together the pepper, baking powder, and garlic powder. Place the drumsticks on a plate and sprinkle evenly with the baking powder mixture, turning the drumsticks so they're well coated. Let the drumsticks stand in the refrigerator for at least 1 hour or up to overnight.
2. Sprinkle the drumsticks with salt, then transfer them to the air fryer oven, standing them bone-end up and leaning against the wall of the air fryer basket. Select the AIR FRY function and cook at 375ºF (191ºC) for 30 minutes, or until cooked through and crisp on the outside.
3. Transfer the drumsticks to a serving platter and finely grate the zest of the lemon over them while they're hot. Cut the lemon into wedges and serve with the warm drumsticks.

Prosciutto-Wrapped Asparagus Bundles

Prep time: 5 minutes | Cook time: 16 to 24 minutes | Serves 6

12 asparagus spears, woody ends trimmed
24 pieces thinly sliced prosciutto
Cooking spray

1. Wrap each asparagus spear with 2 slices of prosciutto, then repeat this process with the remaining asparagus and prosciutto.
2. Spray the air fryer basket with cooking spray, then place 2 to 3 bundles in the basket. Select the AIR FRY function and cook at 360ºF (182ºC) for 4 minutes. Repeat with the remaining asparagus bundles.
3. Remove the bundles and allow to cool on a wire rack for 5 minutes before serving.

Lemony Endive in Curry Yogurt
Prep time: 5 minutes | Cook time: 10 minutes | Serves 6

6 heads endive
½ cup plain and fat-free yogurt
3 tablespoons lemon juice
1 teaspoon garlic powder
½ teaspoon curry powder
Salt and ground black pepper, to taste

Wash the endives, and slice them in half lengthwise.
In a bowl, mix together the yogurt, lemon juice, garlic powder, curry powder, salt and pepper.
Brush the endive halves with the marinade, coating them completely. Allow to sit for at least 30 minutes or up to 24 hours.
Put the endives in the air fryer basket.
Select the AIR FRY function and cook at 320ºF (160ºC) for 10 minutes.
Serve hot.

Lemony Cinnamon Pear Chips
Prep time: 15 minutes | Cook time: 9 to 13 minutes | Serves 4

2 firm Bosc pears, cut crosswise into ⅛-inch-thick slices
1 tablespoon freshly squeezed lemon juice
½ teaspoon ground cinnamon
⅛ teaspoon ground cardamom

1. Separate the smaller stem-end pear rounds from the larger rounds with seeds. Remove the core and seeds from the larger slices. Sprinkle all slices with lemon juice, cinnamon, and cardamom.
2. Put the smaller chips into the air fryer basket. Select the AIR FRY function and cook at 380ºF (193ºC) for 3 to 5 minutes, or until light golden brown, shaking the basket once during cooking. Remove from the air fryer oven.
3. Repeat with the larger slices, air frying for 6 to 8 minutes, or until light golden brown, shaking the basket once during cooking.
4. Remove the chips from the air fryer oven. Cool and serve or store in an airtight container at room temperature up for to 2 days.

Broccoli and Spinach Dip
Prep time: 10 minutes | Cook time: 9 to 14 minutes | Serves 4

½ cup low-fat Greek yogurt
¼ cup nonfat cream cheese
½ cup frozen chopped broccoli, thawed and drained
½ cup frozen chopped spinach, thawed and drained
⅓ cup chopped red bell pepper
1 garlic clove, minced
½ teaspoon dried oregano
2 tablespoons grated low-sodium Parmesan cheese

1. Select the BAKE function and preheat MAXX to 340ºF (171ºC).
2. In a medium bowl, blend the yogurt and cream cheese until well combined.
3. Stir in the broccoli, spinach, red bell pepper, garlic, and oregano. Transfer to a baking pan. Sprinkle with the Parmesan cheese.
4. Place the pan in the air fryer basket. Bake for 9 to 14 minutes, or until the dip is bubbly and the top starts to brown.
5. Serve immediately.

Sirloin Cubes
Prep time: 10 minutes | Cook time: 12 to 16 minutes | Serves 4

1 pound (454 g) sirloin tip, cut into 1-inch cubes
1 cup cheese pasta sauce
1½ cups soft bread crumbs
2 tablespoons olive oil
½ teaspoon dried marjoram

1. In a medium bowl, toss the beef with the pasta sauce to coat.
2. In a shallow bowl, combine the bread crumbs, oil, and marjoram, and mix well. Drop the beef cubes, one at a time, into the bread crumb mixture to coat thoroughly. Transfer to the air fryer basket.
3. Select the AIR FRY function and cook in two batches at 360ºF (182ºC) for 6 to 8 minutes, shaking the basket once during cooking time, until the beef is at least 145ºF (63ºC) and the outside is crisp and brown.
4. Serve hot.

Arancini Balls

Prep time: 5 minutes | Cook time: 8 to 11 minutes | Makes 16 arancini

2 cups cooked rice, cooled
2 eggs, beaten
1½ cups panko bread crumbs, divided
½ cup grated Parmesan cheese
2 tablespoons minced fresh basil
16 ¾-inch cubes Mozzarella cheese
2 tablespoons olive oil

1. In a medium bowl, combine the rice, eggs, ½ cup of the bread crumbs, Parmesan cheese, and basil. Form this mixture into 16 1½-inch balls.
2. Poke a hole in each of the balls with your finger and insert a Mozzarella cube. Form the rice mixture firmly around the cheese.
3. On a shallow plate, combine the remaining 1 cup of the bread crumbs with the olive oil and mix well. Roll the rice balls in the bread crumbs to coat. Transfer to the air fryer basket.
4. Select the AIR FRY function and cook at 400ºF (204ºC) for 8 to 11 minutes, or until golden brown. You may need to work in batches.
5. Serve hot.

Chicken and Veggie Meatballs

Prep time: 5 minutes | Cook time: 13 to 20 minutes | Makes 16 meatballs

2 teaspoons olive oil
¼ cup minced onion
¼ cup minced red bell pepper
2 vanilla wafers, crushed
1 egg white
½ teaspoon dried thyme
½ pound (227 g) ground chicken breast

1. In a baking pan, mix the olive oil, onion, and red bell pepper. Put the pan in the air fryer oven. Select the AIR FRY function and cook at 370ºF (188ºC) for 3 to 5 minutes, or until the vegetables are tender.
2. In a medium bowl, mix the cooked vegetables, crushed wafers, egg white, and thyme until well combined.
3. Mix in the chicken, gently but thoroughly, until everything is combined.
4. Form the mixture into 16 meatballs and place them in the air fryer basket. Air fry for 10 to 15 minutes, or until the meatballs reach an internal temperature of 165ºF (74ºC) on a meat thermometer.
5. Serve immediately.

French Bistro Salad with Dijon Dressing

Prep time: 15 minutes | Cook time: 6 minutes | Serves 4 to 6

Salad:
1 (11- to 12-ounce / 312- to 340-g) log goat cheese
1 head butter lettuce
1 head radicchio
2 Belgian endive
1 cup panko bread crumbs
1 egg beaten with 1 tablespoon water
½ pint raspberries

Dressing:
1 tablespoon minced shallot
1 tablespoon Dijon mustard
½ teaspoon granulated sugar
3 tablespoons white
wine or champagne vinegar
½ cup plus 1 tablespoon extra-virgin olive oil
Kosher salt and pepper to taste

1. Place the goat cheese in the freezer for 15 minutes to firm up. Wash and dry the lettuce, radicchio, and endive and tear into small pieces. Place in a large salad bowl.
2. Place the panko on a plate. Using a piece of plain dental floss, slice the goat cheese into 12 rounds. Dunk each piece in the egg mixture until coated and then dredge in the panko, shaking off any excess. Place the breaded slices in the refrigerator for 15 minutes to firm up.
3. Meanwhile, make the dressing. Put the shallot, mustard, and sugar in a medium bowl. Add the vinegar and whisk to combine. While whisking, pour in the oil in a steady stream until emulsified. Add the dressing to the salad and toss. Season with salt and pepper. Add the raspberries.
4. Working in 2 batches, place the breaded goat cheese slices in the air fryer oven. Select the AIR FRY function and cook at 400ºF (205ºC) for 6 minutes, carefully flipping once halfway through. Remove from the air fryer oven with a spatula.
5. Divide the salad evenly among 4 or 6 plates, top each plate with 2 or 3 of the warm goat cheese croutons, and serve.

Blooming Onion with Sweet-Sour Dip

Prep time: 15 minutes | Cook time: 25 minutes | Serves 4

1 large Vidalia onion, peeled
2 eggs
½ cup milk
1 cup flour
1 teaspoon salt
½ teaspoon freshly ground black pepper
¼ teaspoon ground cayenne pepper
½ teaspoon paprika
½ teaspoon garlic

powder
Dipping Sauce:
½ cup mayonnaise
½ cup ketchup
1 teaspoon Worcestershire sauce
½ teaspoon ground cayenne pepper
½ teaspoon paprika
½ teaspoon onion powder

1. Cut off the top inch of the onion, leaving the root end of the onion intact. Place the now flat, stem end of the onion down on a cutting board with the root end facing up. Make 16 slices around the onion, starting with your knife tip ½-inch away from the root so that you never slice through the root. Begin by making slices at 12, 3, 6 and 9 o'clock around the onion. Then make three slices down the onion in between each of the original four slices. Turn the onion over, gently separate the onion petals, and remove the loose pieces of onion in the center.
2. Combine the eggs and milk in a bowl. In a second bowl, combine the flour, salt, black pepper, cayenne pepper, paprika, and garlic powder.
3. Place the onion cut side up into a third empty bowl. Sprinkle the flour mixture all over the onion to cover it and get in between the onion petals. Turn the onion over to carefully shake off the excess flour and then transfer the onion to the empty flour bowl, again cut side up.
4. Pour the egg mixture all over the onion to cover all the flour. Let it soak for a minute in the mixture. Carefully remove the onion, tipping it upside down to drain off any excess egg, and transfer it to the empty egg bowl, again cut side up.
5. Finally, sprinkle the flour mixture over the onion a second time, making sure the onion is well coated and all the petals have the seasoned flour mixture on them. Carefully turn the onion over, shake off any excess flour and transfer it to a plate or baking sheet. Spray the onion generously with vegetable oil.

6. Transfer the onion, cut side up to the air fryer basket. Select the AIR FRY function and cook at 350ºF (180ºC) for 25 minutes. The onion petals will open more fully as it cooks, so spray with more vegetable oil at least twice during the cooking time.
7. While the onion is cooking, make the dipping sauce by combining all the dip ingredients and mixing well. Serve hot with dipping sauce on the side.

Gougères

Prep time: 10 minutes | Cook time: 17 minutes | Serves 6 to 8

3 tablespoons unsalted butter
½ cup water
½ cup milk
Pinch kosher salt
Pinch granulated sugar
1 cup all-purpose

flour
2 eggs
6 ounces (170 g) Gruyère or Comté cheese, grated
Vegetable oil for brushing

1. Combine the butter, water, milk, salt, and sugar in a medium saucepan and melt the butter over low heat. Add the flour and stir to form a cohesive dough. Cook over medium-low heat for 2 minutes to get rid of the raw flour taste. Remove from heat and allow to cool to room temperature. Beat the eggs in one at a time, making sure the first egg is fully incorporated before adding the second. The dough will look curdled at first, but keep beating vigorously until the dough becomes smooth. Once the eggs are fully incorporated, add the grated cheese and beat the mixture again to incorporate.
2. Select the BAKE function and preheat MAXX to 360ºF (182ºC).
3. Brush the air fryer basket with oil. Using a small spring-loaded cookie scoop or a tablespoon, scoop 6 to 8 circles of dough directly onto the air fryer basket. Bake for 15 to 16 minutes, or until the gougères are a deep golden brown and the inside is cooked through. Remove the cooked gougères from the air fryer basket—you may need to use a thin, nonstick-safe spatula to detach them— and add another 6 to 8 scoops of dough to the basket. Cook in the same manner as the first batch. Serve warm.

Chapter 11 Desserts

Baked Buttery Apples
Prep time: 5 minutes | Cook time: 10 minutes | Serves 4

4 small apples, cored and cut in half
2 tablespoons salted butter or coconut oil, melted
2 tablespoons sugar

1 teaspoon apple pie spice
Ice cream, heavy cream, or whipped cream, for serving

1. Select the BAKE function and preheat MAXX to 350ºF (177ºC).
2. Put the apples in a large bowl. Drizzle with the melted butter and sprinkle with the sugar and apple pie spice. Use the hands to toss, ensuring the apples are evenly coated.
3. Put the apples in the air fryer basket and bake for 10 minutes. Pierce the apples with a fork to ensure they are tender.
4. Serve with ice cream, or top with a splash of heavy cream or a spoonful of whipped cream.

Apple Turnovers with Golden Raisins
Prep time: 10 minutes | Cook time: 45 to 50 minutes | Serves 4

3½ ounces (99 g) dried apples
¼ cup golden raisins
1 tablespoon granulated sugar
1 tablespoon freshly squeezed lemon juice
½ teaspoon cinnamon

1 pound (454 g) frozen puff pastry, defrosted
1 egg beaten with 1 tablespoon water
Turbinado or demerara sugar for sprinkling

1. Place the dried apples in a medium saucepan and cover with about 2 cups of water. Bring the mixture to a boil over medium-high heat, then reduce the heat to low, cover, and simmer until the apples have absorbed most of the liquid, about 20 minutes. Remove the apples from the heat and allow to cool. Add the raisins, sugar, lemon juice, and cinnamon to the rehydrated apples and set aside.

2. Select the BAKE function and preheat MAXX to 325ºF (165ºC).
3. On a well-floured board, roll the puff pastry out to a 12-inch square. Cut the square into 4 equal quarters. Divide the filling equally among the 4 squares, mounding it in the middle of each square. Brush the edges of each square with water and fold the pastry diagonally over the apple mixture, creating a triangle. Seal the edges by pressing them with the tines of a fork. Transfer the turnovers to a sheet pan lined with parchment paper.
4. Brush the top of 2 turnovers with egg wash and sprinkle with turbinado sugar. Make 2 small slits in the top of the turnovers for venting and bake for 25 to 30 minutes, until the top is browned and puffed and the pastry is cooked through. Remove the cooked turnovers to a cooling rack and repeat with the remaining turnovers. Serve warm or at room temperature.

Fruity Crisp
Prep time: 10 minutes | Cook time: 12 minutes | Serves 8

1 apple, peeled and chopped
2 peaches, peeled and chopped
⅓ cup dried cranberries

2 tablespoons honey
⅓ cup brown sugar
¼ cup flour
½ cup oatmeal
3 tablespoons softened butter

1. Select the BAKE function and preheat MAXX to 370ºF (188ºC).
2. In a baking pan, combine the apple, peaches, cranberries, and honey, and mix well.
3. In a medium bowl, combine the brown sugar, flour, oatmeal, and butter, and mix until crumbly. Sprinkle this mixture over the fruit in the pan.
4. Bake for 10 to 12 minutes or until the fruit is bubbly and the topping is golden brown. Serve warm.

Banana and Nuts Cake
Prep time: 10 minutes | Cook time: 25 minutes | Serves 6

1 pound (454 g) bananas, mashed	walnuts, chopped
8 ounces (227 g) flour	2.5 ounces (71 g) butter, melted
6 ounces (170 g) sugar	2 eggs, lightly beaten
3.5 ounces (99 g)	¼ teaspoon baking soda

1. Select the BAKE function and preheat MAXX to 355ºF (179ºC).
2. In a bowl, combine the sugar, butter, egg, flour, and baking soda with a whisk. Stir in the bananas and walnuts.
3. Transfer the mixture to a greased baking dish. Put the dish in the air fryer oven and bake for 10 minutes.
4. Reduce the temperature to 330ºF (166ºC) and bake for another 15 minutes. Serve hot.

Brazilian Pineapple Bake with Cinnamon
Prep time: 5 minutes | Cook time: 16 minutes | Serves 4

½ cup brown sugar	cut into spears
2 teaspoons ground cinnamon	3 tablespoons unsalted butter, melted
1 small pineapple, peeled, cored, and	

1. Select the BAKE function and preheat MAXX to 400ºF (204ºC).
2. In a small bowl, mix the brown sugar and cinnamon until thoroughly combined.
3. Brush the pineapple spears with the melted butter. Sprinkle the cinnamon-sugar over the spears, pressing lightly to ensure it adheres well.
4. Put the spears in the air fryer basket in a single layer. (Depending on the size of the air fryer oven, you may have to do this in batches.) Bake for 10 minutes for the first batch (6 to 8 minutes for the next batch, as the air fryer oven will be preheated). Halfway through the cooking time, brush the spears with butter.
5. The pineapple spears are done when they are heated through and the sugar is bubbling. Serve hot.

Chocolate-Hazelnut Croissants
Prep time: 5 minutes | Cook time: 24 minutes | Serves 8

1 sheet frozen puff pastry, thawed	hazelnut spread
⅓ cup chocolate-	1 large egg, beaten

1. On a lightly floured surface, roll puff pastry into a 14-inch square. Cut pastry into quarters to form 4 squares. Cut each square diagonally to form 8 triangles.
2. Spread 2 teaspoons chocolate-hazelnut spread on each triangle; from wider end, roll up pastry. Brush egg on top of each roll. Place in the air fryer basket.
3. Select the AIR FRY function and cook at 375ºF (191ºC) for 8 minutes, or until pastry is golden brown. You may need to work in batches.
4. Cool on a wire rack; serve while warm or at room temperature.

Mixed-Berry Crumble
Prep time: 10 minutes | Cook time: 15 minutes | Serves 4

For the Filling:

2 cups mixed berries	cornstarch
2 tablespoons sugar	1 tablespoon fresh lemon juice
1 tablespoon	

For the Topping:

¼ cup all-purpose flour	unsalted butter, cut into small cubes
¼ cup rolled oats	Whipped cream or ice cream (optional)
1 tablespoon sugar	
2 tablespoons cold	

1. For the filling: In a round baking pan, gently mix the berries, sugar, cornstarch, and lemon juice until thoroughly combined.
2. For the topping: In a small bowl, combine the flour, oats, and sugar. Stir the butter into the flour mixture until the mixture has the consistency of bread crumbs.
3. Sprinkle the topping over the berries. Put the pan in the air fryer basket.
4. Select the AIR FRY function and cook at 400ºF (204ºC) for 15 minutes.
5. Let cool for 5 minutes on a wire rack.
6. Serve topped with whipped cream or ice cream, if desired.

Vanilla and Cardamom Custard
Prep time: 5 minutes | Cook time: 25 minutes | Serves 2

1 cup whole milk	bean paste or pure
1 large egg	vanilla extract
2 tablespoons plus 1	¼ teaspoon ground
teaspoon sugar	cardamom, plus
¼ teaspoon vanilla	more for sprinkling

1. Select the BAKE function and preheat MAXX to 350ºF (177ºC).
2. In a medium bowl, beat together the milk, egg, sugar, vanilla, and cardamom.
3. Put two ramekins in the air fryer basket. Divide the mixture between the ramekins. Sprinkle lightly with cardamom. Cover each ramekin tightly with aluminum foil. Bake for 25 minutes, or until a toothpick inserted in the center comes out clean.
4. Let the custards cool on a wire rack for 5 to 10 minutes.
5. Serve warm, or refrigerate until cold and serve chilled.

Applesauce Brownies
Prep time: 10 minutes | Cook time: 15 minutes | Serves 8

¼ cup unsweetened cocoa powder	½ cup granulated sugar
¼ cup all-purpose flour	1 large egg
¼ teaspoon kosher salt	3 tablespoons unsweetened applesauce
½ teaspoons baking powder	¼ cup miniature semisweet chocolate chips
3 tablespoons unsalted butter, melted	Coarse sea salt, to taste

1. Select the BAKE function and preheat MAXX to 300ºF (149ºC).
2. In a large bowl, whisk together the cocoa powder, all-purpose flour, kosher salt, and baking powder.
3. In a separate large bowl, combine the butter, granulated sugar, egg, and applesauce, then use a spatula to fold in the cocoa powder mixture and the chocolate chips until well combined.

4. Spray a baking pan with nonstick cooking spray, then pour the mixture into the pan. Place the pan in the air fryer oven and bake for 15 minutes or until a toothpick comes out clean when inserted in the middle.
5. Remove the brownies from the air fryer oven, sprinkle some coarse sea salt on top, and allow to cool in the pan on a wire rack for 20 minutes before cutting and serving.

Apple Crumble with Caramel Topping
Prep time: 15 minutes | Cook time: 50 minutes | Serves 6 to 8

4 apples, peeled and thinly sliced	¼ teaspoon ground allspice
2 tablespoons sugar	Pinch ground nutmeg
1 tablespoon flour	10 caramel squares,
1 teaspoon ground cinnamon	cut into small pieces

Crumble Topping:

¾ cup rolled oats	cinnamon
¼ cup sugar	6 tablespoons butter,
⅓ cup flour	melted
¼ teaspoon ground	

1. Combine the apples, sugar, flour, and spices in a large bowl and toss to coat. Add the caramel pieces and mix well. Pour the apple mixture into a 1-quart round baking dish that will fit in your air fryer basket (6-inch diameter).
2. To make the crumble topping, combine the rolled oats, sugar, flour and cinnamon in a small bowl. Add the melted butter and mix well. Top the apples with the crumble mixture. Cover the entire dish with aluminum foil and transfer the dish to the air fryer basket, lowering the dish into the basket using a sling made of aluminum foil (fold a piece of aluminum foil into a strip about 2-inches wide by 24-inches long). Fold the ends of the aluminum foil over the top of the dish before returning the basket to the air fryer oven.
3. Select the AIR FRY function and cook at 330ºF (166ºC) for 25 minutes. Remove the aluminum foil and continue to air fry for another 25 minutes. Serve the crumble warm with whipped cream or vanilla ice cream, if desired.

Sweet Banana Bread Pudding

Prep time: 5 minutes | Cook time: 50 minutes | Serves 4

½ cup brown sugar
3 eggs
¾ cup half and half
1 teaspoon pure vanilla extract
6 cups cubed Kings

Hawaiian bread (½-inch cubes)
2 bananas, sliced
1 cup caramel sauce, plus more for serving

1. Combine the brown sugar, eggs, half and half and vanilla extract in a large bowl, whisking until the sugar has dissolved and the mixture is smooth. Stir in the cubed bread and toss to coat all the cubes evenly. Let the bread sit for 10 minutes to absorb the liquid.
2. Mix the sliced bananas and caramel sauce together in a separate bowl.
3. Fill the bottom of 4 greased ramekins with half the bread cubes. Divide the caramel and bananas between the ramekins, spooning them on top of the bread cubes. Top with the remaining bread cubes and wrap each ramekin with aluminum foil, tenting the foil at the top to leave some room for the bread to puff up during the cooking process.
4. Select the AIR FRY function and cook at 350ºF (180ºC) for 25 minutes. Air fry two bread puddings at a time. Let the puddings cool a little and serve warm with additional caramel sauce drizzled on top.

Black Forest Pies with Cheery

Prep time: 10 minutes | Cook time: 15 minutes | Serves 6

3 tablespoons milk or dark chocolate chips
2 tablespoons thick, hot fudge sauce
2 tablespoons chopped dried cherries

1 (10-by-15-inch) sheet frozen puff pastry, thawed
1 egg white, beaten
2 tablespoons sugar
½ teaspoon cinnamon

1. Select the BAKE function and preheat MAXX to 350ºF (177ºC).
2. In a small bowl, combine the chocolate chips, fudge sauce, and dried cherries.

3. Roll out the puff pastry on a floured surface. Cut into 6 squares with a sharp knife.
4. Divide the chocolate chip mixture into the center of each puff pastry square. Fold the squares in half to make triangles. Firmly press the edges with the tines of a fork to seal.
5. Brush the triangles on all sides sparingly with the beaten egg white. Sprinkle the tops with sugar and cinnamon.
6. Put in the air fryer basket and bake for 15 minutes or until the triangles are golden brown. The filling will be hot, so cool for at least 20 minutes before serving.

Honey Chickpea Brownies

Prep time: 10 minutes | Cook time: 20 minutes | Serves 6

Vegetable oil
1 (15-ounce / 425-g) can chickpeas, drained and rinsed
4 large eggs
⅓ cup coconut oil, melted
⅓ cup honey
3 tablespoons unsweetened cocoa

powder
1 tablespoon espresso powder (optional)
1 teaspoon baking powder
1 teaspoon baking soda
½ cup chocolate chips

1. Select the BAKE function and preheat MAXX to 325ºF (163ºC).
2. Generously grease a baking pan with vegetable oil.
3. In a blender or food processor, combine the chickpeas, eggs, coconut oil, honey, cocoa powder, espresso powder (if using), baking powder, and baking soda. Blend or process until smooth. Transfer to the prepared pan and stir in the chocolate chips by hand.
4. Set the pan in the air fryer basket and bake for 20 minutes, or until a toothpick inserted into the center comes out clean.
5. Let cool in the pan on a wire rack for 30 minutes before cutting into squares.
6. Serve immediately.

Peanut Butter and Chocolate Lava Cupcakes

Prep time: 10 minutes | Cook time: 10 to 13 minutes | Serves 8

Nonstick baking spray with flour
1⅓ cups chocolate cake mix
1 egg
1 egg yolk
¼ cup safflower oil
¼ cup hot water
⅓ cup sour cream
3 tablespoons peanut butter
1 tablespoon powdered sugar

1. Select the BAKE function and preheat MAXX to 350°F (177°C).
2. Double up 16 foil muffin cups to make 8 cups. Spray each lightly with nonstick spray; set aside.
3. In a medium bowl, combine the cake mix, egg, egg yolk, safflower oil, water, and sour cream, and beat until combined.
4. In a small bowl, combine the peanut butter and powdered sugar and mix well. Form this mixture into 8 balls.
5. Spoon about ¼ cup of the chocolate batter into each muffin cup and top with a peanut butter ball. Spoon remaining batter on top of the peanut butter balls to cover them.
6. Arrange the cups in the air fryer basket, leaving some space between each. Bake for 10 to 13 minutes or until the tops look dry and set.
7. Let the cupcakes cool for about 10 minutes, then serve warm.

Traditional Chocolate Cake

Prep time: 10 minutes | Cook time: 55 minutes | Serves 4

Unsalted butter, at room temperature
3 large eggs
1 cup almond flour
⅔ cup sugar
⅓ cup heavy cream
¼ cup coconut oil,
melted
¼ cup unsweetened cocoa powder
1 teaspoon baking powder
¼ cup chopped walnuts

1. Select the BAKE function and preheat MAXX to 400°F (204°C).
2. Generously butter a round baking pan. Line the bottom of the pan with parchment paper cut to fit.
3. In a large bowl, combine the eggs, almond flour, sugar, cream, coconut oil, cocoa powder, and baking powder. Beat with a hand mixer on medium speed until well blended and fluffy. (This will keep the cake from being too dense, as almond flour cakes can sometimes be.) Fold in the walnuts.
4. Pour the batter into the prepared pan. Cover the pan tightly with aluminum foil. Set the pan in the air fryer basket and bake for 45 minutes. Remove the foil and bake for 10 to 15 minutes more until a knife (do not use a toothpick) inserted into the center of the cake comes out clean.
5. Let the cake cool in the pan on a wire rack for 10 minutes. Remove the cake from the pan and let cool on the rack for 20 minutes before slicing and serving.

Honey Peaches, Pears, and Plums

Prep time: 5 minutes | Cook time: 5 minutes | Serves 6 to 8

2 peaches
2 firm pears
2 plums
2 tablespoons melted
butter
1 tablespoon honey
2 to 3 teaspoons curry powder

1. Select the BAKE function and preheat MAXX to 325°F (163°C).
2. Cut the peaches in half, remove the pits, and cut each half in half again. Cut the pears in half, core them, and remove the stem. Cut each half in half again. Do the same with the plums.
3. Spread a large sheet of heavy-duty foil on the work surface. Arrange the fruit on the foil and drizzle with the butter and honey. Sprinkle with the curry powder.
4. Wrap the fruit in the foil, making sure to leave some air space in the packet.
5. Put the foil package in the basket and bake for 5 to 8 minutes, shaking the basket once during the cooking time, until the fruit is soft.
6. Serve immediately.

Molten Chocolate Cake
Prep time: 5 minutes | Cook time: 10 minutes | Serves 4

3.5 ounces (99 g) butter, melted
3½ tablespoons sugar

3.5 ounces (99 g) chocolate, melted
1½ tablespoons flour
2 eggs

1. Select the BAKE function and preheat MAXX to 375ºF (191ºC).
2. Grease four ramekins with a little butter.
3. Rigorously combine the eggs, butter, and sugar before stirring in the melted chocolate.
4. Slowly fold in the flour.
5. Spoon an equal amount of the mixture into each ramekin.
6. Put them in the air fryer oven and bake for 10 minutes
7. Put the ramekins upside-down on plates and let the cakes fall out. Serve hot.

Blackberry Crisp with Granola Topping
Prep time: 5 minutes | Cook time: 20 minutes | Serves 1

2 tablespoons lemon juice
⅓ cup powdered erythritol
¼ teaspoon xantham

gum
2 cup blackberries
1 cup crunchy granola

1. Select the BAKE function and preheat MAXX to 350ºF (177ºC).
2. In a bowl, combine the lemon juice, erythritol, xantham gum, and blackberries. Transfer to a round baking dish and cover with aluminum foil.
3. Put the dish in the air fryer oven and bake for 12 minutes.
4. Take care when removing the dish from the air fryer oven. Give the blackberries a stir and top with the granola.
5. Return the dish to the air fryer oven and bake for an additional 3 minutes, this time at 320ºF (160ºC). Serve once the granola has turned brown and enjoy.

S'mores
Prep time: 5 minutes | Cook time: 3 minutes | Serves 12

12 whole cinnamon graham crackers
2 (1.55-ounce / 44-

g) chocolate bars, broken into 12 pieces
12 marshmallows

1. Select the BAKE function and preheat MAXX to 350ºF (177ºC).
2. Halve each graham cracker into 2 squares.
3. Put 6 graham cracker squares in the air fryer oven. Do not stack. Put a piece of chocolate into each. Bake for 2 minutes.
4. Open the air fryer oven and add a marshmallow onto each piece of melted chocolate. Bake for 1 additional minute.
5. Remove the cooked s'mores from the air fryer oven, then repeat with the remaining 6 s'mores.
6. Top with the remaining graham cracker squares and serve.

Donuts with Chocolate Sauce
Prep time: 5 minutes | Cook time: 8 minutes | Serves 8

1 (8-ounce / 227-g) can jumbo biscuits
Cooking oil

Chocolate sauce, for drizzling

1. Separate the biscuit dough into 8 biscuits and place them on a flat work surface. Use a small circle cookie cutter or a biscuit cutter to cut a hole in the center of each biscuit. You can also cut the holes using a knife.
2. Spray the air fryer basket with cooking oil.
3. Put 4 donuts in the air fryer oven. Do not stack. Spray with cooking oil.
4. Select the AIR FRY function and cook at 375ºF (191ºC) for 4 minutes.
5. Open the air fryer oven and flip the donuts. Air fry for an additional 4 minutes.
6. Remove the cooked donuts from the air fryer oven. Repeat with the remaining 4 donuts.
7. Drizzle chocolate sauce over the donuts and enjoy while warm.

Choux Puffs with Chocolate Sauce
Prep time: 15 minutes | Cook time: 20 minutes | Serves 4 to 5

Choux Puffs:

3 tablespoons unsalted butter	1 cup all-purpose flour
1 tablespoon granulated sugar	2 eggs
1 cup water	Vegetable oil for brushing

Chocolate Sauce:

4 ounces semisweet chocolate, finely chopped	room temperature
	1 cup heavy cream
2 tablespoons unsalted butter at	¼ cup corn syrup
	1 pint vanilla ice cream for serving

1. Combine the butter, sugar, and water in a medium saucepan and melt the butter over low heat. Add the flour and stir to form a cohesive dough. Cook over medium-low heat for 2 minutes to get rid of the raw flour taste. Remove from the heat and allow to cool to room temperature. Beat the eggs in one at a time, making sure the first egg is fully incorporated before the adding the second. The dough will look curdled at first, but keep beating vigorously until the dough becomes smooth. Once the eggs are fully incorporated, let the dough rest for 30 minutes.
2. While the dough is resting, make the chocolate sauce. Place the chopped chocolate and butter in a heat-proof bowl. Heat the cream and corn syrup in a small saucepan over medium heat until the cream is simmering. Remove from the heat and pour the cream mixture over the chocolate in the bowl. Stir until the chocolate and butter have melted and the sauce is smooth. Set aside.
3. Once the dough has rested, place it in a piping bag outfitted with a large, round tip. Lightly oil the air fryer basket. Working in 2 batches, pipe round puffs of dough approximately 2 inches wide and 1 inch tall directly onto the air fryer basket. Use a knife or scissors to cut the dough when you have achieved the desired size. With a damp finger, press down on the swirl at the top of each puff to round it.

4. Select the AIR FRY function and cook at 360ºF (182ºC) for 18 to 20 minutes until the outside of the puffs is golden brown and crisp and the inside is fully cooked and airy.
5. To serve, halve the choux puffs crosswise and place a scoop of ice cream inside each one. Replace the top of the puff and spoon chocolate sauce over the top. Serve immediately.

Chocolate Chips Cookie Sundae
Prep time: 15 minutes | Cook time: 12 to 15 minutes | Serves 4

1 stick unsalted butter, softened	soda
	¼ teaspoon kosher salt
3 tablespoons granulated sugar	½ cup semisweet chocolate chips
3 tablespoons brown sugar	Vegetable oil for spraying
1 egg	Vanilla ice cream for serving
1 teaspoon vanilla extract	Hot fudge or caramel sauce for serving
½ cup all-purpose flour	
¼ teaspoon baking	

1. In a medium bowl, cream the butter and sugars together using a handheld mixer until light and fluffy. Add the egg and vanilla and mix until combined. In a small bowl, whisk together the flour, baking soda, and salt. Add the dry ingredients to the batter and mix until combined. Add the chocolate chips and mix a final time.
2. Select the BAKE function and preheat MAXX to 325ºF (165ºC). Lightly grease a 7-inch pizza pan insert for the air fryer oven. Spread the batter evenly in the pan. Place the pan in the air fryer oven and bake for 12 to 15 minutes, until the top of the cookie is browned and the middle is gooey but cooked. Remove the pan from the air fryer oven.
3. Place 1 to 2 scoops of vanilla ice cream in the center of the cookie and top with hot fudge or caramel sauce, as you prefer. Pass around spoons and eat the cookie sundae right out of the pan.

Fried Breaded Bananas
Prep time: 5 minutes | Cook time: 7 minutes | Serves 6

1 large egg
¼ cup cornstarch
¼ cup plain bread crumbs
3 bananas, halved
crosswise
Cooking oil
Chocolate sauce, for drizzling

1. In a small bowl, beat the egg. In another bowl, place the cornstarch. Put the bread crumbs in a third bowl.
2. Dip the bananas in the cornstarch, then the egg, and then the bread crumbs.
3. Spray the air fryer basket with cooking oil.
4. Put the bananas in the basket and spray them with cooking oil.
5. Select the AIR FRY function and cook at 350ºF (177ºC) for 5 minutes.
6. Open the air fryer oven and flip the bananas. Air fry for an additional 2 minutes.
7. Transfer the bananas to plates. Drizzle the chocolate sauce over the bananas, and serve.

Graham Cracker Chocolate Cheesecake
Prep time: 10 minutes | Cook time: 20 minutes | Serves 8

1 cup graham cracker crumbs
3 tablespoons softened butter
1½ (8-ounce / 227-g) packages cream cheese, softened
⅓ cup sugar
2 eggs
1 tablespoon flour
1 teaspoon vanilla
¼ cup chocolate syrup

1. For the crust, combine the graham cracker crumbs and butter in a small bowl and mix well. Press into the bottom of a baking pan and put in the freezer to set.
2. For the filling, combine the cream cheese and sugar in a medium bowl and mix well. Beat in the eggs, one at a time. Add the flour and vanilla.
3. Select the BAKE function and preheat MAXX to 450ºF (232ºC).

4. Remove ⅔ cup of the filling to a small bowl and stir in the chocolate syrup until combined.
5. Pour the vanilla filling into the pan with the crust. Drop the chocolate filling over the vanilla filling by the spoonful. With a clean butter knife, stir the fillings in a zigzag pattern to marbleize them.
6. Bake for 20 minutes or until the cheesecake is just set.
7. Cool on a wire rack for 1 hour, then chill in the refrigerator until the cheesecake is firm.
8. Serve immediately.

Orange Cornmeal Cake
Prep time: 10 minutes | Cook time: 23 minutes | Serves 8

Nonstick baking spray with flour
1¼ cups all-purpose flour
⅓ cup yellow cornmeal
¾ cup white sugar
1 teaspoon baking
soda
¼ cup safflower oil
1¼ cups orange juice, divided
1 teaspoon vanilla
¼ cup powdered sugar

1. Select the BAKE function and preheat MAXX to 350ºF (177ºC).
2. Spray a baking pan with nonstick spray and set aside.
3. In a medium bowl, combine the flour, cornmeal, sugar, baking soda, safflower oil, 1 cup of the orange juice, and vanilla, and mix well.
4. Pour the batter into the baking pan and place in the air fryer oven. Bake for 23 minutes or until a toothpick inserted in the center of the cake comes out clean.
5. Remove the cake from the basket and place on a cooling rack. Using a toothpick, make about 20 holes in the cake.
6. In a small bowl, combine remaining ¼ cup of orange juice and the powdered sugar and stir well. Drizzle this mixture over the hot cake slowly so the cake absorbs it.
7. Cool completely, then cut into wedges to serve.

Roasted Honey Pears

Prep time: 5 minutes | Cook time: 20 minutes | Serves 4

2 large Bosc pears, halved and deseeded
3 tablespoons honey
1 tablespoon unsalted butter
½ teaspoon ground cinnamon
¼ cup walnuts, chopped
¼ cup part skim low-fat ricotta cheese, divided

1. Select the ROAST function and preheat MAXX to 350ºF (177ºC).
2. In a baking pan, place the pears, cut side up.
3. In a small microwave-safe bowl, melt the honey, butter, and cinnamon. Brush this mixture over the cut sides of the pears.
4. Pour 3 tablespoons of water around the pears in the pan. Roast the pears for 20 minutes, or until tender when pierced with a fork and slightly crisp on the edges, basting once with the liquid in the pan.
5. Carefully remove the pears from the pan and place on a serving plate. Drizzle each with some liquid from the pan, sprinkle the walnuts on top, and serve with a spoonful of ricotta cheese.

Cinnamon Buttery Almonds

Prep time: 5 minutes | Cook time: 8 minutes | Serves 4

1 cup whole almonds
2 tablespoons salted butter, melted
1 tablespoon sugar
½ teaspoon ground cinnamon

1. Select the BAKE function and preheat MAXX to 300ºF (149ºC).
2. In a medium bowl, combine the almonds, butter, sugar, and cinnamon. Mix well to ensure all the almonds are coated with the spiced butter.
3. Transfer the almonds to the air fryer basket and shake so they are in a single layer. Bake for 8 minutes, stirring the almonds halfway through the cooking time.
4. Let cool completely before serving.

Raspberry Jelly Doughnuts

Prep time: 5 minutes | Cook time: 5 minutes | Serves 8

1 (16.3-ounce / 462-g) package large refrigerator biscuits
Cooking spray
1¼ cups good-quality raspberry jam
Confectioners' sugar, for dusting

1. Separate biscuits into 8 rounds. Spray both sides of rounds lightly with oil.
2. Spray the basket with oil and place 3 to 4 rounds in the basket.
3. Select the AIR FRY function and cook at 350ºF (177ºC) for 5 minutes, or until golden brown. Transfer to a wire rack; let cool. Repeat with the remaining rounds.
4. Fill a pastry bag, fitted with small plain tip, with raspberry jam; use tip to poke a small hole in the side of each doughnut, then fill the centers with the jam. Dust doughnuts with confectioners' sugar.
5. Serve immediately.

Caramelized Apple Butter

Prep time: 10 minutes | Cook time: 1 hour | Makes 1¼ cups

Cooking spray
2 cups unsweetened applesauce
⅔ cup packed light brown sugar
3 tablespoons fresh lemon juice
½ teaspoon kosher salt
¼ teaspoon ground cinnamon
⅛ teaspoon ground allspice

1. Select the BAKE function and preheat MAXX to 340ºF (171ºC).
2. Spray a metal cake pan with cooking spray. Whisk together all the ingredients in a bowl until smooth, then pour into the greased pan. Set the pan in the air fryer oven and bake until the apple mixture is caramelized, reduced to a thick purée, and fragrant, about 1 hour.
3. Remove the pan from the air fryer oven, stir to combine the caramelized bits at the edge with the rest, then let cool completely to thicken.
4. Serve immediately.

Cherry, Carrot, and Oatmeal Cups
Prep time: 10 minutes | Cook time: 8 minutes | Makes 16 cups

3 tablespoons unsalted butter, at room temperature
¼ cup packed brown sugar
1 tablespoon honey
1 egg white
½ teaspoon vanilla extract

⅓ cup finely grated carrot
½ cup quick-cooking oatmeal
⅓ cup whole-wheat pastry flour
½ teaspoon baking soda
¼ cup dried cherries

1. Select the BAKE function and preheat MAXX to 350ºF (177ºC)
2. In a medium bowl, beat the butter, brown sugar, and honey until well combined.
3. Add the egg white, vanilla, and carrot. Beat to combine.
4. Stir in the oatmeal, pastry flour, and baking soda.
5. Stir in the dried cherries.
6. Double up 32 mini muffin foil cups to make 16 cups. Fill each with about 4 teaspoons of dough. Bake the cookie cups, 8 at a time, for 8 minutes, or until light golden brown and just set. Serve warm.

Raisin and Oatmeal Bars
Prep time: 15 minutes | Cook time: 15 minutes | Serves 8

⅓ cup all-purpose flour
¼ teaspoon kosher salt
¼ teaspoon baking powder
¼ teaspoon ground cinnamon
¼ cup light brown sugar, lightly packed

¼ cup granulated sugar
½ cup canola oil
1 large egg
1 teaspoon vanilla extract
1⅓ cups quick-cooking oats
⅓ cup raisins

1. Select the BAKE function and preheat MAXX to 360ºF (182ºC).
2. In a large bowl, combine the all-purpose flour, kosher salt, baking powder, ground cinnamon, light brown sugar, granulated sugar, canola oil, egg, vanilla extract, quick-cooking oats, and raisins.
3. Spray a baking pan with nonstick cooking spray, then pour the oat mixture into the pan and press down to evenly distribute. Place the pan in the air fryer oven and bake for 15 minutes or until golden brown.
4. Remove from the air fryer oven and allow to cool in the pan on a wire rack for 20 minutes before slicing and serving.

Chouquettes
Prep time: 5 minutes | Cook time: 17 minutes | Serves 4 to 5

3 tablespoons unsalted butter
1 tablespoon granulated sugar
1 cup water
1 cup all-purpose

flour
3 eggs
1½ tablespoons milk
Vegetable oil for brushing
½ cup pearl sugar

1. Combine the butter, granulated sugar, and water in a medium saucepan and melt the butter over low heat. Add the flour and stir to form a cohesive dough. Cook over medium-low heat for 2 minutes to get rid of the raw flour taste. Remove from the heat and allow to cool to room temperature. Beat in 2 of the eggs, one at a time, making sure the first egg is fully incorporated before the adding the second. The dough will look curdled at first, but keep beating vigorously until the dough becomes smooth. Once the eggs are fully incorporated, let the dough rest for 30 minutes.
2. Select the BAKE function and preheat MAXX to 360ºF (182ºC).
3. Beat the remaining egg together with the milk in a small bowl. Lightly brush the air fryer basket with oil. Using a small, spring-loaded cookie scoop or a tablespoon, scoop 6 to 8 circles of dough directly onto the air fryer basket. Brush the tops of the dough with the egg wash and generously sprinkle on pearl sugar.
4. Bake for 15 to 17 minutes until the outside of the chouquettes is golden brown and the inside fully cooked and airy. Repeat 2 more times with the remaining dough. Serve immediately.

Hot Churros with Chocolate Sauce
Prep time: 15 minutes | Cook time: 14 minutes | Serves 4

Chocolate Sauce:

4 ounces (113 g) semisweet chocolate, finely chopped	syrup
½ cup heavy cream	½ teaspoon cinnamon
¼ cup light corn	¼ teaspoon cayenne pepper

Churros:

3 tablespoons unsalted butter, divided	1 cup all-purpose flour
1 cup water	2 eggs
½ cup granulated sugar plus 1 tablespoon	Vegetable oil for spraying
Pinch kosher salt	2 teaspoons cinnamon

1. To make the chocolate sauce, place the chopped chocolate in a heat-proof bowl. Combine the cream and corn syrup in a small saucepan and bring to a simmer. Pour the warm cream mixture over the chocolate and stir until the chocolate is melted. Add the cinnamon and cayenne pepper. Set aside.
2. To make the churros, combine 1 tablespoon of the butter, the water, 1 tablespoon of the sugar, and the salt in a medium saucepan. Melt the butter over low heat. Add the flour and stir vigorously to form a dough ball. Continue to cook, stirring until the mixture looks dry and thick, 2 minutes. Remove from the heat and allow to cool to room temperature. Once cool, beat in the eggs one at a time, making sure the first egg is fully incorporated before adding the second. Continue beating until the mixture is smooth. Let the dough rest for 30 minutes.
3. Place the churros batter into a piping bag outfitted with an extra-large tip, round or star-shaped. Spray the air fryer basket with oil. Working in batches, pipe churros that are 5 to 6 inches long and ¾ to 1 inch in diameter directly onto the air fryer basket. Do not crowd the basket. Use a knife or scissors to cut the dough when you've reached the desired length. Spray the churros with oil.
4. Select the AIR FRY function and cook at 360ºF (182ºC) for 12 to 14 minutes until the outside is firm and brown and the inside is soft. While the churros are cooking, combine the remaining ½ cup sugar with the cinnamon on a plate and whisk to combine. Melt the remaining 2 tablespoons of butter and place in a small dish.
5. Remove the cooked churros from the air fryer oven and immediately brush with melted butter and dredge in the cinnamon sugar. Repeat the process with the remaining churros. Serve hot with the chocolate sauce.

Coconut Brownies
Prep time: 15 minutes | Cook time: 15 minutes | Serves 8

½ cup coconut oil	anise star
2 ounces (57 g) dark chocolate	¼ teaspoon coconut extract
1 cup sugar	½ teaspoons vanilla extract
2½ tablespoons water	1 tablespoon honey
4 whisked eggs	½ cup flour
¼ teaspoon ground cinnamon	½ cup desiccated coconut
½ teaspoons ground	Sugar, for dusting

1. Select the BAKE function and preheat MAXX to 355ºF (179ºC).
2. Melt the coconut oil and dark chocolate in the microwave.
3. Combine with the sugar, water, eggs, cinnamon, anise, coconut extract, vanilla, and honey in a large bowl.
4. Stir in the flour and desiccated coconut. Incorporate everything well.
5. Lightly grease a baking dish with butter. Transfer the mixture to the dish.
6. Put the dish in the air fryer oven and bake for 15 minutes.
7. Remove from the air fryer oven and allow to cool slightly.
8. Take care when taking it out of the baking dish. Slice it into squares.
9. Dust with sugar before serving.

Chocolate Lava Cakes with Toasted Almonds

Prep time: 15 minutes | Cook time: 13 minutes | Serves 3

Butter and flour for the ramekins	1 tablespoon all-purpose flour
4 ounces (113 g) bittersweet chocolate, chopped	3 tablespoons ground almonds
½ cup (1 stick) unsalted butter	8 to 12 semisweet chocolate discs (or 4 chunks of chocolate)
2 eggs	Cocoa powder or powdered sugar, for dusting
2 egg yolks	
¼ cup sugar	Toasted almonds, coarsely chopped
½ teaspoon pure vanilla extract, or almond extract	

1. Butter and flour 3 ramekins. (Butter the ramekins and then coat the butter with flour by shaking it around in the ramekin and dumping out any excess.)
2. Melt the chocolate and butter together, either in the microwave or in a double boiler. In a separate bowl, beat the eggs, egg yolks and sugar together until light and smooth. Add the vanilla extract. Whisk the chocolate mixture into the egg mixture. Stir in the flour and ground almonds.
3. Transfer the batter carefully to the buttered ramekins, filling halfway. Place two or three chocolate discs in the center of the batter and then fill the ramekins to ½-inch below the top with the remaining batter. Place the ramekins into the air fryer basket.
4. Select the AIR FRY function and cook at 330ºF (166ºC) for 13 minutes. The sides of the cake should be set, but the centers should be slightly soft. Remove the ramekins from the air fryer oven and let the cakes sit for 5 minutes. (If you'd like the cake a little less molten, air fry for 14 minutes and let the cakes sit for 4 minutes.)
5. Run a butter knife around the edge of the ramekins and invert the cakes onto a plate. Lift the ramekin off the plate slowly and carefully so that the cake doesn't break. Dust with cocoa powder or powdered sugar and serve with a scoop of ice cream and some coarsely chopped toasted almonds.

Mixed-Berries Pies

Prep time: 5 minutes | Cook time: 30 minutes | Serves 4

¾ cup sugar	divided
½ teaspoon ground cinnamon	1 teaspoon water
1 tablespoon cornstarch	1 package refrigerated pie dough (or your own homemade pie dough)
1 cup blueberries	
1 cup blackberries	
1 cup raspberries,	1 egg, beaten

1. Combine the sugar, cinnamon, and cornstarch in a small saucepan. Add the blueberries, blackberries, and ½ cup of the raspberries. Toss the berries gently to coat them evenly. Add the teaspoon of water to the saucepan and turn the stovetop on to medium-high heat, stirring occasionally. Once the berries break down, release their juice and start to simmer (about 5 minutes), simmer for another couple of minutes and then transfer the mixture to a bowl, stir in the remaining ½ cup of raspberries and let it cool.
2. Cut the pie dough into four 5-inch circles and four 6-inch circles.
3. Spread the 6-inch circles on a flat surface. Divide the berry filling between all four circles. Brush the perimeter of the dough circles with a little water. Place the 5-inch circles on top of the filling and press the perimeter of the dough circles together to seal. Roll the edges of the bottom circle up over the top circle to make a crust around the filling. Press a fork around the crust to make decorative indentations and to seal the crust shut. Brush the pies with egg wash and sprinkle a little sugar on top. Poke a small hole in the center of each pie with a paring knife to vent the dough.
4. Air fry two pies at a time. Brush or spray the air fryer basket with oil and place the pies into the basket. Select the AIR FRY function and cook at 370ºF (188ºC) for 9 minutes. Turn the pies over and air fry for another 6 minutes. Serve warm or at room temperature.

Maple Pecan Pie

Prep time: 10 minutes | Cook time: 25 minutes | Serves 4

1 pie dough
½ teaspoons cinnamon
¾ teaspoon vanilla extract
2 eggs
¾ cup maple syrup
⅛ teaspoon nutmeg
3 tablespoons melted butter, divided
2 tablespoons sugar
½ cup chopped pecans

1. In a small bowl, coat the pecans in 1 tablespoon of melted butter.
2. Transfer the pecans to the air fryer oven. Select the AIR FRY function and cook at 370ºF (188ºC) for 10 minutes.
3. Put the pie dough in a greased pie pan and add the pecans on top.
4. In a bowl, mix the rest of the ingredients. Pour this over the pecans.
5. Put the pan in the air fryer oven. Switch from AIR FRY to BAKE and bake for 25 minutes.
6. Serve immediately.

Almond Shortbread

Prep time: 5 minutes | Cook time: 12 minutes | Serves 8

½ cup (1 stick) unsalted butter
½ cup sugar
1 teaspoon pure
almond extract
1 cup all-purpose flour

1. Select the BAKE function and preheat MAXX to 375ºF (191ºC).
2. In a bowl of a stand mixer fitted with the paddle attachment, beat the butter and sugar on medium speed until fluffy, 3 to 4 minutes. Add the almond extract and beat until combined, about 30 seconds. Turn the mixer to low. Add the flour a little at a time and beat for about 2 minutes more until well incorporated.
3. Pat the dough into an even layer in a round baking pan. Put the pan in the air fryer basket and bake for 12 minutes.
4. Carefully remove the pan from air fryer basket. While the shortbread is still warm and soft, cut it into 8 wedges.

5. Let cool in the pan on a wire rack for 5 minutes. Remove the wedges from the pan and let cool on the rack before serving.

Bourbon Vanilla Bread Pudding

Prep time: 10 minutes | Cook time: 20 minutes | Serves 4

3 slices whole grain bread, cubed
1 large egg
1 cup whole milk
2 tablespoons bourbon
½ teaspoons vanilla
extract
¼ cup maple syrup, divided
½ teaspoons ground cinnamon
2 teaspoons sparkling sugar

1. Select the BAKE function and preheat MAXX to 270ºF (132ºC).
2. Spray a baking pan with nonstick cooking spray, then place the bread cubes in the pan.
3. In a medium bowl, whisk together the egg, milk, bourbon, vanilla extract, 3 tablespoons of maple syrup, and cinnamon. Pour the egg mixture over the bread and press down with a spatula to coat all the bread, then sprinkle the sparkling sugar on top and bake for 20 minutes.
4. Remove the pudding from the air fryer oven and allow to cool in the pan on a wire rack for 10 minutes. Drizzle the remaining 1 tablespoon of maple syrup on top. Slice and serve warm.

Chapter 12 Holiday Specials

Paprika Black Olives

Prep time: 10 minutes | Cook time: 5 minutes | Serves 4

12 ounces (340 g) pitted black extra-large olives
¼ cup all-purpose flour
1 cup panko bread crumbs
2 teaspoons dried thyme
1 teaspoon red pepper flakes
1 teaspoon smoked paprika
1 egg beaten with 1 tablespoon water
Vegetable oil for spraying

1. Drain the olives and place them on a paper towel–lined plate to dry.
2. Put the flour on a plate. Combine the panko, thyme, red pepper flakes, and paprika on a separate plate. Dip an olive in the flour, shaking off any excess, then coat with egg mixture. Dredge the olive in the panko mixture, pressing to make the crumbs adhere, and place the breaded olive on a platter. Repeat with the remaining olives.
3. Spray the olives with oil and place them in a single layer in the air fryer basket. Work in batches if necessary so as not to overcrowd the basket. Select the AIR FRY function and cook at 400ºF (204ºC) for 5 minutes until the breading is browned and crispy. Serve warm

Holiday Smoky Beef Roast

Prep time: 10 minutes | Cook time: 45 minutes | Serves 8

2 pounds (907 g) roast beef, at room temperature
2 tablespoons extra-virgin olive oil
1 teaspoon sea salt flakes
1 teaspoon black pepper, preferably freshly ground
1 teaspoon smoked paprika
A few dashes of liquid smoke
2 jalapeño peppers, thinly sliced

1. Select the ROAST function and preheat MAXX to 330ºF (166ºC).
2. Pat the roast dry using kitchen towels. Rub with extra-virgin olive oil and all seasonings along with liquid smoke.
3. Roast for 30 minutes in the preheated air fryer oven. Turn the roast over and roast for additional 15 minutes.
4. Check for doneness using a meat thermometer and serve sprinkled with sliced jalapeños. Bon appétit!

Mushroom, Green Bean, and Pork Casserole

Prep time: 10 minutes | Cook time: 15 minutes | Serves 4

4 tablespoons unsalted butter
¼ cup diced yellow onion
½ cup chopped white mushrooms
½ cup heavy whipping cream
1 ounce (28 g) full-fat cream cheese
½ cup chicken broth
¼ teaspoon xanthan gum
1 pound (454 g) fresh green beans, edges trimmed
½ ounce (14 g) pork rinds, finely ground

1. In a medium skillet over medium heat, melt the butter. Sauté the onion and mushrooms until they become soft and fragrant, about 3 to 5 minutes.
2. Add the heavy whipping cream, cream cheese, and broth to the pan. Whisk until smooth. Bring to a boil and then reduce to a simmer. Sprinkle the xanthan gum into the pan and remove from heat.
3. Select the BAKE function and preheat MAXX to 320ºF (160ºC).
4. Chop the green beans into 2-inch pieces and place into a baking dish. Pour the sauce mixture over them and stir until coated. Top the dish with ground pork rinds. Put into the air fryer basket and bake for 15 minutes.
5. Top will be golden and green beans fork-tender when fully cooked. Serve warm.

Air-Fried Snack Mix
Prep time: 10 minutes | Cook time: 10 minutes | Serves 10

½ cup honey
3 tablespoons butter, melted
1 teaspoon salt
2 cups sesame sticks
2 cup pumpkin seeds
2 cups granola
1 cup cashews
2 cups crispy corn puff cereal
2 cup mini pretzel crisps

1. In a bowl, combine the honey, butter, and salt.
2. In another bowl, mix the sesame sticks, pumpkin seeds, granola, cashews, corn puff cereal, and pretzel crisps.
3. Combine the contents of the two bowls.
4. Put the mixture in the air fryer basket. Select the AIR FRY function and cook at 370ºF (188ºC) for 10 to 12 minutes, shaking the basket frequently. Do this in two batches.
5. Put the snack mix on a cookie sheet and allow it to cool fully.
6. Serve immediately.

Hearty Whole Chicken Roast
Prep time: 10 minutes | Cook time: 1 hour | Serves 6

1 teaspoon salt
1 teaspoon Italian seasoning
½ teaspoon freshly ground black pepper
½ teaspoon paprika
½ teaspoon garlic powder
½ teaspoon onion powder
2 tablespoons olive oil, plus more as needed
1 (4-pound / 1.8-kg) fryer chicken

1. Grease the air fryer basket lightly with olive oil.
2. In a small bowl, mix the salt, Italian seasoning, pepper, paprika, garlic powder, and onion powder.
3. Remove any giblets from the chicken. Pat the chicken dry thoroughly with paper towels, including the cavity.
4. Brush the chicken all over with the olive oil and rub it with the seasoning mixture.
5. Truss the chicken or tie the legs with butcher's twine. This will make it easier to flip the chicken during cooking.
6. Put the chicken in the air fryer basket, breast-side down. Select the AIR FRY function and cook at 360ºF (182ºC) for 30 minutes. Flip the chicken over and baste it with any drippings collected in the bottom drawer of the air fryer oven. Lightly brush the chicken with olive oil.
7. Air fry for 20 minutes. Flip the chicken over one last time and air fry until a thermometer inserted into the thickest part of the thigh reaches at least 165ºF (74ºC) and it's crispy and golden, 10 more minutes. Continue to cook, checking every 5 minutes until the chicken reaches the correct internal temperature.
8. Let the chicken rest for 10 minutes before carving and serving.

Eggnog Quick Bread
Prep time: 10 minutes | Cook time: 18 minutes | Serves 6 to 8

1 cup flour, plus more for dusting
¼ cup sugar
1 teaspoon baking powder
¼ teaspoon salt
¼ teaspoon nutmeg
½ cup eggnog
1 egg yolk
1 tablespoon plus 1 teaspoon butter, melted
¼ cup pecans
¼ cup chopped candied fruit (cherries, pineapple, or mixed fruits)
Cooking spray

1. Select the BAKE function and preheat MAXX to 360ºF (182ºC).
2. In a medium bowl, stir together the flour, sugar, baking powder, salt, and nutmeg.
3. Add eggnog, egg yolk, and butter. Mix well but do not beat.
4. Stir in nuts and fruit.
5. Spray a baking pan with cooking spray and dust with flour.
6. Spread batter into prepared pan and bake for 18 minutes or until top is dark golden brown and bread starts to pull away from sides of pan.
7. Serve immediately.

Monkey Bread with Cherry and Pecan

Prep time: 15 minutes | Cook time: 25 minutes | Serves 6 to 8

1 (16.3-ounce / 462-g) can store-bought refrigerated biscuit dough	allspice
	⅛ teaspoon ground cloves
¼ cup packed light brown sugar	4 tablespoons (½ stick) unsalted butter, melted
1 teaspoon ground cinnamon	½ cup powdered sugar
½ teaspoon freshly grated nutmeg	2 teaspoons bourbon
½ teaspoon ground ginger	2 tablespoons chopped candied cherries
½ teaspoon kosher salt	2 tablespoons chopped pecans
¼ teaspoon ground	

1. Select the BAKE function and preheat MAXX to 310ºF (154ºC).
2. Open the can and separate the biscuits, then cut each into quarters. Toss the biscuit quarters in a large bowl with the brown sugar, cinnamon, nutmeg, ginger, salt, allspice, and cloves until evenly coated. Transfer the dough pieces and any sugar left in the bowl to a round cake pan, metal cake pan, or foil pan and drizzle evenly with the melted butter. Put the pan in the air fryer oven and bake until the monkey bread is golden brown and cooked through in the middle, about 25 minutes. Transfer the pan to a wire rack and let cool completely. Unmold from the pan.
3. In a small bowl, whisk the powdered sugar and the bourbon into a smooth glaze. Drizzle the glaze over the cooled monkey bread and, while the glaze is still wet, sprinkle with the cherries and pecans to serve.

Hasselback Potatoes with Parmesan

Prep time: 5 minutes | Cook time: 50 minutes | Serves 4

4 russet potatoes, peeled	to taste
	¼ cup grated Parmesan cheese
Salt and freshly ground black pepper,	Cooking spray

1. Spray the air fryer basket lightly with cooking spray.
2. Make thin parallel cuts into each potato, ⅛-inch to ¼-inch apart, stopping at about ½ of the way through. The potato needs to stay intact along the bottom.
3. Spray the potatoes with cooking spray and use the hands or a silicone brush to completely coat the potatoes lightly in oil.
4. Put the potatoes, sliced side up, in the air fryer basket in a single layer. Leave a little room between each potato. Sprinkle the potatoes lightly with salt and black pepper.
5. Select the AIR FRY function and cook at 400ºF (204ºC) for 20 minutes. Reposition the potatoes and spritz lightly with cooking spray again. Air fry until the potatoes are fork-tender and crispy and browned, another 20 to 30 minutes.
6. Sprinkle the potatoes with Parmesan cheese and serve.

Honey Yeast Rolls

Prep time: 10 minutes | Cook time: 20 minutes | Makes 8 rolls

¼ cup whole milk, heated to 115ºF (46ºC) in the microwave
½ teaspoon active dry yeast
1 tablespoon honey
⅔ cup all-purpose flour, plus more for

dusting
½ teaspoon kosher salt
2 tablespoons unsalted butter, at room temperature, plus more for greasing
Flaky sea salt, to taste

1. In a large bowl, whisk together the milk, yeast, and honey and let stand until foamy, about 10 minutes.
2. Stir in the flour and salt until just combined. Stir in the butter until absorbed. Scrape the dough onto a lightly floured work surface and knead until smooth, about 6 minutes. Transfer the dough to a lightly greased bowl, cover loosely with a sheet of plastic wrap or a kitchen towel, and let sit until nearly doubled in size, about 1 hour.
3. Uncover the dough, lightly press it down to expel the bubbles, then portion it into 8 equal pieces. Prep the work surface by wiping it clean with a damp paper towel (if there is flour on the work surface, it will prevent the dough from sticking lightly to the surface, which helps it form a ball). Roll each piece into a ball by cupping the palm of the hand around the dough against the work surface and moving the heel of the hand in a circular motion while using the thumb to contain the dough and tighten it into a perfectly round ball. Once all the balls are formed, nestle them side by side in the air fryer basket.
4. Cover the rolls loosely with a kitchen towel or a sheet of plastic wrap and let sit until lightly risen and puffed, 20 to 30 minutes.
5. Uncover the rolls and gently brush with more butter, being careful not to press the rolls too hard. Place the rolls in the air fryer basket.
6. Select the AIR FRY function and cook at 270ºF (132ºC) for 12 minutes, or until the rolls are light golden brown and fluffy.
7. Remove the rolls from the air fryer oven and brush liberally with more butter, if you like, and sprinkle each roll with a pinch of sea salt. Serve warm.

Chapter 13 Fast and Easy Everyday Favorites

Broccoli Coated Coconut-Egg Yolk
Prep time: 5 minutes | Cook time: 6 minutes | Serves 1

4 egg yolks
¼ cup butter, melted
2 cups coconut flower

Salt and pepper, to taste
2 cups broccoli florets

1. In a bowl, whisk the egg yolks and melted butter together. Throw in the coconut flour, salt and pepper, then stir again to combine well.
2. Dip each broccoli floret into the mixture and place in the air fryer basket. Select the AIR FRY function and cook at 400ºF (204ºC) for 6 minutes.
3. Work in batches if necessary. Take care when removing them from the air fryer oven and serve immediately.

Jalapeño Poppers Stuffed Cheese
Prep time: 5 minutes | Cook time: 25 minutes | Serves 6

2 slices bacon, halved
¾ cup whole milk ricotta cheese
½ cup shredded sharp Cheddar cheese
1 green onion, finely

chopped
¼ teaspoon salt
6 large jalapeños, halved lengthwise and deseeded
½ cup finely crushed potato chips

1. Lay bacon in single layer in basket. Select the AIR FRY function and cook at 400ºF (204ºC) for 5 minutes, or until crisp. Remove bacon and place on paper towels to drain. When cool, finely chop.
2. Stir together ricotta, Cheddar, green onion, bacon, and salt. Spoon into jalapeños; top with potato chips.
3. Place half the jalapeños in the basket and air fry for 8 minutes, or until tender. Repeat with the remaining jalapeños.
4. Serve immediately.

Hot Capicola and Brie Cheese Sandwich
Prep time: 5 minutes | Cook time: 8 minutes | Serves 2

2 tablespoons mayonnaise
4 thick slices sourdough bread

4 thick slices Brie cheese
8 slices hot capicola

1. Select the BAKE function and preheat MAXX to 350ºF (177ºC).
2. Spread the mayonnaise on one side of each slice of bread. Place 2 slices of bread in the air fryer basket, mayonnaise-side down.
3. Place the slices of Brie and capicola on the bread and cover with the remaining two slices of bread, mayonnaise-side up.
4. Bake for 8 minutes, or until the cheese has melted.
5. Serve immediately.

Buttered Sweet Potatoes
Prep time: 5 minutes | Cook time: 10 minutes | Serves 4

2 tablespoons butter, melted
1 tablespoon light brown sugar

2 sweet potatoes, peeled and cut into ½-inch cubes
Cooking spray

1. Line the air fryer basket with parchment paper.
2. In a medium bowl, stir together the melted butter and brown sugar until blended. Toss the sweet potatoes in the butter mixture until coated.
3. Place the sweet potatoes on the parchment and spritz with oil.
4. Select the AIR FRY function and cook at 400ºF (204ºC) for 5 minutes. Shake the basket, spritz the sweet potatoes with oil, and air fry for 5 minutes more until they're soft enough to cut with a fork.
5. Serve immediately.

Almond-Crusted Green Tomatoes
Prep time: 5 minutes | Cook time: 6 to 8 minutes | Serves 4

4 medium green tomatoes
$^1/_3$ cup all-purpose flour
2 egg whites
¼ cup almond milk
1 cup ground

almonds
½ cup panko bread crumbs
2 teaspoons olive oil
1 teaspoon paprika
1 clove garlic, minced

1. Rinse the tomatoes and pat dry. Cut the tomatoes into ½-inch slices, discarding the thinner ends.
2. Put the flour on a plate. In a shallow bowl, beat the egg whites with the almond milk until frothy. And in another plate, combine the almonds, bread crumbs, olive oil, paprika, and garlic and mix well.
3. Dip the tomato slices into the flour, then into the egg white mixture, then into the almond mixture to coat.
4. Place four of the coated tomato slices in the air fryer basket.
5. Select the AIR FRY function and cook at 400ºF (204ºC) for 6 to 8 minutes, or until the tomato coating is crisp and golden brown. Repeat with remaining tomato slices and serve immediately.

Chicken Wings
Prep time: 5 minutes | Cook time: 19 minutes | Serves 6

2 pounds (907 g) chicken wings, tips

removed
⅛ teaspoon salt

1. Season the wings with salt.
2. Working in 2 batches, place half the chicken wings in the basket. Select the AIR FRY function and cook at 400ºF (204ºC) for 15 minutes, or until the skin is browned and cooked through, turning the wings with tongs halfway through cooking.
3. Combine both batches in the air fryer oven and air fry for 4 minutes more. Transfer to a large bowl and serve immediately.

Green Beans and Bacon
Prep time: 15 minutes | Cook time: 8 to 10 minutes | Serves 4

2 (14.5-ounce / 411-g) cans cut green beans, drained
4 bacon slices, air-fried and diced
¼ cup minced onion
1 tablespoon distilled

white vinegar
1 teaspoon freshly squeezed lemon juice
½ teaspoon salt
½ teaspoon freshly ground black pepper
Cooking spray

1. Spritz a baking pan with oil. In the prepared pan, stir together the green beans, bacon, onion, vinegar, lemon juice, salt, and pepper until blended.
2. Place the pan on the air fryer basket.
3. Select the AIR FRY function and cook at 370ºF (188ºC) for 4 minutes. Stir the green beans and air fry for 4 to 6 minutes more until soft.
4. Serve immediately.

Feta Beet Salad with Lemon Vinaigrette
Prep time: 10 minutes | Cook time: 12 to 15 minutes | Serves 4

6 medium red and golden beets, peeled and sliced
1 teaspoon olive oil
¼ teaspoon kosher
Vinaigrette:
2 teaspoons olive oil
2 tablespoons

salt
½ cup crumbled feta cheese
8 cups mixed greens
Cooking spray

chopped fresh chives
Juice of 1 lemon

1. In a large bowl, toss the beets, olive oil, and kosher salt.
2. Spray the air fryer basket with cooking spray, then place the beets in the basket. Select the AIR FRY function and cook at 360ºF (182ºC) for 12 to 15 minutes, or until tender.
3. While the beets cook, make the vinaigrette in a large bowl by whisking together the olive oil, lemon juice, and chives.
4. Remove the beets from the air fryer oven, toss in the vinaigrette, and allow to cool for 5 minutes. Add the feta and serve on top of the mixed greens.

Sugar-Free Bacon-Wrapped Hot Dog

Prep time: 5 minutes | Cook time: 10 minutes | Serves 4

4 slices sugar-free bacon

4 beef hot dogs

1. Select the BAKE function and preheat MAXX to 370°F (188°C).
2. Take a slice of bacon and wrap it around the hot dog, securing it with a toothpick. Repeat with the other pieces of bacon and hot dogs, placing each wrapped dog in the air fryer basket.
3. Bake for 10 minutes, turning halfway through.
4. Once hot and crispy, the hot dogs are ready to serve.

Bacon-Wrapped Cheesy Jalapeño Poppers

Prep time: 5 minutes | Cook time: 12 minutes | Serves 6

6 large jalapeños
4 ounces (113 g) ⅓-less-fat cream cheese
¼ cup shredded reduced-fat sharp

Cheddar cheese
2 scallions, green tops only, sliced
6 slices center-cut bacon, halved

1. Select the BAKE function and preheat MAXX to 325°F (163°C).
2. Wearing rubber gloves, halve the jalapeños lengthwise to make 12 pieces. Scoop out the seeds and membranes and discard.
3. In a medium bowl, combine the cream cheese, Cheddar, and scallions. Using a small spoon or spatula, fill the jalapeños with the cream cheese filling. Wrap a bacon strip around each pepper and secure with a toothpick.
4. Working in batches, place the stuffed peppers in a single layer in the air fryer basket. Bake for about 12 minutes, until the peppers are tender, the bacon is browned and crisp, and the cheese is melted.
5. Serve warm.

Mexican Chorizo Scotch Eggs

Prep time: 5 minutes | Cook time: 15 to 20 minutes | Makes 4 eggs

1 pound (454 g) Mexican chorizo or other seasoned sausage meat
4 soft-boiled eggs plus 1 raw egg

1 tablespoon water
½ cup all-purpose flour
1 cup panko bread crumbs
Cooking spray

1. Divide the chorizo into 4 equal portions. Flatten each portion into a disc. Place a soft-boiled egg in the center of each disc. Wrap the chorizo around the egg, encasing it completely. Place the encased eggs on a plate and chill for at least 30 minutes.
2. Select the BAKE function and preheat MAXX to 360°F (182°C).
3. Beat the raw egg with 1 tablespoon of water. Place the flour on a small plate and the panko on a second plate. Working with 1 egg at a time, roll the encased egg in the flour, then dip it in the egg mixture. Dredge the egg in the panko and place on a plate. Repeat with the remaining eggs.
4. Spray the eggs with oil and place in the air fryer basket. Bake for 10 minutes. Turn and bake for an additional 5 to 10 minutes, or until browned and crisp on all sides.
5. Serve immediately.

Cheddar Sausage Balls

Prep time: 5 minutes | Cook time: 15 minutes | Serves 6

12 ounces (340 g) Jimmy Dean's Sausage
6 ounces (170 g)

shredded Cheddar cheese
10 Cheddar cubes

1. Mix the shredded cheese and sausage.
2. Divide the mixture into 12 equal parts to be stuffed.
3. Add a cube of cheese to the center of the sausage and roll into balls.
4. Select the AIR FRY function and cook at 375°F (191°C) for 15 minutes, or until crisp.
5. Serve immediately.

Halloumi Cheese with Greek Salsa

Prep time: 15 minutes | Cook time: 6 minutes | Serves 4

Salsa:

1 small shallot, finely diced	½ cup finely diced English cucumber
3 garlic cloves, minced	1 plum tomato, deseeded and finely diced
2 tablespoons fresh lemon juice	2 teaspoons chopped fresh parsley
2 tablespoons extra-virgin olive oil	1 teaspoon snipped fresh dill
1 teaspoon freshly cracked black pepper	1 teaspoon snipped fresh oregano
Pinch of kosher salt	

Cheese:

8 ounces (227 g) Halloumi cheese, sliced into ½-inch-	thick pieces
	1 tablespoon extra-virgin olive oil

1. Select the BAKE function and preheat MAXX to 375ºF (191ºC).
2. For the salsa: Combine the shallot, garlic, lemon juice, olive oil, pepper, and salt in a medium bowl. Add the cucumber, tomato, parsley, dill, and oregano. Toss gently to combine; set aside.
3. For the cheese: Place the cheese slices in a medium bowl. Drizzle with the olive oil. Toss gently to coat. Arrange the cheese in a single layer in the air fryer basket. Bake for 6 minutes.
4. Divide the cheese among four serving plates. Top with the salsa and serve immediately.

Speedy Beef Bratwursts

Prep time: 5 minutes | Cook time: 15 minutes | Serves 4

4 (3-ounce / 85-g) beef bratwursts

1. Place the beef bratwursts in the air fryer basket.
2. Select the AIR FRY function and cook at 375ºF (191ºC) for 15 minutes, turning once halfway through.
3. Serve hot.

Fast Roasted Asparagus

Prep time: 5 minutes | Cook time: 6 minutes | Serves 4

1 pound (454 g) asparagus, trimmed and halved crosswise	Salt and pepper, to taste
1 teaspoon extra-virgin olive oil	Lemon wedges, for serving

1. Select the ROAST function and preheat MAXX to 400ºF (204ºC).
2. Toss the asparagus with the oil, ⅛ teaspoon salt, and ⅛ teaspoon pepper in bowl. Transfer to air fryer basket.
3. Place the basket in air fryer oven and roast for 6 to 8 minutes, or until tender and bright green, tossing halfway through cooking.
4. Season with salt and pepper and serve with lemon wedges.

Colby Cheese Potato Patties

Prep time: 5 minutes | Cook time: 10 minutes | Serves 8

2 pounds (907 g) white potatoes	salt
½ cup finely chopped scallions	½ teaspoon hot paprika
½ teaspoon freshly ground black pepper, or more to taste	2 cups shredded Colby cheese
1 tablespoon fine sea	¼ cup canola oil
	1 cup crushed crackers

1. Select the BAKE function and preheat MAXX to 360ºF (182ºC).
2. Boil the potatoes until soft. Dry them off and peel them before mashing thoroughly, leaving no lumps.
3. Combine the mashed potatoes with scallions, pepper, salt, paprika, and cheese.
4. Mold the mixture into balls with your hands and press with your palm to flatten them into patties.
5. In a shallow dish, combine the canola oil and crushed crackers. Coat the patties in the crumb mixture.
6. Bake the patties for about 10 minutes, in multiple batches if necessary.
7. Serve hot.

Dried Herb-Roasted Veggies
Prep time: 10 minutes | Cook time: 14 to 18 minutes | Serves 4

1 red bell pepper, sliced
1 (8-ounce / 227-g) package sliced mushrooms
1 cup green beans, cut into 2-inch pieces
1/3 cup diced red
onion
3 garlic cloves, sliced
1 teaspoon olive oil
½ teaspoon dried basil
½ teaspoon dried tarragon

1. Select the ROAST function and preheat MAXX to 350ºF (177ºC).
2. In a medium bowl, mix the red bell pepper, mushrooms, green beans, red onion, and garlic. Drizzle with the olive oil. Toss to coat.
3. Add the herbs and toss again.
4. Place the vegetables in the air fryer basket. Roast for 14 to 18 minutes, or until tender. Serve immediately.

Indian Seasoned Sweet Potato Fries
Prep time: 5 minutes | Cook time: 8 minutes | Makes 20 fries

Seasoning Mixture:
¾ teaspoon ground coriander
½ teaspoon garam masala
½ teaspoon garlic
powder
½ teaspoon ground cumin
¼ teaspoon ground cayenne pepper
Fries:
2 large sweet potatoes, peeled
2 teaspoons olive oil

1. In a small bowl, combine the coriander, garam masala, garlic powder, cumin, and cayenne pepper.
2. Slice the sweet potatoes into ¼-inch-thick fries.
3. In a large bowl, toss the sliced sweet potatoes with the olive oil and the seasoning mixture.
4. Transfer the seasoned sweet potatoes to the air fryer basket. Select the AIR FRY function and cook at 400ºF (204ºC) for 8 minutes, or until crispy.
5. Serve warm.

Grits with Cheese
Prep time: 10 minutes | Cook time: 12 minutes | Serves 6

¾ cup hot water
2 (1-ounce / 28-g) packages instant grits
1 large egg, beaten
1 tablespoon butter, melted
2 cloves garlic, minced
½ to 1 teaspoon red pepper flakes
1 cup shredded Cheddar cheese or jalapeño Jack cheese

1. In a baking pan, combine the water, grits, egg, butter, garlic, and red pepper flakes. Stir until well combined. Stir in the shredded cheese.
2. Place the pan in the air fryer basket. Select the AIR FRY function and cook at 400ºF (204ºC) for 12 minutes, or until the grits have cooked through and a knife inserted near the center comes out clean.
3. Let stand for 5 minutes before serving.

Parmesan Brown Rice and Vegetable Fritters
Prep time: 10 minutes | Cook time: 8 to 10 minutes | Serves 4

1 (10-ounce / 284-g) bag frozen cooked brown rice, thawed
1 egg
3 tablespoons brown rice flour
1/3 cup finely grated carrots
1/3 cup minced red bell pepper
2 tablespoons minced fresh basil
3 tablespoons grated Parmesan cheese
2 teaspoons olive oil

1. In a small bowl, combine the thawed rice, egg, and flour and mix to blend.
2. Stir in the carrots, bell pepper, basil, and Parmesan cheese.
3. Form the mixture into 8 fritters and drizzle with the olive oil.
4. Put the fritters carefully into the air fryer basket.
5. Select the AIR FRY function and cook at 380ºF (193ºC) for 8 to 10 minutes, or until the fritters are golden brown and cooked through.
6. Serve immediately.

Bistro Fingerling Potato Wedges
Prep time: 10 minutes | Cook time: 13 minutes | Serves 4

1 pound (454 g) fingerling potatoes, cut into wedges
1 teaspoon extra-virgin olive oil
½ teaspoon garlic powder
Salt and pepper, to taste
½ cup raw cashews, soaked in water overnight
½ teaspoon ground turmeric
½ teaspoon paprika
1 tablespoon nutritional yeast
1 teaspoon fresh lemon juice
2 tablespoons to ¼ cup water

1. In a bowl, toss together the potato wedges, olive oil, garlic powder, and salt and pepper, making sure to coat the potatoes well.
2. Transfer the potatoes to the air fryer basket. Select the AIR FRY function and cook at 400°F (204°C) for 10 minutes.
3. In the meantime, prepare the cheese sauce. Pulse the cashews, turmeric, paprika, nutritional yeast, lemon juice, and water together in a food processor. Add more water to achieve your desired consistency.
4. When the potatoes are finished cooking, transfer to a bowl and add the cheese sauce on top. Air fry for an additional 3 minutes.
5. Serve hot.

Carrot, Celery, and Leek Croquettes
Prep time: 10 minutes | Cook time: 6 minutes | Serves 4

2 medium-sized carrots, trimmed and grated
2 medium-sized celery stalks, trimmed and grated
½ cup finely chopped leek
1 tablespoon garlic paste
¼ teaspoon freshly cracked black pepper
1 teaspoon fine sea salt
1 tablespoon finely chopped fresh dill
1 egg, lightly whisked
¼ cup flour
¼ teaspoon baking powder
½ cup bread crumbs
Cooking spray
Chive mayo, for serving

1. Drain any excess liquid from the carrots and celery by placing them on a paper towel.
2. Stir together the vegetables with all of the other ingredients, save for the bread crumbs and chive mayo.
3. Use your hands to mold 1 tablespoon of the vegetable mixture into a ball and repeat until all of the mixture has been used up. Press down on each ball with your hand or a palette knife. Cover completely with bread crumbs. Spritz the croquettes with cooking spray.
4. Arrange the croquettes in a single layer in the air fryer basket. Select the AIR FRY function and cook at 360°F (182°C) for 6 minutes.
5. Serve warm with the chive mayo on the side.

Avocado Fries with Pomegranate Molasses
Prep time: 5 minutes | Cook time: 7 to 8 minutes | Serves 4

1 cup panko bread crumbs
1 teaspoon kosher salt, plus more for sprinkling
1 teaspoon garlic powder
½ teaspoon cayenne pepper
2 ripe but firm avocados
1 egg, beaten with 1 tablespoon water
Cooking spray
Pomegranate molasses, for serving

1. Select the BAKE function and preheat MAXX to 375°F (191°C).
2. Whisk together the panko, salt, and spices on a plate. Cut each avocado in half and remove the pit. Cut each avocado half into 4 slices and scoop the slices out with a large spoon, taking care to keep the slices intact.
3. Dip each avocado slice in the egg wash and then dredge it in the panko. Place the breaded avocado slices on a plate.
4. Working in 2 batches, arrange half of the avocado slices in a single layer in the air fryer basket. Spray lightly with oil. Bake the slices for 7 to 8 minutes, turning once halfway through. Remove the cooked slices to a platter and repeat with the remaining avocado slices.
5. Sprinkle the warm avocado slices with salt and drizzle with pomegranate molasses. Serve immediately.

Super Cheesy Chile Toast
Prep time: 5 minutes | Cook time: 5 minutes | Serves 1

2 tablespoons grated Parmesan cheese
2 tablespoons grated Mozzarella cheese
2 teaspoons salted butter, at room temperature

10 to 15 thin slices serrano chile or jalapeño
2 slices sourdough bread
½ teaspoon black pepper

1. Select the BAKE function and preheat MAXX to 325ºF (163ºC).
2. In a small bowl, stir together the Parmesan, Mozzarella, butter, and chiles.
3. Spread half the mixture onto one side of each slice of bread. Sprinkle with the pepper. Place the slices, cheese-side up, in the air fryer basket. Bake for 5 minutes, or until the cheese has melted and started to brown slightly.
4. Serve immediately.

Devils on Horseback
Prep time: 5 minutes | Cook time: 7 minutes | Serves 12

24 petite pitted prunes (4½ ounces / 128 g)
¼ cup crumbled blue

cheese, divided
8 slices center-cut bacon, cut crosswise into thirds

1. Halve the prunes lengthwise, but don't cut them all the way through. Place ½ teaspoon of cheese in the center of each prune. Wrap a piece of bacon around each prune and secure the bacon with a toothpick.
2. Working in batches, arrange a single layer of the prunes in the air fryer basket.
3. Select the AIR FRY function and cook at 400ºF (204ºC) for 7 minutes, flipping halfway, until the bacon is cooked through and crisp.
4. Let cool slightly and serve warm.

Corn Kernels Fritters
Prep time: 15 minutes | Cook time: 8 minutes | Serves 6

1 cup self-rising flour
1 tablespoon sugar
1 teaspoon salt
1 large egg, lightly beaten

¼ cup buttermilk
¾ cup corn kernels
¼ cup minced onion
Cooking spray

1. Select the BAKE function and preheat MAXX to 350ºF (177ºC). Line the air fryer basket with parchment paper.
2. In a medium bowl, whisk the flour, sugar, and salt until blended. Stir in the egg and buttermilk. Add the corn and minced onion. Mix well. Shape the corn fritter batter into 12 balls.
3. Place the fritters on the parchment and spritz with oil. Bake for 4 minutes. Flip the fritters, spritz them with oil, and bake for 4 minutes more until firm and lightly browned.
4. Serve immediately.

Indian-Style Masala Omelet
Prep time: 10 minutes | Cook time: 12 minutes | Serves 2

4 large eggs
½ cup diced onion
½ cup diced tomato
¼ cup chopped fresh cilantro
1 jalapeño, deseeded and finely chopped
½ teaspoon ground

turmeric
½ teaspoon kosher salt
½ teaspoon cayenne pepper
Olive oil, for greasing the pan

1. Select the BAKE function and preheat MAXX to 250ºF (121ºC). Generously grease a 3-cup Bundt pan.
2. In a large bowl, beat the eggs. Stir in the onion, tomato, cilantro, jalapeño, turmeric, salt, and cayenne.
3. Pour the egg mixture into the prepared pan. Place the pan in the air fryer basket. Bake for 12 minutes, or until the eggs are cooked through. Carefully unmold and cut the omelet into four pieces.
4. Serve immediately.

Mexican Street Corn
Prep time: 5 minutes | Cook time: 7 minutes | Serves 4

4 medium ears corn, husked	¼ teaspoon kosher salt
Cooking spray	2 ounces (57 g) crumbled Cotija or feta cheese
2 tablespoons mayonnaise	
1 tablespoon fresh lime juice	2 tablespoons chopped fresh cilantro
½ teaspoon ancho chile powder	

1. Spritz the corn with cooking spray. Working in batches, arrange the ears of corn in the air fryer basket in a single layer.
2. Select the AIR FRY function and cook at 375°F (191°C) for 7 minutes, flipping halfway, until the kernels are tender when pierced with a paring knife. When cool enough to handle, cut the corn kernels off the cob.
3. In a large bowl, mix together mayonnaise, lime juice, ancho powder, and salt. Add the corn kernels and mix to combine. Transfer to a serving dish and top with the Cotija and cilantro.
4. Serve immediately.

Okra Slices
Prep time: 5 minutes | Cook time: 8 to 10 minutes | Serves 4

1 cup self-rising yellow cornmeal	½ teaspoon freshly ground black pepper
1 teaspoon Italian-style seasoning	2 large eggs, beaten
1 teaspoon paprika	2 cups okra slices
1 teaspoon salt	Cooking spray

1. Line the air fryer basket with parchment paper.
2. In a shallow bowl, whisk the cornmeal, Italian-style seasoning, paprika, salt, and pepper until blended. Place the beaten eggs in a second shallow bowl.
3. Add the okra to the beaten egg and stir to coat. Add the egg and okra mixture to the cornmeal mixture and stir until coated.
4. Place the okra on the parchment and spritz it with oil.
5. Select the AIR FRY function and cook at 400°F (204°C) for 4 minutes. Shake the basket, spritz the okra with oil, and air fry for 4 to 6 minutes more until lightly browned and crispy.
6. Serve immediately.

Purple Fingerling Potato Chips with Rosemary
Prep time: 10 minutes | Cook time: 9 to 14 minutes | Serves 6

1 cup Greek yogurt	potatoes
2 chipotle chiles, minced	1 teaspoon olive oil
2 tablespoons adobo sauce	2 teaspoons minced fresh rosemary leaves
1 teaspoon paprika	⅛ teaspoon cayenne pepper
1 tablespoon lemon juice	¼ teaspoon coarse sea salt
10 purple fingerling	

1. In a medium bowl, combine the yogurt, minced chiles, adobo sauce, paprika, and lemon juice. Mix well and refrigerate.
2. Wash the potatoes and dry them with paper towels. Slice the potatoes lengthwise, as thinly as possible. You can use a mandoline, a vegetable peeler, or a very sharp knife.
3. Combine the potato slices in a medium bowl and drizzle with the olive oil; toss to coat. Transfer the potato slices to the air fryer basket.
4. Select the AIR FRY function and cook at 400°F (204°C) for 9 to 14 minutes. Use tongs to gently rearrange the chips halfway during cooking time.
5. Sprinkle the chips with the rosemary, cayenne pepper, and sea salt. Serve with the chipotle sauce for dipping.

Chapter 14 Rotisserie

Seasoned Beef Roast

Prep time: 5 minutes | Cook time: 38 minutes | Serves 6

2.5 pound (1.1 kg) beef roast
1 tablespoon olive oil

1 tablespoon Poultry seasoning

1. Tie the beef roast and rub the olive oil all over the roast. Sprinkle with the seasoning.
2. Using the rotisserie spit, push through the beef roast and attach the rotisserie forks.
3. If desired, place aluminum foil onto the drip pan. (It makes for easier clean-up!)
4. Select the AIR FRY function and set the temperature to 360ºF (182ºC). Press ROTATE button and set time to 38 minutes for medium rare beef.
5. Place the prepared chicken with rotisserie spit into the oven.
6. When cooking is complete, remove the beef roast using the rotisserie handle and, using hot pads or gloves, carefully remove the beef roast from the spit.
7. Let cool for 5 minutes before serving.

Ham with Tangy Glaze

Prep time: 10 minutes | Cook time: 45 minutes | Serves 12 to 14

1 ham, bone in and unsliced, 7 to 8 pounds (3.2 to 3.6 kg)
1 cup packed brown sugar
Glaze:
1½ cups orange juice
½ cup honey
2 tablespoons packed brown sugar
¼ teaspoon ground cinnamon
⅛ teaspoon ground nutmeg
⅛ teaspoon ground allspice
⅛ teaspoon ground cloves
⅛ teaspoon white pepper
2 tablespoons unsalted butter

1. To make the glaze: Combine the orange juice, honey, brown sugar, and spices in a saucepan and bring almost to a boil over medium-high heat. Decrease the heat to medium and simmer for 10 minutes, stirring often. The mixture should be a little runnier than real maple syrup. Remove from the heat and add the butter, stirring until melted. Let the mixture cool.
2. Run a long sword skewer through the center of the ham lengthwise to create a pilot hole. There is a bone in the middle of this ham, but generally it is just to one side. The skewer should easily go through, but feel for the bone before you start so you will know how to navigate around it. Run the rotisserie spit through the hole and secure with the forks. Balance the ham on the spit as well as possible.
3. Select the ROAST function and preheat MAXX to 375ºF (190ºC). Press ROTATE button and set time to 45 minutes.
4. Place the ham on the preheated air fryer oven and set a drip pan underneath, if there is room. The ham should not take too long to heat up. Look for an internal temperature around 130ºF (54ºC). The surface should be hot.
5. Baste the ham with the glaze after 20 minutes on the air fryer oven. Repeat the process every 5 minutes and about 3 more times.
6. During the last 5 to 10 minutes of cooking time, the ham should be hot as well as sticky from the glaze. Increase the temperature to 400ºF (205ºC) and sprinkle the brown sugar evenly on the surface of the ham in small amounts until it is completely coated. Continue to cook until the sugar starts to bubble. Move quickly, as sugar tends to burn.
7. Once the sugar is bubbling rapidly, remove the ham from the heat and place on a large cutting board. Remove the rotisserie forks and slide the spit out, loosely cover the ham with aluminum foil, and let it rest for 5 minutes. Carve into thin slices and serve warm.

Whole Roast Chicken

Prep time: 15 minutes | Cook time: 1 hour 10 minutes | Serves 4 to 6

1 whole chicken, 3 to 4 pounds (1.4 to 1.8 kg)
1 medium-size onion, peeled but whole (for cavity)

Barbecue Sauce:
¾ cup ketchup
⅔ cup cherry cola
¼ cup apple cider vinegar
2 tablespoons packed brown sugar
1 tablespoon molasses
¼ teaspoon salt
¼ teaspoon freshly ground black pepper

Rub:
2 teaspoons salt
2 teaspoons onion powder
1 teaspoon mustard powder
½ teaspoon freshly ground black pepper
½ teaspoon garlic powder

1. To make the barbecue sauce: Combine all the ingredients in a medium-size saucepan over medium heat and simmer for 5 to 6 minutes, until the mixture is smooth and well blended. Stir often and watch for burning. Remove from the heat and let the sauce cool at least 10 minutes before using.
2. To make the rub: Combine all the rub ingredients in a small bowl.
3. Pat the chicken dry inside and out with paper towels. Apply the rub all over the bird, under the breast skin, and inside the body cavity.
4. Truss the chicken with kitchen twine. Run the rotisserie spit through the onion and insert it into the chicken cavity. Use a paring knife to cut a pilot hole in the onion to make this easier. Continue to run the spit through the chicken and secure with the rotisserie forks.
5. Select the ROAST function and preheat MAXX to 400ºF (205ºC). Press ROTATE button and set time to 70 minutes.
6. Place the chicken on the preheated air fryer oven and set a drip pan underneath. Roast until the meat in the thighs and legs reaches 175ºF (79ºC). The breasts should be 165ºF (74ºC). Baste the chicken with the barbecue sauce during the last half of the cooking time. Do so every 7 to 10 minutes, until the bird is nearly done and well coated with the sauce.

7. Remove from the heat, carefully remove the rotisserie forks and slide the spit out, and then set the chicken on a large cutting board. Tent the chicken with aluminum foil and let it rest for 10 to 15 minutes before cutting off the twine and carving.

Chicken with Garlicky Brown Sugar Brine

Prep time: 5 minutes | Cook time: 1 hour | Serves 4

1 (4-pound / 1.8-kg) chicken

Brine:
2 quarts cold water
½ cup table salt (or 1 cup kosher salt)
¼ cup brown sugar
½ head of garlic (6 to 8 cloves), skin on, crushed
3 bay leaves, crumbled
1 tablespoon peppercorns, crushed or coarsely ground

1. Combine the brine ingredients in large container, and stir until the salt and sugar dissolve. Submerge the chicken in the brine. Store in the refrigerator for at least one hour, preferably four hours, no longer than eight hours.
2. Remove the chicken from the brine and pat dry with paper towels, picking off any pieces of bay leaves or garlic that stick to the chicken. Fold the wingtips underneath the wings, then truss the chicken. Skewer the chicken on the rotisserie spit, securing it with the rotisserie forks. Let the chicken rest at room temperature.
3. Select the ROAST function and preheat MAXX to 450ºF (235ºC). Press ROTATE button and set time to 1 hour. Set a drip pan in the middle of the air fryer oven.
4. Put the spit on the air fryer oven, start the motor spinning, and make sure the drip pan is centered beneath the chicken. Close the lid and cook until the chicken reaches 160ºF (70ºC) in the thickest part of the breast.
5. Remove the chicken from the rotisserie spit and remove the twine trussing the chicken. Be careful - the spit and forks are blazing hot. Let the chicken rest for 15 minutes, then carve and serve.

Bourbon Ham with Apple Butter Baste

Prep time: 5 minutes | Cook time: 50 minutes | Serves 10 to 12

1 ham, unsliced, 5 to 6 pounds (2.3 to 2.7 kg)

Baste:

⅓ cup apple butter	mustard
¼ cup packed brown sugar	¼ teaspoon ground ginger
2 tablespoons bourbon	¼ teaspoon white pepper
1½ teaspoons Dijon	

1. Run a long sword skewer through the center of the ham lengthwise to create a pilot hole. Run the rotisserie spit through the hole and secure with the forks. Balance as necessary and secure tightly. Place the ham on the preheated air fryer oven and cook for 50 to 60 minutes. If there is room, set a drip pan underneath.
2. To make the baste: Combine all the baste ingredients in a small saucepan and simmer over medium heat for 2 minutes, stirring often. Remove from the heat and let sit for 5 to 10 minutes before using.
3. Select the ROAST function and preheat MAXX to 400ºF (205ºC). Press ROTATE button and set time to 45 minutes.
4. Place the ham on the preheated air fryer oven and set a drip pan underneath, if there is room. During the last 20 minutes of the cooking time, begin basting the ham with the apple butter-bourbon mixture. Make at least 4 or 5 passes with the baste to coat evenly. Focus the coating on the outside of the ham and not on the cut side. The ham should not take too long to heat up. Look for an internal temperature around 130ºF (54ºC). The surface should be hot.
5. Remove from the heat, carefully remove the rotisserie forks and slide the spit out, and then set the ham on a large cutting board. Tent the ham with aluminum foil and let the meat rest for 10 minutes. Carve and serve immediately.

Ritzy Rotisserie Pork Shoulder

Prep time: 30 minutes | Cook time: 4 hours 30 minutes | Serves 6 to 8

1 (5-pound / 2.3-kg) boneless pork shoulder
1 tablespoon kosher salt

For the Rub:

2 teaspoons ground black peppercorns	1 teaspoon onion powder
2 teaspoons ground mustard seed	1 teaspoon garlic powder
2 tablespoons light brown sugar	1 teaspoon paprika

For the Mop:

1 cup bourbon	2 tablespoons brown mustard
1 small onion, granulated	½ cup light brown sugar
¼ cup corn syrup	
¼ cup ketchup	

1. Combine the ingredients for the rub in a small bowl. Stir to mix well.
2. Season pork shoulder all over with rub, wrap in plastic, and place in refrigerator for 12 to 15 hours.
3. Remove roast from the fridge and let meat stand at room temperature for 30 to 45 minutes. Season with kosher salt.
4. Whisk ingredients for mop in a medium bowl. Set aside until ready to use.
5. Using the rotisserie spit, push through the pork should and attach the rotisserie forks.
6. If desired, place aluminum foil onto the drip pan. (It makes for easier clean-up!)
7. Select the ROAST function and preheat MAXX to 450ºF (235ºC). Press ROTATE button and set time to 30 minutes.
8. Once preheated, place the prepared pork with rotisserie spit into the oven.
9. After 30 minutes, reduce the temperature to 250ºF (121ºC) and roast for 4 more hours or until an meat thermometer inserted in the center of the pork reads at least 145ºF (63ºC).
10. After the first hour of cooking, apply mop over the pork for every 20 minutes.
11. When cooking is complete, remove the pork using the rotisserie handle and, using hot pads or gloves, carefully remove the pork tenderloin from the spit.
12. Let stand for 10 minutes before slicing and serving.

Rotisserie Chicken with Teriyaki Sauce
Prep time: 5 minutes | Cook time: 1 hour 10 minutes | Serves 4

1 (4-pound / 1.8-kg) chicken
1 tablespoon kosher salt
Teriyaki Sauce:

¼ cup soy sauce
¼ cup mirin (Japanese sweet rice wine)
¼ cup honey (or sugar)
¼ inch slice of ginger, smashed

1. Season the chicken with the salt, inside and out. Gently work your fingers under the skin on the breast, then rub some of the salt directly onto the breast meat. Fold the wingtips under the wings and truss the chicken. Skewer the chicken on the rotisserie spit, securing it with the rotisserie forks. Let the chicken rest at room temperature.
2. Select the ROAST function and preheat MAXX to 450ºF (235ºC). Press ROTATE button and set time to 1 hour. Set a drip pan in the middle of the air fryer oven.
3. While the air fryer oven is preheating, combine the soy sauce, mirin, honey, and ginger in a saucepan. Bring to a boil over medium-high heat, stirring often, then decrease the heat to low and simmer for 10 minutes, until the liquid is reduced by half.
4. Put the spit on the air fryer oven, start the motor spinning, and make sure the drip pan is centered beneath the chicken. Close the lid and cook until the chicken reaches 160ºF (70ºC) in the thickest part of the breast. During the last 15 minutes of cooking, brush the chicken with the teriyaki sauce every five minutes.
5. Remove the chicken from the rotisserie spit and transfer to a platter. Be careful - the spit and forks are blazing hot. Remove the trussing twine, then brush the chicken one last time with the teriyaki sauce. Let the chicken rest for 15 minutes, then carve and serve, passing any remaining teriyaki sauce at the table.

Lamb Leg with Chili Brown Sugar Rub
Prep time: 10 minutes | Cook time: 1 hour 20 minutes | Serves 6 to 8

1 boneless leg of lamb (partial bone-in is fine), 4 to 5 pounds (1.8 to 2.3 kg)
Rub:

¼ cup packed brown sugar
1 tablespoon coarse salt
2 teaspoons smoked paprika
1½ to 2 teaspoons spicy chili powder or cayenne
2 teaspoons onion powder
1 teaspoon garlic powder
1 teaspoon freshly ground black pepper
½ teaspoon ground cloves
⅛ teaspoon ground cinnamon

1. Trim off the excess fat and any loose hanging pieces from the lamb. With kitchen twine, tie the roast into a uniform and solid roast. It will take four to five ties to hold it together properly. Run a long sword skewer through the center of the roast lengthwise to create a pilot hole. Run the rotisserie spit through the hole and secure with the forks. Balance as necessary.
2. To make the rub: Combine the rub ingredients in a small bowl and apply evenly to the lamb. Make sure you get as much of the rub on the meat as possible.
3. Select the ROAST function and preheat MAXX to 375ºF (190ºC). Press ROTATE button and set time to 80 minutes.
4. Place the lamb on the preheated air fryer oven and set a drip pan underneath. Roast until the lamb reaches an internal temperature of 140ºF (60ºC) for medium or 150ºF (66ºC) for medium well. The lamb will shrink during cooking, so adjust the forks when appropriate.
5. Remove from the heat, carefully remove the rotisserie forks and slide the spit out, and then set the lamb on a large cutting board. Tent the roast with aluminum foil and let the meat rest for 10 to 12 minutes. Cut off the twine and carve. Serve.

Chipotle-Oregano Chuck Roast

Prep time: 10 minutes | Cook time: 2½ hours | Serves 6 to 8

1 chuck roast, 3½ to 4 pounds (1.5 to 1.8 kg)

Marinade:

1 (7-ounce / 198-g) can chipotle peppers in adobo	1 tablespoon ground cumin
1 cup diced onion	2 tablespoons water
½ cup beef or vegetable broth	1 tablespoon white vinegar
3 cloves garlic, cut into fourths	1 tablespoon salt
	2 teaspoons dried oregano

1. To make the marinade: Place the marinade ingredients in a food processor and pulse 8 to 10 times. Everything should be very finely chopped and combined. Reserve 1 cup of the mixture to use as a baste and refrigerate until ready to cook, then bring to room temperature before using.
2. Trim away any loose or excess pieces of fat from the roast. Place in a large glass dish or large resealable plastic bag. Pour the marinade over the meat, making sure all sides are well covered. Seal the bag or cover the dish with plastic wrap and place in the refrigerator for 12 to 24 hours.
3. Remove the roast from the bag, discarding the marinade. Lay the roast out on a large cutting board. With kitchen twine, tie the roast into a round and uniform shape, pulling tightly. Start in the center and work toward the ends until it is tied into a solid round roast. This will take four or five ties. Run a long sword skewer through the center of the roast lengthwise to create a pilot hole. Run the rotisserie spit through the hole and secure with the forks. Balance as necessary.
4. Select the ROAST function and preheat MAXX to 400ºF (205ºC). Press ROTATE button and set time to 2½ hours.
5. Place the roast on the preheated air fryer oven and set a drip pan underneath. Roast until the meat reaches an internal temperature of about 160ºF (70ºC). Baste with the reserved marinade during the last 30 to 40 minutes of cooking.

This roast is intentionally overcooked so that it can be shredded easily. It will be tender and juicy.

6. Remove from the heat, carefully remove the rotisserie forks and slide the spit out, and then set the roast on a large cutting board. Tent the roast with aluminum foil and let the meat rest for 20 minutes. Cut off the twine. Shred into small pieces or carve into thin slices and serve with warmed tortillas, Spanish rice, beans, and fresh salsa.

Chicken with Mustard Paste

Prep time: 5 minutes | Cook time: 1 hour | Serves 4

1 (4-pound / 1.8-kg) chicken

Mustard Paste:

¼ cup Dijon mustard	de Provence
1 tablespoon kosher salt	1 teaspoon freshly ground black pepper
1 tablespoon Herbes	

1. Mix the mustard paste ingredients in a small bowl. Rub the chicken with the mustard paste, inside and out. Gently work your fingers under the skin on the breast, then rub some of the paste directly onto the breast meat. Refrigerate for at least two hours, preferably overnight.
2. One hour before cooking, remove the chicken from the refrigerator. Fold the wingtips under the wings and truss the chicken. Skewer the chicken on the rotisserie spit, securing it with the rotisserie forks. Let the chicken rest at room temperature.
3. Select the ROAST function and preheat MAXX to 450ºF (235ºC). Press ROTATE button and set time to 1 hour. Set a drip pan in the middle of the air fryer oven.
4. Put the spit on the air fryer oven, start the motor spinning, and make sure the drip pan is centered beneath the chicken. Close the lid and cook until the chicken reaches 160ºF (70ºC) in the thickest part of the breast.
5. Remove the chicken from the rotisserie spit and remove the twine trussing the chicken. Be careful - the spit and forks are blazing hot. Let the chicken rest for 15 minutes, then carve and serve.

Greek Rotisserie Leg of Lamb
Prep time: 25 minutes | Cook time: 1 hour 30 minutes | Serves 4 to 6

3 pounds (1.4 kg) leg of lamb, boned in
For the Marinade:

1 tablespoon lemon zest (about 1 lemon)	powder
	1 teaspoon fresh
3 tablespoons lemon juice (about 1½ lemons)	thyme
	¼ cup fresh oregano
	¼ cup olive oil
3 cloves garlic, minced	1 teaspoon ground black pepper
1 teaspoon onion	

For the Herb Dressing:

1 tablespoon lemon juice (about ½ lemon)	thyme
	1 tablespoon olive oil
¼ cup chopped fresh oregano	1 teaspoon sea salt
	Ground black pepper, to taste
1 teaspoon fresh	

1. Place lamb leg into a large resealable plastic bag. Combine the ingredients for the marinade in a small bowl. Stir to mix well.
2. Pour the marinade over the lamb, making sure the meat is completely coated. Seal the bag and place in the refrigerator. Marinate for 4 to 6 hours before grilling.
3. Remove the lamb leg from the marinade. Using the rotisserie spit, push through the lamb leg and attach the rotisserie forks.
4. If desired, place aluminum foil onto the drip pan. (It makes for easier clean-up!)
5. Select the ROAST function and preheat MAXX to 350ºF (180ºC). Press ROTATE button and set time to 1 hour 30 minutes.
6. Once preheated, place the prepared lamb leg with rotisserie spit into the oven. Baste with marinade for every 30 minutes.
7. Meanwhile, combine the ingredients for the herb dressing in a bowl. Stir to mix well.
8. When cooking is complete, remove the lamb leg using the rotisserie handle and, using hot pads or gloves, carefully remove the lamb leg from the spit.
9. Cover lightly with aluminum foil for 8 to 10 minutes.
10. Carve the leg and arrange on a platter,. Drizzle with herb dressing. Serve immediately.

Rotisserie Buttermilk Chicken
Prep time: 10 minutes | Cook time: 50 minutes | Serves 4

2 cups buttermilk	1 tablespoon sea salt
¼ cup olive oil	1 whole chicken
1 teaspoon garlic powder	Salt and pepper, to taste

1. In a large bag, place the buttermilk, oil, garlic powder, and sea salt and mix to combine.
2. Add the whole chicken and let marinate for 24 hours up to two days.
3. Remove the chicken and sprinkle with the salt and pepper.
4. Truss the chicken, removing the wings and ensuring the legs are tied closely together and the thighs are held in place.
5. Using the rotisserie spit, push through the chicken and attach the rotisserie forks.
6. If desired, place aluminum foil onto the drip pan. (It makes for easier clean-up!)
7. Select the AIR FRY function and set the temperature to 380ºF (193ºC). Press ROTATE button and set time to 50 minutes.
8. Once the unit has preheated, place the prepared chicken with the rotisserie spit into the oven.
9. When cooking is complete, the chicken should be dark brown and internal temperature should measure 165 degrees (measure at the meatiest part of the thigh).
10. Remove the chicken using the rotisserie handle and, using hot pads or gloves, carefully remove the chicken from the spit.
11. Let sit for 10 minutes before slicing and serving.

Bacon-Wrapped Beef Roast
Prep time: 5 minutes | Cook time: 45 minutes | Serves 4

1 (4-pound / 1.8-kg) sirloin roast
1 tablespoon kosher salt
4 slices bacon

1. Season the roast with the salt, then refrigerate for at least two hours, preferably overnight.
2. One hour before cooking, remove the roast from the refrigerator. Cut the butcher's twine and lay the strings on a platter, spaced where you want to tie the roast. Put two slices of bacon on top of the string, with a gap between them. Put the sirloin on top of the bacon, then lay the last two pieces of bacon on top of the roast. Tie the twine to truss the roast and the bacon. Trim off any loose ends of bacon so they don't burn in the air fryer oven. Skewer the roast on the rotisserie spit, securing it with the rotisserie forks. Let the beef rest at room temperature until the air fryer oven is ready.
3. Select the ROAST function and preheat MAXX to 450ºF (235ºC). Press ROTATE button and set time to 45 minutes. Set a drip pan in the middle of the air fryer oven.
4. Put the spit on the air fryer oven, start the motor spinning, and make sure the drip pan is centered beneath the sirloin roast. Close the lid and cook the beef until it reaches 120ºF (49ºC) in its thickest part for medium-rare. (Cook to 115ºF (46ºC) for rare, 130ºF (54ºC) for medium.)
5. Remove the sirloin roast from the rotisserie spit and remove the twine trussing the roast, leaving as much bacon behind as possible. Be careful - the spit and forks are blazing hot. Let the beef rest for 15 minutes, then carve into thin slices and serve.

Lamb Leg with Feta and Herb Stuffing
Prep time: 5 minutes | Cook time: 45 minutes | Serves 3

1 (2½-pound / 1.1-kg) boneless leg of lamb roast
2 teaspoons kosher salt

Feta Stuffing:
2 ounces crumbled feta cheese
1 teaspoon minced fresh rosemary
1 teaspoon minced fresh thyme
Zest of ½ lemon

1. Season the leg of lamb with the salt, then refrigerate for at least two hours, preferably overnight.
2. One hour before cooking, remove the lamb from the refrigerator. Just before heating the air fryer oven, mix the stuffing ingredients. Open up the lamb like a book, then spread the stuffing over the cut side of the lamb. Fold the roast back into its original shape. Truss the lamb, then skewer it on the rotisserie spit, securing it with the rotisserie forks. (You're going to lose a little of the stuffing when you tie down the trussing twine; that's OK.) Let the lamb rest at room temperature until the air fryer oven is ready.
3. Select the ROAST function and preheat MAXX to 450ºF (235ºC). Press ROTATE button and set time to 45 minutes. Set a drip pan in the middle of the air fryer oven.
4. Put the spit on the air fryer oven, start the motor spinning, and make sure the drip pan is centered beneath the lamb. Close the lid and cook the lamb until it reaches 130ºF (54ºC) in its thickest part for medium. (Cook to 115ºF (46ºC) for rare, 120ºF (49ºC) for medium-rare.)
5. Remove the lamb from the rotisserie spit and remove the twine trussing the roast. Be careful - the spit and forks are blazing hot. Let the lamb rest for 15 minutes, then carve and serve.

Tapenade Stuffed Lamb Leg
Prep time: 10 minutes | Cook time: 45 minutes | Serves 3

1 (2½-pound / 1.1-kg) boneless leg of lamb
1 tablespoon kosher salt
Tapenade:

1 clove garlic, peeled	ground black pepper
2 basil leaves	1 anchovy fillet,
1 cup pitted Kalamata olives, rinsed	rinsed (optional)
	2 tablespoons
1 teaspoon capers	grapeseed oil or
Juice of ½ lemon	vegetable oil
½ teaspoon fresh	

1. Season the leg of lamb with the salt, then refrigerate for at least two hours, preferably overnight.
2. Drop the garlic clove into a running food processor and process until completely minced. Turn the processor off, add the basil, and process with one second pulses until finely minced. Add the olives, capers, lemon juice, pepper, and anchovy. Process with one second pulses until finely minced, scraping down the sides of the bowl if necessary. Turn the processor on and slowly pour the oil through the feed tube into the running processor. Once all the oil is added the tapenade should be a thick paste. Use immediately, or store in the refrigerator for up to a week.
3. One hour before cooking, remove the lamb from the refrigerator. Right before heating the air fryer oven, spread the tapenade over the cut side of the lamb, fold the roast back into its original shape, and truss it. (You're going to lose a little of the tapenade as you truss the roast; that's OK.) Skewer the lamb on the rotisserie spit, securing it with the rotisserie forks. Let the lamb rest at room temperature until the air fryer oven is ready.
4. Select the ROAST function and preheat MAXX to 450ºF (235ºC). Press ROTATE button and set time to 45 minutes. Set a drip pan in the middle of the air fryer oven.
5. Put the spit on the air fryer oven, start the motor spinning, and make sure the drip pan is centered beneath the lamb. Close the lid and cook the lamb until it

reaches 130ºF (54ºC) in its thickest part for medium. (Cook to 115ºF (46ºC) for rare, 120ºF (49ºC) for medium-rare.)
6. Remove the lamb from the rotisserie spit and remove the twine trussing the roast. Be careful - the spit and forks are blazing hot. Let the lamb rest for 15 minutes, then carve and serve.

Lamb Shoulder Roast with Mustard Herb Paste
Prep time: 5 minutes | Cook time: 2 hours | Serves 4

1 (4-pound / 1.8-kg) boneless lamb shoulder roast
Mustard Herb Paste:

¼ cup whole grain mustard	1 teaspoon minced fresh oregano
1 tablespoon kosher salt	1 teaspoon minced fresh rosemary
1 tablespoon minced fresh thyme	1 teaspoon fresh ground black pepper

1. Mix the paste ingredients in a small bowl. Open up the lamb like a book, then rub all over with the paste, working it into any natural seams in the meat. Refrigerate for at least two hours, preferably overnight.
2. One hour before cooking, remove the lamb from the refrigerator. Fold the lamb into its original shape, truss the lamb, and skewer it on the rotisserie spit, securing it with the rotisserie forks. Let the lamb rest at room temperature until the air fryer oven is ready.
3. Select the ROAST function and preheat MAXX to 375ºF (190ºC). Press ROTATE button and set time to 2 hours. Set a drip pan in the middle of the air fryer oven.
4. Put the spit on the air fryer oven, start the motor spinning, and make sure the drip pan is centered beneath the lamb shoulder. Close the lid and cook the lamb until it reaches 190ºF (88ºC) in its thickest part.
5. Remove the lamb shoulder from the rotisserie spit and remove the twine trussing the roast. Be careful - the spit and forks are blazing hot. Let the lamb rest for 15 minutes, then carve and serve.

Lamb Shoulder Roast with Spice Rub

Prep time: 5 minutes | Cook time: 2 hours | Serves

1 (4-pound / 1.8-kg) boneless lamb shoulder roast

Spice Rub:

1 tablespoon kosher salt	¼ teaspoon chipotle chile powder (or cayenne powder)
1 teaspoon fresh ground black pepper	⅛ teaspoon (a pinch) ground cloves
1 teaspoon ancho chile powder	Fist sized chunk of smoking wood (or 1 cup wood chips)
½ teaspoon garlic powder	

1. Mix the spice rub ingredients in a small bowl. Open the boned lamb and rub all over with the spices, working them into any natural seams in the meat. Refrigerate for at least two hours, preferably overnight.
2. One hour before cooking, remove the lamb from the refrigerator. Fold the lamb into its original shape, truss, and skewer on the rotisserie spit, securing the roast with the rotisserie forks. Let the lamb rest at room temperature until the air fryer oven is Preheated. Submerge the smoking wood in water and let it soak until the air fryer oven is ready.
3. Select the ROAST function and preheat MAXX to 375ºF (190ºC). Press ROTATE button and set time to 2 hours. Set a drip pan in the middle of the air fryer oven.
4. Put the spit on the air fryer oven, start the motor spinning, and make sure the drip pan is centered beneath the lamb shoulder. Add the smoking wood to the fire, close the lid, and cook the lamb until it reaches 190ºF (88ºC) in its thickest part.
5. Remove the lamb shoulder from the rotisserie spit and remove the twine trussing the roast. Be careful - the spit and forks are blazing hot. Let the lamb rest for 15 minutes, then slice and shred into bite sized pieces. Serve.

Marinated Medium Rare Eye Round Beef

Prep time: 15 minutes | Cook time: 1 hour 40 minutes | Serves 6 to 8

5 pounds (2.3 kg) eye round beef roast	thyme leaves
2 onions, sliced	¾ cup olive oil
3 cups white wine	1 tablespoon coarse sea salt
3 cloves garlic, minced	1 tablespoon ground black pepper
1 teaspoon chopped fresh rosemary	1 teaspoon dried sage
1 teaspoon celery seeds	2 tablespoons unsalted butter
1 teaspoon fresh	

1. Place beef roast and onions in a large resealable bag.
2. In a small bowl, combine the wine, garlic, rosemary, celery seeds, thyme leaves, oil, salt, pepper, and sage.
3. Pour the marinade mixture over the beef roast and seal the bag. Refrigerate the roast for up to one day.
4. Remove the beef roast from the marinade. Using the rotisserie spit, push through the beef roast and attach the rotisserie forks.
5. If desired, place aluminum foil onto the drip pan. (It makes for easier clean-up!)
6. Select the ROAST function and preheat MAXX to 400ºF (205ºC). Press ROTATE button and set time to 1 hour 40 minutes.
7. Once preheated, place the prepared lamb leg with rotisserie spit into the oven. Baste the beef roast with marinade for every 30 minutes.
8. When cooking is complete, remove the lamb leg using the rotisserie handle and, using hot pads or gloves, carefully remove the lamb leg from the spit.
9. Remove the roast to a platter and allow the roast to rest for 10 minutes.
10. Slice thin and serve.

Basted Mutton Roast with Barbecue Dip

Prep time: 15 minutes | Cook time: 4½ hours | Serves 8 to 10

1 mutton roast (shoulder or leg), 5 pounds (2.3 kg)

Barbecue Dip:

1 cup water	1 tablespoon packed
¼ cup Worcestershire sauce	brown sugar
	1 tablespoon freshly
¼ cup apple cider vinegar	squeezed lemon juice
	1 tablespoon salt
1 tablespoon freshly ground black pepper	½ teaspoon ground allspice

Baste:

1 cup apple cider vinegar	squeezed lemon juice
½ cup Worcestershire sauce	2 tablespoons freshly ground black pepper
¼ cup freshly	1 tablespoon salt

1. To make the barbecue dip: Combine the dip ingredients in a jar. Cover with a lid and refrigerate, shaking periodically. Warm the dip in the microwave just before serving.
2. To make the baste: Combine the baste ingredients in a small bowl and set aside.
3. Using kitchen twine, tie the mutton roast into a uniform shape. Run a long sword skewer through the center of the roast lengthwise to create a pilot hole. Run the rotisserie spit through the hole and secure with the forks. Balance as necessary.
4. Select the ROAST function and preheat MAXX to 375ºF (190ºC). Press ROTATE button and set time to 4½ hours.
5. Place the roast on the preheated air fryer oven and set a drip pan underneath. Apply the baste mixture every 30 minutes, until the roast reaches an internal temperature of 185ºF (85ºC). The roast will shrink during cooking, so adjust the forks when appropriate.
6. Remove from the heat, carefully remove the rotisserie forks and slide the spit out, and then set the roast on a large cutting board. Tent the roast with aluminum foil and let the meat rest for 20 minutes.
7. Shred or carve the mutton into small pieces. Serve with the warmed barbecue dip on the side.

Prime Rib Roast with Peppery Rub

Prep time: 5 minutes | Cook time: 2 hours | Serves 8 to 10

1 4-bone prime rib roast (8 to 10 pounds / 3.6 to 4.5 kg)

Rub:

3½ tablespoons kosher salt	1½ tablespoons olive oil
3 or 4 cloves garlic, minced	1 tablespoon coarsely ground black pepper

1. Trim off any straggling pieces of meat or fat from the roast. If the fat cap is too thick, cut it down to between ¼ to ½ inch in thickness depending on how you like your prime rib. Run a long sword skewer through the center of the roast lengthwise to create a pilot hole. Run the rotisserie spit through the hole and secure with the forks. Balance as necessary. This is a large roast and it is important that it be well balanced.
2. To make the rub: Combine the rub ingredients in a small bowl and apply evenly to the roast. Concentrate the rub on the rounded end and not the cut sides, though it should still get some. The rub will then be on the edges of the slices once the roast has been carved.
3. Select the ROAST function and preheat MAXX to 400ºF (205ºC). Press ROTATE button and set time to 2 hours.
4. Place the roast on the preheated air fryer oven, set a drip pan underneath, and add 2 cups hot water to the pan if you intend to make gravy; add more water during the cooking time as necessary. Roast until it is near the desired doneness: 125ºF (52ºC) for rare, 135ºF (57ºC) for medium rare, 145ºF (63ºC) for medium, 155ºF (68ºC) for medium well, or 165ºF (74ºC) for well done. The roast will shrink during cooking, so adjust the forks when appropriate.
5. Carefully remove the rotisserie forks and slide the spit out, and then place the roast on a large cutting board. Tent the roast with aluminum foil and let the meat rest for 15 to 20 minutes. The roast temperature will continue to rise an additional 5ºF during the rest phase. Cut away the bones first by passing a knife against the bones and cutting through (save the bones for later). Cut the meat into slices ⅓ to ½ inch thick.

Pork Belly with Fennel-Sage Rub

Prep time: 15 minutes | Cook time: 3½ hours | Serves 6

1 slab pork belly, skin on, 5 to 6 pounds (2.3 to 2.7 kg)
1 boneless pork loin roast, about 3 pounds (1.4 kg)
Rub:

2 tablespoons fennel seeds	ground black pepper
1 tablespoon finely chopped fresh sage	1 teaspoon chopped fresh rosemary
Zest of 1 lemon	1 teaspoon red pepper flakes
4 or 5 cloves garlic	1½ teaspoons coarse salt
2 teaspoons coarse salt	1 teaspoon freshly ground black pepper
2 teaspoons freshly	

1. Lay the pork belly, skin-side down, on a large cutting board. Place the pork loin on top and roll the pork belly together so that the ends meet. Trim any excess pork belly and loin so that it is a uniform cylinder. Do not tie yet.
2. To make the rub: Using a mortar and pestle or spice grinder, crush the fennel seeds to a medium grind. Combine with the remaining rub ingredients in a small bowl and apply all over the pork loin.
3. Roll the pork loin inside the pork belly and tie with kitchen twine every inch into a secure, round bundle. Season the outside of the pork belly with the coarse salt and pepper. Set onto a baking sheet and place in the refrigerator, uncovered, for 24 hours.
4. Run a long sword skewer through the center of the roast lengthwise to create a pilot hole. Run the rotisserie spit through the hole and secure with the forks. Balance as necessary.
5. Select the ROAST function and preheat MAXX to 400ºF (205ºC). Press ROTATE button and set time to 3½ minutes.
6. Place the porchetta on the preheated air fryer oven with a drip pan underneath. Watch for burning or excessive browning and adjust the heat as necessary. Once the porchetta has reached an internal temperature of 145ºF (63ºC), the roast is done. If the skin is not a deep brown and crispy in texture, increase the temperature to 450ºF (235ºC) and roast for an additional 10 minutes.
7. Remove from the heat, carefully remove the rotisserie forks and slide the spit out, and then set the meat on a large cutting board. Tent the roast with aluminum foil and let the meat rest for 15 minutes. Slice the meat ½ inch thick and serve.

Brined Pork Loin with Spice Rub

Prep time: 10 minutes | Cook time: 45 minutes | Serves 4

1 (4-pound / 1.8-kg) bone-in pork loin roast
Brine:

3 quarts water	cup kosher salt)
½ cup table salt (or 1	¼ cup brown sugar

Spice Rub:

4 cloves garlic, minced or pressed through a garlic press	1 teaspoon fresh ground black pepper
1 teaspoon minced rosemary	½ teaspoon hot red pepper flakes

1. Combine the brine ingredients in a large container and stir until the salt and sugar dissolve. Submerge the pork in the brine. Store in the refrigerator for four to eight hours.
2. One hour before cooking, remove the pork from the brine and pat dry with paper towels. Mix the rub ingredients in a small bowl, then rub over the pork shoulder, working the rub into any natural seams in the meat. Truss the pork roast, skewer it on the rotisserie spit, and secure it with the rotisserie forks. Let the pork rest at room temperature.
3. Select the ROAST function and preheat MAXX to 450ºF (235ºC). Press ROTATE button and set time to 45 minutes. Set a drip pan in the middle of the air fryer oven.
4. Put the spit on the air fryer oven, start the motor spinning, and make sure the drip pan is centered beneath the pork roast. Close the lid and cook the pork until it reaches 135ºF (57ºC) in its thickest part.
5. Remove the pork from the rotisserie spit and remove the twine trussing the roast. Be careful - the spit and forks are blazing hot. Let the pork rest for 15 minutes, then slice and serve.

Stuffed Pork Loin with Cider Brine
Prep time: 10 minutes | Cook time: 50 minutes | Serves 4

2 (2-pound / 907-g) boneless pork loin roasts
Apple Cider Brine:
Dried Fruit Stuffing:
2 cups mixed dried fruit, chopped (apples, apricots, cranberries and raisins)

2 quarts apple cider
1 quart water
½ cup table salt

1 teaspoon fresh ground black pepper
½ teaspoon dried ginger

1. Combine the brine ingredients in a large container and stir until the salt and sugar dissolve. Roll cut the pork roasts to open them up like a book. Set a roast with the fat cap facing down. Make a cut the length of the roast, one third of the way from the bottom, which goes almost all the way to the other side of the roast but not through. Open the roast up like a book along that cut, then make another cut halfway up the opened part of the roast, almost all the way to the other side, and open up the roast again. Submerge the pork roasts in the brine. Store in the refrigerator for one to four hours.
2. One hour before cooking, remove the pork from the brine and pat dry with paper towels. Open up the pork with the cut side facing up, and sprinkle evenly with the chopped fruit, ginger, and pepper. Carefully roll the pork back into a cylinder, then truss each roast at the edges to hold the cylinder shape. Truss the roasts together with the fat caps facing out, then skewer on the rotisserie spit, running the spit between the roasts and securing them with the rotisserie forks. Let the pork rest at room temperature.
3. Select the ROAST function and preheat MAXX to 450ºF (235ºC). Press ROTATE button and set time to 50 minutes. Set a drip pan in the middle of the air fryer oven.
4. Put the spit on the air fryer oven and start the motor spinning. Make sure the drip pan is centered beneath the pork roast. Close the lid and cook the pork until it reaches 135ºF (57ºC) in its thickest part.
5. Remove the pork from the rotisserie spit and remove the twine trussing the roast. Be careful - the spit and forks are blazing hot. Let the pork rest for 15 minutes, then slice into ½ inch thick rounds and serve.

Apple and Vegetable Stuffed Turkey
Prep time: 30 minutes | Cook time: 3 hours | Serves 12 to 14

1 (12-pound/5.4-kg) turkey, giblet
For the Seasoning:
¼ cup lemon pepper
2 tablespoons chopped fresh parsley
1 tablespoon celery salt
For the Stuffing:
1 medium onion, cut into 8 equal parts
1 carrot, sliced

removed, rinsed and pat dry

2 cloves garlic, minced
2 teaspoons ground black pepper
1 teaspoon sage

1 apple, cored and cut into 8 thick slices

1. Mix together the seasoning in a small bowl. Rub over the surface and inside of the turkey.
2. Stuff the turkey with the onions, carrots, and apples. Using the rotisserie spit, push through the turkey and attach the rotisserie forks.
3. If desired, place aluminum foil onto the drip pan. (It makes for easier clean-up!)
4. Select the ROAST function and preheat MAXX to 350ºF (180ºC). Press ROTATE button and set time to 3 hours.
5. Once preheated, place the prepared turkey with rotisserie spit into the oven.
6. When cooking is complete, the internal temperature should read at least 180ºF (82ºC). Remove the lamb leg using the rotisserie handle and, using hot pads or gloves, carefully remove the turkey from the spit.
7. Server hot.

Marinated Chuck Roast

Prep time: 15 minutes | Cook time: 1 hour | Serves 8

1 chuck roast, 4 to 4½ pounds (1.8 to 2.0 kg)	1¼ teaspoons salt ½ teaspoon freshly ground black pepper

Marinade:

1 tablespoon olive oil	balsamic vinegar
1 shallot, finely chopped	1 teaspoon Worcestershire sauce
2 or 3 cloves garlic, minced	1 teaspoon chopped fresh thyme
1½ cups tawny port	¼ teaspoon salt
¼ cup beef broth	¼ teaspoon freshly
1½ tablespoons	ground black pepper

1. To make the marinade: Heat the olive oil in a saucepan over medium-low heat and cook the shallot for 3 minutes until translucent. Add the garlic and cook for 30 seconds. Increase the heat to medium-high and add the port. Stir thoroughly and cook for 1 minute. Add the remaining ingredients and simmer the sauce for 5 minutes, stirring occasionally. Remove from the heat and let cool for 10 to 15 minutes. Divide the mixture into two even portions, reserving one half for the baste and one for the marinade. Store in the refrigerator until ready to cook, then bring to room temperature before using.
2. Trim away excess fat from the outer edges of the chuck roast. Place the roast in a resealable plastic bag. Add half of the port mixture to the bag, making sure that all of the meat is well covered. Seal the bag and place in the refrigerator for 6 to 8 hours.
3. Remove the roast from the bag, discarding the marinade, and place on a large cutting board or platter. With kitchen twine, tie the roast into a round and uniform shape, pulling tightly. Start in the center and work toward the ends until it is tied into a solid round roast. This will take four or five ties. Run a long sword skewer through the center of the roast lengthwise to create a pilot hole. Run the rotisserie spit through the hole and secure with the forks. Balance as necessary. Season the roast with the salt and pepper.
4. Select the ROAST function and preheat MAXX to 400ºF (205ºC). Press ROTATE button and set time to 1 hour.
5. Place the roast on the preheated air fryer oven and set an empty drip pan underneath. Roast until it reaches the desired doneness: 125ºF (52ºC) for rare, 135ºF (57ºC) for medium rare, 145ºF (63ºC) for medium, 155ºF (68ºC) for medium well, or 165ºF (74ºC) for well done. Baste halfway through the cooking time, and repeat the process at least 3 times until the roast is done.
6. Remove from the heat, carefully remove the rotisserie forks and slide the spit out, and then set the roast on a large cutting board. Tent the roast with aluminum foil and let the meat rest for 15 to 20 minutes. Cut off the twine. Slice into ¼-inch slices and serve.

Ham with Honey Glaze

Prep time: 20 minutes | Cook time: 3 hours | Serves 6

1 (5-pound/2.3-kg) cooked boneless ham, pat dry

For the Glaze:

½ cup honey	cloves
2 teaspoons lemon juice	1 teaspoon cinnamon
1 teaspoon ground	½ cup brown sugar

1. Using the rotisserie spit, push through the ham and attach the rotisserie forks.
2. If desired, place aluminum foil onto the drip pan. (It makes for easier clean-up!)
3. Select the ROAST function and preheat MAXX to 250ºF (121ºC). Press ROTATE button and set time to 3 hours.
4. Once preheated, place the prepared ham with rotisserie spit into the oven.
5. Meanwhile, combine the ingredients for the glaze in a small bowl. Stir to mix well.
6. When the ham has reached 145ºF (63ºC), brush the glaze mixture over all surfaces of the ham.
7. When cooking is complete, remove the ham using the rotisserie handle and, using hot pads or gloves, carefully remove the ham from the spit.
8. Let it rest for 10 minutes covered loosely with foil and then carve and serve.

Sumptuous Pork Loin

Prep time: 15 minutes | Cook time: 50 minutes | Serves 4

2 (2-pound / 907-g) boneless pork loin roasts
Brine:
3 quarts water
½ cup table salt (or 1 cup kosher salt)
¼ cup brown sugar
Spice Rub:
1 teaspoon coriander seeds, coarsely ground
1 teaspoon fennel seeds, coarsely ground
1 teaspoon garlic powder
½ teaspoon fresh black pepper, coarsely ground
Glaze:
¼ cup honey
2 tablespoons cider vinegar
2 teaspoons minced fresh thyme (or 1
teaspoon dried thyme)
Fist sized chunk of smoking wood (or 1 cup wood chips)

1. Combine the brine ingredients in a large container and stir until the salt and sugar dissolve. Score the fat on the pork loins in a 1 inch diamond pattern. Submerge the pork in the brine. Store in the refrigerator for four to eight hours.
2. One hour before cooking, remove the pork from the brine and pat dry with paper towels. Mix the spice rub ingredients in a small bowl, then pat the rub onto the pork. Truss the roasts together with the fat caps facing out, then skewer on the rotisserie spit, running the spit between the roasts and securing them with the rotisserie forks. Let the pork rest at room temperature. Submerge the smoking wood in water and let it soak until the air fryer oven is ready.
3. Whisk the glaze ingredients in a small bowl.
4. Select the ROAST function and preheat MAXX to 450ºF (235ºC). Press ROTATE button and set time to 50 minutes. Set a drip pan in the middle of the air fryer oven.
5. Put the spit on the air fryer oven, start the motor spinning, and make sure the drip pan is centered beneath the pork roast. Add the smoking wood to the fire, close the lid, and cook the pork until it reaches 135ºF (57ºC) in its thickest part. During the last 15 minutes of cooking, brush the roast with glaze every five minutes.
6. Remove the pork from the rotisserie spit and remove the twine trussing the roast. Be careful - the spit and forks are blazing hot. Let the pork rest for 15 minutes, then slice and serve.

Prime Rib Roast with Mustard Rub

Prep time: 10 minutes | Cook time: 2 hours | Serves 8 to 10

1 4-bone prime rib roast (8 to 10 pounds / 3.6 to 4.5 kg)
Rub:
½ cup grainy mustard
¼ cup olive oil
1 large shallot, finely chopped
3 tablespoons kosher salt
1½ tablespoons chopped fresh marjoram
1 tablespoon chopped fresh thyme
1 tablespoon coarsely ground black pepper

1. Trim off any straggling pieces of meat or fat from the roast. If the fat cap is too thick, cut it down to between ¼ to ½ inch in thickness depending on how you like your prime rib.
2. To make the rub: Combine the rub ingredients in a small bowl and coat the roast thoroughly with it. Loosely cover with plastic wrap and let the roast sit at room temperature for 30 minutes.
3. Run a long sword skewer through the center of the roast lengthwise to create a pilot hole. Run the rotisserie spit through the hole and secure with the forks. Balance as necessary.

4. Select the ROAST function and preheat MAXX to 400ºF (205ºC). Press ROTATE button and set time to 2 hours.
5. Place the roast on the preheated air fryer oven, set a drip pan underneath, and add 1 to 2 cups hot water to the pan. Add more water to the pan as necessary.
6. Roast until it is near the desired doneness: 125ºF (52ºC) for rare, 135ºF (57ºC) for medium rare, 145ºF (63ºC) for medium, 155ºF (68ºC) for medium well, or 165ºF (74ºC) for well done. The roast will shrink during cooking, so adjust the forks when appropriate. Remove the roast when it is 5ºF to 10ºF below the desired doneness. It will continue to cook during the resting phase.
7. Carefully remove the rotisserie forks and slide the spit out, and then place the roast on a large cutting board. Tent the roast with aluminum foil and a kitchen towel and let the meat rest for 15 to 20 minutes. Cut away the bones first by passing a knife against the bones and cutting through (save the bones for later). Cut the meat into thin slices.

Peppery Prime Rib Roast with Whiskey Baste
Prep time: 10 minutes | Cook time: 2 hours | Serves 8 to 10

1 4-bone prime rib roast (8 to 10 pounds / 3.6 to 4.5 kg)
Rub:

¼ cup coarse salt	1 tablespoon coarsely ground black pepper
1 small shallot, finely chopped	Zest of 1 large lemon
2 cloves garlic, minced	1 teaspoon paprika
2 tablespoons olive oil	1 teaspoon sugar

Baste:

⅓ cup whiskey	Juice of 1 lemon
¼ cup water	⅛ teaspoon salt

1. Trim off any straggling pieces of meat or fat from the roast. If the fat cap is too thick, cut it down to between ¼ to ½ inch in thickness depending on how you like your prime rib.
2. Run a long sword skewer through the center of the roast lengthwise to create a pilot hole. Run the rotisserie spit through the hole and secure with the forks. Balance as necessary.
3. To make the rub: Combine the rub ingredients in a small bowl to form an even paste. Use additional olive oil if necessary to get it to a thick but workable consistency. Apply evenly to the roast, focusing on the outer shell of the roast.
4. To make the baste: Combine the baste ingredients in a small bowl and set aside for 15 to 30 minutes to come to room temperature.
5. Select the ROAST function and preheat MAXX to 400ºF (205ºC). Press ROTATE button and set time to 2 hours.
6. Place the roast on the preheated air fryer oven, set a drip pan underneath, and add 1 to 2 cups hot water to the pan. If you intend to make a gravy from the drippings, monitor the drip pan to make sure it does not run dry. Add extra water if needed.
7. During the last hour of cooking time, begin basting. Apply the baste gently so as not to wash away the seasonings on the outside of the roast. Do this 6 to 8 times, until the roast is well coated with the baste. Roast until it is near the desired doneness: 125ºF (52ºC) for rare, 135ºF (57ºC) for medium rare, 145ºF (63ºC) for medium, 155ºF (68ºC) for medium well, or 165ºF (74ºC) for well done. The roast will shrink during cooking, so adjust the forks when appropriate.
8. Carefully remove the rotisserie forks and slide the spit out, and then set the roast on a large cutting board. Tent the roast with aluminum foil and let the meat rest for 15 to 20 minutes. Cut away the bones first by passing a knife against the bones and cutting through (save the bones for later). Cut the meat into thin slices.

Baby Back Ribs with Ketchup and Rub

Prep time: 15 minutes | Cook time: 2½ hours | Serves 4 to 6

2 racks baby back ribs
Sauce:

1 tablespoon vegetable oil
1 cup finely chopped sweet onion
2 cloves garlic, minced
1½ cups ketchup

¼ cup red wine vinegar
¼ cup packed brown sugar
2 tablespoons yellow mustard
⅛ teaspoon salt

Rub:

1 tablespoon paprika
2 teaspoons salt

2 teaspoons freshly ground black pepper
½ teaspoon cayenne

1. To make the sauce: Heat the oil in a medium-size saucepan over medium heat. Add the onions and sauté for 5 minutes. Add the garlic and sauté for 15 seconds. Add the remaining sauce ingredients and simmer for 4 to 5 minutes, stirring often. Remove from the heat and let cool for 15 to 30 minutes before using.
2. To make the rub: Combine the rub ingredients in a small bowl and set aside.
3. Place the ribs on a cutting board and pat dry with paper towels. Cut away any excess fat from the ribs. Remove the membrane from the back of the ribs by using a blunt knife to work the membrane away from the bone in one corner. Grab hold of the membrane with a paper towel for a good grip and gently peel away. With a little practice, this becomes an easy process. Apply the rub all over the ribs' surface, focusing more on the meat side than the bone side.
4. Place one rack of ribs bone-side up on a large cutting board. Place the other rack of ribs bone-side down on top. Position to match up the racks of ribs as evenly as possible. With kitchen twine, tie the racks together between ever other bone, end to end. The whole bundle should be secure and tight. Run the rotisserie spit between the racks and secure tightly with the rotisserie forks. There will be a little movement in the middle, which is fine. As the ribs cook it may be necessary to tighten the forks to keep them secure. Make sure the forks pass through the meat of each rack on each end.
5. Select the ROAST function and preheat MAXX to 375ºF (190ºC). Press ROTATE button and set time to 2½ hours.
6. Place the racks on the preheated air fryer oven and set a drip pan underneath. Roast until the internal temperature reaches 185ºF (85ºC). Test the temperature in several locations. Baste the ribs evenly with barbecue sauce during the last 45 minutes of cooking time.
7. Remove from the heat, carefully remove the rotisserie forks and slide the spit out, and then set the ribs on a large cutting board. Tent the ribs with aluminum foil and let the meat rest for 5 to 10 minutes.
8. Cut away the twine and cut the racks into individual ribs. Serve.

Chapter 15 Casseroles, Quiches, and Frittatas

Cheddar Bacon Quiche
Prep time: 15 minutes | Cook time: 20 minutes | Serves 4

1 tablespoon olive oil	4 eggs, beaten
1 shortcrust pastry	¼ teaspoon garlic
3 tablespoons Greek	powder
yogurt	Pinch of black pepper
½ cup grated	¼ teaspoon onion
Cheddar cheese	powder
3 ounces (85 g)	¼ teaspoon sea salt
chopped bacon	Flour, for sprinkling

1. Select the BAKE function and preheat MAXX to 330ºF (166ºC).
2. Take 8 ramekins and grease with olive oil. Coat with a sprinkling of flour, tapping to remove any excess.
3. Cut the shortcrust pastry in 8 and place each piece at the bottom of each ramekin.
4. Put all the other ingredients in a bowl and combine well. Spoon equal amounts of the filling into each piece of pastry.
5. Bake the ramekins in the air fryer oven for 20 minutes.
6. Serve warm.

Curried Chicken and Mushroom Casserole
Prep time: 15 minutes | Cook time: 20 minutes | Serves 4

4 chicken breasts	florets
1 tablespoon curry	1 cup mushrooms
powder	½ cup shredded
1 cup coconut milk	Parmesan cheese
Salt, to taste	Cooking spray
1 broccoli, cut into	

1. Select the BAKE function and preheat MAXX to 350ºF (177ºC). Spritz a casserole dish with cooking spray.
2. Cube the chicken breasts and combine with curry powder and coconut milk in a bowl. Season with salt.

3. Add the broccoli and mushroom and mix well.
4. Pour the mixture into the casserole dish. Top with the cheese.
5. Transfer to the air fryer oven and bake for about 20 minutes.
6. Serve warm.

Creamy-Cheesy Tomato Casserole
Prep time: 5 minutes | Cook time: 30 minutes | Serves 4

5 eggs	tomato sauce
2 tablespoons heavy	2 tablespoons grated
cream	Parmesan cheese,
3 tablespoons chunky	plus more for topping

1. Select the BAKE function and preheat MAXX to 350ºF (177ºC).
2. Combine the eggs and cream in a bowl.
3. Mix in the tomato sauce and add the cheese.
4. Spread into a glass baking dish and bake in the preheated air fryer oven for 30 minutes.
5. Top with extra cheese and serve.

Macaroni and Cheese Bake
Prep time: 10 minutes | Cook time: 10 minutes | Serves 2

1 cup cooked	Salt and ground black
macaroni	pepper, to taste
1 cup grated Cheddar	1 tablespoon grated
cheese	Parmesan cheese
½ cup warm milk	

1. Select the BAKE function and preheat MAXX to 350ºF (177ºC).
2. In a baking dish, mix all the ingredients, except for Parmesan.
3. Put the dish inside the air fryer oven and bake for 10 minutes.
4. Add the Parmesan cheese on top and serve.

Lush Vegetable Frittata
Prep time: 15 minutes | Cook time: 21 minutes | Serves 2

4 eggs	½ cup red onion,
¼ cup milk	sliced
Sea salt and ground	½ tablespoon olive
black pepper, to taste	oil
1 zucchini, sliced	5 tablespoons feta
½ bunch asparagus,	cheese, crumbled
sliced	4 tablespoons
½ cup mushrooms,	Cheddar cheese,
sliced	grated
½ cup spinach,	¼ bunch chives,
shredded	minced

1. In a bowl, mix the eggs, milk, salt and pepper.
2. Over a medium heat, sauté the vegetables for 6 minutes with the olive oil in a nonstick pan.
3. Put some parchment paper in the base of a baking tin. Pour in the vegetables, followed by the egg mixture. Top with the feta and grated Cheddar.
4. Select the BAKE function and preheat MAXX to 320ºF (160ºC).
5. Transfer the baking tin to the air fryer oven and bake for 15 minutes. Remove the frittata from the air fryer oven and leave to cool for 5 minutes.
6. Top with the minced chives and serve.

Cheddar Sausage Quiche Cups
Prep time: 15 minutes | Cook time: 16 minutes | Makes 10 quiche cups

4 ounces (113 g)	Cooking spray
ground pork sausage	4 ounces (113 g)
3 eggs	sharp Cheddar
¾ cup milk	cheese, grated

Special Equipment:
20 foil muffin cups

1. Spritz the air fryer basket with cooking spray.
2. Divide sausage into 3 portions and shape each into a thin patty.
3. Put patties in air fryer basket. Select the AIR FRY function and cook at 390ºF (199ºC) for 6 minutes.
4. While sausage is cooking, prepare the egg mixture. Combine the eggs and milk in a large bowl and whisk until well blended. Set aside.
5. When sausage has cooked fully, remove patties from the basket, drain well, and use a fork to crumble the meat into small pieces.
6. Double the foil cups into 10 sets. Remove paper liners from the top muffin cups and spray the foil cups lightly with cooking spray.
7. Divide crumbled sausage among the 10 muffin cup sets.
8. Top each with grated cheese, divided evenly among the cups.
9. Put 5 cups in air fryer basket.
10. Pour egg mixture into each cup, filling until each cup is at least ²/₃ full.
11. Switch from AIR FRY to BAKE. Bake for 8 minutes and test for doneness. A knife inserted into the center shouldn't have any raw egg on it when removed.
12. Repeat with the remaining quiches.
13. Serve warm.

Shrimp and Vegetable Casserole
Prep time: 15 minutes | Cook time: 22 minutes | Serves 4

1 pound (454 g)	sliced
shrimp, cleaned and	1 shallot, sliced
deveined	2 tablespoons
2 cups cauliflower,	sesame oil
cut into florets	1 cup tomato paste
2 green bell pepper,	Cooking spray

1. Select the BAKE function and preheat MAXX to 360ºF (182ºC). Spritz a baking pan with cooking spray.
2. Arrange the shrimp and vegetables in the baking pan. Then, drizzle the sesame oil over the vegetables. Pour the tomato paste over the vegetables.
3. Bake for 10 minutes in the preheated air fryer oven. Stir with a large spoon and bake for a further 12 minutes.
4. Serve warm.

Warm Shrimp Quiche
Prep time: 15 minutes | Cook time: 20 minutes | Serves 2

2 teaspoons vegetable oil
4 large eggs
½ cup half-and-half
4 ounces (113 g) raw shrimp, chopped
1 cup shredded Parmesan or Swiss cheese
¼ cup chopped

scallions
1 teaspoon sweet smoked paprika
1 teaspoon herbes de Provence
1 teaspoon black pepper
½ to 1 teaspoon kosher salt

1. Select the BAKE function and preheat MAXX to 300ºF (149ºC). Generously grease a round baking pan with 4-inch sides with vegetable oil.
2. In a large bowl, beat together the eggs and half-and-half. Add the shrimp, ¾ cup of the cheese, the scallions, paprika, herbes de Provence, pepper, and salt. Stir with a fork to thoroughly combine. Pour the egg mixture into the prepared pan.
3. Put the pan in the air fryer basket and bake for 20 minutes. After 17 minutes, sprinkle the remaining ¼ cup cheese on top and bake for the remaining 3 minutes, or until the cheese has melted, the eggs are set, and a toothpick inserted into the center comes out clean.
4. Serve the quiche warm.

Spinach and Double Cheese Casserole
Prep time: 10 minutes | Cook time: 20 minutes | Serves 4

1 (13.5-ounce / 383-g) can spinach, drained and squeezed
1 cup cottage cheese
2 large eggs, beaten
¼ cup crumbled feta cheese
2 tablespoons all-purpose flour
2 tablespoons butter,

melted
1 clove garlic, minced, or more to taste
1½ teaspoons onion powder
⅛ teaspoon ground nutmeg
Cooking spray

1. Grease an 8-inch pie pan with cooking spray and set aside.

2. Combine spinach, cottage cheese, eggs, feta cheese, flour, butter, garlic, onion powder, and nutmeg in a bowl. Stir until all ingredients are well incorporated. Pour into the prepared pie pan.
3. Select the AIR FRY function and cook at 375ºF (191ºC) for 18 to 20 minutes, or until the center is set.
4. Serve warm.

Western Prosciutto Baked Eggs Casserole
Prep time: 5 minutes | Cook time: 10 minutes | Serves 2

1 cup day-old whole grain bread, cubed
3 large eggs, beaten
2 tablespoons water
⅛ teaspoon kosher salt
1 ounce (28 g) prosciutto, roughly

chopped
1 ounce (28 g) Pepper Jack cheese, roughly chopped
1 tablespoon chopped fresh chives
Nonstick cooking spray

1. Select the BAKE function and preheat MAXX to 360ºF (182ºC).
2. Spray a baking pan with nonstick cooking spray, then place the bread cubes in the pan. Transfer the baking pan to the air fryer oven.
3. In a medium bowl, stir together the beaten eggs and water, then stir in the kosher salt, prosciutto, cheese, and chives.
4. Pour the egg mixture over the bread cubes and bake for 10 minutes, or until the eggs are set and the top is golden brown.
5. Serve warm.

Conclusion

As I have shared with you, the Ninja Foodi pro air fryer oven is equipped with many functions and features that make it a highly functional kitchen unit. However, to maximize the features of the Ninja Foodi pro air fryer to the fullest, it's important to know its functions, benefits, features, and all the details on its accessories and tips, which is what this book centers on.

By reading through all the contents in this book, you will be able to effectively maximize your Ninja Foodi pro air fryer and use it in the best way possible.

Have a nice time using your Ninja Foodi pro air fryer oven!

Appendix 1 Measurement Conversion Chart

VOLUME EQUIVALENTS(DRY)

US STANDARD	METRIC (APPROXIMATE)
1/8 teaspoon	0.5 mL
1/4 teaspoon	1 mL
1/2 teaspoon	2 mL
3/4 teaspoon	4 mL
1 teaspoon	5 mL
1 tablespoon	15 mL
1/4 cup	59 mL
1/2 cup	118 mL
3/4 cup	177 mL
1 cup	235 mL
2 cups	475 mL
3 cups	700 mL
4 cups	1 L

VOLUME EQUIVALENTS(LIQUID)

US STANDARD	US STANDARD (OUNCES)	METRIC (APPROXIMATE)
2 tablespoons	1 fl.oz.	30 mL
1/4 cup	2 fl.oz.	60 mL
1/2 cup	4 fl.oz.	120 mL
1 cup	8 fl.oz.	240 mL
1 1/2 cup	12 fl.oz.	355 mL
2 cups or 1 pint	16 fl.oz.	475 mL
4 cups or 1 quart	32 fl.oz.	1 L
1 gallon	128 fl.oz.	4 L

TEMPERATURES EQUIVALENTS

FAHRENHEIT(F)	CELSIUS(C) (APPROXIMATE)
225 °F	107 °C
250 °F	120 °C
275 °F	135 °C
300 °F	150 °C
325 °F	160 °C
350 °F	180 °C
375 °F	190 °C
400 °F	205 °C
425 °F	220 °C
450 °F	235 °C
475 °F	245 °C
500 °F	260 °C

WEIGHT EQUIVALENTS

US STANDARD	METRIC (APPROXIMATE)
1 ounce	28 g
2 ounces	57 g
5 ounces	142 g
10 ounces	284 g
15 ounces	425 g
16 ounces (1 pound)	455 g
1.5 pounds	680 g
2 pounds	907 g

Appendix 2 Air Fryer Cooking Chart

Beef

Item	Temp (°F)	Time (mins)	Item	Temp (°F)	Time (mins)
Beef Eye Round Roast (4 lbs.)	400 °F	45 to 55	Meatballs (1-inch)	370 °F	7
Burger Patty (4 oz.)	370 °F	16 to 20	Meatballs (3-inch)	380 °F	10
Filet Mignon (8 oz.)	400 °F	18	Ribeye, bone-in (1-inch, 8 oz)	400 °F	10 to 15
Flank Steak (1.5 lbs.)	400 °F	12	Sirloin steaks (1-inch, 12 oz)	400 °F	9 to 14
Flank Steak (2 lbs.)	400 °F	20 to 28			

Chicken

Item	Temp (°F)	Time (mins)	Item	Temp (°F)	Time (mins)
Breasts, bone in (1 ¼ lb.)	370 °F	25	Legs, bone-in (1 ¾ lb.)	380 °F	30
Breasts, boneless (4 oz)	380 °F	12	Thighs, boneless (1 ½ lb.)	380 °F	18 to 20
Drumsticks (2 ½ lb.)	370 °F	20	Wings (2 lb.)	400 °F	12
Game Hen (halved 2 lb.)	390 °F	20	Whole Chicken	360 °F	75
Thighs, bone-in (2 lb.)	380 °F	22	Tenders	360 °F	8 to 10

Pork & Lamb

Item	Temp (°F)	Time (mins)	Item	Temp (°F)	Time (mins)
Bacon (regular)	400 °F	5 to 7	Pork Tenderloin	370 °F	15
Bacon (thick cut)	400 °F	6 to 10	Sausages	380 °F	15
Pork Loin (2 lb.)	360 °F	55	Lamb Loin Chops (1-inch thick)	400 °F	8 to 12
Pork Chops, bone in (1-inch, 6.5 oz)	400 °F	12	Rack of Lamb (1.5 – 2 lb.)	380 °F	22

Fish & Seafood

Item	Temp (°F)	Time (mins)	Item	Temp (°F)	Time (mins)
Calamari (8 oz)	400 °F	4	Tuna Steak	400 °F	7 to 10
Fish Fillet (1-inch, 8 oz)	400 °F	10	Scallops	400 °F	5 to 7
Salmon, fillet (6 oz)	380 °F	12	Shrimp	400 °F	5
Swordfish steak	400 °F	10			

Vegetables					
INGREDIENT	AMOUNT	PREPARATION	OIL	TEMP	COOK TIME
Asparagus	2 bunches	Cut in half, trim stems	2 Tbsp	420°F	12-15 mins
Beets	1½ lbs	Peel, cut in ½-inch cubes	1Tbsp	390°F	28-30 mins
Bell peppers (for roasting)	4 peppers	Cut in quarters, remove seeds	1Tbsp	400°F	15-20 mins
Broccoli	1 large head	Cut in 1-2-inch florets	1Tbsp	400°F	15-20 mins
Brussels sprouts	1lb	Cut in half, remove stems	1Tbsp	425°F	15-20 mins
Carrots	1lb	Peel, cut in ¼-inch rounds	1 Tbsp	425°F	10-15 mins
Cauliflower	1 head	Cut in 1-2-inch florets	2 Tbsp	400°F	20-22 mins
Corn on the cob	7 ears	Whole ears, remove husks	1 Tbps	400°F	14-17 mins
Green beans	1 bag (12 oz)	Trim	1 Tbps	420°F	18-20 mins
Kale (for chips)	4 oz	Tear into pieces,remove stems	None	325°F	5-8 mins
Mushrooms	16 oz	Rinse, slice thinly	1 Tbps	390°F	25-30 mins
Potatoes, russet	1½ lbs	Cut in 1-inch wedges	1 Tbps	390°F	25-30 mins
Potatoes, russet	1lb	Hand-cut fries, soak 30 mins in cold water, then pat dry	½ -3 Tbps	400°F	25-28 mins
Potatoes, sweet	1lb	Hand-cut fries, soak 30 mins in cold water, then pat dry	1 Tbps	400°F	25-28 mins
Zucchini	1lb	Cut in eighths lengthwise, then cut in half	1 Tbps	400°F	15-20 mins

Appendix 3 Index

Made in the USA
Las Vegas, NV
18 November 2023

81123880R00109